The Holocaust in Eastern Europe

PERSPECTIVES ON THE HOLOCAUST

A series of books designed to help students further their understanding of key topics within the field of Holocaust studies.

Published:

Holocaust Representations in History, Daniel H. Magilow and Lisa Silverman

Postwar Germany and the Holocaust, Caroline Sharples

Anti-Semitism and the Holocaust, Beth A. Griech-Polelle

Remembrance, Barry Trachtenberg

Witnessing the Holocaust: Six Literary Testimonies, Judith M. Hughes

Forthcoming:

The Perpetrators of the Holocaust: The Folly of the Third Reich, Nathan Stoltzfus

Sites of Holocaust Memory, Janet Ward

The United States and the Nazi Holocaust: Race, Refuge, and

The Holocaust in Eastern Europe

At the Epicenter of the Final Solution

Waitman Wade Beorn

BLOOMSBURY ACADEMIC
LONDON • NEW YORK • OXFORD • NEW DELHI • SYDNEY

BLOOMSBURY ACADEMIC
Bloomsbury Publishing Plc
50 Bedford Square, London, WC1B 3DP, UK
1305 Broadway, New York, NY 10018, USA
29 Earlsfort Terrace, Dublin 2, Ireland

BLOOMSBURY, BLOOMSBURY ACADEMIC and the Diana logo are
trademarks of Bloomsbury Publishing Plc

First published in Great Britain 2018
Reprinted 2018, 2019, 2021 (twice), 2022

Copyright © Waitman Wade Beorn, 2018

Waitman Wade Beorn has asserted his right under the Copyright,
Designs and Patents Act, 1988, to be identified as Author of this work.

For legal purposes the Acknowledgements on p. xi constitute an
extension of this copyright page.

Cover design by Jesse Holborn / Design Holborn
Cover image © Archiv des Hamburger Instituts fuer Sozialforschung/ Archives of the Hamburg
Institute for Social Research

All rights reserved. No part of this publication may be reproduced or
transmitted in any form or by any means, electronic or mechanical,
including photocopying, recording, or any information storage or
retrieval system, without prior permission in writing from the publishers.

Bloomsbury Publishing Plc does not have any control over, or responsibility for,
any third-party websites referred to or in this book. All internet addresses given
in this book were correct at the time of going to press. The author and publisher
regret any inconvenience caused if addresses have changed or sites have
ceased to exist, but can accept no responsibility for any such changes.

A catalogue record for this book is available from the British Library.

Library of Congress Cataloging-in-Publication Data
Names: Beorn, Waitman Wade, 1977– author.
Title: The Holocaust in Eastern Europe: at the epicenter of the Final
solution / Waitman Wade Beorn.
Description: London; New York: Bloomsbury Academic, an imprint of
Bloomsbury Publishing, Inc, [2018] | Series: Perspectives on the Holocaust | Includes index.
Identifiers: LCCN 2017025351 (print) | LCCN 2017025537 (ebook) |
ISBN 9781474232227 (ePDF) | ISBN 9781474232210 (ePUB) |
ISBN 9781474232197 (hardback) | ISBN 9781474232180 (pbk.)
Subjects: LCSH: Jews–Europe, Eastern–History–20th century. | Holocaust,
Jewish (1939–1945)–Europe, Eastern. | Jews–Persecutions– Europe,
Eastern–History–20th century. | Europe, Eastern–Ethnic relations.
Classification: LCC DS135.E83 (ebook) | LCC DS135.E83 B46 2018 (print) |
DDC 940.53/ 180947–dc23
LC record available at https://lccn.loc.gov/2017025351

ISBN: HB: 978-1-4742-3219-7
PB: 978-1-4742-3218-0
ePDF: 978-1-4742-3222-7
eBook: 978-1-4742-3221-0

Series: Perspectives on the Holocaust

Typeset by Newgen KnowledgeWorks Pvt. Ltd., Chennai, India.
Printed and bound in Great Britain

To find out more about our authors and books visit
www.bloomsbury.com and sign up for our newsletters.

For my mother, Leanne, whose love of the written word was a constant in my life.
May her memory be a blessing!

here in this carload

i am eve

with abel my son

if you see my other son

cain son of man

tell him that i

          "Written in Pencil in the Sealed Railway-Car," Dan Pagis[1]

CONTENTS

List of Illustrations viii
Acknowledgments xi

Introduction 1

1 Beyond the Pale: Pre-War Jewish Life in Eastern Europe 9

2 The Origins of the Nazi State 29

3 Nazis and the Imaginary East 49

4 The Soviet Interlude 71

5 Poland: The Nazi Laboratory of Genocide 95

6 War of Annihilation: The Invasion of the Soviet Union 119

7 Ghetto Life and Death in the East 151

8 Hitler's Eastern Allies 179

9 The Final Solution 201

10 The Kaleidoscope of Jewish Resistance 225

11 Perpetrators, Collaborators, and Rescuers 247

Conclusion 273

Notes 283
Index 333

ILLUSTRATIONS

Map

1 Pre-World War II Europe, 1919–29   2

Figures

1 A father watches his son walk to school down a street of the Eisiskes shtetl in Lithuania. Eisiskes, Lithuania, pre-1941   14
2 The Great Synagogue in Slonim. The small buildings in the foreground are Jewish shops. Slonim, Poland/now Belarus, pre-1939   20
3 Excerpt from Eichmann's diagram for the steps required for Jews emigrating from Vienna, ca. 1938–39   44
4 Nazi propaganda slide of a Hitler Youth educational presentation titled "German power in the East," ca. 1934–37   56
5 Local Jews are arrested in Poland. Note *Wehrmacht* photographer in foreground. Ustrony/Opatow, Poland, September 1939   98
6 Famed Nazi filmmaker, Leni Riefenstahl (second from left) and her film crew observe a killing of Jews by German soldiers during the invasion of Poland. Konskie, Poland, September 1941   103
7 Governor-General of Poland Hans Frank (right) hosts Reichsführer SS Heinrich Himmler at a dinner held at Wawel castle during his visit to Krakow. Krakow, Poland, 1940   107
8 Soviet POW camp outside of Minsk, likely the Drozdy camp, showing conditions for prisoners. Minsk, Belarus, July 5, 1941   126
9 The Lietūkis Garage Massacre. Kaunas, Lithuania, June 27, 1941   135
10 Local Ukrainians abuse a Jew near a German Army guard post. June/July 1941   138
11 Jews assembled in the courtyard of Romanian police headquarters during the Iasi pogrom. Iasi, Romania, June 29–30, 1941   140

ILLUSTRATIONS

12 A Latvian policeman walks along the edge of a mass grave toward the bodies of Jewish women and children who have just been executed. Liepaja, Latvia, December 15, 1941   142
13 Shooting and burning pit in the Ponary Forest. Vilnius, Lithuania, 2017   146
14 Jews move into the Kaunas ghetto with their belongings. Kaunas, Lithuania, August 1941   168
15 A young boy caught smuggling in the Warsaw ghetto by a German policeman, October 1940–May 1943   171
16 Performance of the Kaunas ghetto orchestra. Kaunas, Lithuania, 1944   174
17 Hungarian Jews stand by the open door of a cattle car while awaiting deportation to a forced labor battalion. Hungary, November 1940   191
18 Hungarian soldiers look at the corpses of eight Jews they have just executed on the bank of the Danube. Hungary, 1944   194
19 Map of the Treblinka Extermination Center   212
20 Pages from the album of Treblinka deputy, Kurt Franz, titled "Beautiful Times." Treblinka, Poland, 1942–43   214
21 View from atop the train of Hungarian Jews lined up for selection on the ramp at Auschwitz-Birkenau. Auschwitz, Poland, 1944   218
22 Janusz Korczak (center) with children and younger staff members in his orphanage, approximately 1930–39   234
23 Jewish partisan Faye Schulman in the forest. Near Pinsk, Belarus, Winter 1943   243
23a Portrait of female partisan, Sara Ginaite at the liberation of Vilna, August 1944   244
24 Diagram of "continuous-operation corpse incineration oven for mass use" from Topf and Sons patent application, October 16, 1942   250
25 A member of the Lithuanian auxiliary police who has just returned from taking part in the mass execution of the local Jewish population in the Rase Forest auctions off their personal property in the central market. Utena, Lithuania, July–August 1941   261
26 Ukrainian SS auxiliaries in the Plaszow concentration camp outside of Krakow, 1943   263
27 Portrait of Japanese Consul Chiune Sugihara. Kaunas, Lithuania, 1940   268
28 Ruins of the synagogue built in 1852 in Dzialoszyce, Poland, 2009   274
29 Memorial to the victims of the Lietūkis Garage Massacre in what is now a parking lot behind a school. Kaunas, Lithuania, 2017   280

Tables

1 Jewish population of Europe, 1933   13
2 Deportations of individuals from formerly Polish territory   85
3 Einsatzgruppen units and initial commanders deployed to Poland, September 1939   100
4 Einsatzkommando Bromberg Operational Report, November 10, 1939   101
5 Einsatzgruppen and their initial commanders, June 1941   130
6 Personnel breakdown of EG A, October 1941   131
7 Final Solution decision and execution timeline   205
8 Major deportation Aktions to killing centers in the East   220
9 Closing of extermination centers   221
10 Extermination centers and their death tolls   222
11 Righteous Gentiles by country (Eastern Europe)   266

ACKNOWLEDGMENTS

I am very thankful to Bloomsbury Press for asking me to write this volume. Attempting to encapsulate the Holocaust in Eastern Europe in one series, let alone one book was an intellectual challenge, but it has been an incredibly rewarding process. I have dedicated this book to my mother, who did not live to see it in print, but I know she would be incredibly proud to see it. Without her example as a writer, I would likely never have taken the path I have taken. I must thank my wife, Christina, for her support during this process, and particularly for the patience required when one's partner is in the final stages of finishing a manuscript. I am also thankful for the support and encouragement of all my family, immediate and extended. As always, my father's deep love of history in general and recognition of the importance of Holocaust history in particular continues to inspire

I am incredibly fortunate to be able to rely on a fantastic group of scholars when I have a question or need scholarly advice. I am particularly thankful for conversations with and feedback from Christopher Browning, Wendy Lower, Tarik Cyril Amar, Jeffrey Burds, Mihai Poliec, and many others who have helped me with questions large and small. I especially thank my friends at the United States Holocaust Memorial Museum for their kindness and scholarly support. In particular, Geoff Megargee, Juergen Matthäus, Martin Dean, Rebecca Erbelding, and Judy Cohen have been indispensable.

The Corcoran Department of History at the University of Virginia has been a welcoming and supportive environment. Without such an engaging and helpful home in which to teach and write, this book would not have been possible. I am particularly grateful for the help of Paul Halliday, Jeffrey Rossman, Kyril Kunakhovich, and Jolanta Komornicka as well as Whitney Yancey and Kathleen Miller, without whom nothing would get done. I would be incredibly remiss not to thank the amazing staff of Alderman Library who quickly and successfully responded to every one of my requests for obscure materials for this project.

Finally, I would like to thank my editor, Rhodri Mogford, and Beatriz Lopez for expertly guiding me through every step of the process. I would also like to recognize Rudra Krishna and Karthik Ganesh for helping me to polish this final product. All errors remaining in the text are mine alone.

Introduction

If something happens, I would want there to be somebody who would remember that someone named D. Berger had once lived. This will make things easier in the difficult moments.

DAVID BERGER to his girlfriend, Elsa, Vilnius, Lithuania,
March 2, 1941[1]

Six months after David wrote this letter, German killing squads and Lithuanian auxiliaries murdered him and thousands of other Vilnius Jews in an unfinished Soviet fuel storage site in the Ponary Forest. He was 19 years old. A German soldier who witnessed shootings there recalled that "an elderly man stopped in front of the entrance [to the pit] for a moment and said in good German 'What do you want from me? I'm only a poor composer.' The two [Lithuanian] civilians standing at the entrance started pummeling him with blows so that he literally flew into the pit . . . . 400 Jews were shot . . . over a period of about an hour."[2] By July 1944, 75,000 Lithuanian Jews were shot in the Ponary Forest.

Contrary to the image often portrayed to students and the public, Eastern Europe was the epicenter of the Holocaust and the overwhelming majority of Jews killed were Eastern European. The first large-scale killing of Jews began with the invasion of Poland in 1939 and escalated into full-fledged mass murder first in the occupied Soviet Union. The Nazis built industrialized extermination centers in the East because the majority of Jews to be murdered lived there. The Holocaust in the East obliterated a vibrant and diverse Jewish community that had existed for over a thousand years. In addition, Eastern Europe was the focus of the larger Nazi genocidal project (including the Holocaust) that envisioned German colonization of this territory and explicitly planned for the mass deaths of thirty to forty million people, most of them non-Jews. Placing this massive killing in context, the 165,000 German Jews murdered by the Nazis represent less than three percent of those killed in the Holocaust.[3]

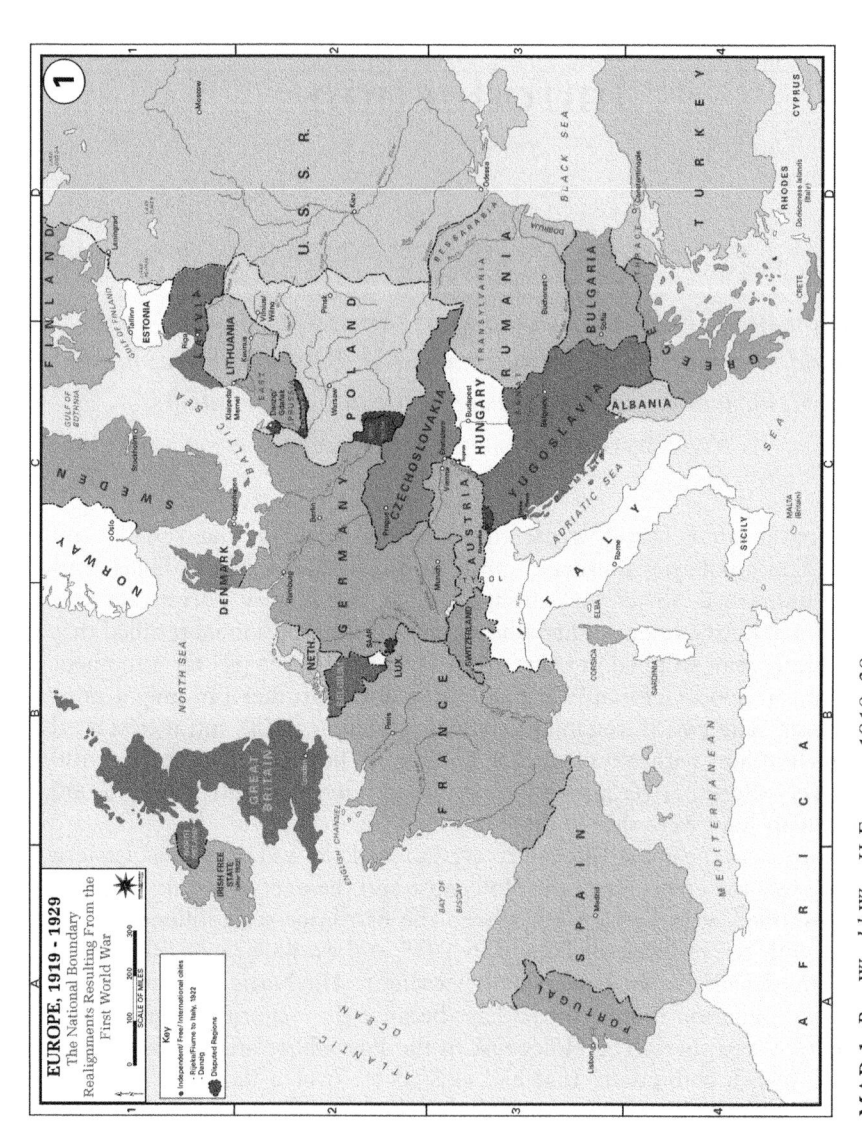

MAP 1 *Pre-World War II Europe, 1919–29.*
Source: United States Military Academy Department of History Military Atlas.

We must shift our gaze from West to East in order to fully understand the Holocaust. Anne Frank's poignant and tragic experience, for example, was not typical of the Holocaust (insofar as *any* experience is "typical.") More Jews lived in the Polish city of Lwów than in all of the Netherlands where Anne hid and wrote her famous diary. Yet, her important story has achieved a level of visibility and awareness that obscures this fact. More Jews lived in the Warsaw ghetto than in all of France. More Jews were murdered on November 14, 1941 in the small Polish town of Slonim than were saved by Denmark's unmatched, massive rescue attempt of its Jewish population. Pointing out the primacy of the East in the Holocaust does not minimize the deaths of those in other places; engaging in any form of competitive suffering is a losing endeavor for all involved. However, the Holocaust in Eastern Europe is critically different from the Holocaust elsewhere, both quantitatively *and* qualitatively.

Several important characteristics distinguish the Holocaust in the East from that in the West, apart from the sheer scale of victims. First, it was conducted largely in public and was no secret to local populations. Second, far more collaborators participated in all aspects of the Nazi genocidal project in the East. Moreover, this collaboration exceeded in severity any in the West, with large numbers of locals acting as killers and co-perpetrators. Third, the Holocaust in the East was a profoundly local affair. Most victims were not deported hundreds of miles to a gas chamber, but were shot near their homes and villages. Finally, unlike Western Europe, which has confronted its Holocaust experience with varying degrees of success, the East remains reluctant to come to terms with the murder of its Jews—at either the public or private level. For all these reasons, we must never neglect Eastern Europe in our study of the Holocaust.

This book, then, tells the story of the Holocaust in Eastern Europe through the voices and documents of those who survived (and died), those who killed, those who watched, and those who helped. It does not seek to be the definitive work on the subject, but to be an open door into a history often overlooked. At its most basic level, this is a story of humanity and inhumanity between individuals. There is no Holocaust; there are six million plus different Holocausts. The murder of an individual was committed six million times. This book, then, seeks to explore the epicenter of the Holocaust in the East—the locations of the majority of victims, of the killing centers, of the majority of collaborators, and of the majority of rescuers. All participants walked the paths that we are challenged to understand here.

Defining the "Holocaust"

Holocaust.
1. A sacrifice wholly consumed by fire; a whole burnt offering.

Oxford English Dictionary[4]

The murder of Jews in Eastern Europe lay at the heart of the Holocaust, but before we address this issue (and the justification for this book) we must define the term "Holocaust" itself, for it often means different things to different people. The word itself originates from the Greek *holos* + *kaustos* meaning "completely consumed by fire." It was often used to mean "the complete destruction of a large group of people," and probably first by the poet Milton in 1671.[5] It was not used to describe the murder of the Jews of Europe until much later, when we came to differentiate between *a* holocaust and *the* Holocaust. Even different institutions and scholars have differing definitions for the term, however. For example, the United States Holocaust Memorial Museum defines the Holocaust as "the systematic, bureaucratic, state-sponsored persecution and murder of six million Jews by the Nazi regime and its collaborators."[6] The Israeli Holocaust museum, Yad Vashem, uses the definition: "the sum total of all anti-Jewish actions carried out by the Nazi regime between 1933 and 1945."[7]

Already, we can see subtle differences in definition. In popular usage, the term has often come to be interpreted more broadly, including non-Jewish victims as well. Indeed, when US president Jimmy Carter established the US Holocaust Memorial Museum, he referred to "eleven million innocent victims exterminated," including some five million non-Jewish victims.[8] More expansive definitions led some to turn to the Hebrew word for "catastrophe": *Shoah*. This term clearly limits its coverage of Nazi crimes to those committed against Jews. Steven T. Katz represents the most extreme version of this, contending "that the Jews alone were targeted for genocide, or total physical annihilation."[9] I will, however, avoid such a narrow use of the term. Not only is it historically imprecise, but it also implies a sense of "competitive suffering" that is simply unhelpful.

I *will* use the term "Holocaust" to refer mainly to the Nazi attempt to murder the Jews of Europe; however, I will also use the more inclusive term "Nazi genocidal project" to capture the larger murderous vision of which the Jews were such a large part. This includes Sinti/Roma (gypsies), the handicapped, political "enemies," Soviet prisoners of war, and—particularly in the East—entire ethnic groups such as the Slavs. One cannot understand the Holocaust in Eastern Europe without placing it in the context of this larger Nazi genocidal project that foresaw murder and demographic engineering on a colossal scale.

This book also contains a lengthy but important discussion of preexisting German histories and fantasies regarding Eastern Europe and their mobilization by the Nazis into an unswerving focus on the conquest of that territory. These intellectual, historical, and popular conceptions of the lands in the East help explain the severity of the Nazi occupation there (as compared to that in the West) as well as the importance of the genocidal project there.

A short chapter provides the important context of the experience of Eastern European populations under Soviet rule. This period between the invasion of Poland and the invasion of the Soviet Union had important repercussions for the course of the Holocaust in the East. The Soviets' own repressive measures and attempts to redesign society affected Jews and non-Jews in similar, yet distinct ways. Perhaps most significantly, the Soviet occupation provided the Nazis with propaganda that enhanced the power of Judeo-Bolshevik antisemitic fervor among non-Jews.

Defining Eastern Europe: Boundaries, Borders, Pasts, and Presents

It was Western Europe that invented Eastern Europe as its complementary other half in the eighteenth century, the Age of the Enlightenment. It was also the Enlightenment, with its intellectual centers in Western Europe, that cultivated and appropriated to itself the new notion of "civilization" . . . Such was the invention of Eastern Europe. It has flourished as an idea of extraordinary potency since the eighteenth century.

Historian LARRY WOLFF, Inventing Eastern Europe[10]

Before we can even begin to discuss the nature of the Holocaust in the East, we must contend with the very fraught definition of that space that we call "Eastern Europe." The notion of civilization or lack thereof mentioned above further complicates matters, as the definition is itself loaded and very much in the eye of the beholder. So, what is Eastern Europe? Which areas are included? How do we define those areas? Do we use the nation state as the basis for our definition? If so, when? What borders do we choose? How do we decide upon the shape of a space containing incredible ethnic, religious, and cultural diversity and whose boundaries have undergone seismic changes in just the past 150 years while holding multiple cultural and historic affinities for centuries? One way of viewing Eastern European history is through the dominance and collapse of four transnational empires: Russian, Ottoman, Austro-Hungarian, and to a lesser extent, Prussian. Poland provides an illustrative example. A series of partitions in the eighteenth century by Prussia, Austria, and Russia tore it apart, only for it to reappear in the nineteenth century, be dismembered by the Nazis and the Soviets in 1939, and then have its boundaries shifted hundreds of miles west at the end of World War II. Thus, those who may claim a Polish background exist in Belarus, Lithuania, Ukraine, and Germany . . . and conversely, inhabitants of those regions may feel a territorial and historical claim to parts of modern-day Poland. Indeed, strong arguments can be made that the division of Eastern and Western Europe is more a relic of the Cold War than a reality in earlier periods of history.

Even the division of Europe into East and West implies an exoticization of the East that in many ways evokes European visions (and divisions) of Africa. It is no coincidence that historian Mark Mazower's book on Europe in the twentieth century is tellingly titled *Dark Continent: Europe's Twentieth Century*. For many at the time and even today, Eastern Europe conjures visions of backwardness, decay, authoritarianism, and stunted growth. While many of these stereotypes stem from the post-Soviet era, others predate it. Thus, much of the richness of the history of Eastern Europe is lost when viewed through these lenses or in comparison to Western Europe where that region is some idealized model of "civilization." Contrary to some popular belief, the sun does shine and the birds do sing in Poland.

Unlike some definitions of Eastern Europe that are primarily political, we will rely on a more spatial approach, for we are more interested in a transnational and territorial approach than a comparative political study.[11] For the purposes of this book, we will consider Eastern Europe to be the territory east of Germany (not including the Czech Republic/Slovakia) stretching to the end of "European Russia" at the Ural Mountains. From north to south, we will begin with the Baltic States and end with Bulgaria.

Here, the Balkans and Greece are notable exceptions that will not be covered in this book.[12] While in some ways this could be seen as an arbitrary distinction, other scholars *have* placed the Balkans and Greece in their own geographic category of "Southeastern Europe." Indeed, the US Holocaust Memorial Museum does not include these areas in Eastern Europe either. The region's common Ottoman past creates deeply important fault lines between this area and an "Eastern Europe," defined mostly as Baltic, Russian, Polish, and Ukrainian territories with the addition of Hungary, Romania, and Bulgaria—as they were the only independent allies of Nazi Germany in the East. Moreover, the death toll in the Balkans of roughly 200,000 pales in comparison to Eastern Europe. This is of importance for the same reason that the study of the Holocaust in Eastern Europe is important compared to that of Western Europe. Even so, our definition of Eastern Europe leaves us with eleven modern-day nations, each with their own histories and experiences in the Holocaust.

The Nazi genocidal project rested on a fluid yet ancient mosaic of cultural conflict, assimilation, and aspirations. Our story is further complicated by the often-intense collaboration of local non-Jews, particularly in killing. Collaboration occurred in the West but never to the same degree or with the same intimacy as in Eastern Europe. This book tells the story of the Holocaust in this region—a region so vital to Nazi expansion and colonial ambitions. In so doing, it brings the Holocaust in Eastern Europe back into our vision and highlights the best new scholarship on the topic.

Constraints of space and accessibility preclude a fully detailed discussion of all aspects of the Holocaust in all of Eastern Europe. However, this book will attempt to touch on as many areas as possible and provide in-depth discussions of themes and experiences common throughout the region, while noting exceptions to those experiences. Chapter 1 focuses on Jewish *life* in Eastern Europe, giving a brief history of Jews there as well as the different forms of antisemitism they experienced. Chapter 2 summarizes the rise of the Nazi state. Chapter 3 critically discusses the mythical position of Eastern Europe in both the German and Nazi mindsets. It helps us understand why the East was so important to the Nazis and how the larger Nazi genocidal project played on an altered view of a German "Manifest Destiny". Chapter 4 discusses the important period of Soviet occupation from 1939–40. This often-overlooked moment was critical in setting the stage for the experience of both Jews and non-Jews under the Nazis. Chapter 5 covers the invasion of Poland, initial mass killings there, and Nazi attempts to answer the "Jewish Question" in the region. Chapter 6 discusses the "War of Annihilation" against the Soviet Union and its relationship to the Holocaust. It includes the *Einsatzgruppen* shootings, local pogroms against Jews, and initial Nazi occupation policy. Chapter 7 addresses both Nazi ghettoization policy and the Jewish struggle to survive in the ghettos, both at the individual and organizational level. Chapter 8 surveys Hitler's independent allies: Romania, Hungary, and Bulgaria. It analyzes how and why these nations sided with Hitler and how their specific approaches to Jews fit (or did not fit) into Nazi anti-Jewish policy. Chapter 9 introduces the incremental steps toward the Final Solution. It explains how the Nazis arrived at the decision to murder Jews and then how that policy was carried out. Chapter 10 highlights the very important topic of Jewish resistance. It helps us define what Jewish resistance looked like, giving examples from camps, ghettos, and the forest. Chapter 11 is more thematic, looking more closely at Holocaust perpetrators, collaborators, and rescuers in Eastern Europe. It discusses the variety of behaviors that took place and offers some explanations as to why individuals made the choices they did. Finally, the book ends with a discussion of the immediate aftermath of the Holocaust in the East as well as a brief overview of attempts at postwar justice, and a discussion of the current state of memory and memorialization there.

For too long, the life and death of Jews and other victims of the Nazis in Eastern Europe have remained in the shadows. It is time to view the East in its own right as the epicenter of both the Holocaust and the Nazi genocidal project.

Selected Readings

Dwork, Deborah, and R. J. van Pelt. *Holocaust: A History*. New York: Norton, 2002.

Hochstadt, Steve, ed. *Sources of the Holocaust*. New York: Palgrave Macmillan, 2004.
Longerich, Peter. *Holocaust: The Nazi Persecution and Murder of the Jews*. Oxford: Oxford University Press, 2010.
Rabinbach, Anson, and Sander L Gilman, eds. *The Third Reich Sourcebook*. Berkeley: University of California Press, 2013.
Sachar, Howard Morley. *A History of the Jews in the Modern World*. New York: Knopf, 2005.

1

Beyond the Pale: Pre-War Jewish Life in Eastern Europe

Introduction

This war over the Jewish Question could continue forever for while both sides are correct concerning details, they have both relied in their arguments on sophistry, both have emphasized quid pro quo *both have missed the larger truth. How will it come to an end? When will the fate of the Jews and of the Slavs be joined together in peace? When will each side acknowledge the other's humanity and join hands for the ascent to human perfection?*

AARON LIEBERMANN, 1877, Vienna[1]

The concept of a "Jewish Question" in Europe, namely, the vague notion that something had to be done with them, was not a new concept—as demonstrated by Aaron Liebermann's plea. In many ways, this idea sprung from the simple geographical fact that, from a nation state perspective, Jews had no homeland. They lived vibrant and varied lives in all countries in Europe but due to antisemitism, xenophobia, political differences, and racism, they often were not viewed as *belonging* to any country.[2] While many Jews saw themselves as French, German, or Polish, local populations often rejected such self-identification.

Jews in Europe generally and in Eastern Europe specifically historically navigated a complicated path between assimilation and individual identity. Any discussion of the Holocaust must, therefore, begin not with Nazis, but with the Jewish history that predated their arrival and was lost or irrevocably damaged. This chapter, therefore, provides an overview of Jewish life and culture *before* the Holocaust. We will examine how and why so many Jews came to live in Eastern Europe, explore the diversity of their daily lives and become familiar with the various forms antisemitism took in this part of the world.

The Other 1492

> In the end, all suffered: some by the sword and some by captivity and some by disease, until but a few remained of the many . . . I, too, chose the way of the sea, and I arrived in the famed Naples, a city whose kings are merciful.
>
> Spanish Jew ISAAC ABRAVANEL[3]

For most Europeans (and Americans), 1492 represents the year in which a middle-class Italian explorer set sail in search of a shortcut to India. However, this year had a darker significance; it also marked the approximate end of a series of massive expulsions of Jews from Western Europe, which had begun in the twelfth century in England. King Ferdinand and Isabella, who sent Columbus on his history-making journey, declared that the Jewish population had "resulted in great damage and detriment of our holy Catholic faith." They "resolved that all Jews and Jewesses be ordered to leave our kingdoms, and that they never be allowed to return." Finally, they decreed that any Jew who remained in Spain after July of 1492 would "incur punishment by death and confiscation of all their belongings." Among those Jews fleeing for their lives was Ferdinand and Isabella's adviser and banker, the above Isaac Abravanel, who coincidentally had helped them finance Columbus' voyage.[4] By 1500, most Jews had emigrated or had fled to Eastern Europe.[5] A combination of antisemitism and political/economic developments drove this migration.

Jews from Spain, known as Sephardic Jews, settled throughout the Mediterranean (and Romania/Bulgaria) while the remainder, known as the Ashkenazi, moved to Central and Eastern Europe. Eastern Europe at this time lagged behind Western Europe in technology and governance, but many rulers in the East had already been receptive to Jews even before the expulsions from the West. In Poland, for example, Jews received some liberties, and the Statute of Kalisz gave them protective rights in 1264.[6] Here, Jews often found rulers willing to take advantage of their business acumen and mastery of languages. For some, this meant managing estates for large landowners. This relatively small number of Jews acquired a not insignificant amount of power, both legally and economically. An agreement from Poland between a landowner and a Jewish manager illustrates this well. The landowners wrote:

> We do hereby lease to the worthy Master Abraham, son of Samuel, our estates, villages, and towns, and the monetary payments that come from the tax on grain, beehives, fishponds, lakes, and places of beaver hunting, on meadows, on forests, and on threshing floors. We also give him the authority to judge and sentence all our subjects, to punish by monetary fines or by sentence of death those who are guilty or who disobey.[7]

Landowners were often willing to delegate the unpopular tasks of both collecting taxes and adjudicating minor legal disputes to their Jewish managers. Naturally, these occupations did not ingratiate Jews with the local populace.

One of the major problems of Eastern European rulers and landowners was cash management. As a result, the nobility employed an even smaller number of Jews to assist in raising and managing the capital necessary for expansion and for increasingly complex governments that relied on large sums of ready cash. With personal connections across Europe, based, ironically, in no small part on the expulsions that dispersed them, Jews were often in a particularly good position to secure loans and cash across state boundaries. These so-called "Court Jews" were, however, dependent upon regimes for support and protection. This placed them in a particularly vulnerable position should the ruler decide to default on his debts and leave his Jewish banker at the mercy of his debtors.

Life looked considerably different for the vast remainder of Jews who did not occupy such privileged positions. Eastern European states prohibited Jews from owning land in almost all cases. This pushed them into towns and cities where they occupied a variety of economic positions. The most well known and problematic of these were moneylending and early forms of banking. Christians (as well as Jews and Muslims) were prohibited, at least theoretically, from lending money to their coreligionists at interest, a practice known as usury. The clearest example of the prohibition against interest lending comes from the Christian Bible via the Gospel of Luke (6:34–5).

The workaround for all three Abrahamic religions became simply lending each other money through a member of another religion. In Europe, this generally meant Jews acting as intermediaries in executing loans between Christians at interest. This somewhat cynical relationship gave some Jews the advantage of wealth while simultaneously making it appear to the local populations that they owed money to Jews, rather than to the Christians who held the debt.

Yet, most Jews in Eastern Europe remained relatively poor and confined to certain occupations, which often varied between nations. In general, Jews lived in towns where they operated as an economic link between the rural Christian countryside and the larger cities. They worked as middlemen for agricultural goods, pawnbrokers, merchants, and craftsmen in the trades in which they were allowed to participate. In Lithuanian villages, for example, there "was almost an absolute correlation between ethnic identity and occupational profile. The vast majority of the Lithuanians were farmers, while most Jews were occupied with the entire range of 'supporting' professions."

handicrafts
petty trade,
supplying of raw material,
machinery for the agricultural needs,
burning woods for heating,
credit,
medical and pharmaceutical services,

transportation services

marketing the farms' crops

selling livestock and horses

small scale industry,

running mills, inns, distilleries, food and alcoholic beverages businesses[8]

Humble beginnings in the trades continued into modern times. In the larger cities of the East, Jews became involved in large industry, banking, and the professions as gradual emancipation allowed. Their relatively high levels of education allowed them to gain solid footholds in these areas once they opened for them. In Russia, the 1897 census reported that 80 percent of Jews were living in towns and villages and engaged in commerce, industry, and various trades.[9] By 1939, for example, in the Belorussian Soviet Socialist Republic (which contained parts of Poland, Lithuania, and Ukraine) Jews were 6.7 percent of the population. However, they accounted for 57 percent of directors of medical institutions; 51.3 percent of physicians; 49 percent of managers and directors of stores; and 24 percent of directors of agricultural and industrial concerns.[10]

Most Eastern European Jews lived in what was known as the Pale of Settlement—a massive swath of land stretching from the Baltic to the Crimea. Jews had been confined to this territory from 1791, when Russian Empress Catherine the Great forced all Jews refusing conversion to Christianity into this region. She was also motivated by a desire to prevent economic competition that engendered political conflict in Russian society. Only exceptional Jews (usually those with money and connections) could move to cities such as Moscow and St. Petersburg. The establishment of the Pale would be decisive for the experience of the Holocaust in the East, as it concentrated the vast majority of Europe's Jews there. While the boundaries of the Russian Empire eventually changed, Jewish populations remained by and large within the shadow of the Pale. Intense overcrowding and limited economic opportunities in the Pale meant that most Jews there were quite poor and scraped by economically in predominantly Jewish towns, called shtetls. Even in the larger cities in the Pale, Jews often represented sizeable percentages of the population. By 1933, an estimated 7,097,500 Jews lived in Eastern Europe, representing 75 percent of Europe's Jewish population and 46 percent of the world's Jewish population.[11]

Jewish Life in Eastern Europe

At Father's place the rejoicing was in true hasidic fashion. Throughout the Sukkot holiday, the very house was carried aloft on the wings of songs and dances lasting entire days and nights. After the hasidim finished praying in

TABLE 1 *Jewish population of Europe, 1933.*

Eastern Europe		Central Europe		Western Europe	
Poland	3,000,000	Germany	525,000	Britain	300,000
Soviet Union	2,525,000	Czechoslovakia	357,000	France	250,000
Romania	756,000	Austria	191,000	Netherlands	156,000
Latvia	95,600			Belgium	60,000
Lithuania	155,000			Spain	4,000
Estonia	4,560			Sweden	6,700
Hungary	44,500			Denmark	5,700
Bulgaria	48,500			Finland	1,800
				Norway	1,400
				Italy	48,000
TOTAL	6,691,260	TOTAL	1,073,000	TOTAL	606,600
Percentage of Jewish Population	80.5	Percentage of Jewish Population	13	Percentage of Jewish Population	6.5

Source: USHMM, "Holocaust Encylopedia: Jewish Population of Europe in 1933: Population Data by Country," http://www.ushmm.org/wlc/en/article.php?ModuleId=10005161.

Note: This excerpt does not include the Balkans.

the shtibl and snatched a hurried meal at their homes, they at once made for Father's place, and then the singing and dancing began.

YEKHEZKEL KOTIK, *Memoirs*, 1913[12]

Contrary to some popular belief, Jewish life in the shtetls of Eastern Europe, while often hard, was also filled with joy and community as Kotik describes above in his memoir. The shtetl represented a vital link between non-Jewish farmers and landowners and the larger markets of the outside world. This resulted in the concentration of Jews in towns and the shtetl and even, to a lesser extent, in the voluntary "ghettoization" of Jews in cities. Religion also encouraged Jews to live together. Orthodox Judaism required ritual bathing at a special bath or *mikvah,* and it also required a kosher butcher to prepare the meat consumed. In addition, there was a great deal of religious diversity in the choice of synagogues, shuls, and prayer houses that Jews could attend. It only made sense that all these things be colocated. Indeed, in many shtetls Jews constituted the majority, and not the minority group, as we often think of them.

Life in Eastern European towns was economically difficult due, in particular, to the prohibition of land owning by Jews. But this did not mean that Jewish life lacked happiness or meaning. Indeed, these communities were tight-knit, many having existed for centuries. Their inhabitants typically

FIGURE 1 *A father watches his son walk to school down a street of the Eisiskes shtetl in Lithuania. Eisiskes, Lithuania, pre-1941.*
Source: United States Holocaust Memorial Museum.

spoke, at a minimum, Yiddish, Hebrew, and the local language, making them exceptionally literate for most time periods. Men worked, while women stayed home preparing meals and raising the children. Jewish children would often attend secular national schools and then attend Hebrew schools that focused on teaching the language as well as providing a religious education. The Sabbath (or *Shabbat*) began on Friday evenings with a ritual meal prepared by the women of the household while the men and boys attended services at the synagogue. The Torah prohibited all work on the Sabbath so Saturdays were most often spent at religious services in the synagogue, where men and women worshipped separately. The strict observance of the Sabbath often differed greatly from its observance in the West.

Indeed, as a rule, Eastern European Jews tended to be more religious than Western European Jews and practiced Judaism differently. Eastern Europe, for example, was home to the Hasidic branch of Judaism. Beginning in the eighteenth century, this new form swept across Eastern Europe, centered on ecstatic prophecy and energetic prayer led by disciples of famous Hasidic rabbis. This form of worship contrasted sharply with the textual rabbinic Judaism that preceded it based on intensive study of the Torah and other Jewish texts as the key to understanding God's design. If nothing else, Hasidism provided hope and respite for Jews suffering from economic difficulty and violent pogroms. A group known as the *Mitnagadim,* which viewed Hasidism as heretical and advocated a return to traditional forms of Judaism, countered the rise of Hasidism—which was most popular in Poland and Ukraine. The *Mitnagadim* had their base in Lithuania, particularly in Vilna—which held a large number of prominent schools for Torah and Talmud study—reinforcing the scriptural basis of Judaism. The ideals of the European Enlightenment chiseled away at all religious belief including Judaism. The Jewish Enlightenment, or *Haskalah*, advocated greater assimilation into the non-Jewish population and the integration of secular studies into a Jewish education that it saw as useless in preparing Jews to live and work in the modern era. This movement found the most adherents in cities, which tended to be more cosmopolitan. Towns and shtetls remained relatively unaffected.

Politically, Jews in Eastern Europe lived under two systems. The first was the political system of the nation state in which they lived. Political influence and participation varied greatly from country to country, into the modern era. Jews began receiving various forms of emancipation in the 18th and 19th centuries. In general, emancipation lagged significantly behind in Eastern Europe. The Austro-Hungarian Empire granted Jews full political rights in 1867. In Poland, emancipation became official only in 1935. In Russia, the rise of Bolshevism ushered in Jewish equality in 1917. After World War I, the Minority Treaties guaranteeing protection for national minority groups and attached to the Versailles Treaty were prerequisites to joining the League of Nations in 1922. It must be said, however, that the extent to which emancipation was real or recognized varied from place to place, and at different levels of government, both positively and negatively. Regardless, by the twentieth century, Jews participated in a variety of political organizations. Many of these tended to be left leaning such as socialist or communist, for several important reasons. First, solidly Christian, agrarian, antisemitic, conservative parties often opposed Jewish emancipation in the first place — and would not admit Jews in any case. Second, leftist parties were more likely to support the kinds of institutional equality that many Jews sought, though the anti-religious stance of communism and socialism was unappealing to observant Jews. For all its many faults, the Soviet Union officially outlawed antisemitism. For this, and other reasons, many Jews chose to vote with the Left; paradoxically, many of the strongest Jewish supporters of communism, like Leon Trotsky (originally Lev Bronshtein), would never consider themselves Jewish, but rather Communists as communism recognized neither religious nor national identity. Jews even created their own socialist labor party in Eastern Europe known as the General Jewish Labor Bund of Lithuania, Poland and Russia or simply as "the Bund." However, the association between Jews and parties on the Left would become problematic as we will see.

Second, alongside the state political system resided a traditional Jewish form of self-government known as the *kahal* or *kehilla*. Historically, the *kahal* represented the Jewish community to the state and administered a wide range of public activities and services. By the beginning of the twentieth century, it had been mostly abolished in Eastern Europe as national governments tightened their control. Yet, its powerful tradition remained alive and well in the many Jewish voluntary and charitable organizations, or *hevras,* that continued to function. These organizations provided social support to the Jewish community, running orphanages, hospitals, soup kitchens, burial services, and a host of other institutions. They operated under the concept of *tzedekah,* or obligation. They were not charities, but instead opportunities for Jews to demonstrate their piety and commitment to their fellow Jews. These organizations, too, would become essential in helping Jewish communities survive under the conditions later imposed by the Nazis.

A third political development of a particularly Jewish nature appeared as well: Zionism. At the end of the nineteenth century, one man came to embody an idea that been percolating throughout Jewish history: the concept of a Jewish homeland. He was a Viennese Jew named Theodore Herzl. His simple yet controversial argument was that Jews required their own homeland. In an 1896 publication titled "The Jewish State," he enumerated why: "The idea which I developed in this pamphlet is a very old one. It is the restoration of the Jewish state. The world resounds with outcries against the Jews, and these outcries have awakened the slumbering idea."[13] Herzl believed that Jews would never be accepted in Europe and required their own nation to escape the evils of antisemitism. Zionism gained traction with Jews across the religious and political spectrum but was violently condemned by those who thought of themselves as assimilated and as citizens of the countries in which they lived, particularly in Western Europe. Zionist organizations sprung up to advocate for the creation of a Jewish state and to prepare Jews to move there. Many of these were youth groups that taught Jewish children and teenagers agricultural skills and provided a source of communal bonding. Such groups frequently provided a core of young leaders for resistance movements later during the Holocaust.

Jews participated actively in both Jewish and non-Jewish cultural spheres. In the realm of high culture, Jewish musicians, composers, and conductors—such as pianist Anton Rubinstein—were prominently represented in the musical life of Eastern Europe, including as professors in some of the best conservatories. Likewise, Jewish artists such as Marc Chagall and Szmul Hirszenberg and writers like I.L. Peretz achieved great acclaim. Alongside these forms of "higher" culture, a particularly Jewish form of cultural and creative life thrived based around the Yiddish language and the klezmer musical form. For example, the Yiddish Theater in Warsaw became a Jewish cultural icon before being destroyed during the Nazi bombardment of the city.[14]

At what would become the epicenter of the Holocaust, Jews had lived more or less peacefully for hundreds of years. Many lived in poverty in the shtetl, but in the larger towns and cities, Jews achieved some degree of economic prominence. Likewise, most Jews were very observant and lived vibrant and diverse religious lives. As they received more and more equal rights, Eastern European Jews became active in those political parties that would accept them and address their concerns, primarily parties to the Left, such as the liberals, socialists, and communists. All the while, Jews contributed to the artistic life of the region in all its forms.

The Long Shadow of Antisemitism

The prejudice of antisemitism in Eastern Europe impacted Jewish-Gentile relations from the very beginning of the Jewish presence there. One cannot understand the experience of Jews in the East during the Holocaust, or the behavior of the Nazis and their allies, without a grounding in the history of antisemitism. The simplest definition of antisemitism is "hostility and prejudice directed against Jewish people."[15] The term itself was popularized by Wilhelm Marr, a nineteenth-century German nationalist, but the concept had existed for over a thousand years. Antisemitism can take many forms, but for ease of discussion, it can be broken down into four: religious, economic, political, and racial.

In addition, antisemitism can be further categorized by the origin or "reality" of the particular trope or stereotype. Scholar Gavin Langmuir gives us a helpful framework here by introducing the concepts of realistic, xenophobic, and chimeric "assertions" that build the framework for different forms of antisemitism. "Realistic" antisemitism is based on an objective analysis of observable difference. For example, a cloth merchant in a particular town could hate Jews because he competes with them and they actually do control the market in which he operates. "Xenophobic" antisemitism takes an observation of a small minority of a group and holds it to be true for all. In our example, then, that same merchant would say that rich Jews control the entire cloth trade because they are all clever and cheating businessmen. Here, the antisemite has taken an observation that may be true for a small number of Jews and applied it to the entire class of people, ignoring poor Jews and not recognizing that they do not control the entire market everywhere. Finally, "chimeric" antisemitism is based on pure fantasies that have no basis in fact or observable evidence. Here, our merchant may claim that all Jews are part of a worldwide economic conspiracy to overthrow the Christian state and that they secretly meet to manage this conspiracy.[16] These levels of antisemitism inform how we look at the phenomenon of antisemitism over the centuries.

Naturally, the oldest form of antisemitism stems from the origins of Christianity and can be called religious antisemitism or anti-Judaism. According to Christian doctrine until as late as 1965 for the Catholic Church, the Jews were directly responsible for the murder of Jesus; not the Roman official, Pontius Pilate. Multiple verses in the New Testament are openly antisemitic or were interpreted that way. For example, in the Gospel of John, Jesus is quoted as telling Jews "ye cannot hear my word. Ye are of your father the devil, and the lusts of your father ye will do. He was a murderer from the beginning, and abode not in the truth, because there is no truth in him . . . He that is of God heareth God's words: ye therefore hear them not, because ye are not of God."[17] Moreover, according to the Church, *all* Jews were responsible and would remain guilty for eternity. These and other similar verses provided a scriptural basis for hatred and discrimination against Jews, particularly when Christianity in its earliest form competed against a much more established Judaism. In the year 313 CE, Roman Emperor Constantine legalized Christianity, which until then had been intermittently persecuted by the Roman government. With this institutional legitimacy and the support of the Roman Empire, Christianity gained the upper hand over its rival, Judaism.

Thus, for Christians throughout much of history, Jews became "Christ-killers." This charge had particular power as Christians tended to be far more devout in earlier times than they are today. The belief that Jews had killed the son of God greatly angered many Christians. The only reason Jews were still allowed to exist, according to Christian doctrine as expressed by St. Augustine, was as a humiliated reminder of the results of rejecting the truth of God.[18] Thus, in what became a self-fulfilling prophecy, the frequent poverty, discrimination, and victimization of Jews proved their great sin which then justified the behaviors that victimized them. Most Europeans were illiterate and all they knew of Christianity came from the priests who told them what to believe, including what to believe about the Jews. Indeed, even the stained glass and architecture of cathedrals visually depicted antisemitic beliefs for the masses who could not read Latin or access the Bible themselves.

Even the coming of the Reformation and the weakening of the Catholic Church that followed did little to ease the plight of Jews or reduce religious antisemitism. The great leader of the Reformation, Martin Luther, initially a supporter of Jews, focused on learning Hebrew and on the Bible as the basis of Christianity, but mistakenly believed that Jews failed to convert to Christianity due to the same flaws he identified in Catholicism and sought to remedy with Protestantism. When Jews still refused to convert, Luther turned on them, unleashing a torrent of antisemitic literature such as *On the Jews and their Lies* (1543), in which he tells Christians that "you have no more bitter, venomous, and vehement a foe than a real Jew."[19] Thus, Christian antisemitism transcended doctrinal differences.

Given the depth of religious belief in earlier periods of history, antisemitic religious doctrine had very real, physical consequences. In 1144, a young boy went missing in Norwich, England. When the boy's body was found, a Benedictine monk named Thomas of Monmouth blamed the Jews for the child's murder. According to Monmouth, Jews murdered Christian children as part of their religious rituals. This charge led to pogroms and the murder of Jews throughout England. It bears noting that that some leaders in the Catholic Church almost immediately rejected the Blood Libel. Indeed, the victim, William of Norwich, was never officially sainted, despite a strong popular cult following. Pope Gregory X (1271–76) wrote a Papal Bull on the blood libel, saying:

> And most falsely do these Christians claim that the Jews have secretly and furtively carried away these children and killed them, and that the Jews offer sacrifice from the heart and blood of these children, since their law in this matter precisely and expressly forbids Jews to sacrifice, eat, or drink the blood, or to eat the flesh of animals having claws.[20]

Popes who opposed victimization of Jews were motivated at least in part by a desire to convert them, a task made impossible if they were killed. However, other popes repeated antisemitic charges and the official position of the Church must be characterized as apathetic at best to anti-Jewish violence, with other popes actively fomenting antisemitic animosity.

Worse still, this chimeric belief spread throughout Europe, where it became widely accepted as true. Christian communities frequently accused Jews of murdering children to obtain their blood as well as defiling the communion host by stabbing it to make it bleed. Ironically, these accusations and the murders that followed may have had more to do with Christianity's insecurity in its own beliefs: by validating religious doctrine regarding transubstantiation and communion. Attacks on Jews also often accompanied societal upheavals such as the plague, economic hardship, or political unrest—where Jews became scapegoats for the real culprits, who remained out of reach. Priests frequently whipped Christian communities into anti-Jewish fervor around religious holidays, particularly Easter. Their parishioners then attacked local Jews. As ridiculous as the blood libel may seem today, it was taken very seriously and persisted for a very long time. In Eastern Europe, which experienced the Enlightenment and the rise of more secular and rational thought later than Western Europe, charges of blood libel and pogroms persisted into the twentieth century.

In 1913, the *New York Times* reported on the trial of Mendel Beilis, a Russian Jew charged with the ritual murder of a Christian boy in Kiev. He was accused of "having killed a boy to get his blood for alleged use in the rites of the Jewish religion." Yet, the *Times* editorial writer noted correctly even at the time that "there was no evidence against Beilis" and, indeed, that a gang of criminals had likely murdered the boy. The reporter called the blood libel "a foolish, blind superstition bred of prejudice upon ignorance" and accused Russia of being "2000 years behind the times."[21] It may be shocking to some readers that such chimeric antisemitism could persist into "modernity." Beilis was eventually cleared after two years in prison and two trials, but the fact that he could be convicted of "ritual murder" by a modern court system in 1913 demonstrates the power that Christian antisemitism possessed in the East. More importantly, across Europe—not just in the

FIGURE 2 *The Great Synagogue in Slonim. The small buildings in the foreground are Jewish shops. Slonim, Poland/now Belarus, pre-1939.*
Source: United States Holocaust Memorial Museum.

East—Christian antisemitism remained a lasting division between Jews and non-Jews—one that could pave the way for other forms of antisemitism.

Economic antisemitism stems from the intersection of stereotype and anti-Jewish fantasy. The basic form of this bias alleges that Jews are naturally ruthless, dishonest, and efficient businessmen and that they seek to use this business acumen to control national and international affairs. The origins of this stereotype likely lie in the Middle Ages or earlier. Economic antisemitism is based, in part, on a self-fulfilling prophecy created by the economic limitations placed on Jews by non-Jews. The most prominent version of economic antisemitism was the view of Jews as economic parasites, taking money from non-Jews via moneylending or banking. This stems from the Christian prohibition on usury, the lending of money at interest.

Usury is mentioned in both the New and Old Testament. One of the clearest prohibitions comes from Ezekiel: "thou hast taken usury and increase, and thou hast greedily gained of thy neighbours by extortion, and hast forgotten me, saith the Lord GOD. Behold, therefore I have smitten mine hand at thy dishonest gain which thou hast made, and at thy blood which hath been in the midst of thee."[22] The message was that Christians should not take advantage of fellow Christians in financial need by profiting via interest. One should note that both the Torah and the Koran also prohibit usury by Jews and Muslims as well. While certainly not all Jews were moneylenders and not all moneylenders were Jews, this became one of the most prominent negative economic stereotypes.

The most extreme and least common form of Jewish banking took the form of the "Court Jew." In the early modern period, as armies and government became larger and required more money, very successful Jewish bankers were called upon to manage the finances of important nobles and kings and to supply loans to finance their wars. Some of these Court Jews became very influential and powerful, though they were always at the mercy of the whims of their Gentile patrons. Compared to the overall Jewish population, however, these men were a tiny minority. As mentioned earlier, as Jews were expelled from Western Europe, some found employment as managers for noble estates. This led many into the unpopular occupation of tax farming, where Jews collected the nobility's taxes from the population in return for a percentage of proceeds.

However, throughout much of Eastern Europe, most Jews were not extraordinarily wealthy and, indeed, were often impoverished. They functioned frequently as wholesale buyers of crops and livestock, a trade that often engendered suspicion by non-Jewish peasants that deceitful Jewish traders took advantage of them. The same was true of Jews who acted as merchants and small shop owners.

As the Industrial Revolution gained momentum, Jews were again the targets of economic antisemitism for several reasons. The first was due to their relationships with capitalism and communism, which will be treated in more detail below. The second was that some Jews—particularly in Western

Europe, but also in the cities of Eastern Europe—were specially poised to take advantage of the changing economic climate. By not owning land, wealthy Jews had immediate access to cash and could invest quickly in the new factory and mass retail economic landscape. As a result, they were often successful in the industrial and large-scale retail spheres. This engendered anger, envy, and frustration among the predominantly non-Jewish small business owners and craftsmen, who could no longer compete with more modern business models. The Nazis would be very popular among German small business owners who viewed the Jews as responsible for their inability to compete. Local populations viewed Jews as being dishonest and as taking advantage of them in their greedy quest for wealth. (And again, most Jews, particularly in Eastern Europe, were not wealthy industrialists or retailers, but the stereotype gained a strong following.)

In short, many non-Jews disliked Jews due to a combination of very real debts owed to them, economic hardship attributed to them, and the fantasy that Jews were part of a world conspiracy to monopolize wealth. This was further connected to the belief that the Jews, as a people without a nation, functioned as economic parasites in the countries in which they lived. These beliefs melded well with political forms of antisemitism.

One of the most central components to political antisemitism was the belief in a "Jewish Question" in Europe beginning in the eighteenth century. This question presupposed that something had to be done with the Jews. Why? According to antisemites (as well as some who were not), the Jews were a problematic group of people because they lacked their own nation state. They were a nationality/ethnicity dispersed throughout Europe, but remained a minority in every country that they inhabited. For many nationalists, this was a problem—in an era when creating states based on shared beliefs and histories was paramount. The Jews represented an obstacle to this in the minds of these theorists because they remained a (relatively) cohesive group that lived in many ways separately from the majority population, particularly in Eastern Europe. The question then, politically, was how to solve this division. Some advocated the expulsion of the Jews and others suggested that the only path to full inclusion was assimilation and conversion to Christianity. This was not a conversation for Gentiles only. In Jewish communities, thinkers like Moses Mendelssohn also suggested that Jews do more to assimilate—speaking the local language, abandoning special forms of dress, and interacting more with their non-Jewish neighbors. Of course, other Jews pushed back against this, particularly in the East, though urban Jews usually tended to be more liberal than the townspeople. Zionists entered into this discussion, advocating that Jews should leave Europe anyway for a homeland in Palestine.

Regardless, the "Jewish question" centered on the modern concept of the nation state; it was here, in politics, that battles for its answer would take place. These battles varied based on local conditions, but political antisemitism became part of national politics throughout Eastern Europe as Jews received more rights and the ability to participate in the political process. Most political antisemitism centered on that fundamental antisemitic belief that Jews sought to control the world through a secret conspiracy and that Jews across national boundaries plotted with one another to accomplish this task. Again, the primacy of the nation state as political framework and the threat of these states being destroyed from the inside in the interests of an international Jewish conspiracy had purchase among some.

One of the best examples of this was the *Protocols of the Elders of Zion*, excerpts of which first appeared in Russia in 1902. This short pamphlet published by Russian writer Sergei Nilus in 1905 purported to be the record of a meeting of a secret organization of powerful Jews, which demonstrated their goals and intent to control the world. Nilus has been described by one scholar as "half prophet and half scoundrel."[23] The preface to the 1921 English edition mirrored the content of the *Protocols* by invoking World War I and saying "it was plotted by Jews, and was waged by Jewry on the Stock Exchanges of the world. The generals and the admirals were all controlled by Jewry." It claimed to explain "how they [the Jews] obtained controlling power for Jewry over all the combatants."[24] The text itself contained such "evidence" of an apocalyptic conspiracy as this quote from an "Elder":

> We will select administrators from among the public, who will be possessed of servile tendencies. They will not be experienced in the art of government and therefore will be easily turned into pawns in our game in the hands of our learned and wise counsellors, who have been, especially trained from early childhood for governing the world.[25]

The *Protocols* were rather quickly proven to be a collection of forgeries, falsehoods, and plagiarism of other existing texts. Indeed, in 1921, the *Times of London* published an article presenting "conclusive proof that the document is in the main a clumsy plagiarism."[26] Despite their exposure as a hoax, however, the *Protocols* held a prominent place in antisemitic propaganda and were accepted by many as legitimate. The *Dearborn Independent* newspaper—owned and published by famed American industrialist and antisemite, Henry Ford—frequently published antisemitic articles that echoed the *Protocols*. On July 20, 1920, an article titled "Does a Definite Jewish World Program Exist?" claimed that "the finances of the world are in control of Jews."[27] The Nazis published twenty-three editions of the *Protocols* from 1919 to 1939.[28] Hitler himself often included concepts from the document in his speeches.

We have already seen that, as Jews gained emancipation and became more politically active, they gravitated toward parties of the moderate to extreme left. This is not to say that there were no Jews who supported other political parties. Regardless, even before the rise of the Soviet Union in 1917, Jews were tarred with the accusation that they supported socialism and communism. The antisemitic logic behind this generalization was that both ideologies espoused the redistribution of wealth and that the world Jewish conspiracy was behind this distribution to its own benefit.

This led to the Judeo-Bolshevist myth in which Jews created Bolshevism to advance their agenda. Part of this myth was founded on the specious argument that Jews were prominent among the first leaders of Communism. It is true that many of the early adherents to Communism (Zinoviev, Kamenev, and Trotsky) had Jewish backgrounds, but they would never have claimed to be Jews. In any case, after Stalin's Great Purge (1936–40), few Jews were left in any prominent positions. Regardless, after what Europe saw as the horrors of Communism—which threatened institutions many Europeans held dear—the connection of Jews and Bolsheviks generated a great deal of animosity. For example, around sixty pogroms took place in Ukraine in November and December 1917, and culminated with the mass killing of Jews in the town of Proskurov in 1919—where 1,200 Jewish men, women, and children were murdered by Ukrainian soldiers for allegedly supporting the communists.[29]

Ironically, despite the Judeo-Bolshevik slander, Jews were also blamed as the driving force behind capitalism, which also sought to accumulate the world's wealth under the control of the "World Jewish conspiracy." A Nazi propaganda book for children, published in 1935, shows an image of a caricatured Jew sitting on a sack of money in front of a stock exchange with the caption "Money is the god of the Jews. He commits the greatest crimes to earn money. He won't rest until he can sit on a great sack of money, until he has become king of money."[30] Hitler, too, saw Jews as behind the economics which, in his view, had lost the First World War and was driving the destruction of the German way of life by extracting Germany's wealth. His 1933 boycott of Jewish businesses was an assault on Jewish economic life in Germany and revealed his "belief" in the economic power of Jews. One of the chief Nazi theorists, Alfred Rosenberg, claimed in 1941 (regarding World War I) that "Now, on Wilson's order, all of the major Jewish and non-Jewish banks and businesses are now being joined in one conglomerate group of Jewish bosses under the kingpin Bernard Baruch. He was in control of the entire industrial infrastructure of the United States."[31] This formulation blended economic antisemitism with political antisemitism by accusing Jews of controlling liberal democratic movements that supported capitalism.

In short, the underlying chimeric belief that there was a Jewish conspiracy to control the world drove politically antisemitic sentiments that blamed Jews in liberal democratic and in communist parties equally for a litany of supposed ills of society. This antisemitism was used to minimize and combat Jewish political mobilization and inclusion in the political process.

Politically active Jews and Jewish political organizations were always subject to deep-seated hatred and antisemitic charges.

The most dangerous and ultimately deadly form of antisemitism arose in the nineteenth century: racial antisemitism. When Charles Darwin published his famous treatise *On the Origin of Species* in 1859, he could not know the ways in which his theory of the evolution of individual species could be harnessed to racist ideologies. Other theorists quickly applied Darwin's work to humanity. Surely, they argued, if natural selection (often misidentified as "survival of the fittest") applied to animals it also applied to humans. Thus, the scientific community began to assign characteristics to ethnic groups and to identify their origins as genetic. In this way, scientists constructed races among humans and began to rank them. They argued that, just as in the animal kingdom, there must be groups within the human species that were superior and destined to prosper while others were doomed to eventual extinction. Whites stood at the top of this racial hierarchy. Jews, blacks, Slavs, native peoples, and others fell beneath white Europeans. Wilhelm Marr, who popularized the term "antisemitism," expressed the urgency of racial politics in his 1879 treatise, *The Way to Victory of Germanism over Judaism*, where he argued that Jews and Germans were locked in a racial death struggle which could only result in the victory of one and the defeat of the other (in a warped comparison to the way natural selection functioned among animal species).

Among racial antisemites, Jews were biological contaminants in countries in where they lived. Most importantly, genetics, not religious practice or cultural tradition, now defined Jews. This made someone a Jew for life, made conversion irrelevant, and assimilation impossible; Jewishness became a matter of blood. Earlier negative stereotypes about Jews (greed, dishonesty, sexual deviance, etc.) now became written into their genetic code. Hitler made clear his views in a 1919 letter viewed by many scholars as the first evidence of his antisemitism. He said, "First, Jewry is absolutely a race and not a religious association."[32] According to Hitler's racial view of Jews, " small doses of German blood could dominate other sorts of blood—except in the case of the Jews, where the opposite was the case. Hitler imagined that even tiny amounts of Jewish blood could assert themselves after many generations."[33]

At about the same time, the pseudo-science of eugenics or racial hygiene gained popularity throughout Europe. Eugenics rested on the concept of social Darwinism: the idea that the "survival of the fittest" required that societies and entire racial groups be in constant competition. Eugenics treated societies and races as one might treat an individual in an attempt to ensure the health of the entire race. Respected institutions such as the Kaiser Wilhelm Institute in Germany and the Eugenics Records Office at Cold Spring Harbor, NY, funded by the Carnegies and Rockefellers, began researching and publishing on hereditary dangers facing society. These included legitimate genetic conditions, but also social ills such as promiscuity, alcoholism, criminality, and other undesirable, but not inherited, behaviors. The eugenics movement advocated selective breeding in the same way livestock were bred for better traits. Forced sterilization would prevent undesirable groups from reproducing. In Germany, legal scholar Karl Binding and psychiatrist Alfred Hoche published a book in 1920 in which they argued for the killing of those individuals who were genetically inferior. Binding wrote, "Again, I find, either from the legal, social, ethical, or religious standpoint absolutely no reason not to permit the killing of these people, who embody the terrible countertype of a true human and awaken horror in nearly everyone."[34] The eugenics movement, its racialization of populations, and advocacy of extreme measures, greatly affected the later development of Nazi anti-Jewish policies. The Nuremberg Laws of 1935 preventing sexual relationships between Jews and non-Jews are but one example. The Nazis drew deeply on racialized views of Jews, where the mixing of races was a threat to the "Aryan" race and where "the Jews constituted a counter-race, the parasitic instincts of which were out to undermine Aryan blood, character, and mind."[35] Indeed, a 1936 SS publication called the Jew "a parasite, the bloodsucker of the world." It simultaneously connected multiple antisemitisms, proclaiming that "three figures are characteristic of the Jews: Ahasver, who has no roots, Shylock the soulless, and Judas the traitor."[36]

This short discussion of Eastern European Jewish history and antisemitism is vital to understanding the Holocaust in the East. Jews in the East had longstanding connections to their countries, and thriving cultures of their own; they were not simply victims of genocide. The complex history of their interactions with other religions and ethnicities formed the experiences from which they approached and attempted to weather the Holocaust. Indeed, Jewish responses to Nazi persecution were often based upon centuries of experience with other forms of antisemitic oppression. However, they had never faced an enemy such as the Nazis, intent on their physical removal from Europe.

In addition, understanding antisemitism is vital as, in many cases, it formed the foundations of relationships between Jews and non-Jews with critical repercussions for the Jewish population. One of the most pernicious characteristics of antisemitism was the many forms it could take, which could reach a wide variety of audiences with wildly different interests. On the other hand, we must be careful not to ascribe all the motivations for the Holocaust to antisemitism. Indeed, there were antisemites who saved Jews and otherwise moral people who murdered them. Antisemitism was one powerful undercurrent that, along with individual motivations and situational factors, provided the energy for the Holocaust. At different times and places, it could be more important, but any search for understanding the Holocaust cannot end with a monocausal explanation based on antisemitism. Indeed, as we will see in the chapter to follow, antisemitism and larger constructs of race theory combined with much older mythical views of the East to directly influence Nazi policy in Eastern Europe and its attitudes toward conquered populations.

Selected Readings

Goldstein, Phyllis. *A Convenient Hatred: The History of Antisemitism*. Brookline, MA: Facing History and Ourselves, 2012.

Langmuir, Gavin I. *Toward a Definition of Antisemitism*. Berkeley: University of California Press, 1990.

Mendelsohn, Ezra. *The Jews of East Central Europe between the World Wars*. Bloomington: Indiana University Press, 1983.

Petersen, Hans Christian, and Samuel Salzborn, eds. *Antisemitism in Eastern Europe*. edited by Samuel Salzborn. Vol. 5, Politische Kulturforschung. Peter Lang GmbH: Frankfurt am Main, 2010.

2

The Origins of the Nazi State

Introduction

The German Reich, as a State, should include all Germans, not only with the task of collecting from the people the most valuable stocks of racially primal elements and preserving them, but also to lead them, gradually and safely, to a dominating position.

ADOLF HITLER, *Mein Kampf* (1923)[1]

Before we can examine the Nazi genocidal project in the East and the unfolding of the Holocaust, we must understand the basic history of Nazism. Specifically, how did the Nazi party become the Nazi state and how did this regime come to be in a position to carry out its policies in Eastern Europe? This entails meeting Adolf Hitler, the man, and the organization he created. For, it is Hitler who wrote above how important the East was to the Nazis. Simultaneously, we must be careful not to ascribe to Hitler a master plan or sole responsibility for the Holocaust.

The Nazis created a state based on a variety of popular causes that appealed to a broader audience and bought together different constituencies. Hitler built a cult of personality around himself in which he and the state were one—an idea that energized many German people. Territorial expansion was a critical plank in the Nazi platform . . . one which Hitler believed could only be realized in Eastern Europe. He was not alone in this belief either, drawing upon a long history of yearning for a German "return" to the East. This chapter brings us to 1939, the point when the Nazis began that return to the East.

The Nazi Rise to Power

National Socialism must, in principle, claim the right to force its principles on the whole German nation and to educate it in its ideas and thoughts . . .

It must determine and reorder the life of a nation, and therefore must imperiously demand for itself the right to overlook boundaries drawn by a tendency which we have rejected.

ADOLF HITLER, *Mein Kampf*[2]

While the Nazi state had many actors, many of whom were at odds with one another, the transformation of Germany into a fascist dictatorship began with one man. He drew many Germans to his side with the promises, illustrated above, of a return to greatness and a new national order. Adolf Hitler (1889–1945) was born in Braunau am Inn, Austria to a domineering father who served as a government customs agent. There is no evidence that his parents were particularly antisemitic. Desiring to be an artist, Hitler moved to Vienna in 1905 to attend art school. The Vienna Art Academy rejected him and Hitler struggled, often penniless, homeless, and selling his mediocre artwork on the street. It is likely that he blamed Jews, who he saw as controlling the art world, for his failure. Looking back, he attributed his antisemitism to this period of his life, though it is unclear if this is accurate. In *Mein Kampf*, Hitler relates some of his early antisemitism. He describes an encounter with an Eastern European Jew, an *Ostjuden,* saying, "I suddenly came upon a being clad in a long caftan, with black curls. Is this also a Jew? was my first thought." More ominously, he then asked, "Is this also a German?"[3] The following pages devolve into derisive and vulgar descriptions of Jews. It is instructive that he attributed his revulsion to an Eastern European Jew and not an assimilated Austrian Jew. According to Hitler, he also recognized at this time the alleged connection between Jews and Marxism. He alluded clearly to this form of antisemitic fantasy saying, "If, with the help of the Marxian creed, the Jew conquers the nations of this world, his crown will become the funeral wreath of humanity."[4] Hitler also dated his hatred of all things communist *and* democratic to this period. Again, in *Mein Kampf*, he wrote, "Democracy of the West today is the forerunner of Marxism, which would be inconceivable without it."[5] He also became disgusted with Viennese cosmopolitanism, which he saw as weakness resulting from racial mixing. Hitler, a constant admirer of all things German, moved to Munich in 1914. It is unclear how much of Hitler's worldview was *actually* formed during his time in Vienna, as he wrote in 1923 after having undergone some substantial life changes. In addition, the book was intended for a public audience. Some scholars argue his antisemitism did not truly mature until much later.

Adolf Hitler might have remained a failed artist in Vienna if not for World War I. In August 1914, Hitler enlisted in a Bavarian infantry unit where he served as a corporal on the Western Front. He worked as a courier, running messages between front-line trenches and headquarters. Hitler appears by all accounts to have served honorably in this relatively dangerous duty. His superior, a Jewish lieutenant, recommended him for the Iron Cross, First Class, though this may have had more to do with his assignment to regimental headquarters.[6] A comrade described him as "a good and eager soldier."[7] Hitler was wounded twice—on the latter occasion by a mustard gas attack in 1918. He learned of Germany's defeat as he lay in a hospital suffering from temporary blindness from that attack. He wrote that upon hearing the news, "I groped my way back to the dormitory, threw myself on my cot and buried my burning head in the covers and pillows."[8]

This moment might be one of the most important in Hitler's life. The war had given Hitler's life a new sense of meaning. He wrote in *Mein Kampf*, "overwhelmed by impassionate enthusiasm I had fallen on my knees and thanked Heaven out of my overflowing heart that it had granted me the good fortune of being allowed to live in these times."[9] For Hitler, the war was a defining moment, a test of will and endurance from which he personally emerged victorious. In equal measure to his pride in his service and his belief in the ennobling qualities of war was his distress and shame at Germany's defeat, which he steadfastly refused to admit. Instead, he quickly subscribed to the "Stab in the Back Theory," blaming Germany's defeat on Jews, war profiteers, communists, and others who he believed had defeated Germany from within. This myth arose almost immediately. General (and later President) Hindenburg declared the day after the Armistice, "We have borne our arms with honor." The commanding general of the 18th Army reported that, "Undefeated, it is coming back home, after having faithfully accomplished her duty." A local newspaper in Köln advised its readers to welcome a unit home with celebration "for the army has not 'lost the battle.'"[10] Former World War I general Erich Ludendorff most vociferously promulgated this false interpretation. Hitler echoed Ludendorff referring to Germany's civilian government as the "wretched party rascals who betrayed the people."[11]

In what must go down as history's worst job placement, the German army assigned Adolf Hitler in 1919 to monitor right-wing extremist organizations. His supervisor in the Army later referred to Hitler as a "stray dog looking for a master."[12] However, this stray dog would *become* the master. On September 12, 1919, Hitler arrived as an informant at a meeting of the right-wing German Worker's Party (*Deutsche Arbeiter Partei-* DAP) in a brewery in Munich. Rather than remaining a silent observer, Hitler delivered a devastating retort to an audience member and, shortly thereafter, joined the party.[13] Within four years, Hitler's fiery oratory and political maneuvering catapulted him to the top. In 1920, the party was renamed the National Socialist German Worker's Party (*Nationalsozialistische Deutsche Arbeiterpartei-* NSDAP, "Nazi" in abbreviation.

Throughout the early 1920s, Hitler consolidated his hold and began building the embryonic organization that would become the Nazi state. He established a group of armed thugs (the *Sturmabteilung* (SA) or Stormtroopers) to protect party events and also battle left-wing paramilitaries in the streets. A small bodyguard force that later became the SS protected Hitler personally. Also, during this period, many of the key players in the

Third Reich gravitated toward Hitler. Among these were former World War I pilot and morphine addict Hermann Göring and failed chicken farmer Heinrich Himmler. Increasing pageantry and incendiary speeches marked Nazi party events. Hitler consciously built a cult of personality, where he as *der Führer* or "the Leader" embodied the will of the party and the German race. A guiding principle of the Nazi state imbued the Führer's wishes with the weight of law. The Nazi party generated a steady stream of propaganda condemning the "November criminals" (civilian leaders who had signed the Versailles Treaty ending World War I), Jews, communists, and playing off the instability of the early years of the Weimar Republic.

By 1923, Adolf Hitler believed the time had come for the revolution that would put him in power. He modeled his coup on Benito Mussolini's successful March on Rome. Mussolini, who Hitler greatly admired, had marshaled large numbers of his paramilitary "Black Shirts" and, through a powerful bluff, forced the King of Italy to give him the reins of government. Hitler hoped to accomplish the same in Germany. The reluctance of some party and government officials (*Staatskommisar* Gustav von Kahr, *Reichswehr* General Otto von Lossow, and Bavarian Police Chief Hans von Seisser) to take such a drastic step frustrated him. As a result, on the night of November 8, 1923, he initiated his power grab, arresting Kahr, Seisser, and Lossow, in a Munich beer hall (hence the name "Beer Hall Putsch"). Hitler assembled a large number of party members and declared the national revolution had begun. He even gained the support of well-respected former general Ludendorff. However, things unraveled rapidly from this point leading to the climactic morning of November 9, when Hitler and 2,000 Nazis marched on the Bavarian Defense Ministry but were met with gunfire by *Reichswehr* soldiers—which killed sixteen Nazis. Four Bavarian policemen were also killed putting down the revolt. This decisively marked the end of Hitler's abortive attempt to seize power. Though conservative, the Bavarian government and military was in no mood for the chaos of revolution and remained loyal to the state. Without their support, the coup was doomed before it could begin. Hitler was arrested three days later with a dislocated shoulder. As his biographer wrote, "Hitler was finished. At least, he should have been."[14]

On February 26, 1924, Hitler's trial for high treason began in Munich. He faced serious charges but, instead of portraying Hitler as an extremist and traitor, the trial provided him with a national platform from which to address the people of Germany. A pro-Nazi journalist described the trial in the following melodramatic but also apt way:

> And Hitler speaks. Speaks for four and a half hours. The courtroom sinks, the court sinks, the walls sink—only one man is left standing and hundreds of thousands listening—millions—this man is not the accused, by God, he is an inexorable accuser, and his sentences burn like flames.

... "I left Vienna a confirmed anti-Semite, a deadly foe of Marxism." The statement sweeps through the room like a peal of thunder.[15]

Hitler's fame grew immensely thanks to his performance at his trial. The judge lost control of the proceedings and only barely succeeded in convincing the jury that they could not acquit Hitler. As a result, he received only five years in prison with the possibility of early release ... for attempting a violent overthrow of the government.[16]

Bavarian authorities remanded Hitler to Landsberg Prison along with his co-conspirators. His time there was very comfortable as he was attended upon by his personal secretary, Rudolf Hess, and frequently received visitors. Most importantly, Hitler reexamined his political strategy and wrote *Mein Kampf* (My Struggle): a rambling combination of biography and political philosophy. The book also laid out some of Hitler's plans for the future, though historians differ over the extent to which these should be considered as actual plans. Hitler walked out of prison a free man, pardoned by the court in December 1924 after barely a year's incarceration. The biggest change in the Hitler who left Landsberg that cold morning was his coming to realize that he would need to take power through legal, democratic means.

This, Hitler set out to do almost immediately. In his absence, the various fringe right-wing parties that had begun uniting under his leadership had fragmented. He absorbed them again into the NSDAP while molding it into a modern political party with a complete platform—in contrast to fringe single-issue antisemitic parties. In this way, he broadened his base to include more mainstream voters and he began to move more freely in conservative circles of power and with greater legitimacy.

Hitler and the Nazi party succeeded at the ballot box because they tailored their message to different constituencies. Perhaps surprisingly, anti-Communism formed a larger part of Nazi propaganda in the early days than vulgar antisemitism. This made good political sense as most Germans had witnessed the terrifying collapse of the Russian Empire in 1917 as well as the very real violence in their own streets as left-wing extremists battled right-wing extremists; after all, a communist state had briefly taken over Bavaria. Nazi propaganda urged a Germanization of the population, a removal of corrupting influences, making Germany great again, and combating the terror of Communism. As economic depression swept through Germany, the Nazis organized soup kitchens and dangled prosperity in front of people crushed by poverty.

This political platform gained traction. The NSDAP went from 6.6 percent of the vote in national elections in May 1924 to a high point of 37.3 percent in July 1932; their number of seats in the Reichstag increased from six to 230.[17] In the July 1932 election, Hitler directly challenged the incumbent president, former general Paul von Hindenburg, and was only narrowly defeated. Despite electoral success, the Nazis could not create a governing coalition. Unfortunately, neither could anyone else. The Social

Democrats and Communists failed to see a common threat in the Nazis and thus did not combine their significant electoral power to block the NSDAP. At the same time, President Hindenburg also could not form a working government and ruled from crisis to crisis through emergency decrees. Hitler refused the position of Vice Chancellor in July 1932, guessing correctly that he could hold out for a higher position in return for delivering Nazi support and stability. Thus, despite the fact that the Nazis actually lost ground in the last democratic elections of the Weimar Republic, Franz von Papen convinced Hindenburg to name Hitler Chancellor, despite Hindenburg's obvious detestation of the "bohemian corporal." Conservatives believed that Hitler was a political blowhard who could be controlled. They were dreadfully wrong.

Adolf Hitler, failed Austrian painter and convicted traitor, was named Chancellor of Germany by one of the country's most respected war heroes on January 30, 1933. Serendipitously for Hitler, less than a month later, a Dutch communist set fire to the *Reichstag* (parliament) building. Hitler leapt at this opportunity to further paint his left-wing opposition as clear and present dangers to the German people. This was his "God-given signal" to "crush out this murderous pest [Communists] with an iron first."[18] Seizing upon an unfortunate clause in the Weimar Constitution, Article 48 allowing the Chancellor to take all measures to maintain national security, Hitler issued the "Reichstag Decree" or the Decree for the Protection of People and State. This decree "suspended the personal liberties enshrined in the Weimar Constitution" and centralized power in the hands of the federal government.[19]

Hitler followed this decree with an immediate wave of assaults on the German Communist Party (KPD) and Social Democratic Party (SPD). He now prepared for a full and permanent seizure of power. After ejecting the KPD from the Reichstag, Hitler sought the passage of the Enabling Act, which granted the Chancellor unlimited executive and legislative powers for a period of four years. With the KPD removed and the SPD cowed, Hitler needed only the support of the Catholic Center party to achieve his aim. On March 23, 1933, the Enabling Act was passed and Hitler became an absolute dictator. Social Democrat Otto Wels stood out as a voice in the wilderness. Speaking on the floor of the Reichstag, he noted that

> Never before . . . has the control of public affairs by the elected representatives of the people been eliminated to such an extent as is happening now and is supposed to happen even more through the new Enabling Act. Such omnipotence of the government must have all the more serious repercussions inasmuch as the press, too, lacks any freedom of expression.[20]

Thus, less than ten years after his revolution was literally gunned down in the streets of Munich, Adolf Hitler achieved his goal of absolute control over Germany . . . through mainly political means.

The Evolution of the Nazi State

> Membership in the Greater German Chess Association which from now on will be the [country's] sole chess organization, is to be determined in accordance with an Aryan paragraph.
>
> German Chess Association, July 9, 1933[21]

From the moment Hitler took power, the Nazis began a campaign to consolidate control of every aspect of German private and public life, including in such mundane areas as a game of chess. Central to this was building support among the local population through massive propaganda campaigns. Hitler dedicated two full chapters in *Mein Kampf* to the "Significance of the Spoken Word" and "Propaganda and Organization." In order to realize his most extreme visions, Hitler knew that incessant and powerful messages explaining the Nazi worldview and ideology must saturate Germany. The mission of indoctrinating the country fell to the short, sickly, and clubfooted Josef Goebbels. He articulated the goal of Nazi propaganda in a 1933 speech saying, "We, on the other hand, intend a principled transformation in the worldview of our entire society, a revolution of the greatest possible scope that will leave nothing out, changing the life of our nation in every regard."[22] Goebbels's adoration for the Führer was complete. As he wrote in 1926, "I love him ... He's a man, taking it all round. Such a sparkling mind can be my leader. I bow to the greater one, the political genius."[23]

In 1933, Goebbels was appointed the Minister of Propaganda in Hitler's cabinet. He had a keen mind for propaganda and frequently spoke at Nazi party events. He also understood how to leverage the new technology at his disposal such as radio and film. In a speech titled "Radio as the Eighth Great Power," he proclaimed, "It is, in fact, a modern revolution, and it has used the most modern methods to win and use power ... the government resulting from this revolution cannot ignore the radio and its possibilities."[24] The Nazi propaganda machine also incorporated print media; from the official newspaper, the *Völkischerbeobachter* (People's Observer), to the odiously antisemitic *Der Stürmer* (The Attacker) published by the even more odious Julius Streicher. Nazi indoctrination also utilized film and all manner of material aimed at specific audiences such as children, students, and women. For example, propaganda targeted children in school and in the Hitler Youth and men in the military via small "knapsack books" on a variety of topics. In addition, Goebbels organized elaborate public events, the most famous of which were the carefully staged and orchestrated Nuremberg rallies, drawing hundreds of thousands of participants for fiery speeches, torch lit ceremonies, and parades. Perhaps the most famous of these was the 1934 rally—the subject of the Leni Riefenstahl film *Triumph of the Will*, a classic in propaganda filmmaking.

The Nazis gained strong support among ordinary Germans, in large part because they presented a variety of issues to the populace. Nazism promised a return to greatness after the humiliating defeat of World War I, playing on simple nationalism. It added a racial component and the concept of the *Volksgemeinschaft,* or national racial community. Nazi propaganda also offered economic relief to Germans suffering the effects of the depression while simultaneously blaming those misfortunes on Jews, communists, and other "enemies of the state." It appealed to more conservative Germans by its rejection of liberal social values, as can be seen in actions against homosexuals and modern art—which it termed "degenerate." Nazi propaganda outlets also violently condemned communism and promised to protect Germany from this threat; a threat that many could relate to given the chaos of the immediate postwar years. When Soviet massacres of Polish prisoners of war were discovered in 1940, Goebbels ordered that the event would "now be exploited in a major way for anti-Bolshevik propaganda."[25] A related vein of propaganda was the lure of the East, the promise of self-sufficiency guaranteed by the destruction of the Soviet Union and the inferior races of Eastern Europe. Lastly, but certainly not least, the Nazis offered a wide array of antisemitic messages, from the most vulgar to more refined arguments, with racial, economic, and political underpinnings.

The Nazi governing apparatus, however, did not clearly delineate the responsibilities of the government. Areas of authority often overlapped, leaving Hitler's subordinates to sort out conflicts among themselves. As one historian points out, "Hitler's way of operating was scarcely conducive to ordered government."[26] Indeed, the Führer preferred maintaining power in his own hands, preventing his subordinates from accumulating too much of their own. Nazi luminaries like Goebbels, Göring, Himmler, Speer and others constantly jockeyed for Hitler's approval. Indeed, the Nazi cabinet never met during most of the twelve years the Nazis were in power. While this system helped maintain Hitler's power base, "the Hitler regime was inimical to a rational order of government and administration. Its hallmark was systemlessness, administrative and governmental disorder, the erosion of clear patterns of government, however despotic."[27] This government structure created two important characteristics of the Nazi state and its plans for the future. The first was a tendency to "work toward the Führer."[28] This concept of "working towards the Führer" meant that Hitler rarely gave explicit or written directives to his subordinates; indeed, they attempted to divine his wishes and intent. Those best able to anticipate Hitler's desires experienced the most success and favor. This system also meant that no single subordinate remained permanently in Hitler's favor and so competition to best understand their leader was continuous. As one Nazi official recognized as early as 1934, "anyone who really works towards the Führer along his lines and towards his goal will certainly both now and in the future one day have the finest reward in the form of the sudden legal confirmation of his work."[29]

The second important characteristic of the Nazi state and its policies arose from the first. This was the phenomenon of "cumulative radicalization."[30] Cumulative radicalization resulted from Hitler's tendency to be most receptive to the most ambitious, extreme, and far-reaching plans that mirrored his intent. This drove subordinates to seek ever grander, ever more extreme solutions to state dilemmas of all kinds. This had important consequences regarding the Nazi genocidal project and the Holocaust, as we will see later.

The chaotic nature of Nazi government allowed for a complex merging of state and party apparatuses as the Nazis took power in Germany, from village government to the highest national offices. Beginning in Bavaria, for example, Heinrich Himmler took control of the German police force, moving from a party official to a government official, and then combining party and police forces. The Communist and Social Democratic parties were outlawed and their members arrested and placed in "protective custody"—in makeshift camps like the one in Dachau (established March 22, 1933), fashioned from an abandoned munitions factory. Throughout Germany, Nazis interned and sometimes killed their political enemies in a series of "wild camps," ranging from basements in local party headquarters to river barges. The first prisoners of the concentration camps were German, not Jewish (though Jews were interned if they were also political enemies.) The goal was to terrify the political opposition into silence. In 1936, *Reichsführer-SS* Heinrich Himmler consolidated the concentration camp system under SS Lieutenant General Theodor Eicke, a formerly disgraced SS officer released from a mental hospital.[31] This second chance guaranteed Eicke's loyalty, and he began building a series of organized camps using Dachau as a model. Himmler placed what would become a massive system of camps and subcamps under his control, enhancing his own power within the regime.

Himmler, an awkward and unprepossessing young man who had watched World War I from the sidelines, maneuvered himself into a position of incredible power, beginning in 1929 when he took over Hitler's personal bodyguard. An opportunist and true believer in Nazi *Volkisch* and racial policy, he rose to prominence by bringing all German police organizations under his control by 1936. In 1939, he created the *Reichssicherheitshauptamt* (RSHA) or Reich Security Main Office. This contained the *Geheimstaatspolizei* (Gestapo) or Secret State Police, the *Sicherheitsdienst* or Security Service (SD), and the *Kriminalpolizei* or Criminal Police (Kripo). The Gestapo and the SD would be most deeply involved in carrying out the Holocaust while the Kripo functioned more or less as regular police. His protégé, the ambitious and talented Reinhard Heydrich, headed the RSHA. His relationship with Himmler was characterized by "deep trust, complementary talents and shared political convictions."[32] Likewise, Himmler "was the man who enabled Hitler actually to exercise his position as a dictator with, in principle, unlimited power through the deployment of state terror."[33] By the end of World War II, Himmler's SS empire spanned the continent and influenced innumerable areas of Nazi policy. Chief among these would be the murder of the Jews of Europe.

Hitler took advantage of his newfound powers and the instrument of the SS to eliminate potential opponents and settle scores with those he felt had wronged him in the past, as exemplified by the "Night of the Long Knives"—a series of personal and political killings that took place from June 30 to July 2, 1934. To cement the vital support of the military (which he had lacked during the Putsch), Hitler agreed to neuter the SA and eliminate its leader, Ernst Röhm, who envisioned a people's army that was completely unacceptable to the existing conservative military. The SS and Gestapo murdered Röhm, who had stood by Hitler during the Putsch. Among other political enemies were Nazi party dissenter Gregor Strasser and, the man who had stood in Hitler's way in 1923, Gustav von Kahr. Hitler's strike succeeded. The *Reichswehr* minister, Blomberg, praised "the soldierly determination and exemplary courage" shown by Hitler in destroying the "traitors and mutineers."[34]

The Nazi consolidation of power did not stop at governmental agencies or at the national scale. Germany was a nation of clubs, associations, and groups of all kinds and all political stripes, and the Nazis coopted them all. Soon, there was an official Nazi version of each that Germans were forced to join as their other options vanished. This process, known as *Gleischaltung* (coordination, bringing into line), was the Nazi attempt to simultaneously unite the *Volk* and control all aspects of public and private life. Catholic singing clubs became Nazi singing clubs, shooting clubs became Nazi shooting clubs (and socialist shooting clubs were disbanded.) Importantly, local authorities made many of these changes without prompting from higher authorities. Thus, the Nazi state gradually narrowed the separation of the public and private spheres in an attempt to create the *Volksgemeinschaft*: a unified racial community with Nazi values.

Nowhere was this clearer than in Nazi anti-Jewish policy in Germany. With Hitler's seizure of power, he and the Nazis took their first steps against the Jews, taking advantage of the Führer's ability to unilaterally dictate policy. Nazi officials organized a boycott of Jewish businesses on April 1, 1933. The attempt had mixed results, as reported by Jewish doctor Paula Tobias:

> from across the road came two young fellows in full array and told me in the most embarrassed manner that they were supposed to stand in front of our property and not to [let] any patient in . . . . it did not work that way everywhere. In Holzminden for example there had been bloody riots with plenty of arrests and shattered windows.[35]

The boycott caused damage across Germany, but only partially succeeded economically; yet it represented an important step in the escalation of

Nazi anti-Jewish policy. Nazi antisemitism was plain to see in the slogans painted across Jewish businesses and, while some ignored the boycott, Germans in general seemed indifferent, if annoyed, by the interruption in normal affairs.

A week later, on April 7, 1933, the "Law for the Restoration of the Civil Service" removed Jews and political opponents from all government positions—from the bureaucracy to schools. The language was very clear: "Civil service officials of non-Aryan descent are to be retired."[36] The only exception, for the time being, was World War I veterans.

The Nazis went a step further in 1935, issuing the "Law for the Protection of German Blood and German Honor," forbidding marriage and sexual relations between Jews and non-Jews. The introduction to the statute claimed that the laws were "compelled by knowledge of the fact that the purity of the German blood is the prerequisite for the continued existence of the German *Volk*, and inspired by the unbending will to secure the future of the German nation in perpetuity."[37] Violators of these so-called "Nuremberg Laws" were subject to arrest and confinement in a concentration camp. A flurry of other laws and restrictions followed, restricting Jewish social and economic freedoms and personal liberties and slowly removing them from public life, even chess clubs. Many German Jews moved from smaller towns—where they were more vulnerable—to larger cities. In this way, over 400 Jewish communities disappeared.[38] The examples below illustrate both local initiative and the escalation of discrimination:

> The City Health Insurance Institute will as of April 1 1933 no longer reimburse the costs for treatment by Jewish physicians.
> Berlin Commissioner of Health, March 31, 1933

> Non-Aryan students will not be permitted to take the examination to become teachers of dance.
> President of the Reich Chamber of Theater, July 27, 1934

> Entrance of Jews to public bathing and swimming facilities is forbidden.
> The City Council of Augsburg, July 19, 1935

> All streets named after Jews . . . are to be immediately renamed. The old street signs are to be removed forthwith and exchanged with new signs.
> Minister of the Interior of the Reich, July 27, 1938

> Jews are not permitted to use public libraries.
> President of the Reich's Chamber of Writers, August 2, 1941

> As of September 15, 1941, all Jews over the age of six are forbidden to appear in public without wearing a Jewish star.
> Ministry of the Interior of the Reich, September 1, 1941[39]

Gradually increasing antisemitic measures enabled the Nazis to gauge public opinion and also to "encourage" Jews to emigrate from Germany. Many Jewish families made this agonizing choice; however, the Nazis extracted practically all wealth before allowing exit. This made it very difficult for most Jews to enter countries like England and the United States; the rest left for other countries in Europe—which would eventually fall into Nazi hands.

1938 witnessed another major turning point in Nazi anti-Jewish policy. In November, a Polish Jew named Herschel Grynzspan was angered at the treatment of his parents, who were trapped between Poland and Germany by the antisemitic immigration policies of both countries. On November 7, he walked into the German embassy in Paris and shot a low-level diplomat, Ernst vom Rath, and was arrested shortly thereafter. Vom Rath died two days later.

Rath's assassination gave the Nazis another opportunity to escalate anti-Jewish violence. What was to appear as a spontaneous outburst of righteous anger at Jews was, in fact, a planned and coordinated assault known as *Kristallnacht* (or the Night of the Broken Glass). Goebbels announced in a speech that Hitler would not intervene in anti-Jewish demonstrations.[40] Heydrich issued more specific instructions to the police, noting that "places of business and apartments belonging to Jews may be destroyed but not looted." He also ordered that "as many Jews in all districts—especially the rich—as can be accommodated in existing prisons are to be arrested."[41] Jewish businesses, synagogues, and homes were damaged and destroyed while the police, firemen, and population looked on. 267 synagogues were burned, 7,500 Jewish-owned businesses were vandalized and looted, and at least 91 Jews were killed during the violence.[42] The Nazis billed the Jewish community for the damage caused. The vulgar Nazi propagandist, Julius Streicher, invoked the "Stab-in-the-back" myth as justification for *Kristallnacht* in a speech the next day. He ranted,

> Today we heard of a "lady" who sighed that it was heartbreaking to see all the destroyed shops. Who had pity for us when, after the war, the Jew brought down enormous misery on the German people, as the Jew stole our savings during the great inflation, as Germany was blockaded during the World War by Jewish orders and hundreds of thousands of women and children starved?[43]

For the first time, the Nazis arrested and interned large numbers of Jewish men in concentration camps. They aimed to extort money for their release and to further encourage emigration. *Kristallnacht* represented an important turning point, being the most violent and most public violence against Jews yet—and it was, again, more or less tolerated, if not applauded, by most Germans.

We should pause here to briefly discuss the first mass killings conducted by the Nazis. Its victims were not Jews, but Germans. In 1938, the parents of a badly deformed child wrote the Führer, asking him to authorize the "mercy killing" of their infant. Hitler ordered his personal physician, SS Dr. Karl Brandt, to investigate the case, and, if necessary, kill the child. Brandt authorized the killing.[44] Hitler then signed a letter authorizing Brandt and his Chief of the Chancellery, Phillipp Bouhler, to expand the program. What followed was a policy of so-called "euthanasia" that was, in fact, the killing of mentally and physically handicapped Germans who were considered to be "useless eaters" and "life unworthy of life." This was the practical application of the eugenics and racial hygiene theories of Binding and Hoche and others. In late 1938, the Nazis began a secret program to murder the handicapped, known as Operation T-4, after the address of its headquarters—Tiergartenstrasse 4. Panels of doctors analyzed and passed judgment on hundreds of patients a day, based solely on their records, without ever examining them. Special buses transported patients to several designated mental hospitals in Germany and Austria where they were gassed to death. Relatives received ashes with a false cause of death—and were billed for the shipping and handling. This process was not without its mistakes; some families received two sets of ashes or were told their loved one had died of appendicitis when the appendix had been removed years earlier. In short, it became impossible to maintain the secrecy of the operation. This failure became painfully clear when Catholic Bishop Clemens von Galen took to the pulpit on August 3, 1941, in brave opposition to T-4, saying, "we are concerned here with human beings, our fellow human beings, our brothers and sisters! With poor people, sick people, unproductive people, if you will. But does that mean they have forfeited the right to life? Have you, have I, the right to live only so long as we are productive, so long as we are recognized by others as productive?"[45] Hitler himself promised to kill Galen at the end of the war. Seeking to avoid a public relations disaster, however, Hitler agreed to—at least publicly—end the program; it continued in a decentralized manner, resulting in the murder of over 70,000 German men, women, and children by the end of the war. The staff that helped carry out this program would not be idle for long, as we shall see later.

The Wars that Hitler Won: Nazi Foreign Policy, 1933–40

"Well, Ribbentrop," I asked him while we were walking in the garden, "What do you want? The Corridor or Danzig?" "Not any longer"—and he fixed on me those cold . . . eyes of his—"We want war."

From the Diary of COUNT CIANO, Italian Foreign Minister, August 11, 1939[46]

There are some who prefer to look at Adolf Hitler as insane or living in a dark fantasy world of his own creation. Yet, for a good portion of his rule, Hitler was an adept politician and accomplished diplomat. Indeed, from 1933 to 1940, he faced international (and some domestic) opposition and prevailed repeatedly. He understood very well the geopolitical and strategic climate and quite effectively achieved his foreign policy goals; goals that further solidified his support at home. It was not until the failed Battle of Britain and the invasion of the Soviet Union that Hitler's worldview drove Germany toward eventual defeat. Moreover, as Ribbentrop clearly recognized above, Hitler wanted war, for he knew that only war would allow him to gain what he sought. What follows is a brief summary of the "wars" that Hitler won up to his invasion of the Soviet Union, which we will discuss in detail later.

Hitler's foray into foreign policy began with reversing the effects of the Versailles Treaty that ended World War I and so humiliated Germany. The Allies sought to prevent future German aggression by reducing its army to 100,000 men, without heavy naval ships or airplanes. They also took land from Germany—in an attempt to both extract reparations and reduce the power of Germany's territorial position in Central Europe. The Treaty split eastern Germany, granting the so-called "Danzig corridor to the sea" to Poland. It also created the state of Czechoslovakia, partly from German-speaking lands. In addition, the Treaty demanded the area bordering the Rhine river, known as the Rhineland, be demilitarized to further protect France from any future German attack.

Hitler sought to reclaim lands these lands and to rebuild Germany's military might, which many Germans viewed as synonymous with Germanic pride. Hitler and many others blamed these penalties on the failures of the "November criminals"—German politicians who had signed the treaty of Versailles. However, Hitler also had much grander plans; reclaiming the lost land of Versailles would never ensure German self-sufficiency and the *lebensraum* (living space) he believed was required for his future conquests. He never intended to stop at returning to the 1914 status-quo.[47] However, Hitler shrewdly started small. He violated the terms of the Versailles Treaty almost immediately. In the interwar period, treaties with the Soviet Union allowed Germans to train on tanks and aircraft in the East. At home in Germany, civilian organizations such as the *Nationalsozialistischenfliegerkorps* (NSFK), or National Socialist Flying Corps, allowed pilots to conduct military flight training in secret.

The Führer openly violated the Versailles Treaty first on March 7, 1936 when he remilitarized the Rhineland. Against the advice of his generals and advisors, Hitler ordered thirty thousand German troops to occupy the territory while he addressed the Reichstag. When he announced the operation underway in the Rhineland, the deputies went wild. "The Messiah plays his role superbly," American journalist William Shirer noted with foreboding.[48] Hitler recognized the risk he was running by so openly flaunting his disdain for Versailles; he had already ordered his troops to withdraw if they met with any resistance. But they were unopposed. Hitler had gauged his enemies correctly; none of the Allies had been willing to risk a war over Germany returning its own soldiers to its own territory. Hitler justified his actions as a response to French diplomatic overtures to his enemy, the Soviet Union. He then offered to participate in peace talks "to avoid any misinterpretation of [his] intentions and to establish beyond doubt the purely defensive character of these measures."[49] In addition, in his mind, he defied the conventional wisdom of his advisors and succeeded through force of will and prophetic vision.

Nine days later, Hitler drove another nail into Versailles' coffin, announcing the return of military conscription and an increase in the size of the Army. This ushered in a period of rapid rearmament and military buildup. These developments were just the beginning for Hitler, as he acknowledged in a secret 1936 memo casting Germany as Europe's defense against Bolshevism. The memo proclaimed, "If we do not succeed in developing the German Army as quickly as possible into the best army in the world—in training, in the number of troops, in armaments, and above all, in mind and spirit—Germany will be lost!"[50] Indeed, Hitler aimed to rebuild a powerful army; for him, the new *Wehrmacht* would be the "victorious sword" that would conquer all of Europe.[51] Naturally, such a program pleased both the generals and the industrialists. It also pleased the populace. An opposition report noted that "Hitler has again gained extraordinary ground among the people. He is loved by many."[52] For many, Hitler had erased some of the shame of the defeat in World War I. More importantly, the Führer had gambled successfully that the Allies would not act. France was certainly alarmed, but Britain was preoccupied and not interested in punishing Germany. The United States had forsworn any overseas entanglements. In fact, some of the former allies felt in hindsight that the Versailles Treaty had been too harsh. Regardless, Hitler correctly read the tea leaves and knew that no one would risk another world war over his rearmament program.

Hitler's next move came in March of 1938, when he "occupied" Austria in what came to be known as the *Anschluss*; again demonstrating his keen ability to manipulate his adversaries. One of the central principles of the Versailles peace had been the right to national self-determination, which argued that people of like nationalities should have the ability to choose to be together. After Austrian Nazi agitation, the German Army entered Austria and incorporated it into the greater Reich. What had been known as Austria became the province of *Ostmark* after a "plebiscite." Again, international reaction was decidedly lackluster.

Hitler next targeted the newly formed Czechoslovakia. Initially, he sought to reclaim only the *Sudetenland*, an area in western Czechoslovakia with a majority German population. He used the Minorities Treaties that resulted from the Versailles Treaty as a justification. The Nazi party had secretly funded the Sudeten German Party—an ally that wanted a return to Germany

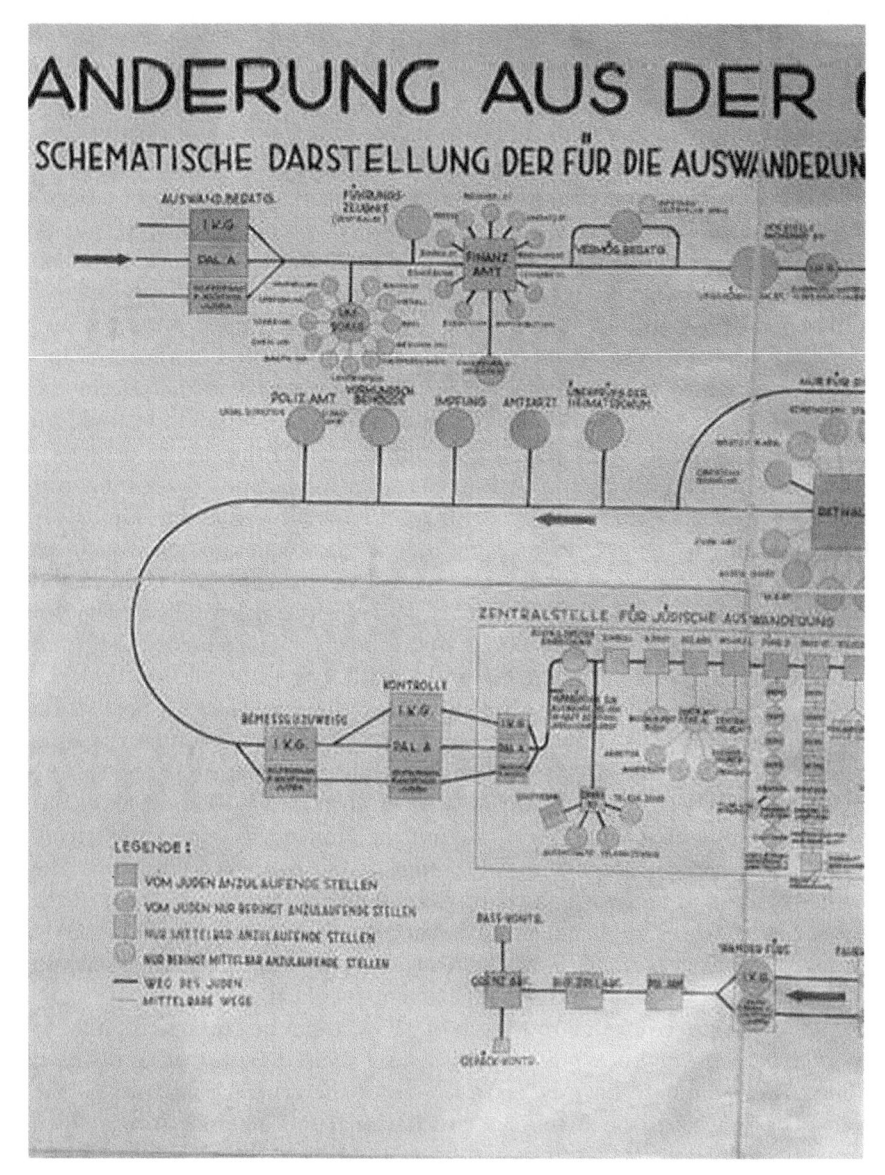

FIGURE 3 *Excerpt from Eichmann's diagram for the steps required for Jews emigrating from Vienna, illustrating the complexity of the process. Many of these organizations were involved in expropriating Jewish wealth and property before they could leave Austria, ca. 1938–39.*
Source: Israelitische Kultusgemeinde Wien.

and that applied pressure to the Czechoslovakian government. Hitler intentionally manufactured a crisis in Czechoslovakia. His saber rattling did not go unnoticed: his own advisors, including Göring, advised against war.

Still wishing to avoid a general war, the Prime Minister of Great Britain, Neville Chamberlain traveled urgently to Munich in September 1938 for negotiations.

With Hitler threatening war and the former allies having no stomach for it, Germany, France, Italy, and Britain signed the Munich Agreement on September 29, giving Hitler control of the *Sudetenland*. No one consulted the Czechoslovakian government. Neville Chamberlain declared "Peace in our time" while Hitler told his generals that "it must be possible to smash at any time the remainder of the Czech State."[53] By March of 1939, Hitler had bullied Czech President Hàcha into surrendering the remainder of the Czech state. German troops entered the country unopposed and it became the Protectorate of Bohemia and Moravia in the Greater Reich. Hitler claimed this would be Germany's last demand for land.

Thus, after only six years in power, Hitler had reversed almost all the humiliations of Versailles and regained most of the lost territory without a shot fired or negative diplomatic repercussions. He had also done it largely against the advice of his closest advisors and generals, a fact that he never forgot and which gave him great confidence moving forward. He now turned toward Poland, which to Germany was more important than any of the previous territories had been. Unlike his previous acquisitions, parts of Poland would be part of the *lebensraum* or "living space" that Hitler sought in the East. It would also greatly exacerbate his "Jewish Problem" by increasing Jews under German control from around 300,000 to 3,000,000. Unlike previous conquests, this one would not come easily. The Nazi government asked Poland, in October 1938, to return the annoying Danzig corridor to Germany, uniting Eastern Prussia with the rest of the country.[54] It was a demand that Poland could never agree to. Hitler may have hoped to bully Poland as he did Czechoslovakia, so he was enraged when the British government allied itself with Poland on March 31, 1939. Sir Neville Chamberlain addressed the House of Commons saying:

> In the event of any action which clearly threatened Polish independence . . . His Majesty's Government would feel themselves bound at once to lend the Polish Government all the support in their power.[55]

Sensing that war was becoming inevitable, German diplomats in Poland increasingly pressed for ever more unrealistic concessions. Italian Foreign Minister Galeazzo Ciano correctly wrote in his diary in August 1939 that "I am certain that even if the Germans were given more than they ask for they would attack just the same because they are possessed by the demon of destruction."[56]

Meanwhile, Hitler was determined to protect Germany from the two-front war that had ruined Germany in World War I. On August 23, 1939, his Foreign Minister, Joachim von Ribbentrop, signed the Nazi-Soviet

Non-Aggression Pact with the Soviet Union. Outwardly, it appeared to be a standard non-aggression treaty, but inside secret protocols divided Poland in case of war and handed half of Poland and the Baltic States to the USSR. On the same day, Hitler received a letter from Chamberlain stating that "whatever may prove to be the nature of the German-Soviet Agreement, it cannot alter Great Britain's obligation to Poland, which His Majesty's Government have stated in public repeatedly and plainly and which they are determined to fulfill." He further warned, that Britain was "resolved and prepared to employ without delay all the forces at [its] command."[57] At this point, it seems that Hitler was ready for war. By April 3, 1939, "Case White," the plan for the invasion of Poland, was finalized and the *Wehrmacht* was instructed to be prepared to invade no later than September 1. In addition, while there may have been some doubters, Hitler's generals seemed to now believe in his vision. Chief of the General Staff Franz Halder practically gushed about the "outstanding, I might say, instinctively sure policy of the Führer."[58] In truth, Hitler had proved the skeptics wrong every time so far. Despite last-ditch diplomatic attempts by others to prevent hostilities, he was determined to go to war. And *this* war would have ominous implications for Nazi Jewish policy. On January 30, 1939, Hitler had spoken before the Reichstag:

> Today I will again be a prophet and say, if international finance Jewry in and outside Europe succeeds in plunging nations into another world war, then the end result will not be the Bolshevization of the planet and thus the victory of the Jews—it will be the annihilation of the Jewish race in Europe.[59]

The audience roared. While this does not indicate a decision at this point to murder all the Jews of Europe, it does represent the importance of the war in Hitler's mind to increasingly extreme measures against Jews.

On the night of August 31, a group of SS men staged a mock attack on a German radio station at Gleiwitz, on the German-Polish border. Early the next morning, on September 1, 1939, the German Army poured into Poland. Hitler addressed the Reichstag the same day, saying, "I have once more put on the uniform which was once the most holy and precious to me. I shall only take it off after victory or I shall not live to see the end."[60] The British and French governments issued ultimatums demanding the immediate withdrawal of German troops in order to avert war. Upon the news, Hitler "sat completely silent and unmoving," according to his government interpreter.[61] Nevertheless, there was no going back; war had already started. On September 17, the Red Army invaded Poland from the East, completing its downfall. The Soviets occupied the Baltic States and their half of Poland and began immediately to implement their communist revolution.

Unfortunately for the Poles, while England and France declared war on Germany, words remained largely the extent of the help Poland received from the West. Geography was the third ally of Nazi Germany and the British or French simply could not reach Poland, certainly not with any hope of impacting the outcome in any way. The period after the surrender of Poland until the invasion of France in 1940 was a period of military inactivity, known as the "Sitzkrieg" while both sides prepared for the inevitable attack on France.

That moment ended when Germany invaded France on May 10, 1940—again employing its superior tactic of blitzkrieg. The French, relying on a series of massive static defenses known as the Maginot Line, were unprepared for the German assault through Belgium that had rendered their fortifications useless. Despite the aid of a British expeditionary force, the French capitulated in less than two months, with the British barely escaping from Dunkirk. Hitler then ordered an aerial assault on Britain in preparation for an invasion. He hoped to eliminate his enemies in the West before focusing on his true targets in the East—and thus avoiding a two-front war scenario. The *Luftwaffe* campaign under Hermann Göring, however, proved a disastrous failure. It soon became clear that there were, indeed, "bitter weeds in England," and that the campaign against Churchill would be far more protracted than Göring had promised. Yet, Hitler had already been ordering preparations for an invasion of the Soviet Union in May 1940. The failure of the Battle of Britain encouraged him to continue with these plans, as he believed that the British were only staying in the war in "expectation of the Soviet Union and United States replacing France as Britain's continental ally."[62] Thus, what Hitler expected would be a quick and decisive destruction of the Soviet Union would isolate Britain and hasten their surrender. However, when the Germans invaded the Soviet Union in June 1941, they would soon see how wrong this particular prophecy was. And so began the war that Hitler lost.

Naturally, the Nazi state was essential for the Holocaust. However, its byzantine organization and competitions for favor would drastically impact the *way* in which it and the larger Nazi genocidal project unfolded in the East; the consent—overt or passive—of the German people for the regime enabled an ever-expanding set of imperial and racial policies. While Hitler and his beliefs have been highlighted here, thousands of Nazi leaders at all levels influenced and altered Nazi policy. The outcomes were usually the same for the victims. Policies, ideologies, and even personnel developed in Nazi Germany from 1933–9 would be exported to occupied territories in the East so that the Holocaust there took place with important roots in the Reich. Finally, Hitler's foreign policy successes (and failures) created the landscape upon which the Holocaust took place. The Holocaust was not a purely ideological, Hitler-driven event, nor was it created solely by actors and situations on the ground. Situation, ideology, and personalities merged in complex ways to enable genocide.

Selected Readings

Bergerson, Andrew Stuart. *Ordinary Germans in Extraordinary Times: The Nazi Revolution in Hildesheim*. Bloomington: Indiana University Press, 2004.

Friedländer, Saul. *Nazi Germany and the Jews: The Years of Persecution, 1933–1939*. Vol. 1, New York: HarperCollins, 1997.

Kershaw, Ian. *Hitler: A Biography*. New York: W.W. Norton & Company, 2008.

Leitz, Christian. *Nazi Foreign Policy, 1933–1941: The Road to Global War*. London: Routledge, 2004.

Longerich, Peter. *Heinrich Himmler: A Life*. New York: Oxford University Press, 2012.

3

Nazis and the Imaginary East

Introduction

We are ceasing the perpetual German movement toward Southern and Western Europe and leveling our gaze at the land in the East.

ADOLF HITLER, *Mein Kampf*[1]

When someone asked noted historian Robert Citino what would have happened if Hitler had decided *not* to invade the Soviet Union, he replied, "He wouldn't have been Hitler." This succinctly describes, in part, the importance of Eastern Europe to Hitler, to the Nazis, and, historically, to the Germans. Hitler drew upon much older Germanic dreams when he leveled his gaze at the East, a subject he covered extensively in *Mein Kampf*. After all, the invasion of the Soviet Union was code-named *Operation Barbarossa*, after a medieval emperor who, legend had it, would one day rise from his deep sleep to return Germany to greatness. It is *impossible* to truly understand the nature of the Holocaust and the Nazi genocidal project in the East without examining long-held German obsessions with Eastern Europe as the natural source of its *lebensraum*; an obsession that long predated the Nazis. Eastern Europe was not simply a geographical location in Nazi and German minds. It was much, much more. Indeed, it was fundamentally different spatially from the rest of Europe. For Germans, the East beckoned as a land of untapped wealth begging for "civilization" in much the same way that the West did for Americans. These visions did not remain abstractions. However, there are fundamental differences in how Germans treated Eastern peoples over the years, especially when comparing occupation during World War I and World War II. We do not draw a straight line from German views of the East to the eventual Holocaust and genocidal projects there, but the Nazi colonization of the East and the Holocaust deeply influenced one another. Even within the Nazi leadership, opinions differed on the manner of colonization and "Germanization" to be carried out in the East.² What is so important about German mindsets about the East is that they became very real policies that spilled large amounts of very real blood.

The Nazi built their gaze toward the east upon centuries of myth and revisionist history placing Eastern Europe at the center of both a German past and a Nazi future. Fundamental revisions of history and not-so-subtle racial prejudices provided a framework for a colonial and imperial attitude toward Eastern Europe that was never directed at the West. Understanding this explains why Nazi policy *and* the Holocaust were executed so fundamentally differently in the East. These attitudes also situate the relationship between Nazi authorities and their non-Jewish partners and collaborators in the East, as well as the extremity and brutality of their behavior there. This chapter, then, seeks to answer the question "Why Eastern Europe (in the context of the Holocaust and the Nazi genocidal project)?" It will also help us to understand the concrete and incredibly lethal plans developed by scholars and bureaucrats within the Nazi state to depopulate and then colonize the East.

Selective Memory: Historical Germandom in the East

To the East Land we want to ride, we want to come along to East Land—
Well over the green heath, fresh over the heath, there is a better place
for us.

"Song of the East Land," traditional German folksong[3]

While the above folksong harkens back to some much earlier and idyllic time when Germans ruled the east, some readers might be surprised to learn that there were, indeed, Germans living in Eastern Europe, some for centuries. These people were distinguished from Germans living within the political boundaries of Germany by the term *Volksdeutsche*, or "ethnic Germans." Citizens of Germany proper were called *Reichsdeutsche*. Beneath centuries of myth and misrepresentation lies the real history of ethnic Germans in Eastern Europe. One must be careful even with the term "German," for no German state as such existed until 1871—when Otto von Bismarck united a vast and disparate group of smaller Germanic territories into the modern state of Germany; some came willingly, others much less so.

Before that time, there were, of course, groups of people called Germans (or who were *called* Germans by later scholars). One of the earliest and most famous discussions of Germans comes from the Roman historian Tacitus in his work, *Germania*, written in 98 CE. Indeed, the Romans were first to use the term "Germans." Having never been to Germanic lands, Tacitus nevertheless sought to describe them for his Roman audience. This "peculiar people," Tacitus wrote, fought in kinship groups and were fearless on the battlefield.[4] Later German historians could be proud of both these descriptions, though Tacitus is certainly not full of glowing praise throughout his work. His work was "an artful mosaic, mostly composed of stereotypes, casting the Germanic warrior as simple, moral, honest, and brave."[5] Himmler himself read *Germania* on a train in 1924 and "the glorious image of the loftiness, purity, and nobleness of our ancestors" inspired him.[6] The ancient history of the "Germans," in descriptions by Tacitus and events such as the annihilation of three Roman legions by Germanic tribes in 9 CE formed the basis for a belief in the continuity (and superiority) of German race and culture.

For German nationalist historians, one piece of evidence of this superiority was the spread of "Germanic" peoples throughout Eastern Europe, where they supposedly brought *Kultur* (German culture) and improvements to eastern lands and peoples. Here, it is important to separate fact from later backward-looking invention. In the medieval period, German settlers *did* move east, many at the invitation of Slavic rulers. Often, they established their own towns; one historian has estimated that between 1200 and 1400 CE, over 1,500 new Germanic settlements arose east of the Elbe River.[7] Thus, new Germanic settlers brought with them trade and economic opportunity. These migrations took ethnic Germans across Eastern Europe, to modern-day Hungary, Poland, Czech Republic, Slovakia, and as far as the Volga in Russia.

One element in this German relationship in the east was the Teutonic Order of Knights, founded in 1202 CE. In addition to its crusading duties in the Holy Land, the Order actively fought in northern and Eastern Europe.[8] These battles were not so much a defense of the West as they would later be painted. Rather, they were often more temporary protection missions for various kingdoms, as well as a form of colonialism. Yet, they formed the basis for a myth of a German right to the East. One ultra-nationalist historian in the nineteenth century would see them as "in all things presaging the German Great Power of Prussia."[9]

In 1721, when Russia took control of the modern-day region of the Baltic States (Latvia, Lithuania, and Estonia), the German nobility in the region was guaranteed their traditional powers and land; ironically for later historians of German history, these "Baltic Barons" became known for their loyalty to the Tsar, which "would become legendary in the following centuries."[10] Tsarina Catherine the Great, the same monarch who confined Jews to the Pale of Settlement, also extended an invitation to German settlers in 1763. Around 30,000 arrived, settling mainly in southern Russia. These came to be known as the Volga Germans.[11] Russia gave these colonists special privileges and the task of bringing modern agricultural techniques.[12]

The last major German migration of consequence was markedly different from the rest. During World War I, contrary to plans, the Germans were militarily far more successful in the East than in the West. While soldiers were dying by the hundreds of thousands in the trenches of France and Belgium, the German army made massive gains in the East, transforming large swathes of land into German occupied territory. The German military government, named the *Ober Ost*, administered it. Ironically, the Germans conquered their *Lebensraum* in World War I only to lose it. *Ober Ost* was more a kingdom than a military area; its overlords, Hindenburg and Ludendorff, ruled absolutely and carried out both a population and "civilizing" policy. Yet this occupation, paternalistic and harsh as it was, particularly in its economics, was not simply a precursor to the Nazis. For example, it did not seek to completely destroy the state of Poland. The general in charge of the Government General (occupied Poland) wrote to his wife in 1915 that Poland was

> Beautiful beyond all expectations and favoured by nature but also lacking good government and the superior intelligence of an intellectually distinguished people . . . they don't know what they want and the cleavage amongst the inhabitants, especially as well the unfortunate Jews, hinder the growth of progress. It's a pity about this land, but about its people too, who are certainly gifted . . . What will one day become of all this is still completely unclear.[13]

This letter encapsulates much of the *Ober Ost* mentality toward its new fiefdom: anticipation of natural resources, latent antisemitism, and a paternalistic but somewhat optimistic approach that hoped to "improve" the Polish people. This extended to Jews as well, with attempts to give them a "fair [political] representation" in Warsaw elections.[14] Ludendorff, an early supporter of Hitler, later reflected on his "German Work" in the East, saying, "The work has not been in vain. It had at least been useful to the homeland, army, and the land itself during the war. Whether seeds remain in the ground and later will bear fruit, that is a question of our hard fate, which only the future can answer."[15] The migration of Germans east, of course, never materialized, but it lived on among academics and the population alike. It also proved a bitter reminder of the lost opportunities of World War I, as large parts of *Ober Ost* would be awarded to the newly reconstituted state of Poland. As one analysis notes, "thus, when German armies crossed the Polish border in September 1939, they brought with them legacies of the nineteenth century, but also animosities of a far more recent historical vintage."[16]

Yet, historically, the issue of ethnic German settlement of the East remains somewhat unresolved. Multiple generations of skewed scholarship obscured the scope and nature of German migration to the East. Some scholars have suggested that the numbers of German settlers were neither particularly large nor particularly German. One wrote, "Germans were drawn to Poland virtually uninterruptedly for a thousand years, and in general succumbed rather quickly to Polish cultural influences."[17] This highlights the dilemma of modern historians as well as that of the occupying Nazis in attempting to identify who was "still" ethnically German among a diverse and mixed population in Eastern Europe.

In the nineteenth century, as nation states began fully developing, formerly "German" settlers often found themselves living in countries that were foreign and nationalistic in different ways. This facilitated Hitler's later claims that he was simply seeking to bring Germans back into their home country. The important point in this discussion of German settlement in Eastern Europe is that there were, indeed, groups of people who exhibited varying levels of "Germanness" throughout the region. This was also common for other ethnic groups. Eastern Europe was, after all, a massive mix of ethnicities and religions; it was not uncommon for five or more languages to be spoken in one country. Poland, for example, contained Poles, Ukrainians, Germans, Russians, and Lithuanians who were Catholic, Protestant, Jewish, and Orthodox. Later German historians, however, would stray from the historical truth and embrace a much more romanticized and more dangerous view of the German past in the East.

German Conceptions of the East

The Slav himself doesn't understand how to seize and exploit the easily accessible resources of their land. He merely uses nothing other than the forest, the meadow, beekeeping, fishing, and hunting like the crude nomads in Asia or the Indians in America.

MORITZ HEFFTER, *The World War of Germans and Slavs*, 1847[18]

German "histories" of the East were consciously racist—as in the case of the Slavs above—but also cognizant of very real comparisons to colonial endeavors such as those in the United States, as we see above. Indeed, German scholars, particularly from the nineteenth century on, sought to rewrite the history of "Germandom" in the East. A new discipline of *Ostforschung* or Eastern Research endeavored to nominally uncover the roots of the German past there but, in reality, served only to supply "detailed evidence to substantiate the political claims."[19] Among both among German scholars and the public, there *were* different ideas of what a German conquest of the East could and should look like. However, a relative consensus began to emerge—in which *Ostforschung* played fast and loose with the facts and only bolstered an already mythical history. We have already mentioned the avid appeal of Tacitus's work as expressing some true ideal of Germanness. German historians envisioned a united German culture and realm from a distant past that simply did not exist. This, then, fueled the theory that this land had been lost to Slavic peoples now living in the East. That a later German settler would be called a *Rückkehrer*, or "one who returns to his lands after a long absence," captures perfectly the German view of a lost land, rightfully theirs.[20]

Historically, Germans, particularly academics, but also the public, viewed the East as a primitive, backward place inhabited by inferior populations. One historian has argued that such views represent the "complement" to the Enlightenment concept of civilization in "shadowed lands of backwardness, even barbarism."[21] This view of the East as a land without culture, without civilization, and populated by primitive peoples permeated German thinking and decisively influenced later policies there. However, Nazis did not create these stereotypical visions of the East. Already in the late eighteenth century, a German travel writer described the "filthiness in the moral and physical sense" of Lithuania while referring to Poles as "millions of cattle in human form."[22] This view was endemic: "filth was emblematic of eastern lands and peoples."[23] Yet paradoxically, it was the very rich, black earth of the East that was so attractive to potential settlers.

A new academic discipline added another layer to German ideology of the East. In the nineteenth century, as professional academia grew, Germans became some of the leading thinkers in the field of geography. Friedrich Ratzel, a famous geographer, coined the phrase *Lebensraum* or "living space" in 1901.[24] By this, he meant territory required for national self-sufficiency. The new work of Charles Darwin deeply influenced Ratzel and others; however, they erroneously applied his theory of natural selection to nation states, contending that countries were like the species Darwin studied, struggling over resources in a war for survival that only the fittest would win. Naturally, then, the East was wasted on the Slavic people who lived there. As one German publication stated in 1916, "we Germanic people build up – create – the Slav broods and dreams – like his earth."[25]

As a result, many Germans initially adopted a paternalistic but not entirely hostile attitude to the people. They believed in a mission to bring *Kultur*, to Eastern peoples; a German form of the White Man's Burden. This attitude dovetailed perfectly with a darker vision of eastern ethnicities as people *without* culture and, later, as threats to German *Kultur*. In the ancient and medieval context, revisionist historians argued that whatever culture and civilization existed in Eastern Europe remained from the days of Teutonic knights and the Germanic settlers. The best example in the modern period was *Ober Ost* itself, which, while domineering, also worked very hard on *Kulturarbeit* or "cultural work." This entailed educating local peoples, putting on shows, and publishing newspapers in local languages. The command even went so far as cataloguing and attempting to preserve historic landmarks, even wooden synagogues in Lithuania.[26]

Yet, racist beliefs also deeply permeated German thought on the East. In 1901, the Chancellor warned of a "Slavic flood" overtaking Germany due to a high Polish birth rate.[27] Increasingly, Eastern Europe began to be seen as a region populated by an inferior species of human. This racial bias included antisemitism as well. A cholera epidemic that ravaged Hamburg in

1892 was blamed on Eastern European Jewish immigrants.[28] *Ostjuden*—or Eastern European Jews—with their traditional clothing, stood out compared to assimilated, less observant German Jews. Even renowned Jewish diarist, Viktor Klemperer, reacted with revulsion to Eastern Jews, writing, "I thanked my Creator I was German."[29] When Jews later became associated with Bolshevism, antisemitic fervor among those yearning for the East only increased.

The end of World War I, and the accompanying loss of the massive new area conquered in the East, was painful to Eastern theorists and Germans as a whole. After all, Germany lost a seventh of its pre-war territory and ten percent of its population.[30] The fact that graves of German soldiers now lay in foreign lands was also unacceptable. One poem summed up this attitude, saying "The earth, consecrated by German blood / be German forever."[31] The German colonial experiment did not end peacefully, however. Thousands of World War I veterans and those too young for the war joined the *Freikorps* (volunteer troops) to fight Bolshevists, seeking to maintain the German Empire in the East. The deep sense of loss over having the German dream of the East slip through their fingers intensified German thought and plans for the East as the Nazis came to power—they would take these older perspectives to new extremes.

Nazi Conceptions of the East

The Poles: a thin Germanic layer, underneath frightful material. The Jews, the most appalling people one can imagine. The towns thick with dirt . . . Above all, if Poland had gone on ruling the old German parts for few more decades everything would have become lice-ridden and decayed.

JOSEPH GOEBBELS, 1939[32]

In many ways, the Nazis—both theorists and general party members—brought forward the stereotypes mentioned above, intensifying some and adding others. These mindsets critically led to real behavior and policies that would have a devastating effect on Eastern peoples, Jew and non-Jew alike. What follows is a brief summary of some of the primary lenses through which Nazi theorists and leaders—but also many lower level individuals—viewed the East. The Nazis fed on a mythologized past. They defined a German nation defined by blood. They gazed enviously at the resources and land available in the East, and they viewed with fear the rise of Bolshevism and, with it (in their eyes), Jewish power.

Even more perhaps than their predecessors, the Nazis adhered to a myth of the East where it had always historically belonged to Germany. Indeed, foundational to this was the idea that there was such a thing as a German community in earlier times. An SS magazine claimed Goths as early Germans and argued that there had been a "Germanic Reich" in the steppe, "a first bulwark of Europe against the racially foreign eastern areas."[33] SS-Chief Heinrich Himmler viewed himself as the reincarnation of Henry the Fowler, theoretically the founder of the German state. He claimed in a speech that King Heinrich "has never forgotten that the strength of the German *Volk* lay in its blood."[34] Himmler was so fixated that he directed his lackey archaeologists to find Henry's lost burial site—which, not so surprisingly, they did—at least, they found *some* bones. "Himmler has dug up the bones of Henry I," Propaganda Minister Goebbels sardonically wrote in his diary, with more than a little derision.[35] When a Catholic Cardinal sermonized that there had been no civilization among the Germans of the pre-Christian era, Nazi party members roared in outrage that he had "dared to 'attack our Germanic forebears and thus also our Germanic race and culture.'"[36] The SS, above all, imbibed an idealized view of the German past. However, they were not alone. The military High Command published a booklet titled "The East: A Special Course of Instruction" in 1941 and issued to common soldiers. Romantic (and mostly heavily modified) notions of a past German colonization of the East and its attempt at civilization there filled its pages.[37] Perhaps more interestingly, in 1943, renowned and prolific travel writer Baedeker published *Baedeker's Generalgouvernment*, a travel guide for the intrepid German tourist wishing to visit the former Poland (and current

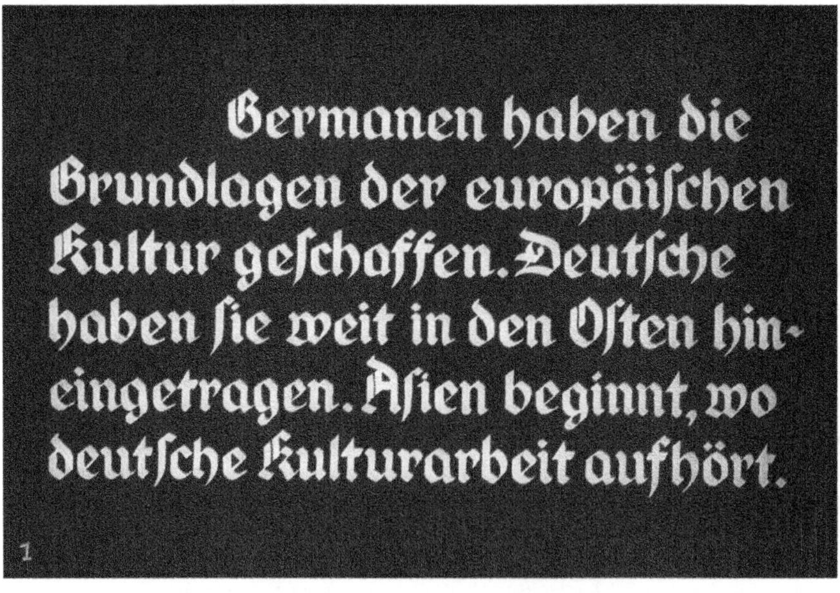

FIGURE 4 *Nazi propaganda slide of a Hitler Youth educational presentation titled "German power in the East." Text reads, "Germans have laid the foundations of European culture. Germans have carried it far to the East. Asia begins where German culture work stops," ca. 1934–37.*
Source: United States Holocaust Memorial Museum.

center of the Final Solution.) This guide, a kind of *Lonely Planet* for the first half of the twentieth century, routinely credited any positive elements to Germanic influence, down to the "typically German "square in Żółkiew.[38]

Building on the racial science of the late nineteenth and early twentieth centuries, Nazi theorists defined Germandom genetically: the *Blutgemeinschaft* or "community of blood." With this definition, Nazis saw German populations throughout Eastern Europe living isolated in the midst of oppressive and inferior nations. A 1939 text summed up this idea, saying that "The German Volk is not defined by the borders of the Reich, but a *Volks- und Schicksalsgemeinschaft* [community of the people and of destiny] spread out over the whole earth, but bound together by blood and race."[39] This feeling of belonging was so strong that it drove German émigré populations in Nebraska and Mexico to "prove to our German fatherland that it can always rely on its brothers abroad."[40] A racial definition, of course, also served as a useful excuse for Hitler's earlier acquisitions of territory lost at Versailles but populated by Germans. He himself wrote in his second, unpublished, book, "I see before me no class or rank, but rather a community of people who are connected by blood, united by language, and subject to the same collective fate."[41] When the Nazis advanced into the Soviet Union, they sought to "recover" Germans from the local population, often to their own deep frustration. The assumed racial inferiority of Slavs justified the harsh treatment accorded them and the planned enslavement of such people. As for Eastern European Jews, they suffered under doubly strong antisemitism, being both Jewish and Eastern.

Many Germans viewed Eastern Europe as an untapped resource required for German self-sufficiency. Hitler and many other Germans remembered all too clearly the hundreds of thousands of their compatriots who had died of starvation due to the British blockade during World War I. The Nazis intended to ensure such a thing would never again be possible. Hitler wrote, "The German people is today even less in a position than in the years of peace to feed itself from its own land and territory."[42] In 1936, he said, "If the Urals with their incalculable raw materials, Siberia with its rich forests, and the Ukraine with its incalculable farmlands lay in Germany, it would under Nazi leadership swim in surplus . . . every single German would have more than enough to live."[43] Later, in 1941, Hitler would speak of the "wonderful soil, which, however, owing to the primitive cultivation to date has yielded less than would have been possible under German management."[44] Such beliefs were not limited to the elites; ordinary soldiers, too, felt a deep connection to the East. In a collection published by the Nazis of real letters from German soldiers, one lieutenant wrote, "No one felt himself responsible for the soil, no one felt the love we Germans have for our homeland, for soil that is ours."[45]

Eastern resources were more than physical; Himmler intended to harness the very labor of its inhabitants. In October 1943, he told an audience that "we can mine endless quantities of value and energy from the human mass of this Slavic people."⁴⁶ The harvesting of resources would thus fall upon a new German population overseeing a helot class of Slavic slave labor. For the new Nazi state controlling all of Europe, the East would supply enough food and resources to render Germany immune from the maritime blockades it had suffered during World War I while providing it with an inexhaustible amount of raw materials to support its military goals. Here, too, the Jew was seen as a threat. A pamphlet written by a *Volksdeutsche* for the Nazis was titled *The Jew is the Parasite of Farming Culture*. After a history of this supposed Jewish threat to agriculture dating back to the Middle Ages, the document ends by declaring that "this terrifying example of the unfortunate Russian agriculture shows clearly that Jewry is and will be the worst enemy of agriculture in all countries of the world."⁴⁷

For the Nazis, the prospect of Ratzel's *Lebenraum* in the East became an essential element in their conception of the territory. Himmler wrote in a 1943 SS pamphlet, "for this global Germanic *Volk*, we will have a space in the East, where we will have at least some air to breathe and a place to live, a space prepared to become the German Germanic land of settlement."⁴⁸ Hitler wrote that Germany should "[concentrate] all of its strength on marking out a way of life for our people through the allocation of adequate *Lebensraum* for the next one hundred years."⁴⁹ This desire for space was, of course, dependent on the resources there and their potential cultivation. Thus, we see racial and economic planning coming together in the desire for *Lebensraum*.

One of the most compelling images marshaled by the Nazis was that of the "Soviet Paradise," a desolate, dirty place of oppression and misery that threatened all things German. One soldier wrote in 1941 that "we all thank the Führer that he let us see the Bolshevist 'paradise.' We swear to extirpate this plague root and branch."⁵⁰ The rise of Bolshevism aroused great fear across Europe, but especially in Germany, which had already seen extremist violence during the Weimar period.

The Soviet Union served admirably as a pan-European existential threat that promised to literally dismantle and alter every aspect of traditional life. Thus, many Nazis and Germans viewed the East as a land of danger that must be defeated (in addition to being a source of resources.) In September 1939, a German historian wrote that the German people had protected Western culture and "for centuries . . . constituted a barrier in the East against the lack of culture (*Unkultur*) and protected the West against barbarity."⁵¹ Such thoughts were echoed in pamphlets such as *Germany: Europe's Bulwark in the East—Germanic Achievements for European Security*, published by the Nazis in 1939.⁵² A German soldier wrote in July 1941, "I always think how fortunate we are that this scourge of humanity never made it to our country."⁵³

Such sentiments express the feelings of many that Bolshevism transcended ideology as a kind of biological contaminant that could not be cleansed.

This would justify the mistreatment of Soviet POWs who Hitler said were "no comrades"—meaning not equal to the German soldiers or deserving of proper care. Indeed, the racist worldview of the Nazis extended beyond Jews to include Slavs as an inferior race who would have to be dealt with at some point in the colonization of the East. Even during the Nuremberg trials, one prominent SS official said "I am of the opinion that when, for years, for decades, the doctrine is preached that the Slav race is an inferior race and Jews not even human, then such an outcome [genocide] is inevitable."[54] The broad range of racist perspectives like this is another reason that the Holocaust must be seen as part of a more comprehensive Nazi genocidal project.

Alfred Rosenberg, the top Nazi theorist on Eastern issues, was himself a Baltic *Volksdeutsche*. Rosenberg had been lobbying for a crusade against "Judeo-Bolshevism" since the 1920s. He played an influential role in articulating Nazi eastern policy and later served as Reich Minister for Occupied Territories, where he would have a chance to realize his theories. Rosenberg wrote of the supposed corrosive power of Bolshevism, saying, "Bolshevism has brutalized and deadened the minds of the people in the East, and therefore their conduct cannot be compared with that of Europeans, who place value on the unfolding and development of the individual personality."[55] He went on to note that not just Communists should be punished, "But it is not Bolshevism alone, rather [it is] the Russian people that must be held responsible for Stalin's course of action."[56]

This almost racialized view of Bolshevism became even deadlier when paired with antisemitism and the age-old myth of Judeo-Bolshevism. Nazi thinkers viewed Eastern Europe, and particularly the Soviet Union, as a land controlled by Jews . . . and they went to great lengths to cement the two groups together. Himmler summed up many of these ideas in 1936, when he said, "We are a country in the heart of Europe surrounded by open borders, surrounded by a world that is becoming more and more Bolshevized, and increasingly taken over by the Jew in his worst form, namely the tyranny of a totally destructive Bolshevism."[57] In this one sentence, we can identify the Bolshevik threat to western society, the horrors of the Soviet state, and the Jewish responsibility for the ideology.

Propaganda instructions from Rosenberg's office in 1941 highlighted that Germans must be seen as "liberators from the Jewish-Bolshevist government" and that the "clique in the Kremlin is nothing but a group of Jewish criminal despots."[58] Nazi official educational materials supported this false connection between Jews and Communism. One need only look at the table of contents for the manual *Jewry and Bolshevism* for a taste of the Judeo-Bolshevik myth: The Jew as instigator of the Bolshevik Revolution, Jewish attempts at settlement, and the Jews in leading positions in the Soviet Union.[59] What is significant here is the conjunction of anti-Bolshevik and antisemitic thought. This concept of Judeo-Bolshevism, highlighted by the Nazis, would have important repercussions in broadening the appeal for

Nazi policies to a larger audience, for whom raw antisemitism may not have been sufficient.

The Nazi thinkers and leaders brought few *new* concepts or ideas to their conceptions of Eastern Europe. What they *did* do was highlight and radicalize existing ideas, officially incorporating them into state policy; whereas before, they had remained in academia or on the fringes of German culture. These intellectual origins formed the ideological underpinnings for policies that resulted in the murder of millions and the planned murder of millions more.

The "Nazi Manifest Destiny"

The settlement of the North American continent was similarly a consequence not of any higher claim in a democratic or international sense, but rather a consciousness of what is right . . . which has its sole roots in the conviction of the white race . . . to organize the rest of the world.

ADOLF HITLER to the Industry Club in Düsseldorf, January 27, 1932[60]

Nazi expansion plans for Eastern Europe may have originated from a "primordial German *Drang Nach Osten*, a drive to the East" but their execution would be much more modern.[61] Indeed, Nazi plans for the settlement and administration of the East should be seen through the lens of imperialism and colonialism. This, too, was not a new concept. After all, Hitler consciously referred to the colonization of America as a model—as we see above. However, the scale and cruelty with which the Nazis conquered was unparalleled.

Germany came much later to the imperial game than its rivals throughout Europe. As such, opportunities for colonies were limited. One important expansionist wrote in 1885 that Germany should seek colonies "not in distant parts of the world, but in our immediate proximity."[62] Bismarck reluctantly *did* get in the colonial game in distant places, most importantly, German East Africa and German Southwest Africa (where the Germans committed the first genocide of the twentieth century.) Neither of these territories were financially or strategically viable concerns, and all were lost with the defeat in World War I.

Partially due to Germany's almost utter colonial failure, expansionists focused even more strongly on the East. As early as 1938, Himmler presented the concept of a "greater Germanic Reich, the greatest empire that has ever been achieved by human beings and that the earth has ever seen."[63] This empire in the East would, indeed, be massive and ordered by racial hierarchy. Here, the Nazis drew on the models of other European powers and America. Rosenberg told a gathering of civil administrators, "It took the British Empire three centuries to shape India. But I believe that just 10 years from now we will be able to look back full of pride at the achievement in the East."[64] Himmler, too, referenced the British Empire, confident that Germans "understand how to govern foreign peoples numbering a hundred million at least as well as the English do today."[65] Hitler himself noted in 1941: "What India was for England, the territories of the Russia will be for us."[66] The Nazi leadership also knew that it could never reasonably challenge Britain on the ocean, yet another reason for the Germans to focus on the landlocked East.

Perhaps most influential, however, as a model for German empire and colonization in the East was the United States. A nineteenth-century German scholar compared the Slavs to "'the Indians in America' in their incapacity to cultivate the environment and shape it by their own efforts."[67] Another proclaimed, "We have our backwoods as well as the Americans, the lands of the Lower Danube and the Black Sea, all of Turkey, the entire Southeast beyond Hungary is our hinterland."[68] The image of the "Wild West" depicted by people like popular novelist Karl May influenced the worldviews of many Nazis, high- and low-ranking. His sales of books on a mythologized American west reached into the hundreds of millions.[69] We know that Hitler avidly read them. He called the Volga "our Mississippi," referencing the American expulsion of Native Americans to the western side of that river.[70]

Germany's "Manifest Destiny" lay in the East, and their "Indians" were the Slavic peoples and Jews that lived there. As Hitler himself said, "[I]n the East a similar process will repeat itself for a second time as in the conquest of America."[71] The American influence was clear. Inferior races would be destroyed, driven out, or used as slave labor. Hitler was very explicit: "the American 'Nordics' had colonized 'the West' after they had 'shot down the millions of redskins to a few hundred thousand.'"[72] It is no mistake that initial plans for dealing with Jews called for "reservations," with the expectation of a large loss of life. Hitler compared his genocidal plans with American history. During one of his "table talks," he ranted, "there's only one duty: to Germanize this country [Russia] by the immigration of Germans and to look upon the natives as Redskins."[73] He further noted the apparent lack of concern among imperial powers for genocidal acts by saying, "When we eat wheat from Canada, we don't think about the despoiled Indians."[74] In his second book, Hitler noted with envy that "the American union itself, motivated by the theories of its own racial researchers, established specific criteria for immigration."[75]

The Nazis justified and to some extent modeled their imperial project in the East on those already conducted elsewhere by the great powers. It is no coincidence that Hitler thought Slavs should be treated as "Redskins" or that local auxiliaries were called "Askaris," as they had been in German African colonies or that these colonies had seen the first German concentration camps.[76] Göring's father, Heinrich, had been an abject failure as the first Governor General of the German colony of German Southwest Africa (present-day Namibia). Franz Ritter von Epp, an early supporter and advisor to Hitler, had served as an Army officer in the same colony. Indeed, the Nazi administrator of the General Government, Hans Frank, explicitly drew the comparison, saying, "The imperialism we are developing here is beyond all comparison with the miserable efforts undertaken by former weak German governments in Africa."[77]

Hitler lamented in 1943 that "one thing the Americans have, and which we lack, is the sense of the vast open spaces."[78] The Nazis planned to remedy this in their God-given *Lebenraum* in the East by populating the region with German colonists of good racial stock. Preferably, these would be former soldiers settling down on orderly fortified farms. The Nazis even subscribed to their own version of the famous American "Turner thesis," in which historian Frederick Jackson Turner argued that the crucible of the frontier had made democracy (and Americans) great.[79] For Hitler and the Nazis, their frontier would be the border between European Russia (once colonized) and central Asia. This border between civilization and the barbarians would blood German colonists, who would defend it and then settle: "The new territories would be colonized by soldier-farmers, their settlements and spacious farms forming a living wall in the East."[80] Himmler told his leadership in 1943 that "I have asked the Führer today that the SS have the honor of holding the extreme eastern German frontier as a defensive border." He then suggested that Germany's military-aged men should fight on this border and that SS divisions should spend a year there so that "we will never grow soft."[81] Hitler himself believed that the "black earth" of the East "could be a paradise, a California of Europe."[82]

Where would these colonists come from? The Nazis hoped that they would be *Reichsdeutsche* and that an emphasis on increasing birthrates would help create this new class of settlers. In actuality, many of them would be *Volksdeutsche*. One group of a dozen former German settlers from East Africa began farming in occupied Poland, a phenomenon further illustrating the historical continuity between other imperialist policies and the Nazi Eastern project.[83] So, too, a bizarre 1940 Hitler Youth letter-writing campaign targeting 15,000 Russian-German farmers in South Dakota, asking that they return to settle in newly conquered territory; one doubts if there were many takers.[84] The rather larger problem, however, was the vast population already living in these lands, which would have to be "removed."

We should recognize that the German colonial past in Africa did not differ significantly in its methods and aims from that of other European nations. Indeed, the above comparisons between America/Britain and Germany emphasize similarities in colonial thought rather than differences. However, a fundamental difference between Nazi plans for the East and previous German ideas was that there would be no civilizing mission, however paternalistic. For the Nazis, no amount of German *Kultur* could change the racial inferiority of the peoples of the East. Hitler viewed earlier German attempts at colonization as failures precisely because "wherever [the German] showed himself, he began to play the teacher."[85] He continued,

"[I]t is not our mission to lead the local inhabitants to a higher standard of life."[86] Himmler made this even clearer. He wrote to Hitler that the only goal of any education in the East should be "Simply arithmetic up to 500 at the most; writing of one's name; the doctrine that it is a divine law to obey the Germans and to be honest, industrious, and good. I don't think that reading is necessary."[87] In fact, most inhabitants would not be alive to receive this meager education in the Germanized East. Indeed, another major difference between the German colonization of Africa and the Nazi colonization of Eastern Europe was that there would be no civilian government or left-leaning political parties to successfully lobby for an end to murderous practices there (as had happened in Africa).

Nazi Plans for Eastern Europe

Many tens of millions of people in this territory will become superfluous and will have to die or migrate to Siberia . . . With regard to this, absolute clarity must reign.

Economic Policy Guidelines for Economic Organization East, May 23, 1941[88]

Nazis planned a massive demographic engineering project in the East whose death toll would dwarf that of the Holocaust, but in which the Holocaust was a critical component. They boldly put this in writing in the memo above. As in the American West, "indigenous peoples" would have to be cleared out to make way for German settlers. As time progressed, the more abstract visions discussed above coalesced into explicit plans for the Nazi reorganization of the East. These designs show us the lethal combination of ideology, racism, misused history, and war, as well as the frankness with which Nazi leaders recognized the genocidal impact of their actions.

Two related plans encapsulated the grand Nazi future in the East: the *Generalplan Ost* (General Plan East) and the so-called "Green Folder." The first dealt primarily with the movement of populations in German occupied territories and the second laid out a *Hungerpolitik* or "hunger policy," which would rob local people of their food. Both plans merit discussions in some depth, as they were key components of the Nazi genocidal project in the East.

Hitler had decided already in 1940—in spite of his newly signed alliance with Stalin—that he would invade the Soviet Union. As soon as he expressed his wishes, Nazi officials began drawing up plans to manage the land and people of soon-to-be-occupied eastern territories of the Soviet Union (the Baltic States, Soviet Poland/Belarus, Ukraine). This *Generalplan Ost* had two architects: Dr. Konrad Meyer (a professor of agriculture and geographer) and Dr. Hans Ehlich (a physician). Together, they crafted a plan for the movement and removal of millions of people; the authors also represent the depth to which Nazism had penetrated the scholarly and intellectual life of Germany. The two men were assigned to the SS Planning Office of the Reich Commissar for the Strengthening of Germandom, which itself was part of the *Reischssicherheitshauptamt* (RSHA) under Heinrich Himmler. Their task was not easy: prepare the massive territory in the East for settlement. This meant two things: removing undesirable populations like Jews, Sinti/Roma, and Slavs, and moving in racially acceptable Germans.

The *Generalplan Ost* was very much a work in progress, going through multiple iterations as situations and opinions of key leaders changed. No copy of the actual plan exists; the Nazis seem to have been successful in destroying all original copies. However, we can reconstruct much of it through existing documents that discuss it. One scholar has suggested that there are at least 14,000–15,000 documents relating to *Generalplan Ost*, only a small fraction of which have been analyzed by scholars.[89] Planning began in 1940 and continued through May 1942, when the most detailed version was completed.

This plan revolved around the creation of thirty-six German settlements, which would also serve as bases for security forces and centers for larger agricultural communities.[90] As mentioned earlier, the Ural Mountains would function as an active, defended border between Eurasian Russia and the new Germanized East. Eight million German settlers would be required to adequately settle the new territory. However, the plan also calculated that 45 million foreign peoples existed, of whom 31 million would have to be "resettled."[91] Some of these resettlements reflected the fickle personal preferences of high Nazi leaders and their callous contempt for life. Hermann Göring ordered the Białowieża Forest (in modern-day Belarus and Poland) be cleared of all population to become his private hunting preserve.[92] Likewise, Hitler ordered the deportation of the entire population of the Yalta coast to create a "German Riviera" there. As for where these people should go, Hitler remarked, "I couldn't care less. Russia is big enough."[93] These two examples demonstrate clearly the contempt the Nazi leadership held for the peoples of the East and the intersection of this attitude with actual planning.

In an earlier meeting, it had been determined that "racially undesirables must be evacuated from the East while racially desirable people in Germany or Germanized peoples should be employed [as settlers.]" Another official at the meeting "advocated in the harshest way this position in which he advised that the undesirables must be evacuated to west Siberia."[94] Among these were to be 20 million "racially undesirable" Poles.[95] Some of these would serve as slave labor for German estates to be established in the East. Himmler planned that the remaining "inferior population . . . will, as a people of laborers without leaders, be at our disposal and will furnish Germany annually with migrant workers and with workers for special tasks."[96]

How would this massive demographic project be accomplished? An integral part of *Generalplan Ost* was the intentional deaths of local populations.

Himmler told a group of senior SS leaders in mid-June 1941 that the purpose of the invasion of Russia was "the decimation of the Slavic population by thirty million."[97] In the written documents mentioned here, planners anticipated the deaths of "tens of millions." This was acceptable because "racial-biological considerations will be of decisive importance for future German policies."[98] In a memo dated June 12, 1942, Heinrich Himmler himself wrote, "I have looked over the *Generalplan Ost* which has very much pleased me. I would like to give this plan to the Führer at some point in time."[99]

Where did Meyer hope to find eight million settlers for the newly opened East? One of the most utopian elements of the *Generalplan Ost* was perhaps the expectation that millions of ordinary Germans would abandon comfortable lives in Germany to settle in what, to them, must have seemed like a wild Third World country. The planners, however, had other sources of manpower. First, they relied heavily on the *Volksdeutsche* or ethnic Germans already living there. By the end of 1942, officials could report that 629,000 *Volksdeutsche* settlers had been mustered from the Baltic States, Belarus, Romania, Yugoslavia, and South Tyrol, with another 400,000 coming from South Tyrol and Ukraine.[100] Of course, not all of these settlers chose to move of their own free will exactly. A second source for settlers would be those inhabitants of the east who could be Germanized, that is, who possessed enough German racial characteristics that they could be reincorporated into the *Volksgemeinschaft*. Teams of Nazi "experts" would fan out across the East seeking these remnants of German *kultur*. Even this process was described in agricultural terms. Alfred Rosenberg told officials that "The cultivating of certain *völkisch* sprouts and the restraining of other sprouts, *that* is history in the making" [emphasis mine].[101] A particularly cruel element of this process was the search for children "capable of Germanization" who were forcibly taken from their parents in German occupied territories and sent to be raised by German families via the Nazi Welfare Organization; a Polish estimate puts the number of children abducted for this reason at between 150,000 and 200,000.[102] Himmler laid out his plan for harvesting children in 1940:

> The parents of such children of good blood will be given the choice of either giving their child away—in which case, they will not likely produce any more children so that the danger of this subhuman people of the east obtaining a class of leaders that, since it would be equal to us, would also be dangerous for us, will disappear—or the parents pledge themselves to go to Germany and to become loyal citizens there.[103]

Himmler was also concerned that 10,000–12,000 children fathered by German soldiers with local women may be racially pure enough to also be sent back to Germany.[104] Lastly, Meyer also hoped to bring back Germans who had left Germany to serve as settlers. Recall the letter-writing campaign to German immigrants in Nebraska. Indeed, the German immigrant community in Mexico expressed its support. It reported that "by means of our unity in Mexico, we want to prove to our German fatherland that it always can rely on its brothers abroad."[105]

In summary, German academics and scholars like Meyer, Ehrlich, and Wetzlich drew up plans for a massive project of demographic engineering that required the displacement of literally millions of people as lands were cleared of indigenous populations and replaced by German settlers of one kind or another. This was not a process expected to take place overnight, but one that planners envisioned happening over twenty to thirty years. Even so, the logistics required and the death toll involved in this utopian vision are almost impossible to grasp.

Yet, the *Generalplan Ost* was not the only plan with far-reaching and lethal consequences being developed for the German-occupied East. As we know, Hitler and the Nazis were incredibly concerned about the economic self-sufficiency of the Reich, which was expected to last for a thousand years. Hitler had already stated before the invasion of Poland that Germany needed "the Ukraine in order that no one is able to starve us again as in the last war."[106] The resulting plan for the economic exploitation of Eastern Europe came to be known as the "Green Folder" or the "Hunger Plan."

In reality, the plan was a moving target, evolving and changing over time as the course of the war and development of the Nazi genocidal project dictated. The Nazi bureaucrat responsible for the Green Folder was Herbert Backe. Like Nazi eastern theorist, Alfred Rosenberg, Backe was a *Volksdeutsche* from the Caucasus in Russia, where he spent the first twenty years of his life before fleeing to Germany during World War I.[107] His experiences as a prisoner of the Czar may well have colored his attitudes toward Russians and Slavs. Backe attempted a PhD in agronomy and wrote a dissertation on the Russian grain market, which was rejected—likely because it was too politically radical. Backe became a dedicated Nazi, writing his wife in March 1933 that he "saw Hitler's gaze on him and knew that 'this man would force me to fight until the end.'"[108] He joined the SS and found employment in the Ministry of Food and Agriculture in Göring's Office of the Four-Year Plan, an organization established in 1936 to prepare Germany economically for war. As was common in Hitler's government, Herbert Backe politically outmaneuvered his boss, Walther Darré, the Minister of Food and Agriculture, and worked around him with senior Nazi leadership. In this way, he became the Nazi food expert with the ability to greatly influence policy and implementation.

By November 1940, Backe had been informed of plans to invade the Soviet Union and began to work up a plan for the economic exploitation of the territories to be conquered.[109] On April 12, 1941, a secret order from Hitler gave additional powers to Backe for the implementation of a "special task" regarding the invasion of the Soviet Union.[110] Presumably, this was his authorization to go forward with ever more extreme planning. This plan had several important elements. First, it divided the occupied Soviet territories into two sections. The first was Ukraine, a "surplus territory." By this, he simply recognized a fact of Russian geography: Ukraine was the breadbasket of Eastern Europe and produced the vast majority of food for the rest of European Russia. This latter area (the Baltic States, Belarus, and Russia proper) Backe categorized as "deficit territories," meaning that they took from the surplus created in Ukraine.[111] Backe's Green Folder plans were as simple as they were horrifying. First, the Nazis would cease distributing food to the "deficit territories." Second, they would supply Germany with food produced in Ukraine through forcible extraction. Backe is said to have noted wryly that the "Germans would have had to introduce the collective farm if the Soviets had not already arranged it."[112] This would ensure that Germany remained fully fed and unaffected by any blockade. Third, more food from the "surplus" zones would be used to supply the *Wehrmacht*, which planners recognized would have to live off the land. Backe reminded the military leadership of this in May 1941, emphasizing that the Army should plan on the "complete feeding of the army from [the] occupied territories."[113] Finally, shipments of food to most large cities were to be cut off.

Of course, "surplus" food grown in Ukraine was not really surplus at all; rather, it fed the rest of the Soviet Union in the same way that agricultural regions everywhere feed non-agricultural regions. Thus, the outcome of the Green Folder plans was entirely predictable: mass starvation of local populations cut off from their usual source of food. This was not a concern for Backe or the rest of the leadership. In fact, the Nazis explicitly acknowledged this many times. On May 23, 1941, the Economic Policy Guidelines for Economic Organization East were published. They noted that "the population of the cities, will have to face the most terrible famine . . . Many tens of millions of people in this territory will become superfluous and will have to die or migrate to Siberia . . . With regard to this, absolute clarity must reign."[114] The commander of an *Einsatzgruppe* mobile killing unit commented in July 1941 that Hitler "intended to decimate the around thirty million Russians living in this strip through starvation, by removing all foodstuffs from this enormous territory."[115] Backe's fingerprints were everywhere. Thus, in the *Generalplan* Ost and the Green Folder, the Nazis plotted a course of forced population movement and planned starvation that would result in the deaths of millions of Eastern Europeans; an outcome fully acceptable and in agreement with their ideological views of the East.

What about Western Europe? If the Nazis seemed to have devoted most of their intellectual capital to the East, it is because that territory was by far the most important—and the one where they planned to exercise a murderous plan of colonization and demographic engineering. Different racial and political considerations tempered their attitudes and plans with regard to Western Europe. As early as 1922, Himmler had written: "The east is the most important thing for us. The west is liable to die. In the east we must fight and settle."[116] A Nazi administrator transferred from Poland to the

Netherlands remarked that "In the east we have a National Socialist mission; over there in the west we have a function. Therein lies something of a difference!"[117] There were, indeed, several differences requiring a different policy toward Western Europe. First, while the German race was (in the Nazi mind) certainly superior to other Western European peoples, the distinction was not nearly as stark as in the east. Western Europeans were, in the eyes of the Nazis, civilized peoples who could function in concert with Nazi wishes and manage their own countries, which had *some* legitimacy in Nazi eyes. The Nazis had no desire to colonize or fundamentally reorganize the West. Instead, they were content to install puppet states that would be cooperative with Nazi political and economic demands. Such relationships did not require the decimation of local populations. Indeed, the Nazis envisioned a sort of forced European Union with Germany as continental hegemon. Western European countries would be bound to Germany in this union and obliged to comply with its desires. Nazi occupation of Western European lands could be relatively benign, insofar as they behaved.

It should be clear at this point why both German and Nazi conceptions of their "manifest destiny" are crucial to understanding both the larger Nazi genocidal project and the Holocaust in the East. The Nazis built upon a long and rich history of idealized German pasts in the East, and employed anti-Slavic, antisemitic stereotypes as they viewed the East. These prejudices and imagined histories combined with a strategic requirement for an economically self-sufficient Germany and complete dominance of the European continent; a goal that would only be possible with German (re)settlement in the East and "proper" exploitation of the land and resources. This included a demographic expansion of the German people in order to provide soldiers to defend the Reich.

Yet while older *Volkisch* yearnings for the past remained in a more abstract, romantic sphere, Nazis translated these desires into organized, bureaucratically (and "scientifically") created plans for how such massive population change would be executed, with the *Generalplan Ost* and the Green Folder or "Hunger Plan" being most prominent. This radical step by the Nazi state illustrates the dangerous combination of ideology and bureaucracy that would have lethal effects on the ground.

The Holocaust was certainly an important part of the Nazi genocidal and demographic projects in the East. After all, Jews constituted one of many "undesirable" elements to be eliminated there to make way for German settlers. However, one should not mistake this convergence in goals with an equality of emphasis. Jews (and their extermination) became a central goal of the Nazi state separate from colonization of the East. While there were parallels, those planning the settlement of East themselves recognized the differences. Eberhard Wetzel, from the Eastern Ministry, and from whom we know much about *Generalplan Ost*, admitted that "one cannot solve the Polish question in the sense that one can liquidate the Poles like the Jews is obvious."[118] Indeed, as we shall see shortly, the eventual plans to murder the

Jews of Europe would be far more successful in the end than any attempt at German colonization.

Selected Readings

Burleigh, Michael. *Germany Turns Eastwards: A Study of Ostforschung in the Third Reich*. New York: Cambridge University Press, 1988.

Kakel, Carroll P. *The American West and the Nazi East: A Comparative and Interpretive Perspective*. New York: Palgrave Macmillan, 2011.

Liulevicius, Vejas G. *The German Myth of the East: 1800 to the Present*. Oxford: Oxford University Press, 2009.

Matthäus, Jürgen, and Frank Bajohr, eds. *The Political Diary of Alfred Rosenberg and the Onset of the Holocaust*. Lanham, MD: Rowman & Littlefield, 2015.

Mineau, Andre. *SS Thinking and the Holocaust*. Amsterdam: Rodopi B.V., 2012.

4

The Soviet Interlude

Introduction

Where was this gray army decorated with red stars going? Was it bringing us assistance or final defeat? What was the meaning of all this?

ANNA GIMZEWSKA, Poland, September 1939[1]

Anna's uncertainty of the implications of the 1939 Soviet occupation echoes both contemporary feelings and the strange absence of this period from many Holocaust texts. Frequently, they ignore the period of Soviet occupation of large parts of the region from September 1939 to June 1941. One must understand Soviet actions and their effects on the areas of the East that would eventually become the graves of most Holocaust victims. Even today, this twenty-one-month period is etched into the landscape of the East: the eastern border of Poland remains the one negotiated between Hitler and Stalin in 1939, for example.

If it feels as if we are taking a detour, remember that the Holocaust took place predominantly on territory occupied by the Soviet Union from 1939–41, and that this occupation colored many aspects of the Nazi genocidal project there. We must first, then, explore the varied approaches the Soviet government under Stalin took to securing and controlling these new areas and the impact on both Jews and non-Jews. We must also identify the effects Soviet occupation would have on both the execution of anti-Jewish measures in the East and on the attitudes of the local population to their Jewish neighbors.

While both Stalin and Hitler ruled over incredibly murderous and repressive regimes, this chapter does not argue one was worse than the other or propose that Stalin's policies brought about the Holocaust. They did not. However, seismic changes and upheaval caused by the Soviets help us to place the Holocaust in its proper historical context. The period of Soviet occupation (much of which was in Polish territory) had several important effects on the local populations, Jewish and non-Jewish. The Soviet state destroyed existing political systems and, often, the traditional social order. It also exacerbated ethnic tensions between various groups by privileging some and victimizing others. Jews often found themselves caught between both groups and unfairly blamed for the hardship of occupation. Finally, in places like Poland, Ukraine, and the Baltic States, Soviet occupation fanned the flames of already powerful nationalist movements whose hatred for the regime and anyone associated with it burned ever brighter.

Friends with the Devil: The Molotov-Ribbentrop Pact and the Collapse of Poland

The sinister news broke upon the world like an explosion.

WINSTON CHURCHILL[2]

On August 23, 1939, the Nazis and the Soviets stunned the world (and clearly Churchill) by announcing they had signed a non-aggression pact, agreeing to "refrain from any belligerent action, and any attack on each other, either severally or jointly with other powers."[3] Two days earlier, Stalin had said, "I hope that the German–Soviet non-aggression pact will mark a decided turn for the better in political relations between our countries."[4] Italian Foreign Minister Ciano wrote with foreboding in his diary: "the European situation is upset" and American newsman William Shirer "had the feeling that war is now inevitable."[5] This treaty was shocking for several reasons. Nazi Germany and the Soviet Union had been ideological bitter enemies. The bulk of Nazi propaganda for years vilified the "Bolshevist menace" in the East as an existential threat to Western civilization that must be defeated. Conversely, Soviet propagandists painted the Nazis and fascism as the natural expression of the capitalist system as predicted by Marx and other Communist theorists, bent on the enslavement of the working class and war mongering. And yet now these two seemingly implacable enemies declared their "friendship?" The second reason the so-called Molotov-Ribbentrop Pact (named after the Soviet and Nazi foreign ministers, respectively) came as such a surprise to the West was that the USSR itself had proposed an alliance with Britain and France in April 1939 and was in negotiations toward that end.[6]

How do we understand this 180-degree turn in diplomacy? First, we must (briefly) look at the strategic picture for both Germany and the Soviet Union. The Nazi viewpoint was relatively simple. Because Hitler intended to invade Poland or obtain a beneficial arrangement with it, he needed to avoid a two-front war with Britain and France on one side and the Soviet Union on the other. Thus, a non-aggression pact taking the USSR out of the picture would allow Hitler to invade Poland without interference. Stalin's motivations were based on a combination of ideological and realistic understandings of the situation. He, too, recognized that Hitler would invade Poland. He also correctly assumed that this would cause a larger European war, given that Britain and France had pledged to support Poland. Stalin hoped this European war between Germany and France/Britain would be long and costly, leaving the capitalist countries of the West weakened and ripe for a communist revolution and/or unable to stop his own territorial ambitions. Second, Stalin viewed the pact pragmatically as a way to buy time to improve and build up his military.

Outwardly, the treaty simply pledged non-aggression and friendship, but the meat of the agreement, the offerings which truly brought these two enemies together, were the secret "Supplementary Protocols" that divided Poland and the Baltic States between Nazi Germany and the Soviet Union "in the event of a territorial and political restructuring of the regions that are part of the Polish state."[7] This "restructuring" meant war, and the two nations were laying out their claims for "spheres of interest" prior to that war taking place. The terms of the secret protocols divided Poland roughly in half along the San, Narew, and Vistula rivers. Through the Molotov-Ribbentrop Pact, the Soviets stood to acquire 201,000 square kilometers and 13.2 million people (of whom about 5 million were Poles).[8] Lucrative economic arrangements accompanied the agreement. All that was required was war. Hitler happily obliged.

In the early hours of September 1, 1939, the Germans attacked Poland. The fortuitous (and conveniently timed) war began and the secret protocols were placed into effect, with both sides aligning their forces in accordance with the Molotov-Ribbentrop Pact whose ink was barely dry. Almost immediately, the two invaders amended their territorial deal. The Germans quickly agreed to extend the Soviet sphere of influence to include Lithuania and the Baltic States while the Soviets granted Germany more territory in central Poland. In 1940, the Soviets would annex Bessarabia and Bukovina from Romania and solidify their hold on the Baltic States and Western Poland, Belarus, and Ukraine. These land grabs from Romania and Hungary would later become important in those countries' decisions to align with the Nazis (even though the Germans themselves had pressured them to submit to Soviet demands.)

Liberation, Conquest, and Uncertainty: The Red Army Marches In

We come not as conquerors but as liberators of our brother Belorussians and Ukrainians and the workers of Poland.

> Order No. 005 of the Military Council of the Belorussian Front to the Troops on the Goals of the Red Army's Entry into Western Belorussia, September 16, 1939[9]

The Soviets (like the Germans) had never truly recognized Poland's right to exist and were very happy to take control of it, not least as a buffer between themselves and the increasingly powerful Nazi state. Soviet Foreign Minister Vyacheslav Molotov happily announced the demise of "this ugly offspring of the Versailles treaty" in an address on October 31, 1939.[10] Yet, to the world and their new populations, the Soviets justified their actions by portraying themselves as helping their fellow communists—as the order above indicates. The Soviet Union had a duty to intercede and protect the workers and national minorities. The Polish ambassador in Moscow was informed that "the Soviet government intends to take all measures to liberate the Polish people from the disastrous war into which they have been dragged by their unwise leaders and to give them the opportunity to live a peaceful life."[11] Red Army soldiers were told that "the Polish landowners and capitalists have enslaved the working people of Western Belorussia and Western Ukraine."[12] Declaring that the Polish state ceased to exist conveniently relieved the USSR of any lingering duties it might have had to Poland under previous treaties.

Despite its claims of liberation and protection, the Red Army received quite different responses to its arrival that often reflected the treatment different groups had received under the Polish government. Many villages gave Red Army troops the traditional welcome offering of bread and salt, but that does not mean everyone greeted occupation in the same way. While we can make *some* generalizations about the responses of these groups to the Soviet invasion, we must also remember that each individual response arose from a complex mixture of experience, ethnicity, and ideology. Yet, these reactions as a whole would have important and long-lasting repercussions (particularly for Jews) when these territories changed hands yet again in 1941. Indeed, the Soviet occupation would at least partially shape the experience of both victims and local collaborators in the coming Nazi storm.

The Poles viewed the invasion as a crime and a devastating defeat. Poland was a nation defined by Polish ethnicity and staunch Catholicism, and the Communist system promised to destroy that. Indeed, the Soviet regime viewed Poles as the least trustworthy of the national groups in Eastern Europe precisely because of their organization and sense of nationalism. During Stalin's Great Terror in the late 1930s, a Communist party official suggested that national minorities (such as Poles) "should be forced to their knees and shot like mad dogs."[13] Thus, Poles throughout the Soviet zone (including Belarus and Western Ukraine) viewed the invasion with deep apprehension and disgust. One Polish citizen stated unequivocally that "the Russians were barbarians, rabble, Asians, another world. When the Bolsheviks entered Brzezany, terrible times started for us Poles. They arrived as our diehard enemies."[14] In areas such as Galicia in Eastern Poland, Poles were especially wary for, under the Austrian empire, they had enjoyed cultural and political superiority despite their minority status and had repressed Ukrainian influence and culture. Polish fears of Soviet retribution would prove to be well justified.

Likewise, ethnic Lithuanians, Latvians, and Estonians had much the same reaction as the Poles when the Soviets annexed their territories. They, too, had a well-established sense of nationalist identity steeped in ethnicity and religion. Nationalist parties here, as in Poland, also often included antisemitic political platforms. At the end of World War I, these nationalities had fought hard against the Soviets for their independence. Now, ten years later, they watched as the Soviet monolith trampled their newfound freedom. They established resistance organizations and suffered under the Communist occupation. In fact, even leftist organizations including the Communist Party of Lithuania were outlawed, not least because they actively opposed the Soviet occupation.

Ukrainians had a slightly more complex reaction to the arrival of the Soviets in Western Ukraine and what would become Western Belarus. Eastern Ukraine, of course, had been a territory of the Soviet Union and had suffered through what can only be described as a genocidal, partially manmade famine carried out by Stalin's government in 1932–3, which killed at least 2 million people. This did not endear Ukrainians to Soviet power. Thus, Ukrainian nationalism was particularly strong. Yet, in some areas of Eastern Poland like the large city of Lvov, Ukrainians were happy to see what they saw as Polish domination overthrown. Perhaps too optimistically, they hoped that Ukrainians might receive some greater autonomy under Soviet control. Some greeted the arriving Red Army with the yellow and blue colors of Ukraine until the first Soviet official they encountered told them to "put away their 'rags' and to put up instead a red banner."[15] Recognizing the Soviets were no friends, other Ukrainian nationalists attacked the Red Army arriving in Lvov and Chodorow . . . with little effect.[16] Ukrainians would find Soviet occupation policies toward them to be complex and, at times, contradictory.

The Jewish reaction (both actual and perceived) to the Soviet occupation of Poland and the Baltic States was the most complex and also the most important of all the national minorities in forming a background for the Holocaust to follow. First, we must distinguish between those happy to see Soviets instead of Germans for obvious reasons and those Jews who were politically communist. For the former, joy at Soviet arrival likely was short-lived, though they still saw them as better than Germans. Politically, Jews found themselves in an impossible situation in most places in Poland, Ukraine, and the Baltic. As we have seen, Jews were precluded from participating in most parties. Regardless, both Poles and Ukrainians sought Jewish support. Attempting to avoid taking sides, most Jewish leaders remained neutral . . . and were condemned by both sides.

It follows, then, that when the Soviets arrived, there were significant numbers of Jews who were happy to see them. In one small town, the Red Army "was welcomed by friendly crowds composed mainly of young Jews and Ukrainians."[17] Yet their motives were complex. Some were, indeed, ideologically communist. Others "particularly the young and the educated, harbored a grudge against the Polish state because of its discriminatory policies in education and employment."[18] Some took a small amount of pleasure in the turn of events on the Poles, turning a pre-war antisemitic sentiment against them: "'You wanted Poland without Jews," they joked, "so now you have Jews without Poland."[19] Indeed, there was a significant influx of Jews from Poland into the Soviet zone. As Jewish diarist Chaim Kaplan wrote from Warsaw in November 1939, "There is no present and no future for young Jews. They escape for their lives."[20] Yet even Communist Jews were quickly disappointed with their "liberators." As one recalled, "First contacts with the Russians . . . struck us with something strange and unpleasant. We thought that every soldier was a Communist and therefore it was also obvious to us that each must be happy . . . I noticed that they were preoccupied with worldly goods, and we were waiting for ideals."[21] Still others were refugees fleeing the Nazi occupation of western Poland; knowing that the Germans were murdering Jews there. One refugee wrote "Who cared about Communism? Who paid any attention to theoretical problems of national economy, when one faced an immediate danger to life?"[22] In Bessarabia (formerly part of Romania), a Jewish Red Army officer recalled that "we found all the sidewalks on the main street . . . filled with Jews. They greeted us with delight, applauded as we passed and showered us with wreaths of flowers."[23]

We must, however, recall that most Jews belonged to traditionally conservative Orthodox communities and had no more reason to welcome an atheistic, socially disruptive state than their devout Polish or Lithuanian counterparts had. A society devoid of religion and lacking traditional Jewish communal leadership did not appeal to observant Jews. Regardless, from the beginning, the popular image in the minds of non-Jews was of Jews welcoming and supporting the oppressive Soviet regime despite the fact that in Poland, for example, only between five and seven percent of the Jewish population supported communism before the war.[24] This misconception blended easily with the antisemitic Judeo-Bolshevist myth to greatly heighten tension in Soviet occupied territories, as we will see. Many non-Jews could not easily separate the different reasons that that Jews might welcome Soviet control, they saw only treason.

The Soviets themselves encouraged some ethnic violence from the beginning, as they entered the occupied territories. During the military advance, the Soviets dropped leaflets encouraging Ukrainians and Belorussians to rob and murder Poles.[25] One Polish citizen, a child at the time, recalled the violence between Polish and Ukrainian nationalist groups that immediately followed the Soviet invasion:

One day, the principal of the local Polish school, who headed the Narajow branch of the Polish Riflemen's Association [a Polish paramilitary organization], grabbed a machine gun and started shooting at a group of Ukrainians from a second-floor window of the school building.[26]

As one scholar has noted, "slogans disseminated by the entering Soviets encouraged the local population to rectify the wrongs it had suffered during twenty years of Polish rule"; these exhortations to violence fell on "eager ears." A Polish survivor in Eastern Poland remembered that "Ukrainian villages assaulted Polish settlements, such as our hamlet . . . for example. The landowner was tied to a pole, two strips of skin peeled off and the wound covered with salt, and he was left alive to watch the execution of his family."[27] Such violence was not only traumatic for the local populations, but also appeared to reinforce the Soviet official claim that it was intervening in Poland to protect so-called "national minorities." Another historian concluded that "Ukrainian peasants took revenge on Polish estate owners and Polish settlers for past humiliations and state violence. Political units of the Red Army exploited social and ethnic conflict, encouraging Ukrainian peasants and the lower stratum of the urban population to form village committees and a militia and to destroy the old social and political structures 'from below.'"[28] In Lithuania in 1940, the Soviet-controlled newspaper, *Darbo Lietuva,* demanded that the population be watchful for "enemies of the people."[29] Jews were not spared this violence. One Jewish resident remembered a close call during the invasion, when "the Ukrainians had a list of fifty Jews who they wanted to get. We were lucky. The Russians came that night."[30] The Soviet occupation would bring both violence and opportunity.

Revolution from Abroad? Soviet Occupation Policy

We will not aim at sovietizing them . . . There will come a time when they will do this themselves.

JOSEPH STALIN, October 25, 1939[31]

Stalin believed his newly occupied territories would one day be important as a first line of defense against a German attack. He also wanted to eventually make them active members of the Soviet Union, but with the appearance of homegrown initiative, hence the statement above. He sought then to carry out a "revolution from abroad," bringing the Soviet system to the newly occupied territories and binding them tightly to the state. Therefore, Soviet occupation policy reached into all aspects of life: political, economic, cultural, religious, and social.

The first order of business was to solidify political control of the newly acquired territories. Borders were sealed and population movement restricted. The Soviets took over most directly at first by removing all pre-war leadership that they viewed as potentially disloyal. This usually meant all nationalist leadership; in Poland, it meant most Poles were removed from their positions. The Soviet authorities and the secret police (NKVD) intentionally targeted intelligentsia and any potential leadership for elimination. Very often, they were often deported deep into the Soviet Union, which we will discuss later. Even among prisoners of war, the Soviets searched for these individuals as an NKVD memorandum instructed in 1939. Specifically, "professors, journalists, physicians, artists . . . who served in the Polish Army as officers, as well as intelligence agents, counterintelligence agents, gendarmes, police, provocateurs, prominent military and state officials, secret agents of the police and the counterintelligence, active figures in anti-Soviet political parties and organizations, landowners, and princes" were to be separated and detained.[32]

Into this vacuum, the Soviets placed individuals they considered more trustworthy. Often, these were local communists, political prisoners, and minority ethnicities including Jews. This replacement of local leaders allowed the Soviets to begin the "Sovietization" of the state that Stalin had mentioned. As the situation stabilized, however, vetted Soviet officials replaced many of these new appointments. At the national level, however, the Soviets wished to appear less heavy-handed. They therefore called for national elections that would validate their takeover. In Western Belarus and Western Ukraine, these elections were held in 1939, but were not democratic. They offered only Soviet candidates, were held in public, and required high voter turnout. In Lvov, residents of a particular neighborhood or building were actually marched together to the polling station to vote.[33] Not surprisingly, once elected, these national assemblies asked to be taken into the Soviet Union. One of those drumming up the vote in Ukraine was future premier, Nikita Kruschev. The Supreme Soviet granted these "requests" on November 1–2, 1939.[34] Likewise in Lithuania, the puppet People's Diet proclaimed in July 1940 that " . . . expressing the unanimous will of the toiling people . . . the Soviet system shall be introduced in Lithuania."[35]

For local populations, however, the Soviet presence offered little cause for celebration. The new government began with a campaign to issue Soviet passports to its new citizens. While this registration was optional, refusal to do so resulted in discrimination in housing and employment and possible deportation.[36] The registration served two other more sinister purposes than inclusion in the great Soviet Union. First, it allowed the Red Army to conscript 150,000 of its new citizens.[37] Second, the detailed information collected in this process could easily be used to identify potential enemies of the state for deportation; failure to register served the same purpose.

Once some semblance of political control had been established, the Soviets began the all-important process of bringing the communist economic system to their new holdings. In accordance with communist doctrine, the government seized large private enterprises in both manufacturing and retail and began instituting strict controls. The unsurprising effect was massive economic turmoil and shortages. As one example, of the 8,500 small shops in Lvov, 6,400 sold out of all their merchandise and, unable to replenish their supplies, closed.[38] In Lithuania by June 1941, only one-tenth of private shops remained in the hands of their original owners; all large factories employing more than twenty people had already been seized.[39] The Soviet system of quotas and economic shock work was introduced to a population unused to such harsh measures. Professionals such as doctors and lawyers were forced to work for the state or in state-run institutions.

For those living in the countryside, the situation was not much better. Soon, the Soviets instituted collectivization (where all land was communally owned and worked). This fundamentally and violently altered rural and peasant life, which had been centered around land ownership. Land and livestock were confiscated to create these collective farms whose harvests were then to be distributed to the people. These *kolkhozes* or collective farms were created in both occupied Poland and the Baltic States. Fortunately for many, the Soviets did not have enough time to fully implement collectivization, but it still served as a major and traumatic change accompanying Soviet governance.

In reengineering their new territories, the Soviets sought to change more than the political and economic systems: they aimed to create Soviet citizens. This meant removing any vestiges of the former regimes. In Lithuania, "The symbols of independent Lithuania—the flag, the national hymn, the knight on horseback—were now illegal."[40] In Poland, Soviet authorities "took medallions with images of saints off children's necks and gave them ones with Stalin's picture instead."[41] Street names were changed. The alphabet was changed from Latin to Cyrillic. Citizens were instructed in communist theory and were taught to sing the communist anthem. Local Soviet officials forced them to attend propaganda sessions designed to introduce them to the Soviet way of life. These measures aimed to reeducate the people in the new way of doing and thinking. The removal and replacement of physical reminders of the past began this process. Other cultural activities such as theater, film, music, and writing were curtailed or brought in line with communist policies. Unapproved newspapers were censored or shuttered. Soviet-style art replaced national artists.

Nowhere was the "revolution from abroad" more apparent than in education. Children were very important to Soviet authorities and sweeping changes appeared in the school system. The Soviets abolished private schools (and religious schools). In Poland, one of the goals of this and other cultural changes was "de-polonization," an attempt to erase Polish history and culture, which was deemed subversive. As a result, teachers were expected to teach in Ukrainian or Belarusian (or Russian in other places). They were required to learn new Soviet curricula and Marxist-Leninist thought.[42] Non-Polish parents could choose the language of instruction for their children, a perk that was not unappreciated. However, within the schools, children were also made to be part of the Soviet system of sowing distrust in the local population: they were encouraged to inform on their parents and others who may be "class enemies." In this way, even the youngest in the new territories could be enlisted in Soviet repression.

Though eventually interrupted by the German invasion in 1941, the Soviets began to implement rather systematically the systems they used in their own territories. They sought to make these new lands extensions of the Soviet state, founded on Marxist communist ideals, members of the Soviet command economy, and with ethnic and social distinctions erased. On this last point, the Soviet state seemed willing at least initially to privilege certain groups to certain extents, but the end goal remained a classless, nationless Soviet state, by either relatively benign or more severe methods.

Mixed Feelings: Jews under Soviet Occupation

The unexpected events were met by the Jewish population with mixed feelings. First of all there was a sense of relief, we were spared the agonies of Hitlerism . . . The truth is that the communist regime also presented its own dangers, but these were of a different kind.

Jewish resident, Tarnopol (Ukraine), 1939[43]

For Jews in the Soviet occupied territories, governmental change brought a complex mix of positive and negative experiences, as noted by our witness in Tarnopol. Ironically, for example, a large number of Jews survived the Holocaust by being forcibly deported from their homes by the Soviets from 1939–41. Though antisemitism certainly existed, the Soviet Union distinguished itself as being one of the only places where antisemitism was officially condemned and actively combated. Of course, this freedom often coincided with a loss of Jewish identity and a strong pressure to assimilate into secular Soviet society. In any case, the relative freedom of opportunity in the Soviet Union meant that many Soviet Jews rose to positions in the professions, government, academia, and the police that were out of reach elsewhere in Europe. In 1927, for example, 23,000 Jewish students attended Soviet universities; this made up 14.3 percent of the student body even though Jews represented only 1.8 percent of the Soviet population.[44]

Some of this opportunity extended to the newly occupied territories. Positions previously forbidden for Jews became available. For example, a Jew named Poldek from the small town of Brzezany had studied medicine in Vienna but returned home after Austria was incorporated into Nazi Germany in 1938. He was unable to find work in Poland. However, after the Soviet invasion, Poldek was admitted to the medical school at Lvov University and given a scholarship. He remembered, "They didn't care whether I was a Jew or anything else. They gave me a chance to finish my studies."[45] Similar stories of economic and social advancement (or at least equality) could be seen throughout the new Soviet territories. Unfortunately, as Jews became more prominent, they also became more vulnerable to anger from non-Jews.

Culturally, the Soviet occupation was also a mixed bag. All Jewish newspapers in Poland were banned, replaced by the *Bialystoker Stern* (Star of Bialystok), which was little more than a mouthpiece for Soviet propaganda and provided no reporting on the plight of Jews in the German zone of occupation.[46] The existing Jewish education system of Hebrew schools was completely destroyed. Religious education was driven underground. The Soviets also declared war on the Hebrew language itself. It was viewed variously as a bourgeois, nationalist, or a religious language and, thus, antithetical to Soviet ideology, which sought to make class the only distinction between peoples. On the other hand, the Soviets elevated Yiddish from a lower, more utilitarian status to that of a preferred language. In Soviet eyes, Yiddish was a proletarian language. Thus, somewhat ironically, Yiddish writing, theater, and culture could be expressed in ways they were not before.

On the religious front, Jews received similar treatment to their Christian counterparts. As mentioned, religious schools were shut down. Synagogues, too, were very often shuttered and repurposed by the Soviets. They became meeting halls, barns, warehouses, movie theaters. Training for rabbis and religious leaders was officially stopped. Naturally, the Soviet state could not be omnipresent and so many of these changes were more evident in larger towns and cities. Often, churches and synagogues were forced to pay a tax to the Soviets. These anti-religious policies did not destroy Jewish religious life, but they did force it underground or out of public view. Families still observed religious rituals and even prayer services, but often these could only take place in private homes.

Jewish political organizations were treated in the same manner as those of their non-Jewish neighbors. The Jewish communist party, the Bund, was dissolved and merged with the existing party apparatus. The Soviet authorities also attacked Zionism, which they saw as a Jewish nationalist organization with international ties and a threat to the state. A KGB report claimed that "the Jewish bourgeoisie and intelligentsia in Poland were influenced by the Zionist-Revisionist party—a Jewish fascist organization."[47] Another report in June 1941 claimed that "All the Jewish nationalist organizations used all means available to sabotage the Soviet regime. By maintaining close ties with the American JDC [Joint Distribution Committee] . . . they collected intelligence information which they passed on to the Americans. British Intelligence, too, made frequent use of the Zionists."[48] Here, the endemic paranoia in the Soviet system worked to dismantle a previously powerful Jewish organization. Anti-Zionist measures would have some effect in weakening Jewish resistance during the Holocaust as Zionist leaders were deported or killed. Even the unofficial *kehila* system of self-help that provided a social safety net for Jewish communities was dismantled or driven underground, hampering efforts to help those under stress from the Soviet "reforms."

Economically, the Jews fared little better (and often worse) than non-Jews. While they had a much smaller stake in land and so were insulated from collectivization, the basis for their economic lives was shattered. For merchants and factory and department store owners alike, the Soviet system was a wrecking ball. Wealthy Jews, viewed as bourgeois "class enemies," lost most of their businesses along with their Gentile countrymen. In Lvov, for example, Leon Wells' father, who had owned an apartment building was fortunate to keep a job as the caretaker for his own building, which become nationalized by the Soviet state.[49] Even for small shopkeepers (many of whom were Jewish) the Soviet occupation was destructive. They quickly ran out of goods and were driven out of business. In Lithuania, Jews owned 83 percent of commercial firms.[50] In factories, wages did not increase but workers were now subjected to the often brutal and unrealistic quota system of the Soviet Five Year Plan. Fortunate Jews were allowed to remain as superintendents in their own factories, working under Soviet leadership.

Under Soviet occupation, as in the Soviet Union itself, Jews faced a complex landscape of some positive and many negative developments. On the positive front, the egalitarian Soviet system offered Jews opportunities politically and professionally that they had never had access to. Similarly, the relatively small number of Jews who had a history of communist activity could realize significant political mobility under the watchful eyes of the Soviet state. However, the price for these reforms was too much for many Jews to bear. The destruction of their spiritual communities and communal life was traumatic and certainly unwelcome. The Soviets offered economic, social, and political advancement at the price of assimilation and secularism. Most Jews refused this deal. For many, this evoked a similar program of assimilation that they had already experienced under their national governments: assimilate or leave.

Soviet Repression: Detention, Deportation, and Death

They asked about my wedding ring, which I . . .
> Last diary entry by Polish officer ADAM SOLSKI before his execution in the Katyn Forest[51]

The third postcard was written in early March. It came at the same time as a returned parcel with photos that my Mom had sent. We were upset by this, but my Mom thought that he must have been transferred somewhere.

> Remembrances of the daughter of Katyń victim Jewish Second Lieutenant
> MIECZYSŁAW JULIAN PRONER[52]

Some of the measures taken by the Soviets were far more extreme than cultural change. Perhaps the most extreme was the murder of "state enemies" as evidenced by the above remembrances from the Katyń massacre of Poles. Shortly after arrival, Soviet authorities carried out brutal repression against perceived enemies across Eastern Europe: imprisonment, deportation, and murder. This, too, was an import of Soviet policy under Josef Stalin. These policies had been carried out for years in the USSR and were relatively easy to bring to the new territories shortly after occupation. The People's Commissariat for Internal Affairs or NKVD was pivotal in carrying out Soviet repression. This organization is best known as the secret police that would also operate in Stalin's new lands. The Soviets already knew the kinds of people who were likely to be "class enemies:" large landowners, the wealthy, large commercial owners, intelligentsia, nationalists (and political activists of all stripes—such as Zionists and even local communists), and existing government officials and elites, including local political and religious leaders. Stalin recognized that successful implementation of "sovietization" and "depolonization" required the elimination of any individuals who could organize resistance. Polish resistance fighter Jan Karski relayed a message to the Polish Government in exile in London from Lvov about the Soviet security forces. It was an insightful analysis. A law professor told Karski:

> There is one thing you must understand and tell the men in Warsaw. Conditions here are very different, indeed. For one thing, the Gestapo and GPU [Soviet Secret Police] are two entirely different organisations. The men of the Russian secret police are more clever and better trained. Their police methods are superior. They are less crude, more scientific and systematic.[53]

Soviet repression began almost immediately after Soviet occupation in Poland and the Baltic States. Stalin needed to turn these nations into loyal members of the Soviet Union as soon as possible to build his buffer against future Nazi aggression. In 21 months in eastern Poland, the Soviets arrested and deported 109,400 Polish citizens and sentenced 8,513 to death.[54]

This drastic demographic engineering was founded on the removal of potential "enemies of the state," accomplished by arrest, deportation, and murder. "Enemies" was a broad category. A Jewish survivor characterized the process saying, "The arrested people were chiefly police officials and people who were known to have carried out anti-Soviet activity before the occupation or after. Most of the arrested belonged, of course, to the well-to-do classes of the town, employers and leading officials."[55] One witness in Bialystok recalled, for example:

> On the first day they arrested the town's mayor, Seweryn Nowakowski, the deputy mayor, K. Piotrowski, who died in jail two months later, the chief judge of the district, Ostruszko, the chief prosecutor, as well as all judges and deputy prosecutors, court clerks, employees of the voivodeship office, police functionaries, officers, etc. On the next day the following were arrested: the party leadership 'of the SN [National Democratic party], the NPR [National Workers' party], the OZN [Camp of National Unity], the Bund [Jewish Socialist party], and other parties. Then it was the turn of politically and socially prominent citizens, teachers, priests, capitalists, merchants, upperclassmen from high schools, etc.[56]

A Soviet tribunal found a Polish POW guilty as a class enemy for "being in the former Polish state from 1936 to 1939, [serving] in the police ..., where he conducted an active struggle against the revolutionary movement."[57] If he was guilty of anything, it was arresting communists in the course of his duties as a Polish policeman. Nationalist movements were also heavily targeted. The Organization of Ukrainian Nationalists (OUN) had already been active under the Polish government in advocating an independent Ukraine. Naturally, this movement directly threatened Soviet rule. The NKVD ruthlessly pursued and arrested or executed its members. Those who survived fled west where they found sympathetic ears in Nazi Germany. Even leaders and members of the Jewish Socialist Zionist Youth Organization, *Hashomer Hatzair*, were targeted.

The Soviets relied on a combination of investigations, interrogations, and denunciations to find their targets. This offered the local population the opportunity to both turn in "real" class enemies, but also to settle personal grudges that had no political motive whatsoever. This created a climate of suspicion and fear that divided society even further and, thus, served Soviet needs quite well. It would also serve Nazi needs when directed in another direction.

In the territories they occupied, the Soviet secret police apparatus often found prison facilities lacking for the massive influx of political prisoners they arrested and so established ad hoc prisons in local buildings. Soviet occupiers encouraged local populations to "unmask" and hand over potential enemies.[58] Prisons filled to the point of extreme overcrowding. One prisoner in Lvov recalled that "I was frightened by the prisoners' faces and by their looks" and that "I couldn't tell the difference between 40-year-old and 70-year-old men."[59] Similar experiences were common throughout the newly acquired Soviet territories.

The next step for many was deportation. The Soviets continued the trend of using population displacement as a solution for opposition. From the establishment of the Soviet Union in 1917, they had sent hundreds of thousands to GULAGs (Soviet prison camps) or simply to settlements in the desolate Soviet hinterlands. They even created a supposedly autonomous Jewish province called Birobidzhan east of China. Conditions in the GULAGs and in settlements in Central Russia and Siberia were brutal and resulted in the deaths of hundreds of thousands through starvation, exposure, disease, and mistreatment. Yet, deportation did not affect just the alleged "class enemies." Whole families were deported. It also caused great fear and angst among the population; a Polish woman recalled that "A Polish girl from Kuropatniki was in my class, and one day she just didn't come to school. Their whole family was deported to Siberia."[60] The NKVD or other Soviet authorities arrived, often at night, giving the family a short time to pack. Then, they were taken by truck to a train station and literally disappeared overnight. Journeys in these freight cars could take several weeks to reach their destinations.

From 1939–41, the Soviets carried out a series of four distinct deportations in eastern Poland (western Ukraine and western Belarus), below:

TABLE 2 *Deportations of individuals from formerly Polish territory.*

Date	Composition	Estimates from Polish Embassy in USSR (wartime)	Estimates from Documents of Soviet Convoys	NKVD Data
I- Feb 1940	Civil servants, local government officials, judges, members of the police force, forest workers, settlers, and small farmers-Polish, Ukrainian, and Belorussian	220,000	139,000–141,000	140,000–141,000
II- Apr 1940	The families of persons previously arrested, the families of those who had escaped abroad or were missing, tradesmen (mostly Jews), farm laborers from confiscated estates, and more small farmers of the three nationalities	320,000	61,000	61,000

Date	Composition	Estimates from Polish Embassy in USSR (wartime)	Estimates from Documents of Soviet Convoys	NKVD Data
III- Jun–Jul 1940	Practically all Polish citizens who in September 1939 had, in thousands, sought refuge in eastern Poland from the ruthless Nazi forces which were then invading Poland from the west; small merchants (a great many of them Jews), doctors, engineers, lawyers, journalists, artists, university professors, teachers, etc.	240,000	76,000	78,000–79,000
IV- May–Jun 1941	All belonging to the categories enumerated above and who had so far evaded deportation; children from summer camps and orphanages.	220,000	34,000–41,000	37,000–42,000
TOTAL		980,000	309,000–318,000	316,000–323,000

Source: Dates and Numbers from Wróbel, "Class War or Ethnic Cleansing?" 27. General description of deportees from Gross, *Revolution from Abroad: The Soviet Conquest of Poland's Western Ukraine and Western Belorussia*, p. 197.

These deportations terrorized local populations. As one can see above, often refugees were included in deportations, the majority of whom were Jews fleeing the Nazis. In a twist of cruel irony, these Soviet deportations often saved the lives of Jews who would have fallen into Nazi hands. Jews constituted 84 percent of the third deportation.[61] A Jewish girl from Eastern Poland recalled that her family escaped the Soviet roundup which was "very bad luck because we could have survived in Siberia. Many of our friends and relatives who were taken there survived—in very bad circumstances, true—but they survived."[62] For Jacob Pesate in Romania, however, opting for flight to the Soviets was immediately lifesaving; he narrowly avoided pogroms by the fascist Romanian Iron Guard on the train and "was among those who received the Red Army with flowers in Czernowitz."[63] Overall numbers of those deported are not altogether clear; however, it is likely that the number from former Polish territories is between 500,000 and 1,000,000. This does not include ongoing individual deportations or deportations the Baltic States.

Again, Jews were placed in a difficult position. Many families were divided between those who had fled to the Soviet zone and those who remained in German-occupied Poland. The former were often reluctant to take a Soviet passport for fear that they would be unable to return to relatives in the West. This often targeted them for deportation. In the spring of 1940, a German repatriation commission arrived in Soviet Poland to sign up volunteers to return to the German zone. It is likely that the Nazis were seeking ethnic Germans to help settle occupied Poland. However, there were many Poles and Jews who wanted to return, either to reunite with family or to escape Soviet repression. However, the Germans soon announced that the limit had been reached and no one else could cross over.[64] The Soviets now had a list of people that they clearly viewed as disloyal and potential enemies. They added them to the June deportation list. Some, like Chaim Hades in Brzesc, had second thoughts and were lucky. He describes the German registration, "I stood long hours in line and I finally got the authorization card for departure, which was considered at the time a pot of luck. A German officer turned to a crowd of standing Jews and asked: 'Jews, where are you going? Don't you realize that we will kill you?'"[65] He chose *not* to take the train to Łodź.

Deportations also took place in the other occupied Soviet territories, though perhaps less systematically. In Lithuania, Jewish deportees disproportionately outnumbered non-Jews proportionally by three to one. On the night of June 13–14, 1940, 100,000 people were deported from the Baltic States to locations deep within the Soviet Union.[66] 35,000 Lithuanians were deported in the last week of the occupation.[67] Among those deported by the Soviets, 6,000 were Latvian, 500 Estonian, and 7,000 Lithuanian Jews.[68] Ten days before the German invasion, mass deportations also took place in the territory seized from Romania.[69]

Executions accompanied mass arrests throughout the Soviet occupied territory. Many of these occurred in NKVD prisons or at specific shooting sites. Some were large and others small. A prisoner in Lvov described the daily horror of living in a working execution prison: "Every night they call out some of the condemned: some of them are given hard labour for life, others are taken into the cellars where the executioners carry out the death sentence with a shot in the back of the skull. If you stay in the death cell for a month it gives you hope that your sentence will be changed."[70]

The most infamous of Soviet executions was the mass murder of Polish prisoners of war taken by the Red Army during the 1939 invasion. These POWs were protected by the 1907 Hague Convention to which Russia was a signatory, but not the Soviet Union. A large number of the officers from this POW group were interned at three main camps in the Soviet Union as well as in several smaller camps. These Polish officers were not just military men; many were reservists and held important positions in Poland's elite classes. The NKVD recognized the dual threat these individuals posed to its new territories, as can be seen in this memo to the commander of the Putivl camp:

> As a supplement to No. 14028, we clarify that professors, journalists, physicians, artists, and other specialists being detained in the Putivl camp, who served in the Polish Army as officers, as well as intelligence agents, counterintelligence agents, gendarmes, police, provocateurs, prominent military and state officials, secret agents of the police and the counter-intelligence, active figures in anti-Soviet political parties and organizations, landowners, and princes . . . that are discovered among the specialists are subject to detainment in the camp.[71]

Soviet authorities clearly targeted political and social elites of Poland and those most likely to actively resist the state. NKVD officials removed priests, pastors, and rabbis from the POW camps on Christmas Eve 1939.[72] They were never seen again. This was an ominous hint of what was to come as similar selections took place throughout the Polish POW camps. The NKVD also received permission to arrest all former Polish officers who may have returned to their pre-war occupations as civilians, including retired senior officers. Finally, convinced of the threat posed by these elites, Lavrenty Beria (chief of the NKVD) directly proposed their elimination. He wrote that, as these men (and one woman) were "all sworn enemies of Soviet power, filled with hatred for the Soviet system of government," the Soviets should "apply to them the supreme punishment, [execution by] shooting . . . [and] Examine [these] cases without calling in the arrested men and without presenting [them with] the charges, the decision about the end of the investigation, or the document of indictment . . ."[73] The Soviet Politburo accepted this proposal on March 5, 1940, and a mass killing operation swung into motion. 97 percent of those "examined" were marked for death.

Beginning in April 1940, the NKVD loaded the first group of Polish prisoners of war onto trucks. The prisoners expected that they were being sent home. Instead, the trains stopped at a small rail station in the forest of Katyń, near Smolensk. Descending the stairs into a small cell in an NKVD building, the men were forced to their knees and shot by NKVD officers. Their bodies were buried in nearby mass graves. Similar mass killings took place across the Soviet Union, near the three main POW camps and also in local prisons. The final death toll was 21,892. The Soviet executioners also murdered somewhere between 600 and 1000 Jews at various sites, including Katyń.[74] Among them was the Chief Rabbi of the Polish Army, Baruch Steinberg.[75] He was 42 when he was shot at Katyń. In the camps, he had led services for Jewish soldiers and officers. Similar executions of smaller magnitude occurred throughout Soviet occupied territory, including 52,000 Lithuanians murdered by the Soviets.[76]

The final act of Soviet terror played out in the very last weeks and days of the occupation. As the Nazi invasion began in 1941, many Soviet officials began to flee. This massive evacuation included the removal of industrial equipment, scientists, experts, and other vital elements for military resistance. However, no plan existed to evacuate the large numbers of inmates overcrowding Soviet prisons. Instead, the NKVD and other police agencies began a systematic mass killing, even as the German army marched ever closer. In Lvov, for example, as truck engines revved to mask the shooting, the NKVD killed all but 600–700 of 13,000 inmates in one prison.[77] There wasn't even time to bury the bodies—which filled the basements and were left in heaps in prison yards. Similar killings occurred throughout the Soviet east in the twilight hours of the occupation. In Lithuania, 9,000 were murdered.[78] During the German attack, a Soviet tank machine-gunned women and children in a camp near Kaunas and 76 high school students were shot by the NKVD near Telsiai.[79]

Jews and Communists, Jewish Communists, and the Myth of Judeo-Bolshevism

Most of the people (at least those whom I meet) are simply craving for the Germans to come. And then the real slaughtering of the Jews would start. Fury at the Jews for their outrageous sympathies to the Bolsheviks, for their internationalism, and for their arrogance is great.

History Professor ZENONAS IVINSKIS, diary entry, June 1940 (Lithuania)[80]

I thought that I lived in Ukraine, but it looks as though I am in Palestine.

Anonymous Ukrainian, 1939–41[81]

The reception, real and perceived, with which various groups met first the Soviets and then the Germans played a significant role in the fate of Jews in both periods. One of the most pernicious outcomes of the period of Soviet rule was the substantial support it lent to the antisemitic Judeo-Bolshevist myth. Many non-Jews in newly occupied Soviet territory became convinced that the Jews were driving influences behind the Soviet regime, and hence, their own suffering. This was not at all a new form of antisemitism brought by the Red Army, but instead simply another context and permutation of existing prejudice. Various aspects of the occupation exacerbated anti-Jewish feeling to be sure, but they did not create it. Regardless, sometimes the distinction between myth and reality matters little and it was so in the East. The effects of this Judeo-Bolshevist perspective would be violently felt with the arrival of the Germans.

A somewhat blinkered view of both Jewish reaction to Soviet occupation and its participation in the regime exacerbated this division between Jews and non-Jews. First, we have seen that there *were* certainly some Jews who were happy to greet the Red Army as liberators, from both pragmatic and ideological standpoints. Not surprisingly, Jews were quite relieved to avoid the horrors the Nazis were visiting upon western Poland; this drove even more Jews East as refugees. Older, more traditional Jewish communities, though wary of the Soviets, viewed them as the lesser of two evils. After all, the Soviet government was the only one of its time that actively combated antisemitism. And the evidence clearly indicates that Jews did not thrive in any real way under Communism.

Second, the more complex aspect of the Judeo-Bolshevik myth held by local populations concerned the role of Jews in the newly established Soviet regimes. Many non-Jews had long believed that all Jews closely identified with Communism. As with all stereotypes, there was a kernel of truth to this. In the Soviet Union itself, "Jews held 33.7 percent of the posts in the central apparatus of the People's Commissariat of Internal Affairs (NK VD), 40.5 percent of its top leadership and secretariat, and 39.6 percent in its main State Security Administration (GUGB)" between 1934 and 1941.[82] The prevalence of Jews in the hated NKVD or secret police, far above their proportion of the population, was not helpful; however, again, it was visibility that hurt because, after all, well over 60 percent of posts were occupied by non-Jews ... and those Jews who did serve were nothing like most of their countrymen. In Poland before the war, it is estimated that most Jews supported the popular Pilsudski government and that only five to seven percent supported the Communists.[83]

When the Soviets arrived, those Jews who were already Communist as well as some of the younger and more secularized Jews did seek positions in the new governments being formed. As mentioned, the Soviets offered professional and educational opportunities that had been out of reach under previous regimes. Local populations mostly failed to appreciate this. As one scholar wrote, "the fact that any of them occupied these positions of authority at all changed Lithuanian thinking about the nature of the ethnic hierarchy."[84] That is to say, this challenged the notion that only those of Lithuanian ethnicity should be in power. A Lithuanian Jewish witness captured the meaning of Judeo-Bolshevism perfectly when he said that "relatively few Jews got those new jobs, but to the Lithuanians it looked like an invasion . . . when one thought of the fact that there was not a single Jew before in those places, every Jew looked unreasonably conspicuous."[85] In Poland, the emissary of the Polish government exile, Jan Karski, analyzed the plight of Jews. Karski was certainly no enemy of the Jews but he reported the following disturbing impression:

> In principle, however, and in their mass, the Jews have created here a situation in which the Poles regard them as devoted to the Bolsheviks and—one can safely say—wait for the moment when they will be able simply to take revenge upon the Jews. Virtually all Poles are bitter and disappointed in relation to the Jews; the overwhelming majority (first among them of course the youth) literally look forward to an opportunity for "repayment in blood."[86]

Karski describes here the explosive tension created by Poles who believed that all Jews had become lackeys of the Soviets. This was, of course, not the case. Most Polish Jews were not communist, nor did they serve the Soviet state.

Indeed, in Lithuania (and elsewhere), there is evidence that Jews were not really overrepresented in government. In 1939, before the Soviet invasion, of the 1,120 members of the Lithuanian Communist Party, Jews made up 35 percent. In the official Communist Party of January 1, 1941, only 16.6 percent were Jews.[87] These numbers show an overrepresentation of Jews, but certainly not dominance of the Soviet regime. It is also telling that Lithuania turned away Jews fleeing the Nazis in 1939 *before* it fell to the Soviets. One Jewish refugee recalled an acquaintance who "after reaching the Lithuanian side of the border . . . was cruelly driven back by Lithuanian soldiers."[88] It is more than a little ironic that by 1939, the Soviets had already begun purging Jews from high party positions. This included the replacement by Stalin of the Jewish Soviet Foreign Minister Litvinov with Molotov who would go on to sign the pact with Hitler. It is thought this was done to appease the *Führer*.[89]

Significantly, while Jews did rise to prominence both in the Soviet Union and in the occupied territories, it was not necessarily due to any special affinity with Soviets. In one instance near Pinsk in eastern Poland, the Polish police chief turned the town over to a known Jewish communist, shook hands, and fled.[90] The occupiers sought trustworthy officials and, therefore, would certainly not rely on national majority ethnicities such as the Poles or Lithuanians. They knew that Jews were rarely strong supporters of local nationalist organizations, were motivated to avoid capture by the Germans, and so had a vested interest in the Soviet state. We should add that many were excited about political, economic, and social opportunities. So, receptive Jews were a natural choice in local government for the Soviets. But they were never a permanent solution, either in the USSR or the occupied territories. In general, Jews merely served as placeholders until Soviet officials could arrive from the Soviet Union proper at which time "local Jews were relegated to inferior posts or removed altogether."[91] In Lithuania, "very few native Lithuanians, Jewish or otherwise, played significant roles in the Sovietization and governance of their country" according to one scholar.[92] Indeed, the Soviets did not always show themselves to be above antisemitism. A *pro-Soviet* Lithuanian group proclaimed that there was "no place for Jewish oppressors" in the "ranks of honorable Communists."[93] Indeed, Lithuanian Jews made up more than 10 percent of the "political activists" arrested in July 1940 and 13.5 percent of those deported immediately before the Nazi invasion.[94]

Often, Judeo-Bolshevik antisemitism manifests itself in family anecdotes that may or may not reflect reality. For example, a Pole recalled that "Two NKVD officers, accompanied by three young Jews wearing red armbands, came at night and arrested my uncle. They made offensive and disgracing remarks, pointing to a painting of Jesus and a picture of Pilsudski."[95] How this witness knew the three men were Jews is unclear, but the association in his mind is clear. Certainly, some Jews *were* collaborators with the Soviet state in these most painful areas of the police and NKVD. But so too were non-Jews. Jews were simply more visible. In the memory of some, this connection between Jews and Soviets became almost pathological. One man interviewed long after the war contended that the arrests of family members by the NKVD were "facilitated by Jews" and that his father had been arrested by a "malicious Jew."[96] This is, of course, possible, but it is much more likely that we are hearing the expression of the Judeo-Bolshevik myth as a way for this individual to make meaning of his own suffering.

The role of Jews in Soviet occupation regimes remains a contentious topic, but mainly for nationalist writers seeking to deflect responsibility for later anti-Jewish atrocities. The historical consensus is that there *were* Jews in positions in Soviet governments and that at times they *were* even overrepresented, but that they rarely played significant roles and certainly did not drive Soviet policy. Local collaboration by non-Jews was assuredly more important, but less visible; it also did not fit as easily into a nationalist anti-Soviet narrative. Instead, for those in the occupied territories who had suffered the painful and deeply personal loss of family, livelihood, and position, "the Jews" as a group served as scapegoats. Judeo-Bolshevist antisemitism ceased to be a vague concept; to its adherents, it had a very specific face and very personal repercussions. On December 8, 1939, a member of the local Polish underground sent the chilling message that "all the Poles here, from the elderly to the women and children, will take such a horrible revenge on the Jews as no anti-Semite has ever imagined possible."[97]

This blaming of the Jews for the actions of the Soviets was not a new phenomenon; indeed, in some ways, it hearkens back to the days when any kind of political or economic upheaval could result in a pogrom. The violent hatred that many in the East held for the Jews did not spring from a vacuum, but it *was* greatly exacerbated by the actions of the Soviets during the short two years in which they occupied Poland and the Baltic States. It was also a hatred that the Germans did not overlook.

The period of Soviet occupation of eastern Poland, the Baltic States, and Ukraine had important repercussions for both non-Jews and Jews. The experience of occupation was also vital in laying some of the groundwork for the nature of the Holocaust there. Some scholars, particularly in Eastern Europe, have sought to blame the Soviet period for all that followed which is a mischaracterization. However, the period from 1939–1941 *was* important. First, it created a period of instability while destroying state structures that had maintained order, if an authoritarian often antisemitic one. Second, it provided very real grievances for nationalists in these countries to rally around real losses of family and friends that would engender a very real hatred of the Soviets and communism. This strengthened both the position of nationalists (who were often antisemitic) and a willingness to collaborate with the Germans. Third, the actual behavior of Jews and, more importantly, the gross exaggerations of it according to the Judeo-Bolshevik myth created populations that were at least more disposed to anti-Jewish violence. This last point does not in any way suggest that there was not sufficient latent antisemitism in Eastern Europe to provide motivation for later anti-Jewish violence by collaborators, but it recognizes that the Soviet experience stoked the fires of antisemitism either in reality or in the mind and made those fires burn brighter when the Nazis arrived in June 1941.

Selected Readings

Gross, Jan Tomasz. *Revolution from Abroad: The Soviet Conquest of Poland's Western Ukraine and Western Belorussia*. Princeton, NJ: Princeton University Press, 1988.

Levin, Dov. *The Lesser of Two Evils: Eastern European Jewry under Soviet Rule, 1939–1941*. Trans. Naftali Greenwood. Philadelphia: Jewish Publication Society, 1995.

Roberts, Geoffrey. *Stalin's Wars: From World War to Cold War, 1939–1953*. New Haven, CT: Yale University Press, 2006.

Snyder, Timothy. *Bloodlands: Europe between Hitler and Stalin*. New York: Basic Books, 2012.

Sword, Keith, ed. *The Soviet Takeover of the Polish Eastern Provinces, 1939–41*. New York: St. Martin's Press, 1991.

5

Poland: The Nazi Laboratory of Genocide

Introduction

As for the Jews, their danger is seven times greater. Wherever Hitler's foot treads there is no hope for the Jewish people.

CHAIM KAPLAN, Diary Entry September 1, 1939, Warsaw[1]

When the German Army invaded Poland on September 1, 1939, the plans and systems that would become the Final Solution were not envisioned, let alone agreed upon by most Nazi leaders, but, as Kaplan noted with foreboding, there could be no positive outcome for Jews. What the German occupation of Poland *became*, however, was a learning laboratory for those involved in the larger Nazi genocidal project and the Holocaust in the East. For the first time, the Nazis had occupied eastern territory. They had taken the first steps toward realizing his vision of *Lebensraum* in the East with the conquest of the part of Poland allocated to Germany by the Molotov-Ribbentrop Pact. While the Soviets sought to reimagine their new territories, the Nazis did the same in theirs. The Nazis divided the western half of Poland into several sections: incorporated and occupied territories. Incorporated territories deemed most historically (and ethnically) "German" immediately became part of the Greater Reich. These were East Prussia, Danzig-West Prussia, Upper Silesia, and the Warthegau. The Nazis designated the remaining portion, the *Generalgovernment*, an occupied territory that might one day be incorporated into the Reich proper. In the meantime, it would function as a sort of colony under the control of Hitler's former lawyer, Hans Frank. In Poland, we see the first instances of the mass killing of Jews and unwanted Slavs, the expropriation of property for use by the Greater Reich, and attempts by local Nazi leaders to implement anti-Jewish policy. This often meant conflict between administrators as local considerations clashed with ideological priorities. We must keep in mind that, for all the virulent Nazi antisemitism, German Jews represented less than 0.75 percent of the population (roughly 505,000 out of a population of 67 million.) By 1939, that number had decreased by half through emigration. When the Nazis took their Polish territories, they became responsible for over 1.7 million Jews, not to mention Ukrainians and Poles. The "Jewish Question" and Nazi racial policy ceased to be abstract concepts and became pressing reality.[2] So, too, did notions of "Germanization" and the daunting prospect of demographic engineering facing the Nazi conquerors. This chapter will discuss the invasion and occupation of Poland up to the invasion of the Soviet Union in 1941. It explores the fits and starts with which Nazi policy toward Jews and other "inferior" people proceeded. It briefly examines the initial stages of ghettoization, which will be covered in depth later. Finally, it reveals the "lessons" learned by the Nazis at the local and national level and how they influenced later anti-Jewish policy. Indeed, some of the cast of characters introduced here become key figures later, in part, due to their experience in Poland.

"Have No Pity:" The German Invasion of Poland

Destruction of Poland in the foreground. The aim is elimination of living forces, not the arrival at a certain line: Even if war should break out in the West, the destruction of Poland shall be the primary objective ... In starting and making a war, not the Right is what matters but Victory. Have no pity. Brutal attitude. 80 million people shall get what is their right. Their existence has to be secured. The strongest has the Right. Greatest severity.

ADOLF HITLER, August 22, 1939[3]

Sometime during the night of August 31, 1939, failed mechanic turned SD Agent Alfred Naujoks drove with five or six other men to a small radio station flanked by two tall radio antennas near the small town of Gleiwitz on the German-Polish border. On Heydrich's orders, they arranged the dead bodies of German concentration camp prisoners from Dachau (callously code-named "canned goods") around the station. Gestapo chief Heinrich Müller supplied the bodies that were dressed in Polish army uniforms. Naujoks broadcast a short message in which the "Poles" called for confrontation with the Germans. Then he and his men fired several pistol shots and left.[4] This "attack" by Poland served as Hitler's pretense for war.

The following morning the German Army or *Wehrmacht* crossed the German-Polish border. Echoing his feelings on the fate of Poland above, Hitler had informed the commander in chief of the German Army, Walther von Brauchitsch in March that "Poland would have to be so thoroughly beaten down that, during the next few decades, she need not be taken into account as a political factor."[5] At 4 am on the 1st, three million German soldiers, 400,000 horses, 200,000 vehicles, and 5,000 trains hurled themselves at Poland.[6] The Poles fought back with what one Waffen-SS officer called "enormous tenacity."[7] The innovative German *Blitzkrieg* (lightning war) tactics based on fast and deep combined arms assaults overwhelmed the poorly equipped Polish Army and Air Force. Though an oft-repeated story, Polish cavalry only engaged German tanks twice and not on purpose (and the Germans had their fair share of horse-mounted units.)[8] Some Polish reactions were less than honorable as they fell upon ethnic Germans living among them, killing thousands. The most egregious of these was in the town of Bydgoszcz (Bromberg) where Poles murdered several thousand ethnic Germans.

From Berlin, CBS Correspondent William Shirer noted that "there is no excitement here . . . no hurrahs, no wild cheering, no throwing of flowers . . . It is a far grimmer German people that we see here tonight than we saw last night."[9] This was not August 1914. Ironically, the capitals of France and Britain buzzed with indignation and promises to support their Polish allies. However, tough talk and a small French advance into Germany were the sum total of Allied guarantees of Polish security. The Allies provided no tangible support. The Poles fought and fell alone, their fate firmly decided by the Soviet invasion on September 17.

It soon became clear that this war would be more brutal than perhaps anticipated. Some Nazi propaganda had filtered into the ranks of ordinary soldiers. After the beginning of the attack, the commanding general of the *Wehrmacht* issued a pamphlet to his soldiers. "The German soldier," he wrote, "in the occupied territories is a representative of the German Reich and its power. He should think and act as such. [. . .] Each insult and each attack on the German *Wehrmacht* and the German people should be dealt with through the harshest means . . . It is not necessary to mention how the soldiers are to behave toward the Jews."[10]

The behavior of at least some soldiers bore out that the intent of these instructions was clear. The Army began almost immediately to violate the most basic laws of war for, in the eyes of many, these racially inferior people did not count. After the battle for the town of Ciepelow, regular German soldiers machine-gunned three hundred captured Polish soldiers.[11] German military brutality was not limited to combatants. Four days into the invasion, in Częstochowa, German soldiers murdered more than three hundred civilians in reprisal for what was likely friendly fire. *Luftwaffe* planes frequently strafed civilians. One Polish officer recalled a teacher trying to lead her class to shelter when a German plane attacked. "The children scattered like sparrows . . . but on the field some crumpled and lifeless bundles of bright clothing remained." He concluded that "the nature of the new war was already clear."[12] That officer, Wladislaw Anders, would go on to command a Polish army fighting for the Soviets

FIGURE 5 *Local Jews are arrested in Poland. Note* Wehrmacht *photographer in foreground. Ustrony/Opatow, Poland, September 1939.*
Source: Bundesarchiv.

against the Nazis. Undisciplined looting also accompanied the invasion. A Jewish schoolboy in Łódź recalled that "Every few days there would be a knock on the door and invariably there would be a German soldier, often with a *Volksdeutsche* (a Pole of German origin) with a swastika on his lapel, and they would simply come and rob: the wedding ring from my mother's finger, look into a cupboard and take whatever they wanted."[13] A Pole remembered a German officer looting the neighbors' house of "radios, mattresses, comforters, carpets" and taking the family's only down quilt.[14]

Warsaw surrendered on September 28. All organized resistance ceased by October 5. After an air raid on Krzemieniec, a Pole observed a lone Jew mourning his wife, killed by the bombs. "There is no God," he screamed," Hitler and the bombs are the only gods! There is no grace and pity in the world!"[15] The Polish people, Jew and non-Jew alike, would soon discover just how prophetic this lamentation was.

Decapitation: The *Einsatzgruppen* in Poland

I hear of events from the "colonization" of the east that frighten me.

Diary Entry, Commanding General of Army Group North,
FEODOR VON BOCK, 1939[16]

Accompanying the general brutality of the military invasion was a more calculated organ of violence: the *Einsatzgruppen* (EG) or "operational groups." Von Bock's frightening events are the murders they carried out. These small groups of Security Service (SD) personnel had deployed in Austria in 1938 and Czechoslovakia a year later. Then, their task had been to secure sensitive material, set up an initial SD presence, and locate potential enemies of the Nazis. The *Einsatzgruppen* that entered Poland in September 1939 were vastly expanded in size and mission.

Five *Einsatzgruppen* (I-V) were initially established for the Polish campaign, though this number eventually expanded to seven, with the inclusion of EG VI and an *Einsatzgruppe für besondere Verwendung* (EG z.b.V.) or EG for special assignment. Each EG was made up of smaller *Einsatzkommandos* (EKs). The approximately three thousand of the EG came from the three German police organizations: Criminal Police (*Kriminalpolizei* or *Kripo*), Secret State Police (*Geheime Staatspolizei* or *Gestapo)*, and the intelligence service (*Sicherheitsdienst* or *SD*).

The choice of leadership was much less haphazard. Twenty-one commanders came from leading *Gestapo* offices in Germany. These leaders represented the "the cream of the crop in Himmler's circle of executive leaders."[17] Devout National Socialists, a third of them were World War I veterans and almost all had experience in the right-wing *Freikorps*.[18] They were also surprisingly well educated: fifteen of twenty-five *Einsatzgrupppen* and *Einsatzkommando* leaders held PhDs in law or the humanities.[19]

The mission of these groups was inextricably Intertwined with Nazi plans for Poland. Hitler and his leading subordinates never recognized Poland as a legitimate state, seeing it as an aberration of the Versailles treaty and in the historical context of its many dissolutions. Hitler wrote in his 1928 second book that "The ethnic state, in contrast, could under absolutely no circumstances annex Poles with the intention of turning them into Germans one day." It would be necessary to "isolate" or "have them [Poles] removed entirely."[20] On March 25, 1939, Hitler told his generals that, "Poland would have to be so thoroughly beaten down that, during the next few decades, she need not be taken into account as a political factor."[21] Speaking later, a Nazi administrator called his area of Poland "the first colonial territory of the German nation."[22] Moreover, he emphasized "that this area remains firmly under German control, that the backbone of the Poles remains broken for all time and that never again can there be even the slightest resistance from this area to German Reich policy."[23] The goal of removing any and all potential resistance drove the *Einsatzgruppen* in their murderous activities in Poland.

The *Einsatzgruppen* executed Operation Tannenberg (named after a great German World War I victory). Tannenberg demanded the decapitation of Polish leadership, intelligentsia, and anyone deemed a potential resister. Highly mobile EGs followed closely behind military units, carrying out their deadly tasks. Here, the ideological goals of the SS and the military coincided. The *Wehrmacht* suffered from an almost pathological fear of armed civilian

TABLE 3 *Einsatzgruppen units and initial commanders deployed to Poland, September 1939.*

Unit	Commander(s)
Einsatzgruppe I	SS-Standartenführer Bruno Streckenbach
Einsatzkommando 1/I	SS-Sturmbannführer Ludwig Hahn
Einsatzkommando 2/I	SS-Sturmbannführer Bruno Müller
Einsatzkommando 3/I	SS-Sturmbannführer Alfred Hasselberg
Einsatzkommando 3/I	SS-Sturmbannführer Karl Brunner
Einsatzgruppe II	SS-Obersturmbannführer Emanuel Schäfer
Einsatzkommando 1/II	SS-Obersturmbannführer Otto Sens
Einsatzkommando 2/II	SS-Sturmbannführer Karl-Heinz Rux
Einsatzgruppe III	SS-Obersturmbannführer und Regierungsrat Hans Fischer
Einsatzkommando 1/III	SS-Sturmbannführer Wilhelm Scharpwinkel
Einsatzkommando 2/III	SS-Sturmbannführer Fritz Liphardt
Einsatzgruppe IV	SS-Brigadeführer Lothar Beutel SS-Standartenführer Josef Albert Meisinger (Oct 1939)
Einsatzkommando 1/IV	SS-Sturmbannführer und Regierungsrat Helmut Bischoff
Einsatzkommando 2/IV	SS-Sturmbannführer und Regierungsrat Walter Hammer
Einsatzgruppe V	SS-Standartenfürer Ernst Damzog
Einsatzkommando 1/V	SS-Sturmbannführer und Regierungsrat Heinz Gräfe
Einsatzkommando 2/V	SS-Sturmbannführer und Regierungsrat Robert Schefe
Einsatzkommando 3/V	SS-Sturmbannführer und Regierungsrat Walter Albath
Einsatzgruppe VI	SS-Oberführer Erich Naumann
Einsatzkommando 1/VI	SS-Sturmbannführer Franz Sommer
Einsatzkommando 2/VI	SS-Sturmbannführer Gerhard Flesch
Einsatzgruppe z. B.V	SS-Obergruppenführer Udo von Woyrsch and SS-Oberfürer Otto Rasch
Einsatzkommando 16 (recruited from ethnic Germans)	SS-Sturmbannführer Rudolf Tröger

resistance behind the lines and appreciated the help securing those areas. To this end, the SS coordinated with the German Army. In an agreement of July 31, 1939, the army High Command (OKH) confirmed that "the mission of the Security Police *Einsatzkommandos* is to combat all elements hostile to the Reich and to Germans in enemy territory to the rear of the combat troops."[24] This suited the military just fine.

Einsatzgruppen commands themselves were to "perform certain ethnic-political tasks in the occupied territory on behalf of the Führer and in accordance with his instructions." What were these tasks? The military informed its members that "The Führer's tasks encompass, above all, ethnopolitical measures. The details of the performance of these tasks are left to the discretion of the commanders of the Einsatzgruppen and are outside the responsibility of the military commanders."[25] If these instructions seem vague, it is because they are. Indeed, after the war, the leader of *Einsatzgruppe IV*, Lothar Beutel, recalled that "no clear directive to kill the Polish intelligentsia had been issued." Rather, Himmler and Heydrich had explained that the overall goal was "pacifying" the occupied area.[26] A bit more specific was the September 7 order by Heydrich that "The leading strata of the population should be rendered harmless."[27] Explicit orders were likely not required because Himmler and Heydrich knew their men and knew that they would work toward the Führer. Himmler trusted his underlings to grasp the true meaning of his guidance.

EG leaders did this and directed their violence against broadly defined categories of potential resisters: intelligentsia, politicians, party leaders, clergy, academics, and professionals. At times, they had actual lists of individuals to be hunted down. Actions taken ranged from arrest to executions. For example, on November 10, 1939, EK Bromberg reported the following:

TABLE 4 Einsatzkommando *Bromberg Operational Report, November 10, 1939.*

	Liquidated	Evacuated	Released
Teachers	73	68	66
Lawyers and Notaries	3	2	1
Pharmacists	2	-	5
Judges	-	1	1
Tax Officials	13	3	10
City Administration	1	-	4
Miscellaneous Professions	2	1	4

Source: "Situation Report by Einsatzkommando Bromberg, November 10, 1939," in *War, Pacification, and Mass Murder, 1939: The Einsatzgruppen in Poland*, ed. Jürgen Matthäus and Jochen Böhler (Lanham: Rowman & Littlefield, 2014), p. 150.

Another EG report from Warsaw in October 1939 reported the arrest of 354 clergymen and teachers. "Because of their demonstrated Polish chauvinism," it continued, "they represent a danger, not to be underestimated, to the security of the German troops, German civilian officials, and the German civilian population." It continued, noting that the EG had acquired a list which "shows the elite of Warsaw, who naturally have to disappear!"[28] Sometimes charges of resistance were tenuous at best, as illustrated by a September 1939 report: "Among those arrested is Father Trzaskome. He was arrested because he told German troops that within a week they would disappear like dust. He also stated that the French have already occupied half of western Germany. Within his close circle of friends, he accused the German military of looting." For these transgressions, the Nazis deported Father Trzaskome to a concentration camp.[29] A Polish woman recalled the September 12 murder of her husband by the EGs:

> Around 3:00 p.m., Germans entered our house . . . The Germans had a list with names of Limanowa inhabitants, and at the top of this list was my husband, Jan Semik. The other names on the list were those of Jews, rich craftsmen, and businessmen from Limanowa . . . [My brother] came to my house around 5pm, he told me that the Germans had murdered my husband and ten Jews, and that the corpses were in the quarry at Mordarka.[30]

One hundred Polish civilians were executed in Wawer near Warsaw as a reprisal for the killing of two German policemen.[31] Exact death tolls are difficult to come by. For the early period, the best estimates are that 10,000 Polish civilians were executed during the fighting. The *Wehrmacht*, SS, police, and EGs murdered 16,000 Poles (and an unknown number of Jews) by October. Estimates of civilians murdered in former Polish territory by the end of 1939 exceed 60,000.[32] As the war ended and a more stable occupation began, the liquidation of the Polish leadership did not stop.

While most of the initial actions were directed at non-Poles, thousands of Jews were attacked and murdered by the EG, the military, and police. Polish leadership capable of resistance had to be eliminated to facilitate immediate occupation and destroy future resistance; Jews and their leadership had to be eliminated as part of the larger Nazi genocidal project of removing Jews from a space intended for German settlement. As such, EG leaders correctly interpreted their orders to include Jews, predominantly male, and those in leadership positions. As one former EG member stated after the war, "Our EK was deployed in Białystok to round up all male Jews between about 15 and 60 years of age in a schoolyard."[33] The largest killing during the initial period took place in Przemyśl around September 20, when members of EG I and EG z.b.V. killed more than 500 Jews. An eyewitness later stated that these were "mostly from the intelligentsia."[34] It is an important distinction.

The wholesale murder of Jewish men, women, and children was not yet Nazi policy, so Jews murdered by the EGs in Poland still fell loosely into the category of elites and "potential resisters." However, murders of Jews were often more brutal and horrifying, as one survivor testified. In the town of Mielec, EG members "doused the synagogue with gasoline and set it on fire. The Jews in the bathhouse and the slaughterhouse were locked inside, and the buildings were set on fire. Those who tried to escape and save themselves were shot at and thrown back into the fire."[35] The burning of synagogues had become part of standard Nazi anti-Jewish violence since *Kristallnacht* in 1938, and frequently accompanied the murder of Jews in Poland. The problem became so bad that only a week into the campaign, Himmler prohibited the burning of synagogues in major urban areas to prevent fire from spreading and destroying non-Jewish property.[36]

Actions against Jews in 1939 had a secondary motive that may partially explain their brutality and public nature. As the Nazis were still pursuing a territorial solution to the "Jewish Question," many hoped they could free their newly acquired territories of Jews by driving them into Soviet territory. This may have been part of the motivation at Przmyśl, which straddled the border. The commander of EK 3/1 drove 18,000 Jews across the river into the Soviet zone.[37]

FIGURE 6 *Famed Nazi filmmaker Leni Riefenstahl (second from left) and her film crew observe a killing of Jews by German soldiers during the invasion of Poland. Konskie, Poland, September 1941.*
Source: Bundesarchiv.

It should be noted that the mass murder of both Jews and Poles did not go without objection in Poland, though these complaints were not numerous. The violence distressed several *Wehrmacht* officers. Some inquired if orders had been given to shoot Jews. Army colonel Helmut Stieff wrote his wife that "this extermination of entire families with women and children is only possible through subhumans who do not deserve the name German. I am ashamed to be a German."[38] (He would go on to participate in the July 20, 1944, plot to kill Hitler.) One general reported to his commander that "The selection [of those to be executed] in these instances was completely disparate and often incomprehensible, and the carrying out of the shootings was often dishonorable."[39] Another decried the "incomprehensible lack of human and ethical sensitivity" on the part of the police and suggested the problem could only be solved if all police units and their officers were removed from Poland.[40]

One of the most outspoken was General Johannes Blaskowitz, commander of occupied Poland. He wrote several reports which made their way to Hitler himself. Blaskowitz noted that "surprisingly quickly the like-minded and the deviant personalities come together, as is the case in Poland, in order to give full vent to their animalistic and pathological instincts."[41] He also marshaled a utilitarian disagreement, saying that the EGs had "so far accomplished no visible task of keeping order but rather only spread terror among the population."[42] An Army major refused to hand over 180 Polish civilians to the SS when he learned they would be shot.[43]

Clearly, such resistance, though rare, required a response. It was swift and unequivocal. Hitler dismissed Blaskowitz's criticisms as "a childish attitude" and derided his military as operating with "Salvation Army methods."[44] Blaskowitz was the only Army colonel general from the Polish campaign to not receive the rank of Field Marshal; he was removed from Poland and relegated to the backwaters of the German military. On October 25, 1939, Army commander in chief, Field Marshal Brauchitsch, ordered his officers to "refrain from any form of criticism of the actions of the state leadership," even going so far as to suggest their wives do the same.[45] Brauchitsch reiterated this guidance in February 1940, telling his generals that "harsh measures against the Polish population" were "made necessary by the forthcoming battle of destiny of the German people."[46] General Keitel, chief of the Armed Forces (OKW) put it even more cynically. "The *Wehrmacht*," he said, should be glad if it can distance itself from administrative questions in Poland."[47] Himmler himself addressed the generals a month later commenting that "I do not do anything that the Führer does not know about."[48] The implication was clear: Hitler had approved the actions of the EGs and any resistance to them was resistance to the *Führer*. On the whole, resistance to the more murderous Nazi policies in Poland was in short supply, but its presence in 1939 ensured that extra measures would be taken in 1941 to avoid the same problem.

Regardless, the German military did actually support the mission of the *Einsatzgruppen*. Cooperation rather than resistance predominated. Moreover, at least some objections to EG behavior stemmed not from moral objections to Nazi policy but from questions of decorum, practical effects on the local population, or impacts on troop morale. Indeed, in some instances, Army officers requested that EGs be deployed to their areas to "pacify" the population. A directive from the commander of the 14th Army, Wilhelm List, serves as a damning counterpoint. "You are asked," he told his commanders, "to explain this to the subordinate units in an appropriate way. Extensive support for the *Einsatzkommandos* in their border policing and their state security tasks is in the interest of the troops."[49]

The *Einsatzgruppen* experience in Poland from 1939–41 differed greatly from Czechoslovakia or Austria. In Poland, these units engaged for the first time in the mass shooting of targeted civilians. While the magnitude of future killings in the Soviet Union would drastically increase, the EGs and their leaders gained valuable experience in the practical and administrative tasks required in Poland. SS leadership also recognized the need for a clearer relationship with the Army, one allowing for greater support. They also learned how to carry out these mass shootings and became acclimated to the levels of sheer brutality necessary. It should come, then, as little surprise that many of the same men who directed and committed murder in Poland would do the same in the Soviet Union.

The Division and Occupation of Poland

All of them want to unload their rubbish into the *Generalgovernment*. Jews, the sick, slackers, etc. And Frank is resisting. Not entirely wrongly. He wants to create a model country out of Poland. That is going too far. He cannot and should not.

JOSEF GOEBBELS, diary entry, November 1940[50]

The occupation and dissection of Poland brought Nazi ideologues and officials face to face with practical challenges to their massive demographic project. Conflict was not always cordial, as Goebbels indicates regarding the *Generalgovernment*. In Poland, the Nazis attempted to make their vision of *Lebensraum* a reality on the ground. They also honed their skills at moving large groups of people; skills that would be particularly useful as the Holocaust progressed.

When the Germans occupied Poland, they were immediately confronted with a set of competing demands stemming from their own ideological goals. They wanted to "Germanize" these new territories as quickly as possible through the settlement of ethnically acceptable Germans and the "salvaging" of any such individuals in the local population. They also wanted to remove undesirable "races" like the Poles to make space for these new arrivals. Finally, they also had to solve the "Jewish Question" as soon as possible by removing the new, 1.7 million Jews Germany had now added. All of these aims required a demographic engineering project of massive proportions and, logistically and politically, all of them could not be accomplished at once. This resulted in conflict between Nazi leaders.

All of occupied Poland was not treated equally. The Nazis considered certain areas of western Poland to be originally German or sufficiently German that they were immediately annexed and became formally part of the Greater Reich with the same standing as existing provinces or *Gaus*. The following regions constituted the incorporated territories established by Hitler orders in 1939:

- Danzig-West Prussia—*Gauleiter* Albert Forster
- Wartheland or *Warthegau*—*SS-Obergruppenführer and Reichsstatthalter (Reich Governor)* Arthur Greiser
- Silesia—*Gauleiter* Josef Wagner

The leaders of these territories focused on making their province a model German state as soon as possible, and this inevitably led to conflict between *Gauleiters* and also with the administrator of the final region: the *Generalgouvernement* (GG), Hans Frank. Civilian administrators took control from the military of these regions on October 25, 1939.

The Polish territory remaining after the annexation of the incorporated territories became the *Generalgouvernement,* an area not directly annexed by the Reich, but seen more as a colonial holding, at least for the time being. The GG was placed under the control of Hans Frank, thirty-nine year old veteran of the *Freikorps* and early Nazi party follower. As the German Army invaded Poland, Hitler summoned Frank to Potsdam to offer him the position of governor of the forthcoming GG. He accepted on September 15.[51] Frank arrived in Krakow on November 7 after a grand torchlit parade through town. He took up residence in the ancient royal Wawel Castle, a stone's throw from the church where the kings of Poland were buried, and overlooking the historic Jewish quarter of Kazimierz. He and his wife, Brigitte, filled the castle with valuable objects looted from his new fiefdom. As one visitor noted, the fourteenth-century castle "was now crammed full, from the subterranean caves to the top of its highest tower with furniture stolen from the palaces of the Polish gentry" as well as objects acquired via "crafty raids through France, Holland and Belgium." His own son, Niklas, derisively wrote after the war that "ghettos had to be created so that Mother could have all her tailors in one place."[52]

We will focus primarily on the GG, but also touch on the incorporated territories. After all, the massive ghetto of Łódź was located in the *Warthegau*. Governor-General Frank, however, controlled a massive region. He further

FIGURE 7 *Governor-General of Poland Hans Frank (right) hosts Reichsführer SS Heinrich Himmler at a dinner held at Wawel castle during his visit to Krakow. Krakow, Poland, 1940.*
Source: United States Holocaust Memorial Museum.

divided this area into districts: Krakow, Lublin, Radom, and Warsaw Districts. District Galicia in eastern Poland would be added in 1941, after the invasion of the USSR. Approximately 11.5 million people lived in the GG, a third of Poland's pre-war population. This included 1.3 million Jews and around 500,000 Ukrainians. Unfortunately, Frank only had 100,000 ethnic Germans at his command.[53] This was a huge obstacle, as he hoped at some point to sufficiently Germanize his territory to be incorporated into the Reich. Goebbels recognized Frank's ambition and discounted it. In any case, Frank had another more pressing central problem. The incorporated territories considered the GG a dumping ground for their unwanted, racially inferior populations (mainly Jews). Frank would spend much of the next two years fighting off these deportations.

Initial priority for Nazi leadership was Germanization of the incorporated territories. While ideally this would have involved large immigration of Reich Germans, at least initially, administrators would have to settle for the movement of ethnic Germans to their territories. Himmler, in his capacity as Reich Commissioner for the Consolidation of German Nationhood, ordered on October 30, 1939, that all Poles and Jews be removed from the incorporated territories.[54] The Higher SS and Police Leader (HSSPF) for

Greiser's *Warthegau* elaborated on these plans in November 1939, stating that their purpose, according to Himmler, was "a) cleansing and securing of the new German territories, b) creation of dwellings and work opportunities for the ethnic Germans immigrating."[55] Suddenly, everyone wanted to send their unwanted populations to the GG, from not just the incorporated territories, but also Germany proper. Adolf Eichmann hoped to deport his Viennese Jews. A Nazi police official asked if he could add Berlin's Sinti/Roma to Eichmann's transports.

In the minds of many, the GG was a Jewish "reservation" where Europe could dump its unwanted Jewish populations and a "Polish work camp" for a steady supply of slave labor. This concept crystallized into the first of three territorial solutions to the "Jewish Question." Territorial solutions sought to remove Jews by physically transporting them someplace else. The first of these, known as the Nisko or Lublin plan ultimately encompassed several intermediate deportation plans. Under this plan, the Nazis would deport all the Jews of Europe to a specific region near Lublin, where they would be consolidated, much like Native Americans reservations in the United States. The Nisko/Lublin plan was no more benign than the American one. While Nazi planners did not aim to systematically murder the Jews, they certainly recognized that confining so many people to a small region would result in a large loss of life. This was absolutely acceptable to them. Almost immediately, the gulf between Himmler's imagination and the realm of possibility in occupied Poland became apparent. The GG was simply not prepared to handle the influx of people required by Germanization and anti-Jewish policies. 45,000 Jews arrived in this Lublin reservation in November 1939. There were no facilities for them. An SS officer told them matter-of-factly that "There are no dwellings. There are no houses. If you build, there will be a roof over your heads. There is no water; the wells all around carry disease. There is cholera, dysentery and typhoid. If you bore and find water, you will have water."[56] The resulting high number of fatalities was entirely predictable.

Governor-General Frank fought these deportations, arguing not without reason that he was simply unprepared to accommodate such an influx. He also did not want his territory to become a squalid, poverty-stricken land of refugee camps and sickness. Dr. Fritz Arlt, head of "Population Affairs" in Krakow, later described the days of the Lublin plan, saying: "The people were thrown out of the trains, whether in the marketplace or on the train station or wherever it was and nobody cared about it . . . We received a phone call from the district officer and he said, 'I don't know what to do any more. So and so many hundreds have arrived again. I have neither shelter nor food nor anything.'"[57]

Hans Frank impressed upon Hermann Goering the problems deportations caused and successfully halted them in 1940. Himmler cited "technical difficulties."[58] Gestapo chief Heinrich Müller killed Eichmann's plan of deporting Austrian Jews, stating that "that the resettlement and deportation of Poles and Jews in the territory of the future Polish state requires central coordination. Therefore permission from the offices here must on principle be in hand."[59] Frank himself described the conditions of the first transports, reminding his officials in 1942:

> You remember those terrible months in which day after day goods trains, loaded with people, poured into the *Generalgovernment*; some wagons were filled to overflowing with corpses. That was terrible when every District Chief, every County and Town Chief, had his hands full of work from early morning to night to deal with this flood of elements which had become undesirable in the Reich and which they wanted to get rid of quickly.[60]

By early 1940, Himmler conceded that all future deportations would require Frank's approval. This effectively ended the future of the Nisko/Lublin plan. In addition, the Germany victory over France in May 1940 breathed new life into another proposal. This territorial solution would deport European Jews to the formerly French island of Madagascar off the eastern coast of Africa. This plan also helped pause deportations to Poland, as it seemed that the Jewish question would be solved in Madagascar. In any case, by the time deportations more or less ended, 400,000 Poles and Jews had been deported into the GG. The Nazis floated a plan to send their Jews to the Soviet Union, which had an "autonomous Jewish province" in Birobidzhan. The Soviets politely declined.

Massive deportations planned for the *Generalgouvernment* in 1939 and 1940 failed for a variety of reasons. First, the scale and scope of demographic change desired by Himmler and the civil administrators simply failed to match the reality of the logistically possible. Second, Frank mounted a vigorous and ultimately successful campaign to oppose deportations of Poles and Jews into his area. He based his objections both on the real unfeasibility of the project as well as on his own ambitions for the region. Third, Himmler placed a greater emphasis on the movement of ethnic Germans to newly occupied territories, and devoted more of his resources and attention there. The deportation of Poles, and particularly Jews, received lower priority in 1939 and 1940. Finally, the Madagascar Plan, which the Nazis took very seriously, seemed to better solve the Jewish problem and therefore removed the urgency of deporting Jews to the GG.

Frank's Kingdom: Occupation Policy in the *Generalgovernment*, 1939–41

We have decided to behave, as officials, exactly the other way round than at home, that is, like bastards.

FRITZ CUHORST, *Stadthauptmann*, Lublin, December 1939[61]

Hans Frank's *Generalgovernment* served as an incubator for a variety of policies that would be replicated elsewhere in Eastern Europe, but as Cuhorst's statement shows, these policies would be carried out with brutality and indifference. While some of the same policies would appear in the incorporated territories, Frank had a degree of freedom to operate in the GG precisely because it was technically not part of Germany. Conversely, many of his policies did not appear from thin air but reflected previous experience, particularly, domestic German anti-Jewish policy. For these reasons, the unfolding of the Holocaust and the larger Nazi genocidal project in the GG add critical elements to our understanding of the evolution of these processes over time.

As time progressed, the *Einsatzgruppen's* mobile killing mission ended. They were officially dissolved on November 20, 1939. The leaders and men of the EGs shifted into a more stationary, permanent role in the police bureaucracy of the four districts of the GG: Warsaw, Lublin, Radom, and Krakow. The position of Higher SS and Police Leader (HSSPF) was carried over from the Reich. In the GG, the HSSPF was forty-five-year-old *SS-Obergruppenführer* Friedrich Wilhelm Krüger. His immediate superior was the *Reichsführer SS* (RFSS) himself, Heinrich Himmler, but, in the usual byzantine Nazi bureaucracy, he was also theoretically under the control of Frank. Each district had its own SS and Police Leader (SSPF) as well as a police office headed by a Commandant of Police (KdS). In turn, major cities and regions had their own police offices. Former EG members held a large number of these positions. *Einsatzgruppen* or *Einsatzkommando* leaders from the Polish campaign led all KdS district offices in the GG.

However, the killing did not stop. The clearest example of this was the so-called AB Aktion, from the German *Ausserordentlich Befriedungsaktion* or "Extraordinary Pacification campaign." It began in May 1940 and, again, targeted Polish leadership. The start date was no coincidence. Frank hoped the military campaign in France would distract the world from events in the GG. HSSPF Krüger led this operation, which killed several thousand people. Frank addressed his men plainly, saying, "I confess quite openly that it will cost several thousand Poles their lives, above all from the intellectual leadership of Poland. But for us all as National Socialists this time brings the obligation to make sure that no more resistance emerges from the Polish people." Oddly, he concluded by saying, "Gentlemen, we are not murderers."[62] In the same speech, he referred to the mass arrest of professors from the famous Jagiellonian University in November 1939 and their deportation to the Sachsenhausen concentration camp, which had generated significant public protest. "The trouble we had with the Kraków professors was terrible," he lamented. "Had we dealt with the matter here, it would have gone differently. I would therefore urgently entreat you to deport no one else to the concentration camps in the Reich but to undertake the liquidation here or to impose a proper punishment."[63] And so began the second wave of decapitation of Polish intelligentsia.

The SS and police conducted other mass killings as well in Poland. They marked the mentally and physically handicapped in the GG and the incorporated territories for death. This was in keeping with the Aktion T-4, which murdered these same people in Germany proper. However, in occupied Poland, the killings lacked most of the subterfuge associated with their German counterparts. In Pomerania (part of Danzig-West Prussia), a psychiatric hospital in the town of Swiece became a killing site when an SS unit and an ethnic German militia arrived and murdered 1,000 patients, including the hospital director.[64] In Chełm in the *Wartheland*, an SS unit murdered 300 men, 124 women, and 17 children in the local psychiatric hospital on January 12, 1940. The SS men threw those who resisted out the windows.[65] One SS man recalled a mass killing in the port city of Gdynia, in Danzig-West Prussia: "On another occasion, between 80 and 90—as I recall, 82—Polish women and men from the Hospital for Epidemic Diseases at Hexengrund near Gdynia, who had venereal diseases, were shot. So far as I know, this execution took place in November 1939." He then went on to explain that "To my knowledge, they were shot because the Navy wanted to establish a torpedo school in the building."[66] This last statement illustrates an important difference between the T-4 program and similar killings in the East. Often, the killings had little to do with eugenics and much more to do with the cold calculus of creating space for the German military, civil administration, and civilian "settlers." The hospital in Chelm, where 400 had been murdered, became an SS barracks and military hospital.[67] Another important historical moment in the murder of the handicapped in Poland was the use of gas vans by SS-*Obersturmführer* Herbert Lange. Lange, a veteran of EG VI, commanded his own *Sonderkommando*, or special detachment, which murdered over 4,000 mentally ill individuals in the *Wartheland*. Some of these people were murdered in specially constructed gas vans where victims were placed in a sealed compartment into which carbon monoxide gas from the exhaust was piped. Some of the vans had "Kaiser Coffee Company" painted on the side in order to deceive victims. Historian Henry Friedlander described one killing in East Prussia: "The Lange Kommando loaded forty patients into its gas van on each trip, killed the victims during the trip, disposed of their bodies in the surrounding countryside, and returned with the empty van about three hours later."[68] Lange's operations were the first use of mobile gas vans in occupied Poland but not the last. Gas vans would be employed at the Chełmno extermination camp, which would be commanded by Herbert Lange. In addition, carbon monoxide would be the gas of choice for most of the extermination centers.

For Frank, occupation of the *Generalgovernment* also meant attempts at Germanization. This required two tasks: the suppression of Polish life and culture and the cultivation of German culture and settlement. Both proved to be daunting. A Central Emigration Office (UWZ) was set up in order to find ethnic Germans among the general population. The SS Race and Settlement Office (RuSHA) included racial "examinations" of the local population to rate the ethnic value of individuals and seek "valuable bloodlines."[69] Academics and scientists such as anthropologists and ethnologists actively participated in this task. At least some of their equipment and resources had been stolen from the Jagiellonian University in Krakow.[70] The quality of the *Volksdeutsche* or ethnic Germans found in occupied Poland did not always impress the SS. Often, they did not speak German or act particularly German at all. Good *Volksdeutsche* were given privileged positions in local government and police forces.

Himmler was particularly interested in finding ethnic German children who could be raised German, a special kind of brutality that saw children ripped from their parents' arms and taken to families in Germany. In May 1940, Himmler wrote that "The basis of our considerations must be to fish out of this mush the racially valuable, in order to bring them to Germany for assimilation."[71] These children were renamed and often left with no knowledge of their parents or origins. Sometimes, this abduction of children was haphazard. As this policy was carried over into the Soviet Union, a member of the *Einsatzgruppen* there found an eleven-year-old "Aryan looking" Belarusian girl and sent her home to live with his parents in Berlin.[72] Attempts at the settlement of ethnic Germans in occupied Poland had mixed results by January of 1941. 500,000 *Volksdeutsche* had been identified to take over Polish land, but most of them remained living in less than comfortable transit camps awaiting placement.[73]

The uprooting of Polish culture was perhaps more successful than the fertilization of the German. As noted, many of the human pillars of Polish culture had been murdered, forced to flee, or driven underground by deadly attacks on the intelligentsia and leadership. The Nazis suppressed education and the Polish language. Clergy were not systematically targeted for extermination, but a very large number had been murdered or deported to concentration camps. The occupiers removed Poles from all but the lowest level of government and cultural institutions. In addition, Frank directed a physical assault on Polish culture, what the Polish government in exile in London called "the war on statues." In Krakow, a statue commemorating a Teutonic defeat by Poles and Lithuanians in *1410* was demolished.[74] Hitler, through Frank, ordered the Royal Castle in Warsaw destroyed. Throughout Poland, German art historians and experts systematically looted of cultural treasures from museums and private collections, not least those owned by Jews.

The attempted destruction of Polish culture was not limited to "high" art and architecture. Cities were renamed: Rzeszów became Reichshof, Gdynia became Gottenhafen, Łódź became Littmanstadt, Częstochowa became Tschenstochau, and so on. Streets were renamed. Cities and towns in the GG abounded with Adolf Hitler Streets and Adolf Hitler Squares. German was the official language and German culture the only accepted form of expression. With the suppression of Polish culture came a deluge of all things German. Jan Karski, emissary for the Polish government in exile, visited Poznan (then renamed Posen) and reported that "the city with the finest historical tradition in all Poland was now, to all appearances, a typical German community. Every sign on stores and banks and institutions was in German. The street names were in German. German newspapers were being hawked on the corners."[75]

Hans Frank himself later asked for a special volume of the popular German tourist guidebook, Baedeker's, to be printed for tourists to the *Generalgovernment*. The preface of the guide aimed to introduce the reader to "the extensive ... reconstruction that has already been achieved or is still in progress, under difficult wartime conditions, in the three and one half years since Germany took over the administration of the Vistula Region", and "to point out the innumerable vestiges, often hidden, of old German cultural and pioneering activities-above all, the creations of German architecture."[76] Intrepid tourists to the *Generalgovernment* in 1943 learned that Krakow was "a predominantly German city, in which one everywhere encounters the traces of German labour and German culture." The St. Mary's Church, home to the Trumpeter of Krakow, now located on Adolf-Hitler-Platz, was the "most magnificent construction of Kraków's German citizenry in which German was preached until 1537."[77] Such revisionist history was certainly wishful thinking, but clearly demonstrated the Nazi elimination of Polish culture from a future Germanized space.

Several Polish resistance movements sprung up to oppose the Nazis in Poland, the most well known being the Polish Home Army (AK). In this early period of occupation, resistance, severe reprisals, and repression drove most resistance underground. Though the Polish Underground State wrote in December 1939 that "preparations [should be made] for an armed uprising at the rear of the armies of occupation, to occur at the moment of entry of regular Polish forces into the country," it also recognized that any major actions before that time "would in no way be proportionate to the repression that it would necessarily bring down on the country, giving the occupant an excuse for the ruthless extermination of the Poles."[78] Frank's decree on Polish Freedom Day (November 10, 1939) that one male would be shot in any house that displayed Polish flags or symbols exemplified this repression. He also ordered that 120 civilian hostages be taken in Krakow to prevent any unrest.[79]

On April 30, 1940, a young SS captain arrived in the town of Oświęcim to build a concentration camp from a set of abandoned Polish military barracks.[80] The German name for the town was Auschwitz and the thirty-nine-year-old SS captain was Rudolf Höss. The camp was intended to hold Polish political prisoners who first arrived on June 14 and were assigned numbers 31–758.[81] Many of these first prisoners were university students and their first task was to construct their own prison.[82]

In order to govern and police the GG, a flood of Nazi functionaries arrived to handle every facet of public life from music to lumber. One of the most important functions was the economic management, or better, exploitation of the new territory. In the incorporated territories, the path was perhaps clearer, as businesses and the economy were expected to be integrated into Germany as quickly as possible. Hans Frank, on the other hand, in the *Generalgovernment* faced a conflict between the desire of some to simply loot and strip his territory of everything of value and his goal of creating a valuable, functioning state worthy of eventual inclusion in the Reich. Frank succeeded in halting the wholesale destruction of the Polish economy via exportation to Germany. He was able to show that he could harness the economic resources of the region on the ground to benefit the German economy. This is not to say that Nazi occupation did not devastate Polish and Jewish businesses. The occupiers established an office known as the *Treuhandstelle Ost* or Trust Office East, which took control of economic concerns, distributed them to German ownership, and brought them in line with larger German economic policy. The *Treuhandstelle Ost* was quite effective in its work; by February 1941, it had seized 5,246 industrial concerns and 121,120 commercial businesses from the Poles.[83] As one scholar puts it, the result was "the attempted subjugation and reorientation of the entire Polish economy for the purpose of its consistent exploitation to the benefit of the German war effort."[84] This policy privileged businesses that could be used in the defense industry over non-defense operations, many of which were closed down. Here, the government either directly controlled defense industries or handed them to contractors such as Oskar Schindler who were able to buy distressed Jewish, businesses and produce items for the military.

The severest of the economic measures in the *Generalgovernment* was the shipment of Poles to Germany to perform forced labor. Though, as we will see, the use of slave labor would have the most drastic influence on Jews, the conscription of Poles was no small matter. In June 1940, authorities deported 20,000 Polish forced laborers to Germany. Initially, the Germans hoped to entice Polish volunteers, but this soon failed as word of the treatment of foreign workers reached Poland. The labor policy was, itself, closely connected to Nazi racial conceptions of the East, which we have already seen. Slavs were useful only as forced laborers for the superior Germans. In Poland, we see that abstract concept became harsh reality. By August 1944, there were 7.5 million foreign forced laborers from across Europe working for the Reich. Even the labor terms Frank chose were based on race: Poles had *Arbeitspflicht* (a duty to work) while Jews had *Arbeitszwang* (forced labor.)[85] These were not idle words; while conditions for Polish laborers were harsh, they were worse for Jews.

Darkening Skies: Initial Anti-Jewish Policy in the *Generalgovernment* and Incorporated Territories

The gigantic catastrophe which has descended on Polish Jewry has no parallel, even in the darkest periods of Jewish history.

CHAIM KAPLAN, diary entry, March 10, 1940[86]

For two long years, the *Generalgovernment* would be at the heart of Nazi planning and discussions on how to solve the so-called "Jewish Question." It would also begin the catastrophe that Chaim Kaplan so feared. It was logical that many important parts of anti-Jewish policy evolved here, as Polish Jews constituted half the future victims of the Holocaust. However, Nazi administrators also imported many of the discriminatory policies that had already been tested in Germany. Thus, anti-Jewish policy in the *Generalgovernment* (as throughout the occupied East) was a combination of local initiatives and guidance from Berlin. This is often described by scholars as a sort of symbiotic relationship between center and periphery: the center being Berlin and the high-level leadership while the periphery represents the distant lands where local officials developed their own initiatives. At times, these two forces pulled together and, at times, they pulled apart. Sometimes, directives from the top drove policy while at others, experimentation and local choices on the ground deeply influenced those same directives. The Holocaust and larger Nazi genocidal project were thus connected with events and individuals across Europe.

As we have already seen, anti-Jewish violence accompanied the German invasion of Poland, beginning with the military itself. German soldiers routinely humiliated Jews by cutting their side locks or shaving their beards. In another town, soldiers gathered Jews in the courtyard of the synagogue and burned them with hot wax.[87] These humiliations often turned deadly. On September 4, 1939, members of an infantry unit killed Jews in retaliation for what was likely friendly fire.[88] In Wroclawek, unidentified Germans (likely soldiers) broke into a house where Jews were praying and killed five or six of them.[89] One Jewish survivor recalled the impunity of soldiers and others after the invasion of Poland, saying, "Any German who wore a uniform and had a weapon could do whatever he wished with a Jew in Warsaw. He could compel him to sing or to dance or to shit in his trousers, or to go down on his knees and beg for his life."[90]

The *Wehrmacht* also actively persecuted Jewish soldiers among its prisoners of war. Approximately 60,000 Jewish soldiers in the Polish army were captured. By the spring of 1940, 25,000 of them were dead. Jewish prisoners were separated and given the most exhaustive labor. Unlike their Christian counterparts, Jews were often transferred from POW camps into civilian Nazi custody, where they almost certainly would be killed.[91] Regular German military units often established ghettos and instituted antisemitic measures in the areas under their control as well. This military complicity with the murderous policies of the regime would only escalate later.

In addition to the deadly violence that accompanied the invasion and then tapered off, Nazi authorities began implementing familiar antisemitic regulations on the Jewish population. From his palace in Krakow, Hans Frank and his administrators issued a steady stream of rules and decrees aimed at removing Jews from the social, cultural, and economic life of the GG. On November 23, 1939, Jews were required to wear a blue star on a white background. In typical Nazi fashion, the orders specified that the armband be at least ten centimeters wide and appear on the right sleeve.[92] Regulations forbid Jews from changing residences and curfews limited Jews to very short periods of time in which they could shop and leave their houses. Jewish doctors could not see non-Jewish patients. In Łódź, one survivor remembered that "Jews were not allowed to walk on the main street which was renamed Adolf Hitler Strasse. They were not allowed to go into parks, swimming pools, or cinemas and theatres."[93] Mandatory slave labor was required on October 26, 1939, for all Jews between the ages of 14 and 60.[94] The *Aryanization* of businesses began in conjunction with the larger economic exploitation described above. This process entailed the registration of Jewish business assets and their forced handover to the Nazi state. This included cash in bank accounts as well. Jews were allowed to keep some personal belongings and 1,000 RM, by Göring's decree.[95] As ghettos were established, Jewish homes and apartments were stolen, complete with their contents. During one three-day period, the SS men responsible for this systematic eviction and theft "cleared" 399 apartments in Łódź in the *Wartheland*; similar activities were taking place across the GG.[96]

These apartments became available as Jews were increasingly forced into Nazi-designated areas of towns and cities. This policy was known as ghettoization. We will examine both the policy and life in the ghettos in a future chapter, but it is important to briefly discuss the origins of the policy here as the GG and the incorporated territories provided the testbed for the concept. Nevertheless, before we can approach the topic of ghettos, we must first examine (briefly) the larger Nazi policies regarding the "Jewish Question" in Europe as they are directly tied to ghettoization.

Nazi antisemitic ideology, as noted, rested on a belief that the continued existence of Jews in Europe was unacceptable. The "Jewish question" was very simply how to remove the Jews from Europe. The answer evolved through several iterations, influenced both by events, as well as by shifts in the approach of Nazi leaders, above and below. The first solution proposed to rid Germany (and eventually) Europe of Jews was forced emigration. Adolf Eichmann's systematic efforts at forcing the emigration of Jews from Vienna as well as the intolerable conditions created by the Nazis in Germany are excellent examples of this policy in action. In many ways, this policy was stymied, at least in terms of emigration out of Europe. More than half of Germany's Jews *did* manage to escape Nazi Germany, but only to areas which would later be conquered. A combination of antisemitic foreign immigration policies and the Nazi demands that Jews be stripped of all wealth before emigration (which made them even more unattractive to potential areas of refuge) denied Jews access to Britain, America, and other countries safely off the European continent. This was the first territorial solution, meaning a solution that involved the movement of Jews but not their complete extermination. The second territorial proposal, the Lublin or Nisko plan, involved the permanent and forced consolidation of Jews in the *Generalgovernment* on a reservation. This plan was derailed by Nazi administrative resistance, not least, on the part of Frank himself. Finally, during this period, the last idea was the Madagascar Plan that, after the fall of France in 1940, suggested the mass deportation of Jews to the east African island of Madagascar. This plan was delayed and eventually shelved when Germany failed to master the seas. And so, ghettoization in Poland was a policy affected by the tension between applying permanent solutions to the Jewish question and stopgap measures until a final solution could be agreed upon.

In any case, the forced collection and confinement of Jews first began in occupied Poland to consolidate the Jewish population in preparation for whatever final plan would be decided upon. The impetus for ghettoization came from Reinhard Heydrich, chief of the RSHA and eventual architect of the Final Solution. Less than a month after the invasion of Poland, he wrote to EG commanders on September 21, 1939, that "For the time being, the first prerequisite for the final aim is the concentration of the Jews from the countryside into the larger cities." He noted that this was a short-term measure prior to an undescribed "final aim."[97] Heydrich also ordered the consolidation of smaller Jewish communities into larger ones and the creation of Jewish councils.

The first ghetto was established in Piotrków Trybunalski in October 1939, but the process of mass ghettoization proceeded in fits and starts, with the Łódź ghetto being established in February 1940, Warsaw in October, and, in the large cities of Krakow, Lublin, and Radom, only in the spring of 1941. As one scholar has noted, fewer than thirty ghettos were established by September 1940.[98] This phenomenon owed as much to the decentralized role of local Nazi authorities as it did to evolving plans for the final disposition of the Jews. Hans Frank, for one, hoped to avoid the creation of large permanent Jewish residential areas in his territory, particularly as it seemed that they would soon be sent elsewhere. Eventually, ghettos became seen as a necessary evil to consolidate Jews as new plans were made. As Adolf Eichmann made clear in December 1940, the final solution to the Jewish question "will be achieved by way of transfer of the Jews out of the European economic space of the German people to a still-to-be-determined territory." He projected that 5.8 million Jews would need to be deported.[99]

Nazi authorities established ghettos either in the poorest and most run-down areas of town or in areas which already had a large Jewish quarter. Non-Jews were evicted (but compensated by the Jews forced to move in). As we will see later, not all ghettos fit the stereotypical image of Warsaw or Łódź; many were quite small, temporary, or unguarded. Overcrowding, mass theft, disease, hunger, and forced labor characterized them all. In addition to the loss of homes and apartments, often, Jewish communities were forced to pay exorbitant sums for their own confinement. When Hans Frank attempted to "cleanse" his capital city of Kraków of Jews, he demanded that the Jews pay for their own deportation.[100]

Jews could no longer be owners or decision-makers in economic affairs, but they were increasingly forced to function as slave labor, particularly as ghettoization began to appear more permanent and Nazi administrators sought to benefit. At first, such slave labor was demeaning and not particularly productive. In fact, the main goal appeared to be humiliation. Jews were forced to clean streets, gutters, and toilets with their bare hands. Eventually, however, as we will see, ghettos across Eastern Europe were transformed into pools of slave labor for a myriad of German economic concerns. For the time being, they served as a way to continue the larger Nazi project of demographic engineering by beginning the process of removing Jews from the local population.

Until the invasion of Poland, Nazi policy—in terms of both the Holocaust and the larger genocidal project—had been relatively limited in its execution. When Germany invaded Poland and a world war began, the regime was free to begin realizing its imperial and racist goals, particularly in the East. Occupied Poland, and especially the *Generalgovernment*, presented Nazi leaders with large populations of non-German "subhuman" Slavs as well as almost two million Jews. For the first time, the Nazi state was faced with actually executing what had been empty rhetoric until September 1939. They soon became personally acquainted with the very real logistical, political, and economic challenges associated with that rhetoric. They quickly discovered the massive gulf that lay between ideology and execution. How they navigated these challenges had important repercussions as the opening act for the massive murderous system that followed. The experimentation with different solutions by Nazi authorities at every level made occupied Poland a laboratory for genocide. The lessons learned here would accompany the Nazis as they moved further east and as their actions became more extreme and more deadly.

Selected Readings

Browning, Christopher R. *Remembering Survival: Inside a Nazi Slave-Labor Camp*. New York: W.W. Norton, 2010.

Dobroszycki, Lucjan, ed. *The Chronicle of the Łódź ghetto, 1941–1944*. Abridged ed. New Haven, CT: Yale University Press, 1984.

Kaplan, Chaim. *The Warsaw Diary of Chaim Kaplan*. Trans. Abraham I. Katsh. New York: Collier Books, 1973.

Kochanski, Halik. *Eagle Unbowed: Poland and the Poles in the Second World War*. Cambridge: Harvard University Press, 2014.

Matthäus, Jürgen, and Jochen Böhler, eds. *War, Pacification, and Mass Murder, 1939: The Einsatzgruppen in Poland*. Lanham: Rowman & Littlefield, 2014.

6

War of Annihilation: The Invasion of the Soviet Union

Introduction

I participated the entire time. The only time I paused was when my rifle was empty and I had to reload. It's impossible for me to say how many Jews I murdered during this three to four-hour period.

SS man, ALFRED METZNER on shooting in Zyrowice, Belarus, ca. fall 1941[1]

I only know one thing: there is something terrible, horrible going on, something inconceivable, which cannot be understood, grasped or explained.

IRYNA KHOROSHUNOVA, diary entry, September 29, 1941, Kiev[2]

According to German legend, the great former Holy Roman Emperor and warrior-king Frederick Barbarossa sleeps deep inside the Kyffhäuser Mountain with his knights, awaiting the moment when he is awakened to restore greatness to Germany. It is no coincidence that the codename for the German invasion of the Soviet Union was "Operation Barbarossa." It *is* a terrible coincidence that the local 339th Infantry Division raised in that same area would participate in the wholescale murder of Jewish men, women, and children during the course of that operation. This program of murder is what brought such horrific experiences to people like Metzner and Khoroshunova.

All Hitler's previous diplomatic and military gambits led to the conquest of the Soviet Union. If one divides World War II into two parts—the war that Hitler won and the war that he lost—the former (Rheinland, Austria, Czechoslovakia, Poland, France) helped breed the optimism seen in the war against the Soviet Union. Joseph Goebbels wrote in his diary on June 16, a few days before the invasion, "The Führer estimates that the operation will take about four months. I reckon on less. Bolshevism is going to crumble like a pack of cards."[3] The poor performance of the Red Army against Finland in the Winter War of 1939–40 no doubt fed his optimism. Hitler was not alone. Coming off indisputable masterstrokes in Poland and France, many of Hitler's generals were also incredibly optimistic about the coming campaign. Less than two weeks after the invasion, Chief of Staff of the German Army, Franz Halder, wrote in his diary that he believed the war had been won.[4] His almost fanatical optimism came from Nazi prejudices against the Soviet Union and an utter failure to gain accurate intelligence.[5]

No doubt, this optimism seemed warranted for the first several months. As three million German soldiers, more than 3,000 tanks, and 2,700 aircraft attacked from the Baltic Sea to the Black, the invasion was, as one historian noted, "the largest offensive in the history of war."[6] And it initially succeeded. Almost inexplicably, the German attack surprised the Soviets, despite increasingly clear indications of its coming. Soviet Marshal Zhukov described a deeply shocked Stalin as "somewhat depressed . . . when his belief that the war could be avoided was shattered." Molotov recalled that, "Stalin was in a very agitated state. He didn't curse, but he wasn't quite himself."[7] Red Army units were overrun before they knew an attack was underway. 4,000 Soviet planes were destroyed on the ground.[8] Fast-moving German units created massive pockets of enemy troops that surrendered in unprecedented numbers: 348,000 near Smolensk in Western Russia and 665,000 near Kiev in Ukraine—put another way, over 1,000,000 prisoners in two operations in September 1941.[9] Massive swathes of Soviet territory quickly fell under Nazi control. In two weeks, leading German formations reached Minsk (320 km from their starting point). By August 22, thirty percent of the Soviet Union's Jewish population was under German control.[10] By September, in Belarus alone, 225,000 sq. km and 9.8 million people were incorporated into the *Reichskommissariat Weissruthenien* occupation region.[11] In this area alone, the *Wehrmacht* conquered a territory half the size of pre-war Germany.

However, it became clear that there would be no swift victory over the Soviet Union, despite Hitler's claims that "what happened to Napoleon would not repeat itself." The length of the campaign quickly exceeded his four-month prediction.[12] Supply lines stretched over 1,000 miles. Contrary to popular mythology, the vast majority of the Army (90%) was not mechanized, and so 600,000 horses accompanied German soldiers into the USSR.[13] Discouragement grew at the top and bottom. A corps commander noted already in September 1941: "no victorious Blitzkrieg, no destruction of the Russian army, no disintegration of the Soviet Union."[14] As the days passed, the brutal Russian winter advanced. The Army had received 50 percent of required gloves and 5 percent of winter boots by November 1941.[15] Hitler, as Supreme Commander of the German Armed Forces, sent his men in conflicting directions, wasting time, resources, and momentum. And so, by December 1941, a combination of strategic blunders, logistical failures, inclement weather, and the increasingly dogged Soviet resistance stopped the *Wehrmacht* in its tracks and confronted it with vicious counterattacks.

When *Wehrmacht* tanks rumbled across the newly established border with the Soviet Union in the pre-dawn hours of June 22, 1941, they turned a disastrous and ultimately genocidal page in the story of the Holocaust in Eastern Europe. Hitler, his generals, and many in the German population yearned for a "crusade" in the East, unlike the pragmatic conflict in the West. This ushered in an unprecedented period of violence including but not limited to the victimization of Jews and escalation in the murderous nature of the solution to the "Jewish Question." Racist ideology and violence dominated both the foreground and the background of the military campaign. For this reason, the war and the Holocaust cannot be separated: threads of ideology, personnel, overlapping interests, situational conditions, and a thousand other common ties bind them together forever. In addition, during the campaign, the first concrete steps toward the Final Solution were made *and* the full colors of the Nazi genocidal palette emerged.

Planning a War of Annihilation: Preparations for Barbarossa

The Führer says whether we are right or wrong, we must win. This is the only way. And it is right, moral and necessary. And once we have won, who will ask us about the methods. In any case, we have so much to account for that we must win; otherwise our whole people—and we in the first place, and all that we love—would be erased.

From GOEBBELS'S diary, June 15, 1941[16]

By the end of July 1940, less than a year after signing his pact with Stalin, Hitler ordered his General Staff to prepare for an invasion of Germany's new ally ... as he always planned to do. Though the loss of the aerial Battle of Britain became clearer by the day, Hitler thought a defeat of Russia instead would bring about England's capitulation. "But if Russia suffered defeat the last hope of England would be gone," he predicted. "Domination of Europe and the Balkans would then be Germany's. Decision: in this conflict Russia must be finished off. Spring 1941. The sooner Russia is destroyed the better. The operation will only have meaning if we destroy this state in one blow."[17]

Vitally important genocidal decisions were made before a shot was fired, alongside purely military planning. This massive cataclysm overshadowed all other theaters of World War II in men, materials, and casualties, and was designed to be unlike any war fought in modern history. Nazi planners intended that the war in the Soviet Union would not follow customary laws of war or applicable conventions (even those to which Germany was a signatory.) The justifications for this were embedded deeply in Nazi ideology. Its very worldview stressed that "life consisted of a constant struggle for survival, in which the best would win, or rather, in which the very fact of victory and survival would show the inherent physical and spiritual superiority of the winner, on the one hand, and the inferiority and moral depravity of the vanquished, on the other."[18] On March 30, 1941, Hitler explicitly told his generals that he "wanted to see the impending war against the Soviet Union conducted not according to customary military principles, but as a war of extermination against an ideology and its adherents, whether within the Red Army or in a non-military function."[19] An Austrian diplomat recorded from a conversation with a future *Einsatzgruppen* commander that "In Russia, all cities and cultural sites including the Kremlin are to be razed to the ground; Russia is to be reduced to the level of a nation of peasants, from which there is no return."[20] The genocidal Green Folder and Hunger Plan that Nazi theorists had developed were now to be implemented.

One might expect some German military resistance to the open and intentional violation of the customs of "civilized" warfare, but most leaders were staunchly conservative, anti-Communist, and more than happy to crush the Bolshevik threat in the East—and many owed their promotions to Hitler, receiving monetary bribes for their support.[21] The Chief of the Army High Command, parroting Hitler, told his senior commanders in March 1941 that "the troops have to realize that this struggle is being waged by one race against another, and proceed with the necessary harshness."[22] That such a proclamation needed to be made suggests that the German Army required preparation for the violence that it would unleash. It also demonstrates quite clearly how Nazi racial ideology and military tactics were inextricably intertwined.

The *Wehrmacht* generated orders directing its troops to support Hitler's vision of a "war of annihilation." These orders contravened all accepted codes and customs of warfare of the time; regardless, senior leaders passed them on to the lowest levels so that each ordinary soldier knew what was expected. Three of these directives are most important: the Jurisdiction Order, the Commissar Order, and the Guidelines for the Behavior of the Troops. These three orders clearly defined the bloody role the *Wehrmacht* would play—both in the Holocaust and in the larger Nazi genocidal project—and each bears a short discussion, given the decisive impact they had on the behavior of the German Army and on the mentality of Nazi organizations in the East.

Military lawyers and commanders together developed the so-called "Jurisdiction Order" to address the issue of military crimes. The language of the final May 13, 1941, document was unambiguous. Citing the "great expanse" of the Eastern front and the staffing problems of military courts, it stated:

> Punishable offenses committed by enemy civilians do not, until further notice, come any more under the jurisdiction of the courts-martial and the summary courts-martial . . .
>
> For offenses committed by members of the *Wehrmacht* and its employees against enemy civilians, prosecution is not compulsory, not even if the offense is at the same time a military crime or violation.[23]

This order told soldiers that crimes against civilians were no longer military crimes and would not be prosecuted. It was a blank check for criminality. The only reason to prosecute was if a crime were detrimental to the war effort. The order also included guidelines for conducting reprisal killings of civilians.

The May 19, 1941, "Guidelines for the Behavior of the Troops," also known as the Barbarossa Decree, addressed the *Wehrmacht* directly. "Bolshevism is the mortal enemy of the German people," it proclaimed, "this war demands ruthless and aggressive action against Bolshevik agitators, snipers, saboteurs, and Jews and tireless elimination of any active or passive resistance."[24] It made no distinction between hostile behavior and the racial category of Jewishness. The message reaching soldiers was that Jews should be treated with the same ruthlessness as enemy combatants; that is, killed.

Finally, the Commissar Order, published on June 6, 1941, required the immediate murder of all Soviet Red Army political officers (or commissars). The murder of captured, uniformed combatants was unquestionably illegal under all the international treaties that Germany had signed. Regardless, the troops were instructed that "In particular, the political commissars of all kinds, who are the real bearers of resistance, can be expected to mete out treatment to our prisoners that is full of hate, cruel and inhumane." As a result, "Political commissars operating against our armies are to be dealt with in accordance with the decree on judicial provisions in the area of Barbarossa. This applies to commissars of every type and rank, even if they are only suspected of resistance, sabotage or incitement to sabotage."[25] "Dealt with" here is a Nazi euphemism for "killed." A memo a day prior declared, "Political commissars of the Army are not recognized as Prisoners of War and are to be liquidated at the latest in the transient prisoner of war camps."[26] On June 18, a military judge told the officers of the 11th Army that "Every officer must know that . . . political commissars are to be taken aside and finished off."[27] Despite postwar protestations, the documentary record suggests that ninety percent of units complied with the Commissar Order, resulting in the reported murders of at least but probably far more than 4,000 men.[28]

A flurry of other directives, some antisemitic and others simply directing brutal treatment of civilians, accompanied these orders. Together, these messages left little to the imagination of the common soldier as to what was expected in this new kind of war. The gloves were off, rules did not apply, and the stakes were higher than ever before in the history of Germany. The involvement of the *Wehrmacht* in the Holocaust also rightly expands our group of perpetrators. In the Army "ordinary men" who were not SS men or Nazi Party functionaries also willingly participated in genocide. The Army became involved in antisemitic policy as well as the disastrous POW policy quite quickly and readily. However, one more vital area of planning based on recent history required addressing for both the Nazis and the *Wehrmacht*: the *Einsatzgruppen*.

The *Einsatzgruppen* in Poland in 1939 had somewhat surprised the Army and caused confusion and consternation. A new and improved version of the *Einsatzgruppen* once again accompanied leading military units into the Soviet Union. However, this time, both the SS and the *Wehrmacht* pledged to reduce any friction before Barbarossa began. Thus began a series of negotiations primarily between the *Wehrmacht* Quartermaster General Eduard Wagner and the SS. At issue were the roles and responsibilities of the EG, vis-à-vis the *Wehrmacht*. These negotiations resulted, on March 26, 1941, in a plan of cooperation between the Army and the killing squads designed to maximize efficiency. The EGs were assigned to the Army for the purposes of logistics (food, fuel, ammunition, repair, etc.). However, their operational missions, described as "executive measures against the civilian population," would come directly from the Reich Security Main Office, from Reinhard Heydrich. The military would be informed of these operations via a liaison officer, but would have no control (and hence no responsibility) for the actions of the SS.[29] Though this agreement may have made it possible for some military leaders to feel separate from the "executive measures" of the EGs, in reality, it simply made them more complicit.

Many mistakenly believe that the war in Eastern Europe was an aberration, resulting from a "barbarization" process of increasing violence, while the war in Western Europe was a "normal" war. In fact, the opposite is true. A war based on racial ideology and the zero-sum annihilation of the enemy was precisely the "normal" state of war for the Nazi state. Western Europe presented an exception to this rule. Hitler told his generals as much, saying "This will be very different from the war in the West. In the east, harshness today means lenience in the future."[30] The Nazi worldview saw the French, for example, as "decadent" or "degenerate" but not racially inferior in the same way as Slavs or Jews, nor were they destined for subjugation or their land for colonization.[31] Likewise, long historical relationships and Nazi racial views toward the British saw them as racially similar to Germans and as potential allies. Indeed, while massive killings took place in the East, German soldiers occupying the British Channel Islands were strictly forbidden from picking the flowers.[32] The fundamental distinctions of the war in the East were the deep penetration of genocidal racial thinking into all aspects of Nazi policy, the unique place the East held in the German imagination, and its position as the focal point of the Holocaust.

German POW Policy: The First Million Victims

I have often thought so when watching yet another one of our prisoners lie dying. No priestly words. Carried out like a corpse. Such deaths occur by the millions. This is truly the work of the devil .

Sergeant KONRAD JARAUSCH, September 20, 1941[33]

The treatment of Soviet prisoners of war as described by Jarausch remains one of the most forgotten elements of the Nazi genocidal project in the East. Approximately 3.3 million Soviet POWs are thought to have died during the war. Of these 3.3 million, 2 million died by February 1942, just eight months after the war began.[34] Sixty percent of Soviet POWs died at German hands. To place this in context, only four percent of Western POWs died in German captivity and, even at the brutal hands of the Japanese in the Pacific, the death rate of Allied prisoners of war was "only" 27 percent.[35] Put another way, "As many Soviet prisoners of war died on a single given day in autumn 1941 as did British and American prisoners of war over the course of the entire Second World War."[36] *Eight times as many Soviet POWs died as American combat casualties.*

After the war, those officers responsible claimed the unprecedented death toll resulted from unpreparedness for the immense number of prisoners. This was self-serving propaganda. The Nazis intended that Soviet POWs die in massive numbers, and it was only a pressing demand for labor that spared some of them (often only to be sent to a GULAG when liberated by their brothers in the Red Army).

Damning evidence remains of these German plans. Hitler's famous phrase that the Soviet soldier is *Keine Kameraden* (no comrade in arms) sought to break down the common feeling of kinship among all soldiers over time. Instead, in the Nazi worldview, Red Army soldiers had been tainted by Communism in almost a biological sense and deserved none of the considerations given to surrendered combatants. This was codified before the first shot was fired. General Quartermaster Eduard Wagner, who negotiated cooperation with the *Einsatzgruppen*, also led the planning for the "care" of POWs. All evidence shows that he and the Army planned for them to die. High-level decisions made their way to lower-level units. For example, the 4th Army Corps issued orders on June 8, *before the invasion*, that "prisoners of war are to be fed with the most primitive rations (for example horseflesh). High quality and scarce food and luxury foods may not be given out to them."[37] By September 8, the general responsible for POWs published the final order for their treatment, reminding soldiers that the "bolshevist soldier has lost all claim to treatment as an honorable opponent in accordance with the Geneva Convention."[38]

The intended suffering of Soviet POWs began at the moment of capture. Commissars were shot on the spot. Prisoners were often forced to march hundreds of miles on foot. Often, commanders refused POWs passage on empty trains returning from the front. The 4th Panzer Army refused access for "hygienic reasons."[39] Those lucky enough to be transported by train were crammed into open cars in the heat of summer and in the cold of winter. Many died there. The rest walked. Soviet prisoner Aleksei Maslov recalled, "The large and long column of prisoners slowly moved westward . . . It moved without stops, without rest, without water, and without food."[40] Another recalled how, during the march, he "watched with horror as they reduced healthy people to a state of complete helplessness and death."[41] Death rates on these transports could be as high as seventy percent.[42]

Those who survived at a transit camp (*Durchgangslager* or DULAG) had little cause to celebrate. These could hardly be called "camps" in any real sense. For example, the Drozdy camp outside of Minsk was simply an open field enclosed by barbed wire, holding 100,000 men. The nearby stream had been cruelly left outside the wire. Even a quartermaster in the 4th Panzer Army found the conditions "untenable" and noted that the "prisoners were

FIGURE 8 *Soviet POW camp outside of Minsk, likely the Drozdy camp, showing conditions for prisoners. It is probable that this was the POW camp visited by Himmler during his August visit to Minsk, when he observed a mass shooting. vic. Minsk, Belarus, July 5, 1941.*
Source: Bundesarchiv.

completely exposed to the searing heat."[43] Shelter was absent, food scarce, and hardly edible; the caloric intake given POWs was simply insufficient to sustain life.[44] German sergeant, Konrad Jarausch, in charge of the kitchens at one of these DULAGs, wrote home in August that "Their hunger drove them to the kitchens. Shots were fired to keep them in order. Some (not many) were killed. Others rolled around in the mud, howling from their hunger pains."[45] Soldiers guarding Drozdy recalled frequently killing prisoners storming the kitchens for food.[46] Soviet prisoner Maslov recalled only receiving 16 ounces of sunflower seeds per day.[47] Things got worse. An Army colonel described coldly "how "these cursed *Untermenschen* have been observed eating grass, flowers and raw potatoes. Once they can't find anything edible in the camp they turn to cannibalism."[48] The more sympathetic Jarausch simply noted "We discovered another case of cannibalism today . . . the whole thing is already more murder than war."[49] Thousands died from rampant disease and starvation.

Killings also took place systematically. The Commissar Order continued to be enforced for those who had survived long enough to end up in a POW camp. Army units separated these men as well as Jewish Red Army soldiers and shot or turned them over to the *Einsatzgruppen* for similar treatment. One former POW recalled that "The Germans were looking for Jews and Red Army commissars, they also promised to reward any prisoners that helped point them out."[50] It is estimated that half a million POWs were shot by German troops and *Einsatzgruppen*.[51]

Lastly, Soviet POWs were subjected to forced labor, both locally and, later, in Germany and elsewhere. General Quartermaster Wagner noted in a meeting that "non-working POWs in POW camps must starve."[52] Indeed, only the recognition of their utility as laborers saved the remaining POWs from eventual death. Even so, the "labor" could be terrifying and brutal. In October 1941, the rear area commander in Belarus ordered that Soviet prisoners, especially Ukrainians and White Russians, be used to assist in mine clearing operations.[53] One German noted that "Of the millions of prisoners only a few thousand are capable of work. Unbelievably many of them have died, many have typhus, and the rest are so weak and wretched that they are in no condition to work."[54]

This discussion of the treatment and systematic murder of Soviet POWs is quite relevant to the Holocaust in the East. In fact, it demonstrates how deeply theoretical racial views of the Nazis became violent reality in the East. It is perhaps no small coincidence that the first people to be gassed—for experimental purposes—with Zyklon-B at Auschwitz were Soviet prisoners of war. Nazi POW policy shows how the SS and the *Wehrmacht* drew on experiences in Poland to improve cooperation and how POW policy incorporated the murder of Jews, tying it to the Holocaust and continuing an escalation of anti-Jewish policy. Of course, the largest escalation can be seen in the new *Einsatzgruppen* deployed to the East during Barbarossa.

The Holocaust by Bullets: the Einsatzgruppen in the Soviet Union

Screams of thousands of people were heard from far away ... They stood surrounded by many policemen and awaited their fate ... The policemen drove groups of people to the ditches, where they undressed. Special SD details and the policemen of our battalion shot them at the nape of the neck. Adults were forced to lie down in the ditches and were shot, while children were torn away from their mothers and shot. Most of the shooters were drunk ... People begged for mercy, mothers begged us to spare their children.

> Company Sergeant ERICH DRACHENFELS (320th Police Battalion) describing the murder of 23,500 Jews of Rovno, November, 1941[55]

The first truly systematic murder of European Jews occurred not in Germany or in Western Europe, but in the occupied East. Here, the first wholesale slaughter of men, women, and children as described in detail by Sergeant Drachenfels took place, and here, anti-Jewish policy evolved with increasing rapidity. Many of the same killers from Poland returned, this time with a larger mandate. In the East, too, however, these killers experienced the traumatic nature of daily face-to-face killing. This experience was one of many factors contributing to the development of the extermination camp. Historians speak of two killing sweeps (to which I would add a third):

- First Sweep (June 1941–end of 1941): Killings of mainly Jewish intelligentsia, leadership, as well non-Jewish Communist leadership but growing to include all Soviet Jews.
- Second Sweep (1942): Liquidation of Jews in ghettos incapable of work and consolidation of remaining Jews.[56]
- Third Sweep (1943–44): Liquidation of all ghettos and most remaining Jews—often carried out by a variety of perpetrators some of whom were *Einsatzgruppen* members who had taken up stationary positions.

The "Holocaust by Bullets" does not dominate our consciousness the same way as Auschwitz. However, it should. Somewhere around 1.5–2 million Jews from the Baltic Sea to the Crimea were murdered. They were marched through their own hometowns where they had lived most of their lives, past their neighbors and colleagues, and were then shot one by one into nearby pits. In fact, a large number of these victims were killed before any systematic gassing occurred.

The performance of the EGs in Poland in 1939 satisfied Himmler, but he sought a larger role for them in the Soviet Union, with its huge Jewish population. The mission of the EGs in the occupied Soviet Union differed fundamentally from their Polish iteration. Rather than simply "pacification" or removing leadership and intelligentsia that could provide resistance, the EGs in 1941 very quickly evolved into organizations tasked with the indiscriminate murder of Jews, though their initial mandate was limited.

That mandate is reflected in a March 13, 1941, memorandum issued by the OKW (Military High Command). It informed the leadership that "within the area of Army operations the Reichsführer SS will be entrusted, on behalf of the Führer, with special tasks for the preparation of the political administration—tasks which derive from the decisive struggle that will have to be carried out between the two opposing political systems. Within the framework of these tasks, the Reichsführer SS will act independently and on his own responsibility." The document went on to order close "collaboration [by the military] to support the Reichskommissar his political tasks."[57] These "political" and "special" tasks were simply Nazi euphemisms for murder by the EG and other organizations under the direction of the SS.

The *Einsatzgruppen* personnel themselves received more specific instructions when they assembled at Preztsch, Germany, for training and organization. Reinhard Heydrich and Gestapo chief Müller visited them on multiple occasions. On June 17, 1941, Heydrich, Himmler's deputy at the RSHA, addressed assembled EG officers in Berlin, and also later at a closing ceremony at Pretszch. In these meetings, he issued their final instructions before Operation Barbarossa. Heydrich summed up his remarks in a July 2 memorandum to the HSSPFs in the occupied territories. "All of the following are to be executed," he ordered:

- Officials of the Comintern (together with professional Communist politicians in general)
- Top and medium-level officials and radical lower-level officials of the Party
- Central Committee and district and sub-district committees People's Commissars
- Jews in Party and State employment and other radical elements (saboteurs, propagandists, snipers, assassins, inciters, etc.)[58]

Regarding Jews, we can see that "the briefings and lectures given at Pretzsch appear to have contained the essential elements for an ideological war that would involve extermination, but the exact shape lacked specificity."[59] However, they were also "open-ended enough in their formulation to have allowed for a rapid expansion of the murder campaign."[60]

Who *were* the *Einsatzgruppen* that followed the German Army into the Soviet Union? These new EGs consisted of four units A, B, C, and D; EG A followed Army Group North, EG B followed Army Group Center, and EGs C and D followed Army Group South. Each EG had a number of subunits, known as *Sonderkommandos* or *Einsatzkommandos*. Not infrequently, even these subunits were broken up into smaller units temporarily, for specific missions.

The leadership of the EGs was carefully chosen, beginning in March 1941 for their experience and political reliability, with most coming from the SD. Some were higher-ranking officers in the SD and others commanded SD and Gestapo offices within Germany. These leaders were certainly out of the ordinary. Three of four EG commanders held four PhDs between them; seven of the SK and EK commanders held PhDs.[61] Ironically, many of these criminals held doctorates in law.

TABLE 5 Einsatzgruppen *and their initial commanders, June 1941.*

Unit	Commander(s)
Einsatzgruppe A (990 men)[a]	*SS-Brigadeführer* Dr jur. Walter Stahlecker
Sonderkommando 1a	SS-Sturmbannführer Dr. Martin Sandberger
Sonderkommando 1b	SS-Obersturmführer Erich Ehrlinger
Einsatzkommando 1b	SS-Sturmbannführer Dr. jur. Hermann Hubig
Einsatzkommando Ic	SS-Sturmbannführer Kurt Graaf
Einsatzkommando 2	SS-Sturmbannführer Rudolf Batz
Einsatzkommando 3	SS-Standartenführer Karl Jäger
Einsatzkommando Tilsit	Kommandoführer Karl Böhme
Einsatzgruppe B (665 men)[b]	*SS-Gruppenführer* Artur Nebe
Sonderkommando 7a	SS-Obersturmbannführer Dr. jur. Walter Blume
Sonderkommando 7b	SS-Sturmbannführer Günther Rausch
Einsatzkommando 8	SS-Sturmbannführer Dr Otto Bradfisch
Einsatzkommando 9	SS-Obersturmbannführer Dr. jur. Alfred Filbert
Vorkommando Moskow	SS-Standartenführer Prof. Dr. Six
Einsatzgruppe C (700 men)[c]	*SS Brigadeführer* Dr. Otto Rasch
Sonderkommando 4a	SS-Standartenführer Paul Blobel
Sonderkommando 4b	SS-Sturmbannführer Günter Hermann
Einsatzkommando 5	SS-Oberführer Erwin Schulz
Einsatzkommando 6	SS-Standartenführer Erhard Kroeger
Einsatzgruppe D (600 men)[d]	*SS-Standartenführer* Otto Ohlendorf
Sonderkommando 10a	SS-Obersturmbannführer Heinz Seetzen

Unit	Commander(s)
Sonderkommando 10b	SS-Sturmbannführer Alois Persterer
Sonderkommando 11a	SS-Sturmbannführer Paul Zapp
Sonderkommando 11b	SS-Sturmbannführer Hans Unglaube
Einsatzkommando 12	SS-Sturmbannführer Gustav Nosske

Sources: a. Wolfgang Scheffler, "Die Einsatzgruppe A: 1941/42," in Die Einsatzgruppen in der besetzten Sowjetunion, 1941/42: die Tätigkeits- und Lageberichte des Chefs der Sicherheitspolizei und des SD, ed. Peter Klein (Berlin: Edition Hentrich, 1997), 44; Helmut Krausnick and Hans-Heinrich Wilhelm, Die Truppe des Weltanschauungskrieges: die Einsatzgruppen der Sicherheitspolizei und des SD, 1938–42 (Stuttgart: Deutsche Verlags-Anstalt, 1981), p. 286.

b. Christian Gerlach, "Die Einsatzgruppe B: 1941/42," in *Die Einsatzgruppen in der besetzten Sowjetunion, 1941/42: die Tätigkeits- und Lageberichte des Chefs der Sicherheitspolizei und des SD*, ed. Peter Klein (Berlin: Edition Hentrich, 1997), p. 63.

c. Dieter Pohl, "Die Einsatzgruppe C: 1941/42," ibid., ed. Peter Klein (Berlin: Edition Hentrich, 1997), pp. 83–4.

d. Andrej Angrick, "Die Einsatzgruppe D: 1941/42," ibid., ed. Peter Klein (Berlin: Edition Hentrich, 1997), p. 105.

The EG selected the rank and file in a much more haphazard way, from the lower ranks of the Gestapo, Waffen-SS, and police. For example, the men of the EGs included a graduating class of SD cadets from Berlin, a class of Criminal Policemen, four companies from Reserve Police Battalion 9, and a battalion of Waffen-SS.[62] Table 6 provides a representative breakdown of the 990 personnel in *Einsatzgruppe A*:

TABLE 6 *Personnel breakdown of EG A, October 1941.*

Affiliation/Position	Number
Security Police (Sipo)	89
Criminal Police (Kripo)	41
Security Service (SD)	35
Order Police (Orpo)	133
Waffen-SS	340
Drivers	172
Auxiliary Police	87
Translators	51
Clerks, Secretaries, Communication specialists	42

Source: Browning and Matthäus, *The Origins of the Final Solution*, p. 460.

Many of these men (and women) were not necessarily rabid antisemites. They had to eventually grow into their roles as killers and either adapt, or attempt to remove themselves from the killing process.

The EGs followed closely behind their supporting Army. Killing began almost immediately. The *Einsatzgruppen* openly sent frequent reports about their activities to Reimhard Heydrich at the RSHA in Berlin. These "*Einsatzgruppen* Reports" are a valuable source as they give us an idea of EG activities as they moved across the East. For example, EK 10 of EG D reported on July 17 that in the town of Belzy in Moldova, "considerable excesses were carried out repeatedly against Jews by Rumanian soldiers."[63] On July 22, EG C reported from Zhitomir in Ukraine that "187 Soviet Russians and Jews turned over by the army, some as civilian prisoners, were shot."[64] From Belarus, EG B informed Berlin that "Another 301 persons were thus liquidated in Baranovichi. This accounts for Jewish activists, officials, and looters."[65] By August 10, EG A reported from Novoselye in the Baltics that "partly with the assistance of Lithuanian and Latvian auxiliary units ... 29,000 persons were liquidated in this district."[66]

Soon after the invasion, the mission of the EGs and their collaborators drifted more and more toward wholesale murder. By July 1941, SS units were murdering men, women, and children regardless of age. This shift becomes apparent by the behavior of killing units, but a uniform order appears *not* to have been given simultaneously across the front. Some commanders seem to have instructed their units differently. The commander of Police Battalion 309, for example, told his men from the beginning that they would be killing all Jews.[67] Elsewhere, it took time for this escalation to occur. It appears that Himmler, Heydrich, and the Higher SS and Police Leaders passed on oral orders to expand the killing process.

Throughout July and August 1941, Himmler visited Lwów, Kaunas, Riga, Baranovichi, and Minsk (cities representing each of the major operational zones.)[68] During these visits, he passed along orders for an escalation of the killings decided upon in Berlin. Thus, a mass killing of all Jewish men in Bialystok occurred shortly after a visit by Himmler and Daluege in July. Likewise, two SS Cavalry Regiments began murdering Jewish men, women, and children in July. The 2nd SS Cavalry Regiment attempted to drown women and children and, remarkably, reported the failure of this technique, noting that "The driving of women and children into the marshes did not have the expected success, because the marshes were not so deep that one could sink."[69] As policy moved toward murdering all Jews across the Eastern front, it became clear that the 3,000 men of the *Einsatzgruppen* would simply not be sufficient. As a result, additional police battalions were called up. All in all, Himmler mobilized 21 battalions of Order Police, including reserve battalions made up of German policemen, adding a force of approximately 11,000 men to assist the EGs in their murderous work.[70] These men, many middle-aged with families and civilian jobs as policemen, were often less ideologically prepared than the rank and file of the EGs, but they would adapt. By the end of the first year, there would be 101 Police Battalions operating with their *Einsatzgruppen* partners in the occupied East.[71]

Incitements to Violence: Pogroms— Homemade or Imported?

Did you see how Germans kill Jews? We will kill them all, and we will kill all Russians as well . . . Romanians and Germans will conquer all the world, while Russians with their hordes have failed.

Local perpetrator in Bessarabian village of Barboieni[72]

In addition to directly carrying out mass killings, the *Einsatzgruppen* were specifically tasked with fomenting pogroms against Jews by the local populations, some of whom felt like this Romanian man in Bessarabia. Himmler and Heydrich planned to leverage existing antisemitism to achieve the murder of Jews. In so doing, they sought to tap into the longer history of the pogrom in Eastern Europe. The future Minister for the East, Rosenberg, expressed this hope prior in the Spring of 1941: "The people itself will probably deal with its real oppressors, for it should be generally assumed that the population, especially in the Ukraine, will proceed to large-scale Jewish pogroms and murders of Communist functionaries." "The Jewish question," he continued, "can be solved to a significant extent by giving the population free rein for a certain length of time after we occupy the country."[73] The EGs were to encourage the local population to carry out these pogroms. Reinhard Heydrich reminded his commanders a week after the invasion that "no obstacle is to be placed in the way of the 'self-cleansing efforts' of anticommunist and anti-Jewish circle in the newly occupied territories. On the contrary, they are to be intensified and if necessary pointed in the right direction."[74]

The extent to which the Germans successfully instigated these pogroms is a matter of some debate, as is the initiative of local populations. Local collaboration plays heavily as well in the national memory of Eastern European countries and how they view their role in the Holocaust. Pogroms varied in level of organization and the role of authorities. They also stemmed from a combination of local antisemitism, anger at Soviet crimes during the occupation, and varying roles of both German and local leadership.

However, without a doubt, pogroms *did* erupt throughout the East as the Germans arrived. A Jewish child from Drohobych in Ukraine recalled that the Germans "didn't take possession of the town immediately, but let the Ukrainians run wild and start the first pogrom of the Jews." "I never realized how antisemitic they were," she remembered, "they also hated the Russians and smashed the figures of Lenin and Stalin in the middle of the town."[75] A Romanian witness in Bukovina observed that "the ringleaders provoked a panic in the village by shouting, 'Jews and Bolsheviks are coming to kill Christians.' The pogrom then started. Gentiles broke into the Jews' houses, plundered their property, beat them severely, and robbed them of their belongings. A number of Jews were apprehended . . . were thrashed with pickets and pitchforks, then thrown into the water and drowned."[76] In the next sections, we explore three pogroms from Lithunia to Romania.

Kaunas, Lithuania (Late June 1941)

Even before German troops arrived in Kaunas, nationalists began laying the groundwork for violence. Nazi Germany sheltered members of the Lithuanian Activists Front (LAF) when they fled the Soviets in 1939. The LAF issued a directive in March 1941 providing instructions that "Local communists and other traitors of Lithuania must be arrested at once." Ominously, a traitor could be pardoned if he "proves beyond doubt that he has killed one Jew at least." The directive also carried a dark message for Lithuania's Jews: "Inform the Jews that their fate has been decided upon. So that those who can had better get out of Lithuania now, to avoid unnecessary victims."[77]

When the German Army occupied Kaunas on June 23, 1941, local Lithuanian militias and auxiliaries began taking over. Walter Stahlecker, commander of EG A, met with Lithuanian leadership in order to help instigate anti-Jewish violence. He insinuated that this could be one way to demonstrate their commitment to the anti-Bolshevik crusade underway against the Soviet Union.[78] Violence began with spontaneous beatings, humiliation, and looting, and quickly escalated, as armed groups of the LAF took to the streets. The Lietūkis garage massacre became the most infamous example of this escalation.

This killing is so well known because it was very well documented. Locals drove Jewish men into the courtyard of a garage/gas station and humiliated them before they were brutally attacked by, among others, a man known as the "Death Dealer of Kaunas." A German soldier reported that "a young man . . . with rolled up sleeves was armed with an iron crowbar. He dragged one man at a time from the group and struck him with the crowbar one or more blows on the back of his head. Within three-quarters of an hour he had beaten to death the entire group of forty-five to fifty people in this way. I took a series of photographs."[79] These photographs survived the war and provide a chilling glimpse into a pogrom in progress. In particular, they show a large crowd of Lithuanian men, women, and children watching. Much testimony comes from a passing German Army Bakery unit that witnessed the killings. One soldier remembered that "Lithuanian civilians could be heard shouting out their approval and goading the men on." He also noted that the "soldiers did not express assent or disapprobation for what was happening."[80] Another soldier reported that "I had to leave the square because I could not watch any more. My friends went with me."[81] The photographer reported that the communal killing included an accordionist who would climb on the bodies and play the Lithuanian national anthem. The people would clap and sing, which he found "unbelievable."[82] More systematic murders followed, with EG men and Lithuanian auxiliaries taking part.

EK 3 reported on July 11 that "7,800 have been liquidated, partly through pogroms and partly through shooting by Lithuanian Kommandos."[83] Stahlecker reported on October 15, 1941, that "native anti-Semitic forces were induced to start pogroms against Jews during the first hours after capture [occupation] though this inducement proved to be very difficult." Referring to Kaunas specifically, he wrote "This [local involvement in the killings] was achieved for the first time by partisan activities in Kaunas. To our surprise it was not easy at first to set in motion an extensive pogrom against Jews. Klimatis, the leader of the partisan unit ... who was primarily used for this purpose, succeeded in starting a pogrom on the basis of advice given to him by a small advanced detachment acting in Kaunas, and

FIGURE 9 *The Lietūkis garage Massacre. Lithuanian nationalists beat approximately fifty Jewish men to death with metal bars while local civilians and members of the German military watch. Kaunas, Lithuania, June 27, 1941.*
Source: Bundesarchiv.

in such a way that no German order or German instigation was noticed from the outside."[04]

Thus, we can see the hand of the EG in these pogroms and the difficulty of increasing the scale of homegrown murder. Similarly, brutal pogroms took place in Vilnius and across the country. The German Army commander in Army Group North, Field Marshal von Leeb, referred to the pogroms in Kaunas, advising simply that "the only thing to do is to keep clear of them."[85] As for the Lithuanians, only one member of the Provisional Government objected. The Cabinet minutes read: "Minister [Landsebergis-] Žemkalnis reported on the extremely cruel torture of Jews at the Lietūkis garage in Kaunas." The outcome was simply that "partisans and individuals should avoid public executions of Jews," hardly a condemnation of the killings.[86]

Lwów, Poland (Late June–Early July 1941)

The city of Lwów in Eastern Poland fell under Soviet control in 1939. It was a cosmopolitan city—a former Austro-Hungarian "Paris of the East"—with Poles, Ukrainians, and Jews forming the bulk of the population. In 1941, around 160,000 Jews lived there. The German Army reached the city on June 29th, 1941, and set off a bloody pogrom, made particularly notable by the horrific photos taken of brutalized Jewish women.

Executions of "enemies of the state," mainly local nationalists marked the Soviet occupation as a whole but particularly its end. Eastern Poland was no exception. The NKVD had amassed a huge inmate population in three prisons throughout Lwów and had no way to evacuate them, nor did they plan to. Therefore, they coldly began executions when Operation Barbarossa began. As one survivor recalled from the Brygidki prison, the "sound of shooting could clearly be heard in the cells." By the end of the mass execution period, the NKVD sought to mask the sounds of killing with truck engines. They filled the cellars with dead and were forced to begin shooting prisoners in trenches in the prison yard.[87] Estimates of the dead range from 4,000–10,000.

When Soviet forces retreated, an uneasy silence fell over the city, but only briefly. Soon ethnic Ukrainians flooded the streets, greeting the German Army with "flowers, laughter, joy, full of hope and illusions, as rescuers and liberators."[88] They expected to be granted some form of independence. Poles, meanwhile, warily stayed away, knowing the Nazi attitude toward them. Jews, especially, made themselves scarce, predicting accurately what would soon occur. The Nazis themselves had encouraged a surge of Ukrainian nationalism by harboring and supporting Ukrainian leaders in Germany beginning in the 1930s. Not coincidentally, therefore, two battalions of ethnic Ukrainians entered Lwów with the *Wehrmacht*.

The citizens of the city (Jews included) began flocking to the former Soviet prisons in search of their loved ones. Devastated, they discovered the whole-scale slaughters there. Yet, quickly, word on the street spread that Jewish members of the NKVD were responsible. What followed was at times a carefully staged propaganda event. First, Ukrainian militia and local police rounded up Jews and forced them to bury the bodies of those murdered in Soviet prisons. *Sonderkommando* 4a, supposedly tasked with arranging pogroms, *had not even arrived.*

After it did so, on July 2, violence escalated. Jews were brought to the same prisons and shot to support the idea of vengeance for Soviet killings. Radio and posters passed the message that "dead bodies of Ukrainians and Poles, shot down by 'Bolsheviks and Judas' has been discovered in prisons."[89] One survivor recalled burying the bodies of Jewish victims in a prison yard while German officers and military police "photographed the execution of completely innocent women, children, and the elderly." German officials told him the graves were intended for victims of "Russian soldiers and Bolsheviks" which he knew clearly was untrue as he had just witnessed a mass shooting of Jews there.[90] All the while, Nazis filmed the scene to create the message that Jews had been responsible for NKVD killings. Some of this film footage survived the war and can be seen today.[91] These widely distributed films served to incite (or simply excuse) escalating violence against Jews.

The truth of the Soviet prison massacres did not matter in the Lwów pogroms that followed. As one Polish witness, Tadeusz Zaderecki, wrote, "The prisons that the Soviets left behind opened and dozens, hundreds of mutilated bodies of political prisoners were revealed . . . Who carried out the murders? The Jews! The fact that the murdered prisoners included Jews made no difference to anyone."[92] *Einsatzkommando* member Felix Landau wrote in his diary that Jews he saw leaving a Lwów prison were "under suspicion of having assisted with persecution of Ukrainians and Germans." He observed that "there were hundreds of Jews with blood streaming down their faces, holes in their heads, broken hands, and eyeballs hanging from their sockets."[93]

As the days went on, the violence spread into the streets. Zaderecki watched as "A rabble of drunken farmers flowed in from the countryside to Lvov." "Something," he predicted darkly, "was about to happen and it was planned."[94] In the following weeks known as the "July Days," thousands of Jews were "horribly beaten with wooden clubs and iron rods." Stores were also looted.[95] Women were assaulted and raped. Humiliation of Jews became a common occurrence. A survivor suspected that the presence of German officers indicated that this was "no spontaneous *Aktion*."[96] Similar mob violence took place elsewhere in Galicia. In Jablonica, 143 miles to the south, a parish priest "praised local Ukrainians for drowning the Jews, and assured them that their deed would be 'rewarded with paradise.' "[97] Galician Jews prayed for the best. Adolf Folkmann hoped that "that our life would gradually revert to its normal course in time, and we could see no reason why it should not. It had always been like that before."[98]

FIGURE 10 *Local Ukrainians abuse a Jew near a German Army guard post. This photo was most likely taken during the Lvov pogroms in July 1941. Photographer was a member of a* Wehrmacht *Propaganda unit, June/July 1941.*
Source: Bundesarchiv.

Iasi, Romania (June 26–Early July 1941)

Pogroms took place across the Eastern Front, not all of them instigated by the Germans, as they were in Kaunas and Lwów. The bloody Iasi pogrom is a good example of the different forms and motivations for violence against Jews in the early days of the war. First, Iasi, the capital of Moldavia, was not a territory of the Soviet Union conquered by the Germans. It was a major city already within the borders of Romania, and Romanian troops occupied it, though some Germans were present for the pogrom. Perhaps, more importantly, in comparison with the two pogroms above, neither EG D nor any SS unit was present in Iasi at the end of June 1941. While some German soldiers participated in the pogrom, their behavior has been characterized as "unorganized [and] chaotic."[99]

Romanian authorities, on the other hand, had a very clear plan. Beginning with Romanian Prime Minister, Ion Antonescu, the killings of Jews in Iasi were to be part of a "'greater plan'" that sought to rid Moldova of its Jews, together with the physical extermination of ('cleansing the ground') of the Jews from Bessarabia and Bukovina."[100] He told his Council of Ministers that "I let the mob loose to massacre them. I withdraw to my citadel, and after the massacre, I restore order."[101] Deep-seated, long-held Romanian antisemitism was a key component in driving the Iasi pogrom. Shortly before the invasion, Prime Minister Ionescu instructed his Ministry of Propaganda to ensure that "all Judeo-Communist coffee shops in Moldavia be closed down, all kikes, Communist agents and sympathizers be identified by region." Antonescu ordered that the Ministry of the Interior "be prepared to do with them whatever I shall order at the appropriate moment."[102]

The Romanian authorities also created an organization "modeled on Einsatzgruppen D." The Romanian Secret Service (SSI) created the First Operative Echelon, with 160 men and the official assignment to "protect the home front from acts of espionage, sabotage, and terror."[103] However, a colonel in the SSI testified after the war that "one of the secret and unofficial aims of the expedition of this Operative Echelon was do away with the Moldavian Jews by deportation or extermination."[104] Operation Barbarossa provided the cover for this operation.

After the invasion began, the war came to Iasi in the form of two Soviet bombing raids. The second raid, at 11 am on June 26 was "devastating."[105] Immediately, (unfounded) rumors circulated that some of the downed Soviet pilots were Jews and that Soviet agents and saboteurs were actively aiding the enemy in the town.[106] The conflation of Jews and Communists was just as powerful in Romania as it was in Germany, Ukraine, and Lithuania. 207 Jews were arrested because they owned flashlights (presumably used to signal Soviet planes.)[107] Two days later, on June 28, posters appeared declaring, "Romanians! Each kike killed is a dead Communist. The time for revenge is now!"[108] Anti-Jewish violence began.

The local police, Romanian military, and First Operative Echelon, began carrying out the systematic parts of the pogrom, rounding up Jews and confining them to the *Chestura* or Police Headquarters. Here, and elsewhere throughout the city, mass executions took place. Around 3,500 Romanian Jews were collected in the *Chestura* courtyard on June 29. Around 2pm, German and Romanian soldiers along with local policemen fired into the mass of people.[109] One eyewitness reported that "Soon, the dead and wounded piled up in the middle of the courtyard. Those who continued to be pushed in by the savage sentries at the entrance had no choice but

FIGURE 11 *Jews assembled in the courtyard of Romanian police headquarters during the Iasi pogrom. Iasi, Romania, June 29–30, 1941.*
Source: United States Holocaust Memorial Museum.

to trample them." A Jewish witness described the victims as "frenzied with fear."[110] At least a thousand Jews were murdered in this way.

Romanian authorities then began to deport Jews in two trainloads. German soldiers and Romanian police together loaded the trains, nailed boards over the air vents to make breathing more difficult, and wrote "Communist Kikes" or "Murderers of German and Romanian Soldiers" on the outside of the cars. Conditions inside were dreadful and the trip was intentionally made excruciatingly longer than normal. On the first train, which left on June 30 and arrived at its destination a week later, 1,400 Jews died.[111] A second train with 1,902 Jews was loaded the same day—1,194 died.[112] Romanian authorities intentionally routed these trains on an agonizing journey to kill as many as possible.

Spontaneous and brutal outbursts by the local population accompanied the more organized killing at the *Chestura* and in the trains. On the night of the 28th, "a group of young gentiles led by the coachman Lepioskin, and accompanied by soldiers, went into the outskirts . . . and began plundering and killing."[113] Civilians often joined the police and military in raiding homes and rounding up Jews. One report stated that a group of Jews "were taken from their homes by several Romanian railway employees, who lived in the same neighborhood."[114] Horrific scenes blanketed Iasi. Tauba Greenberg, an eight-year-old girl "was found disemboweled in front of [presumably a

Jewish store]."[115] The violence was so bad that "many Christians who knew of the pogrom in advance left Iasi and went to stay with relatives, so as not to witness the hideous acts of murder."[116]

Estimates of the Iasi pogrom death toll vary between ten and twelve thousand Jews murdered, either directly or on the death trains. The Romanian government explained the violence with an official communiqué claiming that "500 Judeo-Communists, who had shot from houses at German and Romanian soldiers, were executed."[117] Clearly, Romanian authorities played up the Judeo-Bolshevist myth to support a visceral antisemitic pogrom. As for the perpetrators, the head of the SSI called the Iasi massacres "the great deeds I accomplished in Moldavia."[118]

The Iasi pogrom is significant for several reasons. First, it took place within the sovereign borders of Romania. Second, it shows that direct German influence was not necessary while illustrating how Germany's allies could adopt its methods to deal with their own "Jewish Questions." Third, the pogrom demonstrates the different proportions of antisemitism and Judeo-Bolshevism that could be brought to bear along with the varying degrees to which ordinary civilians and government organizations took part.

The vigor, brutality, and widespread nature of pogroms throughout newly occupied territories in the East are not debated. However, scholars and nations continue to dispute the degree to which Germans orchestrated these episodes of mass violence against the motivations and extent of local participation. The historical evidence reveals the following. First, pogroms and their execution differed across time and space. Second, Nazis, particularly the *Einsatzgruppen*, certainly attempted to encourage mass atrocities by local populations. Third, elements in local populations, particularly in the Baltic States and Ukraine, were complicit in murdering and abusing the neighbors. As we saw in Lwów, killings began before the EGs arrived. Fourth, some element of the Judeo-Bolshevist myth was decisive in most pogroms either as an excuse for violence or as a "legitimate" reason for vengeance against Jews. Lastly, pogroms tended to be more extreme in regions with strong feelings of nationalism and accompanying dreams that Nazi success would support nationalist goals.

On the other hand, it also soon became clear to the *Einsatzgruppen* themselves that they would not be able to solve the "Jewish Question" through "spontaneous" local pogroms alone. They were quite explicit on this point. "Spontaneous cleansing actions," a report by Einsatzgruppe A pointed out, "were insufficient to stabilize the rear army area, especially as the eagerness of the local population was quickly waning."[119] In Belorussia, the EG reported in August 1941 that "Pronounced anti-Semitism is also missing . . . In general, the population harbors a feeling of hatred and rage toward the Jews and approves of the German measures . . . but is not able by itself to take the initiative in regard to the treatment of the Jews."[120] Therefore, the EG continued their own escalating mass killings.

Einsatzgruppen Mass Shootings

> Every village is a different crime scene. Every case is particular.
>
> Father PATRICK DESBOIS[121]

Even with mixed success in inciting local populations to do their work, the EG killed the majority of their victims themselves or with the assistance of organized local auxiliary units. As a result, Eastern Europe is a landscape of graves, some of which Father Debois investigated when trying to reconstruct open-air killings there. Pogroms were simply too chaotic, too complex, with the added drawback of generating false hopes of national independence. Mass killings in the "first sweep" (1941) involved the shooting of Jews by EG units which then moved on (as opposed to killing non-workers or the liquidations of ghettos which followed.) Even so, these first steps toward mass murder varied in form and scale, as we will see in detail below.

FIGURE 12 *A Latvian policeman walks along the edge of a mass grave toward the bodies of Jewish women and children who have just been executed. Known as a "kicker," it was his job to push the bodies that did not fall in during the shooting into the mass graves. This was necessary to make room on the edge of the graves for the next group of Jews to be shot. Photo taken by member of the SD. Liepaja, Latvia, December 15, 1941.*
Source: Bundesarchiv.

Babi Yar, Ukraine (June 29–30, 1941)

The city of Kiev fell to the *Wehrmacht* on September 19, 1941, after a bitter struggle that resulted in 600,000 Soviet casualties and an additional 600,000 POWs who disappeared into the deadly Nazi POW system.[122] The German army entered a town that greeted them warmly, with at least some of that warmth provided by the fires set by retreating Soviet forces. The NKVD (Soviet Secret Police) had left more surprises behind. On September 20, a large explosive device detonated in the former arsenal building housing German officers. The artillery commander and his chief of staff were killed.[123] Four days later, another bomb destroyed the Grand Hotel, killing more high-ranking officers. Another exploded in a department store, killing Ukrainians standing in line to register with German authorities. Over two hundred German soldiers died in explosions or while fighting the fires that followed.[124] These were part of a complex plan by the NKVD, including tons of explosives planted throughout the city timed to go off at set intervals.

Angry Germans and Ukrainians alike blamed the Jews for these "cowardly" attacks. They fit perfectly into the narrative of Jews as Bolsheviks and therefore partisans as well as the local anger at mass killings by the NKVD prior to its departure. Even local Jews recognized this scapegoating. One remarked that "They [the Bolsheviks] decided to play on us Jews one last trick. Without these terrible explosions, the Germans would have left us alone."[125] High-level German commanders openly endorsed antisemitic action. The German military commander of the city, General Kurt Eberhard, met with commanders of EG C and SK 4a, Otto Rasch and Paul Blobel, respectively on September 26 and suggested that Jews should be murdered as "retaliation."[126] The Jews had not, of course, planted the explosives. A lieutenant in SK4a recalled the agreed upon division of labor: "We had to do the dirty work. I will never forget how General Eberhard said to us in Kiev: *You* have to do the shooting."[127] The EG C and SK 4a Report for September 28 predicted, "Execution of at least 50,000 Jews planned. German Army welcomes measures and demands drastic procedure."[128]

On September 28, Ukrainian militia posted notices that all Jews were to assemble and that "they must take with them documents, money, and valuables, and also warm clothing, underwear, etc."[129] Rumors spread throughout the Jewish community speculating about the meaning of this gathering. Some thought they were to be resettled or sent for forced labor. Others thought this was the preliminary stage for the creation of a ghetto in Kiev. It was neither. Some Jews suspected as much. A bystander overheard her Jewish neighbor tell her husband, "Khaim, why are you taking that pillow, for we are going to our death?"[130]

On September 29, elements of *Einsatzgruppe C, Sonderkommando 4a*, Police Regiment South, and Ukrainian auxiliaries drove the Jews of Kiev through the streets to a ravine called Babi Yar on the outskirts of town. Regular German Army soldiers guarded the route to prevent escape.[131] There, Jews were forced to remove their clothes and were shot in an ongoing operation that lasted two days. Fritz Hofer, a driver in SK 4a, arrived at the ravine to load up the clothing of the murdered. He witnessed the killing taking place. He testified in 1959:

> How many layers of bodies there were on top of each other I could not see. I was so astonished and dazed by the sight of the twitching blood-smeared bodies that I could not properly register the details. In addition to the two marksmen there was a "packer" at either entrance to the ravine. These "packers" were Schutzpolizisten, whose job it was to lay the victim on top of the other corpses so that all the marksman had to do as he passed was fire a shot.
>
> When the victims came along the paths to the ravine and at the last moment saw the terrible scene they cried out in terror. But at the very next moment they were already being knocked over by the "packers" and made to lie down with the others. The next group of people could not see this terrible scene because it took place around a corner.
>
> Most people put up a fight when they had to undress and there was a lot of screaming and shouting. The Ukrainians did not take any notice. They just drove them down as quickly as possible into the ravine through the entrances.[132]

Kurt Werner, also in SK4a, personally killed during the Babi Yar massacre. He later testified, "It's almost impossible to imagine what nerves of steel it took to carry out that dirty work down there. It was horrible . . . I had to spend the whole morning down in the ravine. For some of the time I had to shoot continuously."[133] Ironically, while admitting to his participation in mass murder, Werner highlights the difficulty *for him*. Large numbers of ethnic Germans and Ukrainians, perhaps up to 1,500, greatly assisted German shooters.[134]

Over two days, the *Einsatzgruppen* and their collaborators murdered 33,771 Jews of Kiev. This constituted the majority of the Jewish population and the largest mass shooting of Jews in the entire war. After the killing, nine elderly Jews returned to Kiev and sat by the Old Synagogue. According to a witness, "there they sat for days and nights. No one gave them food or water and they died one by one." When only two remained alive, a local approached a German guard; "He asked him, while pointing at the bodies, to shoot those two. The guard thought for a moment and did."[135] *Wehrmacht* engineers assisted in burying the bodies and "in concealing the massacre."[136] On October 10, less than two weeks after the massacre, the commander of the Sixth Army, responsible for the Kiev region, General Walter von Reichenau, reminded his soldiers that they "must have full understanding for the necessity of harsh but just punishment of the Jewish subhumans. It has the broader objectives of nipping in the bud any uprisings in the *Wehrmacht*'s rear, which experience shows have always been instigated by Jews."[137] The *Einsatzgruppen* epitaph for the Jews of Kiev was one sentence reporting the execution of 33,771 Jews.

Krupki (September 18, 1941)

Unlike Kiev in Ukraine, Krupki in central Belarus, northeast of Minsk, was a small rural town with a Jewish population of about 870 in 1939 out of a total of 3,455.[138] It served mainly as a market town for the surrounding farmers with little other significance than its location on an important east-west highway. A *Wehrmacht* unit had occupied the town since July 28, 1941. Shortly before September 18, Werner Schönemann, commander of a *Teilkommando* (subunit of an EK) arrived at the battalion headquarters to arrange for the murder of the approximately 1,000 Jews in Krupki. Schönemann was a Gestapo officer who had been ordered from law school to *Einsatzkommando* 8. He often began shootings personally, even jumping into the graves "to set an example and to show that he did not shirk his duty."[139]

He and Army officer, MAJ Johannes Waldow, worked out the details of the upcoming massacre. Waldow supplied manpower to round up, guard, and deliver the victims to the mass graves and Schönemann conducted the killings. An Army lieutenant even personally chose the killing site. The night before the executions, a platoon leader allegedly told his troops, "Men, we have a serious task ahead of us tomorrow. Whoever doesn't trust himself to handle a sensitive and serious assignment does not need to be ashamed and can back out."[140]

The next morning Schönemann said "Let's get started," and the Jews of Krupki were collected in the central square. Soldiers marched them to the killing site about half a mile outside of town. One soldier remembered allowing a Jewish woman to pull up her toddler's pants but still marching her to the killing pits. Victims surrendered valuables at the grave site. The shooting took place all afternoon, with *Wehrmacht* soldiers also participating in the killing. After all the Jews of Krupki had been murdered, the SS left with the valuables. Locals under the supervision of the Belarusian mayor covered the grave. The local population deepened its own complicity with a "fair" organized in the town where "everything was sold off, furniture, clothes."[141] And so the neighbors of the victims participated in the plunder of their property. In the reports of *Einsatzgruppen B*, *Einsatzkommando 8*, the mass killings in Krupki received a short mention:

> Two larger actions were carried out by the unit ... in Krupka and Sholopenitsche [sic]. In the first town 912 Jews were liquidated and in the second 822. With this, the Krupka region can be seen as Judenfrei.[142]

Army records make no mention of the events of September 18, even though the *Wehrmacht* had been deeply complicit in all aspects of the killing.

Einsatzgruppen killings spanned the entire length and breadth of the Eastern Front from Latvia to the Crimea. Numbers ranged from relatively small to large. Some killings were one-time affairs while other sites, like the Ponary Forest outside of Vilna, Lithuania, were used on a continuing basis to kill 50–60,000 people (mainly Jews) over the course of the war.[143] As in Poland, when the first mobile phase of killing ended, the *Einsatzgruppen* transitioned

FIGURE 13 *Shooting and burning pit in the Ponary Forest. Soviet Memorial reads: "Here, the Hitlerite occupiers burned unearthed corpses." vic. Vilnius, Lithuania, 2017.*
Citation/Provenance: The author.

into stationary units responsible for a specific region where they continued to carry out mass killings and assist in anti-partisan efforts. The *Einsatzgruppen* killings must also be seen in the context of the eventual "Final Solution," the decision to physically exterminate all the Jews in Europe. Though initially targeting only men, the EGs very quickly began shooting all Jews in the occupied Soviet Union; this was the first systematic killing of Jews, long before any gas chambers or extermination camps had become operational.

As a result, the logistical and psychological difficulties in murdering so many people one at a time soon became apparent and influenced the unfolding of the later stages of the Holocaust. The experience of the "Holocaust by Bullets" was at least partly responsible for the evolution of the Nazi killing machine. The commander of *Einsatzgruppe B*, Artur Nebe, noted as early as July 1941 that "a solution of the Jewish Question during the war seems impossible in this area [Belarus] because of the tremendous number of Jews."[144] The initial response was the calling up of additional Police Battalions and increased involvement of local auxiliaries, but even this would prove insufficient for the task at hand. Experiments with other methods began.

Himmler and others were also concerned with the traumatic nature of the mission, given the EG men. They recognized that this brutal method of killing affected the men. On December 12, 1941, Himmler secretly informed his EG commanders that "It is the sacred obligation of the higher SS leaders and commanders to see to it personally that none of our men who have to fulfill this heavy duty, become brutalized."[145] He advocated that killing units hold comradeship evenings to counteract the emotional damage of their work. Himmler himself experienced anxiety while witnessing an execution outside of Minsk in August 1941, when the experience shook him up and he fainted. A high-ranking official told him, "Look at the eyes of the men in this commando, how deeply shaken they are. These men are finished for the rest of their lives."[146] For Himmler and others, the trauma of face-to-face killing allowed them to paint the Germans as the victims, suffering from the difficulty of their "work." However, it also appears to have been a concern that contributed to the development of new forms of killing.

The Initial Occupation of the East

Is the goal to permanently secure [these populations] some subsistence, or should they be totally eradicated?

ROLF-HEINZ HOEPPNER, Chief of Resettlement Office-Poznan to Eichmann, September 3, 1941[147]

The Nazi occupation of the Soviet Union would soon answer Hoeppner's question; indeed, some policies had already been prepared in advance. The occupation, by definition, encompassed most of the countries of Eastern Europe with the exception of those allied to Hitler, which we will discuss later; this area included Latvia, Lithuania, Estonia, Belarus, Ukraine, and parts of Poland. Many occupation policies developed in Poland were swiftly instituted in the occupied East. In addition, while the military had been at least somewhat reluctant to participate in anti-Jewish measures in Poland, Barbarossa marked a turning point where the Army fully participated in Nazi anti-Jewish policies. Even before the invasion, the military administration department published guidelines that "All male and female Jews aged 10 years or above in the occupied territories of the Soviet Union must wear a 10-cm yellow star on their left chest and on their back . . . In every settlement in which more than 50 Jews reside, a Jewish council will be established."[148] Thus, on July 8 in Vilna, the military commander ordered that Jews wear special insignia on their chest and back.[149] In Kaunas, the military established a ghetto on July 10.[150] It also began forcing Jews into labor. Throughout the occupied East, similar policies were put into place.

On August 1, 1941, much of the newly conquered territory came under the civilian control of Alfred Rosenberg's *Reichskommissariat Ostland* and was further subdivided into smaller jurisdictions. Ghettoization, forced labor, and establishment of concentration camps continued to evolve under civilian rule.

The occupation of the Soviet Union also saw the uneven implementation of the previously mentioned Green Plan and Hunger Plans. Already, by September 16, Goering had ordered German troops to live "off the land."[151] This, of course, meant depriving local populations of necessary food. In addition, the war itself interrupted harvests, causing starvation across the East. Under Goering's Four Year economic plan, all machinery, heavy equipment, factories, and raw materials were seized, with disastrous effects.[152] The combination of Army food policy and general looting of the East proved lethal in some areas. In Kiev, a resident observed in December 1941 that while Germans celebrated Christmas, "the locals 'all move like shadows, there is total famine.'"[153]

Nowhere were the effects of Nazi destructive economic planning and intended starvation of the local population more evident than in Leningrad and the surrounding region. While the city itself escaped capture, the German Army laid siege, preventing almost any attempt at resupply as it extracted food from the region. The siege began on September 8, 1941 and lasted until January 27, 1944. The Quartermaster General of the Army, Wagner, who had helped craft POW policy and the Hunger Plan, wrote his wife that all 3.5 million inhabitants of Leningrad would have to starve, as "sentimentality would be out of place."[154]

The regions outside Leningrad fared little better. Even German police units noted the destructive effects of the combined military and civilian policy. Already in September, they were reporting that the "area occupied by Army Group North presents a uniform picture of economic and cultural misery . . . In several areas . . . nearly all cattle herds and horses have been carried off. German troops have requisitioned nearly the entire chicken population, so that the food situation is extraordinarily difficult for the civilian population."[155] A German medic reported from the Pavlosk region in December 1941 that:

> A man is lying on the street, a civilian or a prisoner of war. He is completely broken down by exhaustion in the freezing weather, and steam rises off his still warm head. In general, ragged and starving civilians. They stagger and drag themselves till [their death], in –40-degree weather. Their houses are destroyed, either by the Bolsheviks or by us. No one can help them. With weakened arms, they try to hack pieces out of frozen horse cadavers. Many children are dying in the villages, one sees many with prematurely aged faces and with bloated stomachs. Children and women look through the horse excrement on the street . . . in the hope of making something edible.[156]

German authorities discovered multiple cases of cannibalism, including a woman who admitted having eaten five children. She was executed.[157] In Leningrad, around one million men, women, and children starved to death before the siege ended.

Operation Barbarossa, the "Holocaust by Bullets," and the German occupation of the occupied Soviet Union highlight the intimate connection between the war and the Holocaust. These events in the fall of 1941 and early part of 1942 also represent critical moments in the evolution of Nazi policy leading to the Final Solution. We must view Operation Barbarossa and the genocidal policies which accompanied it, directed against Jews and non-Jews, as the norm for Nazi rule. Based on German conceptions of *Lebensraum*, colonial aspirations in the East, and virulent antisemitism and anti-Bolshevism, the war against the Soviet Union was precisely the war the Nazis wanted to fight. Both the conquest and occupation of Western Europe that dominate much of our popular memory must therefore be seen as exceptions to the rule of Nazi terror and domination. As we move on to examine ghettoization, consider as an example of this difference that not a single ghetto was established in Western Europe.

Selected Readings

Arad, Yitzhak. *The Holocaust in the Soviet Union*. Lincoln: University of Nebraska Press, 2009.

Arad, Yitzhak, Schmuel Krakowski, and Shmuel Spector, eds. *The Einsatzgruppen Reports: Selections from the Dispatches of the Nazi Death Squads' Campaign against the Jews, July 1941-January 1943*. New York, NY: Holocaust Library, 1989.

Beorn, Waitman Wade. *Marching into Darkness: The Wehrmacht and the Holocaust in Belarus*. Cambridge: Harvard University Press, 2014.

Browning, Christopher R. *Ordinary Men: Reserve Police Battalion 101 and the Final Solution in Poland*. New York: Harper Perennial, 1998.

Megargee, Geoffrey P. *War of Annihilation: Combat and Genocide on the Eastern Front, 1941*. Lanham, MD: Rowman & Littlefield, 2006.

7

Ghetto Life and Death in the East

Introduction

Nowadays, death rules in all its majesty; while life hardly glows under a thick layer of ashes ... The very soul, both in the individual and in the community, seems to have starved and perished, to have dulled and atrophied.

ABRAHAM LEWIN, Warsaw ghetto, September 31, 1941[1]

Abraham Lewin was forty-seven years old when the Warsaw ghetto was sealed on November 15, 1940. He had been a teacher and historian. In the ghetto, he joined fellow historian Emanuel Ringelblum in an attempt to document for posterity the experiences of Warsaw's Jews. His last entry was dated January 16, 1943, just a few days before an *Aktion* took him to the Treblinka extermination center where he was murdered along with his daughter, Ora.[2] Portions of his diary survived, buried in milk cans in what was left of the ghetto, and parts were discovered in 1946 and 1950. It describes the unbearable conditions in the Warsaw ghetto and the emotional toll ghettoization took on inhabitants. In May 1942, Lewin wrote "An unremitting insecurity, a never-ending fear, is the most terrible aspect of all our tragic and bitter experiences" and that "the most destructive aspect for our nervous system and our health was to live night and day in an atmosphere of unending fear and terror for our physical survival, in a continual wavering between life and death."[3]

The experience of ghettoization—being confined to particular, small portions of cities and towns with insufficient food and the constant threat of deportation—was unique to the occupied East; the Nazis created no ghettos in Western Europe. Ghettos *had* existed across Europe in the medieval and early modern periods: the first official Jewish ghetto was established in sixteenth-century Venice. Often, these were voluntary communities. Indeed, even Jews themselves contested the nature of the ghetto: was it a forced, discriminatory confinement or a rich cultural community that served all Jewish needs?[4] Ghettoization under the Nazis was a completely different process. It represented another development and escalation in Nazi anti-Jewish policy. At the same time, ghettoization should not be seen as a direct preparation for the Final Solution, though it greatly enabled the genocide. Approximately 500,000 Polish Jews died in the ghettos before systematic deportations to the gas chambers began.[5]

This chapter provides an overview of the process of ghettoization across Eastern Europe, highlighting the diversity of ghetto organization and forms as well as differing Nazi viewpoints on the purpose of ghettos. It also explores the experience of life and death there and how Jewish leadership and individuals reacted to ghettoization. Finally, drawing on material from inhabitants themselves, such as Lewin, as well as the Nazis, this section situates the ghetto in the larger context of the Holocaust.

A Difficult Birth: Nazi Ghetto Policy

The best solution would apparently still be the removal of the Jews to some other place. So long, however, as the Jews are still present here, the course of action adopted in Warsaw would seem to be the most appropriate: to seal off the Jews as much as possible from their surroundings, to exploit their labor, according to plan, and to allow them the widest latitude in regulating their own affairs.

HEINZ AUERSWALD, Warsaw Ghetto Commissar, November 24, 1941[6]

Contrary to some conventional wisdom, the ghettos in Eastern Europe were not established to consolidate Jews for extermination. Auerswald here offers an economic rationale, for example. In fact, ghettos were created from 1939 to 1944 across the occupied East, usually by local authorities and often for differing reasons. Part of the confusion over the intended role of the ghetto stems from a 1939 directive from Reinhard Heydrich specifying that the "first prerequisite for the final goal is initially to concentrate the Jews from rural areas in the larger cities." He went on to dictate that

> As far as possible, the area referred to under 1) is to be cleared of Jews; at least, the aim should be to establish only a few cities of concentration. In the areas referred to under 2), as few concentration centers as possible are to be set up, to facilitate the subsequent measures. Here it must be borne in mind that only those cities which either are rail junctions or at least are situated on railroad lines should be selected as concentration points.

As a matter of principle, Jewish communities of fewer than 500 persons are to be dissolved and the people transported to the nearest city of concentration.[7]

This order might be read, with hindsight, as setting the stage for the murder of the Jews. In reality, it highlighted missteps in Nazi anti-Jewish policy more than evidence of a master plan. The creation of permanent ghettos resulted from failures of other plans. Furthermore, certainly in 1939 and even later into 1941, the "final goal" of which Heydrich speaks was still deportation and not murder. Thus, ghettoization would hopefully ease the mass deportation of Jews to a yet undetermined location. When German Jews began being deported, many of them ended up in eastern ghettos until the Nazis made a final decision regarding their fate. Particularly in Poland, the last thing high-level Nazi leaders wanted was a permanent concentration of Jews as they vied to make their territories *judenrein* (free of Jews.) As late as October 1941, Hans Frank, head of the *Generalgovernment*, still believed that his Jews would be resettled somewhere in Russia.[8]

Nazi mayor, Hans Drechsel, established the first ghetto at Piotrkó Trybunalski in the Radom district of the *Generalgovernment* on October 8, 1939. It had no fence and was simply marked with signposts.[9] If we accept that ghettos first appeared as a stopgap measure to consolidate Jews in preparation for some future action, then the actions of the German authorities responsible for managing ghettos must be seen as a form of discovery learning. What were they to do with these concentrated populations, particularly when they were large and in major cities? History shows that individual officials devised different systems and envisioned different purposes for ghettos.

Historian Christopher Browning provides the useful categories of "attritionists" and "productionists" to describe the stances of ghetto managers. These contrasting viewpoints nicely illustrate the local influence on larger Nazi policy and the relative lack of coherence across Nazi occupied territory. "Attritionists" viewed ghettos as areas of confinement in which the largescale death tolls of Jews were inconsequential, or even welcome. For them, "the ghettos were vast concentration camps facilitating the total extraction of Jewish wealth through the leveraging of deliberate starvation" until eventually, the ghetto's population died out. Himmler, unsurprisingly, was a firm attritionist, having stated in 1939 that "the time has come to drive this rabble into ghettos, and then epidemics will erupt and they'll all croak."[10] "Productionists" on the other hand "viewed their task, at least until that future point when the Jews were finally removed, as the minimization of the burden of the ghettoized Jews on the Reich through the maximization of their economic potential," that is through labor.[11] These two perspectives, between temporary labor and decimation, clashed repeatedly, even among leaders of the SS.

This debate played out, for example, in the creation and evolving management of the Łódź and Warsaw ghettos. The ghetto in Łódź in the *Warthegau* was the first of the large, well-known ghettos. It had been established by May

1, 1940, with an estimated 163,777 initial inhabitants.[12] Fences cut off Jews from food, and thus their provisioning quickly became the responsibility of the Nazi authorities. At first, the attritionist Friedrich Uebelhoer controlled ghetto policy in Łódź. His position was clear: "The creation of the ghetto is of course only a transition measure. I shall determine at what time and with what means the ghetto and thereby also the city of Lodź will be cleansed of Jews. The final goal in any case must be that we burn out this plague-boil."[13] However, the ghetto administrator, Hans Biebow, soon altered this extreme position, insisting that the ghetto must contribute economically to the German war effort and thus could not be left to wither on the vine. In this, his own deputy Palfinger opposed him, siding with others who advocated starvation as a tool to extract wealth and a little more. Palfinger, made his position clear, saying that "The rapid dying out of the Jews is for us a matter of total indifference, if not to say desirable."[14] However, Biebow prevailed in setting up the ghetto as a source of slave labor that could contribute both to the cost of its own existence and to German business needs. He created "four principal business subdivisions regulating labor creation and manufacturing, monetary conversion of goods removed from the ghetto, financial administration, and central purchasing."[15] For both Łódź Jews and Biebow, labor and production became necessary to justify the existence of the ghetto. Indeed, the predominance of Jews as skilled workers and craftsmen meant that they were needed in the local economy, despite their racial "inferiority." In many ways, the Łódź ghetto would become the model for the large ghettos, created mainly in the former Polish territories.

The Warsaw ghetto, officially sealed in November 1940, took a slightly different path toward its final structure and purpose. First, in Warsaw, Nazi public health officials played a decisive role in the isolation of the Jewish population. Officials marshaled a military and medical argument. "The German Army and population," they contended, "must in any case be protected against the Jews, the immune carriers of the bacteria of epidemics."[16] This motivation combined the real threat of disease (created by Nazi policy itself) with antisemitic stereotypes about Jews as disease carriers. Ironically, the attritionist Palfinger had left Łódź hoping to bring his perspective to the Warsaw ghetto. Here, too, he was defeated by forces seeking to make the ghetto economically viable in order to sustain itself and to support the Nazi war effort. Even though productionists initially prevailed, their actions did not radically relieve the suffering in the ghettos. Hunger, disease, and abuse remained constant traits of all ghettos.

Another variation in the establishment of ghettos came in Krakow, the capital of the *Generalgovernment* and site of Hans Frank's palatial residence. Frank did not want a large concentration of Jews in "his" city. For him, it was "absolutely intolerable" that "thousands and more thousands of Jews slink around and take up apartments" in Krakow. He therefore sought to create "the most Jew-free city" in the *Generalgovernment* by driving Krakow's Jews into the countryside. He even gave them the incentive of taking their property with them and choosing their destination.[17] Of course, they had to pay their own way, a requirement which led to an official report suggesting the administration pay for transportation in order to speed the process.[18]

Regardless, Łódź became the model for the establishment of many ghettos: a confined space which forced Jews to pay for their own existence and harnessing the captive population to the local economy and the war effort (and often providing funds for the personal accounts and projects of Nazi administrators). Indeed, corruption among Nazi officials such as District Governor in Galicia, Karl Lasch, not infrequently resulted in severe punishment. Lasch was arrested for his corruption as head of the Radom District and forced to commit suicide before his trial in 1942.[19]

Systematic theft of wealth from ghetto populations occurred almost universally. The Nazis believed, not altogether incorrectly, that valuable items, currency, precious gems, and so on, had been brought into the ghettos. They were anxious to force the Jews to surrender this wealth. Starvation was one method by which the Nazis extorted funds from Jewish communities. Ghetto populations paid exorbitant amounts for sustenance, of which only a small amount often went to food for the ghetto (if any.) In May 1941, the military commander of Warsaw reported, for example, on starvation in the ghetto. He noted that "No one has yet been able to deliver potatoes, for which the Jewish council made a prepayment of several millions."[20]

Ghetto administrators frequently took hostages, often the Jewish Councils themselves, and demanded a "ransom." In Lwów in August 1941, ghetto inhabitants were forced to collect 20 million złoty ($5 million in today's currency).[21] They surrendered 1,400 kg (3,080 lbs) of silver as well as gold and jewelry in an attempt to pay.[22] A survivor recalled that Jews gave up wedding rings and gold but that "the people that they held for ransom never came back anyway."[23] In Łódź, a systematic plan of extraction was created. Ghetto administrators sought cash from "(1) the extraction of all currency from the ghetto, (2) the sale of goods produced by skilled Jewish labor, especially textile workers, within the ghetto, (3) the providing of unskilled Jewish labor for construction work in the city, and (4) 'in the future' the sale of goods held" in German warehouses.[24] In Warsaw in January 1940, after an ethnic German was attacked, the Jewish Council was given 24 hours to raise 100,000 złoty in ransom money.[25] In Łódź, the city government attempted to collect 275,000 RM from the Jewish community "to compensate for a drop in the city's real estate and business tax revenues" created by the Nazis' own policy of ghettoization.

Systematic looting of Jewish wealth extended into a myriad of other economic areas. In April 1940, the *Generalgovernment* issued a request for information that included the question: "What property is still in Jewish hands? Where is the Jewish property and of what does it consist?"[26] The theft of residences by Nazis and/or their sale to local non-Jews accompanied the displacement of Jews into ghettos. In this way, valuable real estate was stolen along with most of the property that was left behind. During the first winter of the war against the Soviet Union, Jews were forced to give up furs, ski clothing, and any other warm garments for the woefully unprepared German Army. A survivor of the Krakow ghetto described the event in her memoirs:

> These furs were to be brought to a building on Limanowskiego Street. Whoever did not give up their furs would be put to death immediately ... So on a day that saw the temperature drop well below the freezing point, Jews in painfully thin cloth coats stood in line and handed over the warm furs.[27]

This "Fur Aktion" took place in many ghettos across the East. Systematic thefts of Jewish wealth greatly impacted ghetto inhabitants. As the number of these "ransoms" increased, the Jews became less and less able to pay, as they were unable to acquire new wealth. Second, the wealth they did bring into the ghetto was a vital means to acquire food, firewood, clothing, and other necessities and, as their reserves were depleted, it became increasingly difficult to survive.

In conclusion, ghettoization evolved organically, like many Nazi policies, as leaders on the ground sought to deal with their Jewish "problems" in a variety of different ways. These problems themselves originated from the failure of other options for the removal of Jews from Europe rather than from a set plan ending with their extermination. While ghettoization eventually proved useful in carrying out the murder of Jews, that was not the initial goal.

All Ghettos were Local: The Diversity of Ghettoization in the East

Everything depends on local conditions and on the particular despot on whom our fate depends. There are cities and towns where there is no ghetto, where shrewd authorities are ready to accept bribes. And in places where ghettos have been established, they are not all closed.

CHAIM KAPLAN, Warsaw, March 28, 1941[28]

When most people envision a Holocaust ghetto, they see Warsaw, with its large wall topped with broken glass and bridges over streetcar lines passing through. They see thousands of people packed into a small area. And they see the massive train deportations to the extermination centers. While some of the larger ghettos conform to these iconic images, the diversity in ghetto geographies and experiences is actually quite surprising. Browning emphasizes that "There is no single interpretive framework that encompasses ghettoization in the German-occupied East throughout the war years . . . ghettoization occurred in different places at different times in different forms and for different reasons."[29] As Chaim Kaplan pointed out in 1941, the nature of the ghetto experience depended upon local conditions. The editors of the United States Holocaust Memorial Museum's comprehensive encyclopedia themselves add: "There was no clear definition of what a ghetto was. Even the wartime German authorities themselves had varying conceptions of a ghetto, using it to mean quite different things according to the time and place."[30]

What we do know is that there were at least 1,150 different ghettos throughout occupied Eastern Europe, including in Nazi-allied countries like Romania and Hungary. Size, location, time, and leadership influenced the diversity of these places. No ghetto was like any other and many were wildly different from each other. The Lwów ghetto, for example, like a few others, ceased to become a ghetto entirely and was redesignated a concentration camp (*Judenlager* or JULAG) in February 1943.

Ghettos came in a wide variety of sizes and shapes. The largest, like Warsaw, Łódź, and Lwów, held hundreds of thousands of Jews. Others, like the Mrozy ghetto in Belarus, held only around 1,000, many of whom were refugees from elsewhere.[31] As the Germans moved further east, there were fewer large cities, and ghetto populations dropped away somewhat. Ghettos in more rural areas became collecting points for Jews from even smaller surrounding towns. Two separate ghettos were established in the town of Proskurow in Ukraine to house between 10,000 and 12,000 Jews from the town and surrounding areas.[32] In the town of Slonim in Belarus, the large number of Jews living in the market town plus the influx of refugees from other areas resulted in a majority Jewish population. The Nazi civil administrator, Gerhard Erren, was not at all prepared and lamented that "it was almost impossible to seal the ghetto as there was no barbed wire and insufficient security."[33] Erren's local economic struggles to deal with his ghetto can be seen in his gleeful statement after the first murder of Slonim Jews: "The Juden-Aktion of November 14, 1941 has greatly ameliorated the housing problem and also rid us of 10,000 unnecessary mouths to feed."[34] Most ghettos were smaller than even this, meaning that Jews were often confined in close proximity to their erstwhile neighbors.

The Warsaw and Łódź ghettos were massive and tightly sealed. The Warsaw ghetto, in particular, was enclosed by a brick wall with 28 points of exit and entry for 53,000 inhabitants with the requisite passes.[35] Other ghettos were not closed at all. In the town of Brzezany in Ukraine, the ghetto remained simply a designated area for over a year. Until mid-January 1942, its Jewish residents could "move quite freely in and around town." Even when authorities began controlling their movements, the tactic was simply an announcement in the paper prohibiting Jews from leaving the ghetto area.[36] In Budapest, the capital of Hitler's ally Hungary, no ghetto existed at all (until two small ones were established). Even when Nazi authorities began controlling Jewish policy in Hungary, Jews were confined to individual apartment buildings that were marked as "yellow star houses" but scattered throughout the city. Here, the area the Nazis envisioned as the site of the future ghetto in 1944 was home to many Christians who governmental authorities were reluctant to inconvenience by forcing to move.[37] Individual apartments were also seized in the process of ghettoization to house non-Jewish bombing victims.[38] In other ghettos, a simple barbed wire fence and sign marked the ghetto, but security was rather haphazard. The Kishinev ghetto, created by Romanian officials, was contained via "makeshift barriers" on the streets surrounding the ghetto.[39] It even had Christian residents who refused to move. According to one witness, these neighbors took advantage of Jews, stealing their possessions.[40]

Ghetto populations themselves could be quite diverse. Almost all ghettos forced together groups of Jews who had been divided by class, religious, social, and political status in close quarters. Often, rural Jews were consolidated in urban centers. The Warsaw ghetto contained 5,000 baptized Christian Jews and three working Catholic churches. Baptized Jews, too, were ghettoized because the Nazi definition of Jewishness did not recognize conversion. The head of the ghetto recalled meeting with the priest assigned to minister to these Jews, who told him that "after the war he would leave as much of an anti-Semite as he was when he arrived there."[41] Clearly, this priest cared for his "Christian" congregation only. As the Holocaust progressed, tens of thousands of Western European Jews arrived in ghettos in places like Riga, Minsk, Łódź, Warsaw, and Kaunas. Often, these highly assimilated Jews did not even speak the local language and had no connections outside the ghetto. In just these examples, we can see the local variations in the forms of ghettoization and begin to imagine the impact they had on life and death in these areas.

Chronology also played an important role in the form and function of ghettos in Eastern Europe: when was a ghetto established and how long did it last? The ghetto in Budapest did not appear until 1944 and did not last long. The first ghettos established in occupied Poland lasted the longest while those created as the Nazis moved east had much shorter life spans. This is, in part, due to the three waves of *Einsatzgruppen* killings. The second wave targeted non-working Jews in ghettos and the third consisted of the liquidation of the remaining ghetto populations. The second wave moved from east to west, leaving western ghettos in existence longer. Another reason for the shorter existence of ghettos established after 1940 was the accelerated process of expropriation, selection, and victimization first perfected in Poland. In addition, the (mis)fortunes of the German war effort meant that many ghettos were liquidated or deported as the Germany army retreated, so as to prevent them from falling into Soviet hands. The Vitebsk ghetto lasted only ten to twelve weeks before its 10,000 to 11,000 inhabitants were murdered in a nearby ravine.[42] Likewise, the ghetto in Zhitomir, Ukraine, was established in July 1941 and liquidated in

September.[43] The Warsaw ghetto, on the other hand, lasted four years. The Kaunas ghetto lasted until 1944.

Chronology and location had a very real impact on the lives of its inhabitants. For example, shorter-lived ghettos had fewer opportunities to develop smuggling operations with the outside population or to build effective administrations and resistance movements. Longer-lived ghettos offered the possibility of preparation for liquidation, but also the increased risk of disease or starvation.

Finally, a *Judenrat* or Jewish council, usually headed by a chief managed each ghetto internally. The make-up and nature of these vital organizations, and even the personalities of the leadership, had significant repercussions for the average inhabitant. Particularly in the occupied Soviet Union, the formation, structure, and purpose of ghettos was uneven, inconsistent, and decidedly unsystematic. Thus, we see in this brief discussion that "the ghetto" is not a clearly defined concept that we can use uncritically. Ghettoization varied greatly from place to place and time to time. The evolution of Nazi anti-Jewish policy, the course of World War II in the East, and the individuals (Jewish and German) responsible for administering it all influenced ghetto experience. This great diversity of structure and conditions again highlights the developmental nature of the Holocaust and the importance of studying it at the local level.

"Choiceless Choices:" The Jewish Councils and Their Leaders

It seems that Rumkowski in Łódź issued his own currency "Chaimki." He has been nicknamed "Chaim the Terrible."

ADAM CZERNIAKOW, diary entry, Warsaw, August 29, 1940[44]

He perpetuated his name by his death more than by his life. His end proves conclusively that he worked and strove for the good of his people; that he wanted its welfare and continuity even though not everything done in his name was praiseworthy.

CHAIM KAPLAN, diary entry, July 26, 1942, on the suicide of Adam Czerniakow[45]

Nazi authorities recognized that managing ghettos would be incredibly difficult and that local Jewish assistance would be required. However, as the quotations above illustrate, the nature and quality of ghetto leadership varied, as ultimately it was shaped by individuals. The Nazis still viewed Jewish leadership as necessary. Reinhard Heydrich dictated this in his ghettoization directive of September 21, 1939:

Councils of Jewish Elders
(1) In each Jewish community, a Council of Jewish Elders is to be set up which, as far as possible, is to be composed of the remaining influential personalities and rabbis. The Council is to be composed of 24 male Jews (depending on the size of the Jewish community).

It is to be made fully responsible (in the literal sense of the word) for the exact execution according to terms of all instructions released or yet to be released.

. . .

(3)

The Jewish Councils are to take an improvised census of the Jews of their area, possibly divided into generations (according to age)

. . .

(5)

The Councils of Elders of the concentration centers are to be made responsible for the proper housing of the Jews to be brought in from the country.[46]

These Jewish Councils or *Judenräte* were responsible for the day-to-day operations of the ghetto according to the orders issued by their German superiors. Not all ghettos had a Jewish council. For example, some, particularly in Romania and Hungary but also in the occupied Soviet Union, were controlled by "non-Jewish auxiliary forces (militias, gendarmerie, the municipality.)"[47] The German Army directly administered some Jewish ghettos during the invasion of the Soviet Union until civil administrators arrived.

As the two introductory quotations indicate, the nature of ghetto leadership was as diverse as ghettos themselves. Proskurov (mentioned earlier), for example, had a Jewish council headed by a woman.[48] The Jewish Council, in form and function, was, as Saul Friedländer aptly described it, "a distorted . . . replica . . . of self-government within the framework of the traditional *kehilla*, the centuries-old communal organization of the Jews."[49] Thus, just as the ghetto itself, the Jewish Council had an historic ancestor.

But, of course, the Nazis ultimately determined the work of these Jewish Councils *for* them to serve *their* goals, not those of the Jewish community. This forced cooperation makes the topic of the Jewish Council in the Holocaust a difficult and uncomfortable one. Many, if not most, decisions and actions fell into the category of "choiceless choices," that is, choices between the least, worse alternative, creating a situation which calls into question the very possibility of choice.[50] Councils and their leaders came to diverse decisions and responses to Nazi demands and to their own elevation to authority. Throughout Jewish communities then and now, some Jewish leaders are deeply condemned as having taken advantage of their position and collaborating with the Nazis. Others are seen as having done the best they could under impossible circumstances. Some members of the

Jewish council were called to account by Jewish Courts of Honor after the war. However, lest we be too quick to judge, we should remember that, in the *Generalgovernment*, "of the 146 Jewish elders originally nominated by the Germans, 57 lost their positions because they were not willing to meet the demands that were placed upon them by the Germans: 11 resigned their posts, 26 were replaced, 18 were liquidated and 2 committed suicide."[51] This section examines the leadership of three ghettos and how ghettos were administered.

Historian Isaiah Trunk conducted some of the most in-depth research on the make-up and function of Jewish Councils during the Holocaust. Looking at a group of 740 to 850 members of Jewish councils, he paints a solid picture of who these men were. Most (85%) were older, between 30 and 60 years old. They were married and had at least a high school education, with 39 percent having a higher degree. The majority of Council members were merchants and professionals. They were overwhelmingly locals.[52] Politically, the majority were Zionists of some kind and the vast majority (99.9 %) had been elected officials in the *kehilla* community self-help organization or in city government. They were also active in community organizations from the professional to the philanthropic.[53] The Germans were thus savvy enough to impress into service already respected and influential members of Jewish communities.

The nature of many Jewish Councils began with the leadership, so we will begin by looking at three ghetto leaders and their approaches to governing: Adam Czerniakow in Warsaw, Chaim Rumkowski in Łódź, and Elkhanan Elkes in Kaunas. While this group provides a sample of differing experiences, each ghetto and its leadership was unique. In many ghettos, the decisions and behaviors of Council leaders were well documented, and many kept a diary.

Adam Czerniakow was born in 1880 in Warsaw. He studied chemistry in Warsaw and industrial engineering in Dresden.[54] His time in Germany gave him an understanding of German culture and mastery of the language. Throughout his life, Czerniakow advocated for the rights of Jewish workers and craftsmen, and was a political activist. He was also a renaissance man, "representative of the Warsaw Jewish assimilated middle class," educational activist, poet, teacher, journalist, and engineer.[55] Thus, it is perhaps no surprise that he was chosen to lead what would become the largest ghetto in Europe. Ironically, the Polish mayor of Warsaw first appointed Czerniakow Chairman of the Jewish Council during the German attack on the city. On September 23, 1939, when he took over the task, Czerniakow wrote in his diary: "A historic role in a besieged city. I will try to live up to it."[56] This position did not last long, nor did Poland.

On October 4, *Einsatzgruppe IV* reaffirmed Czerniakow's appointment. He was fifty-nine. He was then ordered to name twenty-four members to the council, which he did, choosing a variety of notable members of the Jewish community. Czerniakow answered to a variety of Nazi officials but, in arguably the most crucial period, to Heinz Auerswald, the Nazi administrator of the Warsaw ghetto, appointed on May 15, 1941. He faced challenges common to all Jewish Councils: the health, feeding, and municipal management of a large group of people with insufficient resources in the face of an unsympathetic Nazi administration. By mid-1941, the Warsaw Jewish Council employed 6,000 Jews in approximately 30 separate departments.[57] As in all large government organizations, the Council included both selfless public servants and corrupt opportunists. Warsaw diarist Chaim Kaplan recorded that "according to rumor, the President is a decent man. But the people around him are the dregs of humanity."[58]

Czerniakow's greatest challenge was balancing the needs of the ghetto with the often-unpredictable cruelty of the German administration. The fundamental question facing all Jewish Councils was how to keep their population alive while simultaneously fulfilling harsh Nazi demands. Czerniakow seems to have chosen to appease German authorities by adhering to their demands as best he could. However, he spent much of his time meeting with SS and city officials in attempts to mitigate those demands. Czerniakow "tried to use logical arguments with the Germans; he used the arts of persuasion, managed to postpone some decrees, paid ransoms and bribes, gave presents."[59] Like all Jewish Council leaders, he always "negotiated" from a position of absolute weakness and zero power.

While Kaplan (and others) saw the council as "an abomination in the eyes of the Warsaw community," those working closely with it and its elderly but tireless leader had different impressions.[60] His personal secretary noted that Czerniakow "believed that the war would end soon, that it was necessary to hold on. He did not believe in the possibility of genocide."[61] It is in this last area, that Jewish Councils were most disadvantaged. Most did not believe that the Nazis intended to murder all Jews, so they chose different courses of accommodation. Czerniakow cultivated relationships with Auerswald and others to make the ghetto run as smoothly as possible. He was "ready to reach a compromise with the Germans in order to save the Warsaw Jews."[62]

As we have seen, Jews in the past had faced violence and discrimination from non-Jewish populations. They responded by accommodating, forging communal bonds, and generally waiting for anger and violence to subside and for life to return to normal. Recognizing that Nazis eventually intended the complete physical annihilation of the Jews and that none of the past tactics could be successful was extremely difficult. Even after word of the extermination centers reached ghettos, it was often dismissed. Contemporary historian of the Warsaw ghetto, Emanuel Ringelblum, wrote in December 1942:

> Initially people did not believe at all in Treblinka, and anyone who spoke about it was shouted down as a spreader of panic, a pessimist who enjoyed wounding Jews. It was not understood that it was possible

simply to murder tens of thousands of innocent men, women, and children . . . Is this possible now, in the twentieth century?[63]

Czerniakow himself did not initially believe this possible and Nazi ghetto administrator Auerswald took advantage of Czerniakow's "naïveté," deceiving him into even reassuring worried ghetto inhabitants.[64] Czerniakow finally came to terms with the harsh reality of the Final Solution during the massive deportations of July 1942. In the end, his desire to compromise with the Germans helped send them to their deaths. He wrote on July 22, 1942, "We were told that all the Jews irrespective of sex and age . . . will be deported to the East . . . The most tragic dilemma is the problem of children in orphanages, etc. I raised this issue—perhaps something can be done."[65] Instead, Czerniakow's concerns were brushed aside and he was referred to the SS officer in charge of the deportations and told that the mass deportations would continue seven days a week. He likely realized neither the children nor the rest could be saved. At this point, Czerniakow resolved not to preside over the murder of his people and killed himself with cyanide in his office. Before committing suicide, he wrote two letters, one to his wife and another to the Jewish Council. He told his wife that "They are demanding of me that I kill the children of my people with my own hands. Nothing is left but for me to die." To his colleagues, he wrote, "I am helpless, my heart is breaking with sorrow and pity; I can bear it no longer. My act will show the truth to all and will perhaps lead them to the right path of action."[66]

Czerniakow's death, like his work on behalf of Warsaw's Jews, received mixed responses. Some, like Kaplan in the quote at the beginning of the section, praised his sacrifice. The leader of the underground, however, suggested that he "could have committed suicide in another way, as a leader of the community warning his people."[67] Another ghetto inhabitant accused Czerniakow of "cowardice," writing angrily, "Believe me, in our circumstances nothing was easier than choosing to die; deciding to survive was harder by far. Czerniakow should have lived and led the rebellion."[68] However, with the availability of Czerniakow's diaries to historians, it appears that under the circumstances, he worked tirelessly with some success to care for his people. Saul Friedländer praised his "basic decency" in a time of "unbridled ruthlessness." Czerniakow "devote[d] every every single day to his community, but he particularly cared for the humblest and the weakest among his four hundred thousand wards: the children, the beggars, the insane."[69]

The man in charge of the second largest ghetto in Poland, Chaim Rumkowski, was a different individual altogether. Born in 1877 in Russia, he was a failed industrialist who then became an insurance salesman and active member of the Jewish community in Łódź, eventually directing an orphanage.[70] Rumkowski was ordered to establish a Jewish Council in Łódź on October 13, 1939. He was the only survivor of the mass murder of that council in November. Nazis sealed the Łódź ghetto on May 1, 1940.

Rumkowski became responsible for over 144,000 Jews crammed into an area of 1.6 square miles with an average of almost six people living in each room.[71]

Chairman Rumkowski took his job as leader of the Jewish community seriously, but also reveled in the massive amount of power he wielded. He "developed a reputation as disputatious, long-winded, fiercely independent, and strong willed."[72] Many noted Rumkowski's ambition as boundless. He worked from well-appointed offices in Jewish Council headquarters and traveled in an "impeccably lacquered" coach with a white horse and a driver "impeccably dressed in white livery."[73] Ringelblum described Rumkowski's visit to Warsaw in 1940. "Today," he wrote, "there arrived from Łódź, Chaim, or as he is called, 'King Chaim' Rumkowski, an old man of seventy, extraordinarily ambitious and pretty nutty." He referred to Rumkowski's "Jewish kingdom" and noted that "he considers himself God anointed."[74] Rumkowski could be quite petty in his exercise of power, demanding, for example, that all cultural organizations be controlled by his council.[75]

Even more problematic was Rukowski's treatment of his own co-workers. When a prominent doctor refused to join the council, Rumkowski became wildly angry, screaming at him, "Do you think you can just do what you like . . . This is war and we are like soldiers, we have to carry out orders, obey without condition and fulfill our tasks unconditionally—or die! If you do not do what I, the president of the Jewish Council, order [you to do], I will crush you like an ant."[76] Such outbursts and megalomania were not the worst of Rumkowski's excesses. Lucille Eichengreen was seventeen when she was deported from Germany to Łódź, where she found work with the Council. Rumkowski sexually assaulted her. She remembered, "And I was alone in the office and he would pull up a chair and we had a couple of conversations. He talked and I would listen, and he molested me."[77] Other accounts corroborate Rumowski's habits of taking advantage of young women. Some even accuse him of having molested the children in his orphanage. He was known to deport people who had angered him in some way. In the summer of 1940, he arrested the leaders of a protest blaming him for ghetto conditions and had some deported to a labor camp.[78]

Thus, Rumkowski was, in many respects, a vile man. Yet, he was also complicated. He did seek to take care of his community as best he could. Rumkowski was legitimately concerned about the plight of ghetto children and worked to help them. He was deeply concerned with hygiene and health in the ghetto and successfully improved life there to the extent he could. His "energetic promotion of the health, welfare, and occupational development of the community, contributed vitally to its collective survival."[79] Rumkowski confronted authorities, attempting to end the practice of "[pulling] people off the street for work."[80] He demonstrated some real courage in this, challenging even the Nazi administrator of the ghetto, Hans Biebow.

He routinely reported Nazis who misbehaved in the ghetto or mistreated inhabitants. One complaint drove Biebow himself to confront Nazi police authorities, saying, "they should in no way allow themselves to be drawn into further insults directed against the Eldest. In my view, no patrolman or sergeant has the right to confront the Jews, and especially not the Jewish Eldest, in such a way or manner that, instead of working to my department's advantage, leads in a considerable degree to its detriment."[81]

How did Rumkowski get away with such behavior? One can point primarily to his strategy for the survival of the ghetto: work. Unlike Czerniakow, Rumkowski was prepared to sacrifice some for the survival of the many. To him, making the ghetto an indispensable economic concern was the only solution. He was undoubtedly clever in this approach, for he "succeeded in engaging his German masters on the plane of reasoning where the authorities' self-serving interests intersected with the immediate requirements of the beleaguered community [he] sought to preserve."[82] For example, while some Jewish councils encouraged smuggling to augment the insufficient rations available, Rumkowski cracked down, jailing and deporting smugglers. In short, he dedicated his full energy to labor in the ghetto. He told inhabitants "We must work in order to be able to exist . . . Do your work fully in peace, do not daydream. I stand watch over our common interests."[83] In another speech, he reiterated that "The plan is work, work, and more work!"[84] Rumkowski's authoritarian rule over the ghetto and single-minded focus on saving at least some Jews through labor bore fruit as it intersected with Biebow's plans of making the Łódź ghetto an important economic force for his own purposes.

The most controversial element of this (and the best example of the "choiceless choices" faced by all Jewish Councils) was Rumkowski's response to German demands for deportations. Most historians agree that Rumkowski knew Jews were being murdered after deportation, but he continued to publicly dismiss such claims. He employed a utilitarian, if brutal, methodology for deportations, selecting those who could not work and could not contribute to his overall strategy for survival. Because he had proved his value, he conducted selections and deportations on his own authority . . . and, in at least one instance in January 1942, was able to decrease the number of victims demanded from 20,000 to 10,000.[85] The most horrifying example of his willingness to sacrifice part for the whole came in September 1942, when the Nazis demanded 20,000 Jews for deportation. Rumkowski appeared before the ghetto and told the assembled crowd:

> Fathers and mothers, give me your children! . . . I must carry out this difficult and bloody operation, I must cut off limbs in order to save the body! I must take away children, and if I do not, others too will be taken, God forbid . . . Common sense requires us to know that those must be saved who can be saved and who have a chance of being saved and not those whom there is no chance to save in any case.[86]

This astounding speech represents clearly Rumkowski's calculations on how to save the most Jews: keep working people by deporting children and the sick and elderly first. He also recognized that had the Nazis been forced to do the selection themselves, anyone was fair game. The roundups began the next day. 6,000 children were deported to the Chelmno extermination center. A sixteen-year-old ghetto resident saw "two wagons full of little children drive past the open gate. Many of the children were dressed in their holiday best, the little girls with colored ribbons in their hair. In spite of the soldiers in their midst, the children were shrieking at the top of their lungs. They were calling out for their mothers."[87]

A child survivor of Łódź ghetto wrote of the Jewish Council that "These people, although they were Jewish, their sympathy had gone. We were being badly treated. We didn't see the Germans any more, they were outside, we just saw our own people mistreating us."[88] Rumkowski's corruption certainly characterized his reign as Chairman and he was usually reprehensible. However, his legacy remains complex. He was proud of his accomplishment of saving Jews, telling a colleague, "All my work here is to save as many as possible. Afterwards . . . if I survive, let them try me. Let them! I don't care."[89] Rumkowski did not survive. In August 1944, he volunteered to accompany his family to Auschwitz, where, according to some accounts, he was murdered by Jews from his former ghetto.[90] The nature of his death remains unclear. However, the Łódź ghetto outlasted any other ghetto in Poland. 68,000 Jews were still alive in July 1944, over a year after the Warsaw ghetto had been completely annihilated.[91] It was only the fortunes of war that prevented the Red Army from liberating those 68,000, as they were but 60 miles away from the city. Thus, while historian Yehuda Bauer states unequivocally that "Of all the men who served on Jewish Councils during the Holocaust years, Rumkowski probably was the nearest thing to a major war criminal," he also asks whether, had those 68,000 survived, "might not Rumkowski, despite all his crimes, have been hailed as a hero?"[92] Thus, Rumkowski is both a stark comparison to Czerniakow and an enigmatic character in his own right.

For a final example of a ghetto leader, we turn to the Kaunas ghetto in Lithuania. Unlike Warsaw and Łódź, this ghetto was established much later, and as part of the "war of annihilation" in the occupied Soviet Union. These factors certainly influenced its leadership, but its leader, Dr. Elkhanan Elkes, was as strikingly different from Czerniakow and Rumkowski as his ghetto was from theirs. Elkes, born in 1879, had been a physician before the World War I and a doctor in the Russian Army in that war before becoming chief of the internal medicine department at the Jewish Hospital in Kaunas. His service as the personal physician to the Lithuanian prime minister and many in the diplomatic community enhanced Elkes' public profile.[93] Kaunas's Jewish community widely respected him.

The German Army arrived three days after the invasion of the Soviet Union. Bloody pogroms against Jews soon broke out. Lithuanian Mayor, Kazys Palčiauskas ordered a ghetto created on July 10 in the poor section of Slobodka. It is noteworthy that the Jewish community of Kaunas elected a Jewish Council and a chairperson *before* they were ordered to do so by the Nazis. Jewish leaders approached Dr. Elkes on August 4, 1941, urging him to accept the position of Chairman. His future deputy, Leib Garfunkel, described the scene after Elke first declined. A respected rabbi rose and said, "please understand, dear and beloved Dr. Elkes, that only to the Nazi murderers will you be 'Head of the Jews,' in our eyes you will be the head of our Community, elected in our most tragic hour, when blood runs from all of us and the murderer's sword is suspended over our heads."[94] Garfunkel recalled that "Dr. Elkes stood pale and silent."[95] Reluctantly, he accepted despite his age and poor health.

Unlike Czerniakow and Rumkowski, who only faced deportations to killing centers much later in their tenure, Elkes confronted the murder of his community rather quickly. Indeed, he had already lived through the mass violence of the early days of occupation. As *Einsatzgruppe A* reported as of July 11, 1941, "in Kaunas, up to now a total of 7,800 Jews have been liquidated, partly through pogroms and partly through shooting by Lithuanian Kommandos."[96]

Eleven days after Elke's election, the 30,000 Jews of Kaunas were moved into the ghetto (which temporarily consisted of a "Large" and "Small" ghetto connected by a footbridge). Dr. Elke faced the same challenges as other Jewish leaders in terms of health and food, but also the Nazis' murderous anti-Jewish policies. By this point in the Holocaust, many of the "standard operating procedures" regarding ghettos had been established by the Germans. In addition, the evolution of Jewish policy was beginning to close in on physical annihilation as the "Final Solution." Finally, the treatment of the Jewish population in the occupied Soviet Union was more violent from the first moments.

On October 27, 1941, the Jewish Council was told that all Jews were to assemble the next morning on an open ground known as "Democracy Square." The Jewish Council, torn over how to respond, finally turned to Chief Rabbi Shapiro for advice. Shapiro spent the night studying Hebrew scripture, searching for an answer to this impossible problem. He determined that, as diarist Avraham Tory recounted, "When an evil edict had imperiled an entire Jewish community . . . communal leaders were bound to summon their courage, take the responsibility, and save as many lives as possible."[97] Elkes made the decision to order the assembly.[98] He hoped, like Rumkowski, to save some portion of his community by allowing others to be "selected." In the end, 9,200 Kaunas Jews were marched out and murdered in the nineteenth century Fort IX, on the outskirts of the city.[99] This became known as the "Great Aktion." Ghetto diarist Tory wrote that "Some

FIGURE 14 Jews move into the Kaunas ghetto with their belongings. Photo by ghetto inhabitant George Kadish. Kaunas, Lithuania, August 1941.
Source: United States Holocaust Memorial Museum.

thirty thousand proceeded that morning into the unknown, toward a fate that could already have been sealed for them by the bloodthirsty rulers."[100] To his great credit, Elkes forbid his Jewish council from giving preferential treatment to friends and relatives.[101]

Elkes wrote later what the responsibility of leadership felt like, saying, "We are steering our battered ship in the heart of the ocean while every day waves of persecutions and harsh decrees hasten to drown it."[102] However, unlike Rumkowski, Elkes personally went to the square to intervene. He successfully saved some families and was nearly beaten to death for his efforts.

Like ghetto leaders elsewhere, Elkes focused on making his ghetto as productive as possible. Tory wrote on March 16, 1943, "Lately, we have been inclined to connect our fate with the growing demand for Jewish labor . . . the Ghetto has eight to nine thousand productive and creative workers, who contribute their part to the German war effort."[103] The Jews of the Kaunas ghetto worked as slave laborers at a variety of locations and this did probably prolong the ghetto's existence, even when it was turned into a JULAG concentration camp. Ultimately, the ghetto was liquidated in 1944, with surviving inhabitants being sent to concentration camps in the Reich.

Two other elements distinguish Elke from his peers: support for resistance and the behavior of his ghetto police. Unlike some ghetto leaders, Elkes supported the underground and resistance in Kaunas. Many ghetto leaders actively opposed armed resistance, fearing collective reprisals against the ghetto population. Elkes, on the other hand, "financed the purchase of arms for the local resistance organization and provided facilities for manufacturing grenades and explosives."[104] In addition, the ghetto police, often corrupt and vindictive elsewhere, were resisters and generally honorable men in Kaunas. Indeed, during the liquidation of the ghetto, the Nazis arrested the remaining policemen and tortured them to discover hiding places in the ghetto. Thirty-six policemen were killed as a result.[105]

The examples of these three men—Czerniakow, Rumkowski, and Elkes—give only a brief illustration of the various tactics taken by ghetto leaders as they faced an impossible situation. Their choices reflect the influence of their own personalities, the disparate times and places in which they served, and differing strategies for ensuring the survival of their communities. Ghetto leaders in the thousands of Eastern European ghettos faced similar circumstances and were forced to navigate local conditions in the face of overwhelming Nazi power.

Ghetto Life: The Daily Struggle for Survival

The ghetto was a captive city-state in which territorial confinement was combined with absolute subjugation to German authority . . . Each ghetto was on its own, thrown into sudden isolation, with a multiplicity of internal problems and a reliance on the outside world for basic sustenance. Fundamental to the very idea of the ghetto was the sheer segregation of its residents . . . Physically the ghetto inhabitant was henceforth incarcerated. Even in a large ghetto he stood never more than a few minutes' walk from a wall or fence.

Historian RAUL HILBERG[106]

All ghettos had much in common, not the least of which was the sheer physical confinement that Hilberg describes above. Hunger, slave labor, and a constant fear of abuse or death meted out at the hands of the Nazis characterized daily life for most inhabitants. On top of this, the ghetto leadership faced the task of essentially running a municipality. As we have seen, the size of these ghetto "city-states" varied from the massive Warsaw ghetto (460,000) to Kaunas (30,000) to Młynów (ca. 1,500). Each had to carry out the normal functions of a city (health, sanitation, education, taxation, etc.) and confront the abnormal challenges presented by the Nazis (starvation, forced labor, deportation, "ransoms.")

Some ghetto administrations were more complex than others. Size and duration of the ghetto helped determine how effective such administrations could be. While the Łódź ghetto lasted from 1939–44, for example, the Młynów ghetto survived less than a year.[107] The Lwów ghetto administration was divided into 22 divisions and employed around 4,000 people, which constituted 4.5 percent of the ghetto population.[108] The Warsaw ghetto had 38 different departments, offices, and agencies, not including subsections. It employed 6,000.[109] Sometimes ghettos were fortunate to have officials with pre-war experience working in their areas of expertise; others, such as the police, often learned on the job.

The most pressing of needs was food. Starvation and malnutrition shadowed every inhabitant of the ghetto. Children and the elderly were particularly vulnerable. German authorities, reluctant to expend German resources on Jews, often supplied the ghetto with insufficient or inedible supplies. For some ghettos, no food was supplied. In most cases, German authorities sought to extract some form of payment in exchange for food. The Polish underground resistance organization reported on May 23, 1941, that, in the Warsaw ghetto, "Groups of pale and emaciated people wander aimlessly through the overcrowded streets. Beggars sit and lie along the walls and the sight of people collapsing from starvation is common . . . Meanwhile the Germans continue to plunder the wealthy Jews."[110] In Lwów, a boy recalled seeing "people fighting in the street below. One guy was running with a knife and stabbed a man in the back for food. Other people were just sitting in the street dying."[111]

Ghetto communities attempted to alleviate suffering in two ways: official and unofficial (smuggling). Official means consisted of the tireless work of the departments responsible for arranging food shipments into the ghetto

FIGURE 15 *A young boy caught smuggling in the Warsaw ghetto by a German policeman, October 1940–May 1943.*
Source: United States Holocaust Memorial Museum.

as German officials grudgingly supplied some food. However, the food was never in sufficient quantity . . . or quality. A German official in Łódź stated that "preferably the most inferior merchandise" should be sent to the ghetto.[112] In addition, the quantity of food supplied never approached the required daily caloric intake. In Łódź, Jews received less than one and a half pounds of meat, twelve pounds of potatoes, and one egg for an entire month.[113]

In the traditional spirit of Jewish self-help (*kehilla*), ghetto organizations eased conditions somewhat. These efforts resulted in varying levels of success, though they never were sufficient to solely guarantee survival. Before America entered the war, some support came from the American Jewish Joint Distribution Committee. Soup kitchens proliferated. In Warsaw, almost 2,000,000 meals were served in March 1940.[114] In the Lwów ghetto, the Food Supply Department managed a total of 49 distribution sites.[115] The ghetto there also supplied packages of food to the Janowska concentration camp in the city . . . for a certain period of time.[116] In Minsk, the Jewish Council operated a canteen where most of the food "consisted of waste from German kitchens; potato peels were a staple."[117]

Almost immediately, however, smuggling became vital in providing food and other supplies to the ghetto. Jewish councils were often divided in their attitudes toward smuggling. On the one hand, they did not want to antagonize their German overlords but on the other, they recognized the ghetto could not survive without additional sources of food (and fuel). Local non-Jews often took advantage of the situation to enrich themselves in exchange for food. As a survivor from Łwów recalled, "rations for Jews were at a starvation level. We were giving away, piece by piece, what we still had at home in exchange for potatoes, flour, vegetables, and other foodstuffs to supplement the inadequate rations. This was a great opportunity for peasants from the nearby villages . . . The farmers were evading the ban [on illegal trading] not for humanitarian reasons but because they got such good deals in these exchanges."[118] Children, often the most adept smugglers, crawled through small holes in the fence or wall and returned with food. Other food sources included workers employed outside the ghetto who had contact with non-Jews. Historian of the Warsaw ghetto, Ringelblum, recorded in January 1941: "Heard marvelous stories of the smuggling that goes on via the Jewish graveyard. In one night they transported twenty-six cows by that route."[119] Smugglers, of course, risked being killed by German or local police. Sometimes, as in the Kaunas ghetto, smugglers were even arrested by Jewish police. Tory recalled the arrest of a man who had taken up the "ignominious business" of black-marketeering. He wrote that the ghetto population was so frightened of Gestapo reprisals that they were moving out of their homes: "they fear that all the inmates of this street will be arrested."[120]

Despite official and unofficial efforts of the Jewish Councils and ghetto populations, starvation and hunger continued to kill. In addition, it weakened immune systems and, combined with poor sanitation and hygiene, led to the outbreak of disease, particularly typhus. Ironically, therefore, Nazi authorities created precisely the conditions in the ghetto for the epidemics they used as an excuse for ghettoization in the first place. Overcrowding simply multiplied the effect. Even in areas with slightly more space, the locations chosen often lacked sanitation and infrastructure.

As a result, Jewish ghetto administration strove valiantly to provide medical treatment, even when facing a constant shortage of medicine and equipment. Dr. Blady-Szwajger, who worked in the children's hospital in Warsaw described the ghetto doctor's task as "superhuman medicine." "We had our duty as human beings," she later wrote, "but first you had to be made of stone."[121] Everything about the ghetto system made medical care extremely difficult. Indeed, in many places, Germans stole all valuable equipment and supplies from Jewish hospitals. In Częstochowa, the building itself was confiscated. Medical personnel established their own hospitals which varied in size and capability. In Krakow, a former prayer house and Jewish school housed the contagious disease hospital. A "primitive wooden shack" was the hospital in Kutno.[122]

Doctors were often in short supply; many had been murdered by the *Einsatzgruppen* as "Jewish intelligentsia." In the smaller ghetto of Brzeziny (ca. 7,000 inhabitants), the local doctor wrote: "I am the only Jewish doctor in the ghetto . . . A house has been given to us . . . Ladies go around from home to home collecting underwear, beds, dishes, and other things for the hospital."[123] The Kaunas ghetto yearbook noted that "doctors and nurses of the Sanitation Service were often called on to attend to patients at night. To walk around in the ghetto after 10pm is forbidden. With the armbands of the Sanitation Service, they can do their work even at night."[124] Knowing the German fear of epidemic, doctors often sought to hide patients with infectious disease for fear they would be murdered. In Brzeziny, this is precisely what happened as typhus patients were rounded up and killed in a gas van in April 1942.[125] Even with the best of efforts, ghettos remained deadly places. In 1942, Warsaw Jewish authorities reported that the death toll "still hovers around 5,000 per month;" in Łódź, 40 percent of the ghetto was ill by 1944. In three years, 83,000 Jews died of "natural" causes in the Warsaw ghetto.[126]

Despite the daily horrors of ghetto existence, life went on. Orphanages were established for increasing numbers of children without parents. Parents and authorities both were concerned with children, often trying to protect them from the horrors around them. Though the Nazis outlawed education, underground schools flourished. Both religious and secular schools were established. One survivor from Warsaw recalled that "we learned all that from books which were pre-war and out of date, but we learnt with great enthusiasm. People learnt foreign languages: Latin, Greek, German, French, English. People were continuing with higher education; there were university professors who were also giving courses in everything."[127] Schools struggled with the unique conditions of ghetto life. One teacher asked, "How do you make an apathetic, hungry child, who is all the time thinking about a piece of bread, interested in something else?"[128]

Cultural life also flourished in many ghettos, despite restrictions placed upon inhabitants. Renowned Jewish artists, musicians, and writers were naturally interned as well. Many continued to practice their art, even in the oppressive setting of the ghetto. Much of the artistic material created in the ghettos of Eastern Europe was destroyed along with its creators, but some has survived. For example, Władysław Szlengel, a well-known journalist and theater director before the war, became a prolific poet during his time in the Warsaw ghetto. He called himself "the chronicler of those drowning."[129] Szlengel was murdered during the ghetto uprising. Official cultural departments arranged events in many ghettos. Photographer George Kadish documented Kaunas ghetto life in a series of photographs which he hid and retrieved after the war. An entry from the Łódź Ghetto Chronicle illustrates the breadth of cultural activities that took place there in 1941:

FIGURE 16 *Performance of the Kaunas ghetto orchestra. Photo by ghetto inhabitant George Kadish. Kaunas, Lithuania, 1944.*
Source: United States Holocaust Memorial Museum.

In 1941, the House of Culture performed its one hundredth in a series of concerts. This jubilee concert took place on the last day of the year and was devoted to a violin recital by Bronisława Rotszat accompanied by maestro [Teodor] Ryder. The program consisted of works by Bach, Glazunov, and Mozart. Aside from the one hundred concerts, the House of Culture, which was created on March 1, has presented 85 revue performances . . . there were two special shows for children.
ŁODŹ GHETTO CHRONICLE, December 29–31, 1941[130]

Theodor Ryder was a famous conductor who had performed at the Lyons Opera House in France. Even Germans attending his concerts reviewed them positively. One stated, "Ryder led the evening with talent."[131] Orchestras and theatrical performances were common. Cultural events allowed both ghetto inhabitants and the artists themselves some freedom of expression and escape from the hardships of daily life as did religion.

Contrary to Western European Jews, Eastern European Jews were generally more religiously observant. Thus, many approached their persecution from a religious perspective. One example of this response comes from the Kaunas ghetto, where observant Jews turned to their rabbi for advice on their behavior. This was an ancient and critical practice of rabbinical Judaism. Individuals with disputes or questions turned to their rabbi, who would research scripture and come to a resolution. In Kaunas, Rabbi Ephraim Oshry and other rabbis sought to give advice on very new problems. Rabbi Oshry kept notes on the questions he was asked. Some examples are below:

Is one permitted to commit suicide?
Can you take the property of murdered Jews who have no surviving heirs?
May a Jew cook on the Sabbath if he was working in the ghetto soup kitchen?
May a woman who has become pregnant have an abortion?
Can one eat in the presence of a corpse?[132]

The nature and seriousness of such questions indicate the new and awful dilemmas Jews faced in the ghetto.

We owe much of our knowledge of ghetto life to the hundreds of individuals and organizations who dedicated themselves to preserving the history of their experience even in the face of their own deaths. The most well known of these projects was that of Warsaw historian, Emanuel Ringelblum, and the Oneg Shabbat archive he and his colleagues assembled and buried in milk jugs. Ringelblum systematically collected information on every aspect of life in the Warsaw ghetto. Similar efforts were conducted elsewhere. Avraham Tory managed to escape the Kaunas ghetto after hiding his diary and other documents.

One of the most controversial organizations in the ghettos was the Jewish Police, sometimes known as the *Jüdische Ordnungsdienst* (JOD). Nazi officials required the establishment of a police force in the ghetto, ostensibly to deal with day-to-day policing. Often, the police came from the privileged class or intelligentsia or had bribed their way into such a position. A position in the police force was desirable for several reasons. First, it protected the policeman and his family from German authorities and from most deportations. Second, the job usually paid well and offered opportunities for other forms of enrichment, some less ethical than others. For example, in the Warsaw ghetto, police took bribes in exchange for letting ghetto inhabitants remain outdoors after curfew.[133] Daily duties included investigating ordinary crime, maintaining law and order, and controlling smuggling. However, often both the Jewish Councils and the Germans used Jewish Police for tasks related to anti-Jewish policy. Police guarded the ghetto interior, collected taxes and ransoms, escorted inhabitants to slave labor, and ultimately, assisted in rounding up their fellow Jews for deportation. Frequently, the police were threatened with a selection of their own families if they failed. A diarist in Łódź, for example, wrote that "To encourage the Jewish police and the firemen to conduct the operation conscientiously, promises that their closest relations would be spared had been made."[134] In Vilnius, ghetto police handed over the elderly and sick for deportation and were so helpful that German officers praised them for "enforcing a strict regime" and for "handing over to the Gestapo 'Jews who had sinned.'"[135] Without the assistance of the Jewish Police, deportations of Jews would have been more difficult for the Germans, but we must recognize that they would have taken place regardless.

While membership in the police could certainly represent a "choiceless" choice, many ghetto inhabitants had little sympathy for those who joined. A survivor from the Warsaw ghetto stated, "We knew they were treacherous and we disliked them for cooperating with the Germans. I wouldn't do it for anything in the world."[136] Samuel Golfard from the Ukrainian town of Peremyshliany described the corruption of the police during deportations in his diary: "For thousands of złoty and for dollars they saved certain people. In this respect, they were not better or worse than many Germans, who for a bottle of vodka or a can of sardines spared one's life. They [Jewish militia] were just somewhat cheaper."[137] In Lwów, a survivor remembered that "the Jewish police often used their truncheons against their fellow Jews. On the whole, the members of this police force were very unpopular, and the gulf between them and the general population widened daily."[138] Indeed, when the Lwów ghetto police were rounded up and brought to the Janowska concentration camp to be shot, the former ghetto inhabitants took revenge. One prisoner recalled the scene, writing angrily "Before the execution, crowds of inmates rushed at the policemen, savagely beating them. These traitors and Judases had earned their punishment at the hands of their own brothers, and their masters' prize for their faithful service."[139]

However, the situation remained complicated. A former member of the ghetto police in Warsaw remembered that "right from the start, the people of the ghetto developed antagonistic feelings toward the Order Service . . . At every step and every opportunity, the Order Service men were made to feel the community's resentment and this naturally led to the Order Service reacting by closing ranks in defense of their own interests . . . This point of view created selfishness within the Service and contributed enormously to its fall into the whirlpool of decadence."[140] Other observers were more forgiving, or at least pragmatic. One survivor frankly characterized their service by saying, "were the Jewish police traitors . . . to their fellow Jewish brothers? I wouldn't call them traitors. I think it was their way how to survive maybe a little longer, hoping that that they can save their families, when frankly they did it. If they didn't do it somebody else would have done it."[141] In the Vilnius ghetto, resistance leader Abba Kovner singled out the Jewish Police as a "blind tool in the hands of our murderers." However, he pointed out that "you, Jewish policemen, have at least a chance to demonstrate your personal integrity and national responsibility!" Among other things, he demanded that "Any act which threatens Jewish life should not be performed!"[142]

Many Jewish policemen across the ghettos of Eastern Europe heeded such calls. In the Kaunas ghetto during its liquidation, "No less than 140 policemen and officers of the . . . police were arrested and tortured to force them to reveal hiding places of the children and the elderly." All refused, and only seven broke under torture.[143] The Kaunas police also had a high representation in the underground. Other police decided individually to refuse to act against their consciences. In Lwów, during an *Aktion*, a Jewish policeman was ordered to murder Jewish children. He refused, telling the Gestapo he would rather be killed himself. The Nazis then killed him and murdered the children.[144] Police often tried to warn people of forthcoming *Aktions* as well. Even during deportations, some policemen behaved honorably, saving their fellow Jews. One inhabitant of Łódź wrote that "Intervention was possible on the spot, and, in many cases, actions taken by our police proved effective."[145] Despite many actions of rescue and charity, the Jewish police remain an organization many view as tarnished by its behavior during the Holocaust.

The deaths of the ghettos, like their lives, took different forms at different times. As we have seen, some ghettos lasted weeks and some lasted years. The precise timing of ghetto liquidations varied. The ghetto in the small town of Skvira near Kiev, for example, lasted little more than month. On Friday, September 20, 1941 (three months after the invasion), the 850 Jews in the partially fenced-in ghetto were taken to the Jewish cemetery and shot by members of *Einsatzkommando 5*.[146] Conversely, the Łódź and Warsaw ghettos lasted much longer. Larger ghettos were generally liquidated via large-scale deportations to extermination centers. For example, the remaining Jews in the Minsk ghetto were gassed at the Sobibor extermination center in September 1943. The Vilnius ghetto was shot at the Ponary Forest mass shooting site. Nazi authorities simply converted remaining ghetto space into a concentration camp for only working Jews. Only a few ghettos received this designation. Kaunas and Lwów ended their days as these so-called *Judenlagers* or JULAGS. In the end, all ghettos were liquidated in one way or another, with surviving remnants escaping or transferred into the concentration camp system. Death tolls were catastrophic. In Lwów, of the estimated 160,000 Jews in the ghetto in 1941, only 800 resurfaced in the city after the war (and they included people from the surrounding countryside). In most smaller towns throughout Eastern Europe, the liquidation of the ghetto meant the vanishing of centuries-old Jewish communities.

The ghetto formed an essential component of Jewish life during the Holocaust and was a singularly Eastern phenomenon. The concentration of Jews began in a relatively haphazard manner as a temporary measure, as the final disposition of the Jews of Europe evolved in Nazi circles. While ghettoization would eventually be very helpful in organizing the Final Solution, ghettos were not initially established with that end state in mind. The conditions and experiences of the ghettos also illustrate the diversity of responses to Nazi oppression by Jewish communities and the various tactics taken in an attempt to survive the intolerable situation in which ghetto Jews found themselves.

Selected Readings

Engelking, Barbara, and Jacek Leociak. *The Warsaw Ghetto: A Guide to the Perished City*. Translated by Emma Harris. New Haven, CT: Yale University Press, 2009.

Lower, Wendy, ed. *The Diary of Samuel Golfard and the Holocaust in Galicia*. Lanham: Altamira Press in association with United States Holocaust Memorial Museum, 2011.

Michman, Dan. *The Emergence of Jewish Ghettos During the Holocaust*. Cambridge: Cambridge University Press, 2011.

Tory, Avraham, Martin Gilbert, and Dina Porat. *Surviving the Holocaust: The Kaunas Ghetto Diary*. Cambridge, MA: Harvard University Press, 1990.

Trunk, Isaiah. *Judenrat: The Jewish Councils in Eastern Europe under Nazi Occupation*. Lincoln, NE: University of Nebraska Press, 1996.

8

Hitler's Eastern Allies

Introduction

It is becoming more and more evident that the Romanians, obviously with the moral support of the Germans, are utilizing the present period for handling the Jewish problem in their own way. I have it on good authority that Marshal Antonescu has stated . . . that "this is wartime, and a good time to settle the Jewish problem once and for all."

FRANKLIN GUNTHER, US Envoy to Romania, November 4, 1941[1]

Hitler was not without friends in the east, as Marshal Antonescu's comments brazenly show. These allies contributed both to the German war effort and to the Nazi genocidal project. Yet their reasons for joining with Hitler represented a commonality of aims rather than lockstep ideological agreement. Indeed, relations between Hitler and the states allied to him were rarely congenial and usually unequal. By the end of the war, many of these same friends refused to cooperate with Hitler, albeit rarely for humanitarian reasons. As one scholar has noted, "The overpowering image of Hitler dominating Europe and his fixation on the destruction of the Jews hides the actual diversity that existed in Nazi-dominated Europe."[2] This chapter will explore the complexities of Hitler's diplomatic alliances in Eastern Europe and the impact they had on the execution of the Holocaust in each, specifically Romania, Hungary, and Bulgaria. I am intentionally not covering places like Croatia and Slovakia, which, while nominally allies of the Nazis, are better described as puppet states.[3] While these states were willing collaborators in Nazi plans, such collaboration derived mainly from the dominant German influence there. Likewise, Nazi occupied states in which substantial collaboration took place (such as the Baltics and Ukraine) will be discussed later when we examine collaboration. Nazi-allied countries, however, retained a much greater degree of independence and were legitimate nation states; as such, they require a different treatment. I am also not addressing Hitler's main allies of Italy and Japan as they are of lesser importance regarding the Holocaust in Eastern Europe. Italy focused its conquests on North Africa and, to a lesser extent, along the Adriatic while Japan, of course, was focused on Southeast Asia and the Pacific.

The chaos of the end of World War I resulted in the spread of conservative, totalitarian states in Eastern Europe with sizeable far right-wing organizations. These organizations and the authoritarian states in the East became more radical and more violent as a result. Only Czechoslovakia stood out with its democratic government. As a result, overtures of Nazi friendship fell on receptive ears in the East, not least due to the potential threat posed by the Soviet Union. In the interwar period, Germany cast about for allies and made inroads with its future allies through economic influence. Faced with the threat of Soviet influence, these countries reluctantly accepted German alignment instead, often agreeing to arrangements that benefited Germany. As a result, by 1939, a third of Romania's exports went to Germany, half of Hungary's and over two-thirds of Bulgaria's. In addition, Germany became the primary supplier of these countries, providing 40 per cent of Romania's imports, half of Hungary's, and almost two-thirds of Bulgaria's.[4]

Such economic dominance was exacerbated by the abandonment of these countries, particularly Romania, by their former allies, the French. The de facto concession of a sphere of influence in this region to Germany can even be seen in official documents. In January 1936, a British diplomat wrote:

> Since I think everyone is now agreed that it is dangerous to sit indefinitely on the safety-valve, and that Germany must expand somewhere, I feel that there is an overwhelming case for the view that the direction in which Germany can expand with a minimum of danger and inconvenience to British interests (whether political or economic) is in Central and South-Eastern Europe.[5]

Such policies made Germany the only major power with which the dictatorships of Eastern Europe could ally. Indeed, the idea of a "safety valve" evokes the policy of appeasement and the hope that Germany's ambitions could be satisfied by concessions in Eastern Europe.

While Hitler's eastern allies (Romania, Hungary, and Bulgaria,) approached their relationships with Nazi Germany in different ways, we *can* begin with some generalizations that apply to all in varying degrees. First, these states were autonomous and had a great deal of freedom of action. Nazi Germany could not easily dictate their behavior and had to employ at least a minimum of diplomacy. This is important, as we will see that these states had the ability to refuse Nazi demands. Second, while antisemitism was alive and well in these countries, each looked to an alliance with Germany mainly to gain specific, local territorial concessions. They did not share a vision of massive expansion or global domination. Nor was the murder of the Jews a primary motivation. The threat of Soviet expansion proved a much greater motivator. Of course, the Nazi attitude toward the Jews allowed these nations to deal with their own "Jewish problems" as they so chose. Third, each of these countries featured an extreme right wing antisemitic revolutionary movement that would figure prominently in anti-Jewish measures and political responses. Powerful themes of national purification and ethnic community existed in all three. Finally, Romania, Hungary, and Bulgaria, were all governed by forms of authoritarian, dictatorial, monarchies that, while deeply conservative, did not easily align with more extremist right-wing elements. With these general characteristics in mind, however, it is enlightening to examine how and why each of these nations came to be an ally of the Nazi state.

Romania—An Enthusiastic Partner

The way in which the Romanians are dealing with Jews lacks any methods. No objections could be raised against the numerous executions of Jews, but the technical preparations and the executions themselves were totally inadequate. The Romanians usually left the victims' bodies where they were shot, without trying to bury them.

Einsatzgruppe Report, October 30, 1941[6]

Romania was perhaps the most murderous of Hitler's allies (and often described as more brutal, as in the above report). This situation was compounded by the fact that Romania had one of the largest Jewish populations in Europe. In 1930, 756, 930 Jews lived there, including those who lived in territory taken from Russia, Austria, and Hungary at the end of World War I.[7] Romania was also a nation that demonstrated pronounced antisemitism. Throughout much of its history, antisemitism in the largely rural country had been religious and traditional in nature. Though traditional, it was still virulent and "had been a matter of international concern as far back as the nineteenth century."[8] The ultra-nationalist right-wing paramilitary group, the Iron Guard, included this traditional antisemitism in its platform. Indeed, one of the distinguishing characteristics of the Guard was its "quasimystical identification with Romanian Orthodox Christianity." A 1941 editorial emphasized, for example, that "The anti-Semitism of the young generation was not only racial struggle. It asserted the necessity of spiritual war, the Jews representing in their spirit amoral materialism, and the only salvation being embodied in Christianity."[9] The addition of the more modern "Judeo-Bolshevist" concept strengthened this religious antisemitism. Finally, a key element that enhanced the power of Romanian antisemitism was a desire for national ethnic purity. A right-wing ideologue adhered as early as 1909 to the slogan: "Romania for Romanians, all Romanians, and only Romanians."[10]

The desire to reclaim lost territory also factored heavily in Romanian support for the Third Reich. Ever since the Balkan wars of 1912–13, Romania sought to enlarge its territory. In those wars, it had gained the province of Dobrudja in eastern Bulgaria. As a result of World War I, Romania added Transylvania in eastern Hungary and Bessarabia in western Russia. However, as a result of the Nazi-Soviet Pact of 1939, Romania was forced to cede Bessarabia and Bukovina in southern Ukraine to the Soviet Union in 1940. Both Germany and the Soviet Union pressured Romania into surrendering this territory. Germany then compelled Romania, later that same year, to return the northern part of Transylvania to Hungary as part of a diplomatic arrangement between the Nazis and the Hungarians. Romania's territorial gains were completely reversed when it was forced to also return Dobruja to Bulgaria; Romania had lost a large amount of territory and 30 percent of its population.[11] These were shattering losses to King Carol II and to the Romanians as a whole. The extreme right was infuriated and soon acted.

In the interwar period, right wing nationalism and extremism swept across much of Eastern Europe. In Romania, Corneliu Codreanu capitalized on these sentiments. Born in 1919, Codreanu epitomized a generation of extremists (including Heinrich Himmler) who had been born too late to participate in World War I but harbored deep resentments about the war's outcome and the state of their respective nations. An icon of the Archangel Michael allegedly inspired Codreanu in prison to create the Legion of Archangel Michael in June 1927. New members were given a bag of soil from Romanian battlefields to wear and were sworn in annually on the day dedicated to Saint Michael, thus conflating nationalist and religious meanings.[12] Codreanu also imbued his movement with an intense antisemitism. He feared a Jewish takeover of the state and wrote in his memoirs that "when I say 'communists' I mean Jews."[13] The paramilitary wing of the Legion would come to be known as the Iron Guard, and was established to fight communism, the common enemy of both Romania and the Church. This organization challenged the existing government, which it deemed not extreme enough.

King Carol II headed that authoritarian regime beneath a thin veneer of a constitutional monarchy. For the most part, the prime minister ruled with the consent of the King. This arrangement became legal reality in 1938, when a new constitution put the King at the head of a "royal dictatorship."[14] He attempted to appease the far right with antisemitic legislation, but was ultimately unsuccessful politically. The Iron Guard and the Legion continued to challenge his government. King Carol II then took action against them. The King had Codreanu arrested, along with many of his followers, eventually shooting them and dousing their bodies with acid in November 1938.[15] However, even these harsh measures did not destroy the Iron Guard.

Two men, Horia Sima and Ion Antonescu, led an uprising after the loss of Transylvania. They formed what they called the "Legionary State" and forced King Carol II to abdicate in favor of his son, Michael. Under the Legionary State government, Romania joined the Axis, hoping to regain its lost territory. Antonescu became Prime Minister and commanded the Romanian Army. However, relations soured between him and the Iron Guard—led by Sima—which attempted a coup in January 1941. Antonescu crushed the uprising and much of the Iron Guard. Sima and surviving Iron Guard members fled to a somewhat sympathetic Nazi Germany.

At this point, Antonescu's disagreements with the Iron Guard and Horia Sima were political, not ideological. Antonescu's traditional antisemitic views were supplemented by his firm conviction in the Judeo-Bolshevist myth conflating Jews and Communists. In particular, he (and many other Romanians from all walks of life) blamed Jews for the loss of Bessarabia to the Soviets. He frequently used the term "Judeo-Bolshevik" in reference to the Russian-speaking Jews of that region.[16] So, while Sima and many Iron Guard members sheltered in Germany, their ideology was very much alive in Romania and its new dictator.

Thus, Marshal Ion Antonescu would preside over Romania's alliance with Hitler and involvement in the Holocaust. Ion Antonescu was a career military officer and a committed antisemite. His was a complex legacy. As one historian has commented, "He was a war criminal, sending tens of thousands of Jews to their death in Transnistria, and yet he refused to send other Romanian Jews to the death camps in Poland. He was an antisemite and yet, despite the deportations to Transnistria, more Jews survived under his rule than in any other country within Axis Europe."[17] In 1922, the French military attaché described Antonescu as possessing "a well-tried intelligence, brutal, duplicitous, very vain, a ferocious will to succeed . . . together with an extreme xenophobia."[18]

This enigmatic character led Romania into war as a Nazi ally. Romania officially joined the Axis powers on November 23, 1940, for several reasons. First, it sought German protection from the Soviet Union, to whom it had already lost land (largely by German design). Indeed, a Romanian diplomat remarked to a British diplomat that "Nothing could put Romania on Germany's side except the conviction that only Germany could keep the Soviets out of Romania."[19] Second, and following from the first, was the hope that Romania would regain its lost territory with Germany's help (and influence over Hungary). Third, Romania was already closely tied economically to Germany, having agreed in 1939 to granting Germany 25 percent of its oil exports.[20] Germany's dependence on Romanian oil would increase dramatically as the war progressed. Romania became one of Nazi Germany's closest allies. Hitler liked Antonescu and "no other leader Hitler met other than Mussolini ever received such consistently favorable comments from the German dictator."[21] Hermann Goering declared him to be "quite a stubborn mule but the only one in Romania who sticks to a pro-German line."[22] Romania supplied 585,000 soldiers to Hitler's war on the Soviet Union and has been termed "on par with Italy as a principal ally of Germany and not in the category of minor Axis satellite."[23]

The outbreak of the war on the Soviet Union proved not only Romania's loyalty to Hitler, but also the lethal effects of its national variety of anti-semitism. Romania has been singled out as a particularly brutal ally, not least because it carried out much of its anti-Jewish violence without pressure from the Nazis. When the Nazis attacked the USSR, Romanian Armies invaded and reconquered the territory of Bessarabia they had lost a year earlier. Romanian Deputy Prime Minister Mihai Antonescu (no relation) called for a "complete ethnic liberation." "Let us be ruthless so as not to miss this opportunity. No one should allow himself to be seduced by humanitarian philosophy," he declared, "The act of ethnic cleansing will involve removal or isolation of all Jews in labor camps, from which they will no longer exert their nefarious influence."[24] With this brutal philosophy ringing in their ears, Romanian troops entered Bessarabia. The Iasi pogrom (discussed in Chapter 6), which occurred a week after the invasion and *within* the pre-war borders of Romania, serves as evidence of the power and influence of Mihai Antonescu's message. In addition, orders issued by Antonescu to the Army encouraged anti-Jewish violence as they were authorized to "do with the Jews' lives and property as they saw fit 'within the first 24 hours of the occupation.' "[25] This guidance to the military very much resembled the criminal orders issued to the *Wehrmacht* prior to Operation Barbarossa.

Romania's initial violence against Jews characterized much of their operations in the Soviet Union. In return for its participation in the war, Romania received the area between the rivers Bug and Dniester in what is now the country of Moldova. Included in this territory was the major city of Odessa on the Black Sea. Antonescu dubbed this new Romanian "province" Transnistria, with Odessa as its capital. Transnistria encompassed 24,840 square miles, an area roughly the size of Latvia.[26] Before Romania could consolidate its new territory, disaster struck in Odessa. The city had been tenaciously defended and was not captured until October 16, 1941. Six days later, a delayed bomb left behind by the retreating Soviets exploded. The blast killed 67 people, including the Romanian Army commander of the city and many high-ranking officers. Antonescu responded immediately with fury, ordering on October 23 that "immediate retaliatory action, including the liquidation of 18,000 Jews in the ghettos and the hanging in the town squares of at least 100 Jews for every regimental sector." The surviving chief of staff of the 4th Romanian Army replied the same day, reporting that "Retaliatory action has been taken within the city via shooting [and] hanging . . . the execution of the Jews in the ghettos is well on the way to reaching the aforementioned number." The Romanians had declined the help of an SS Regiment in this endeavor.[27] The Jewish population of Odessa at the time was approximately 80,000. The violence against them was beyond brutal. Jews were crowded into warehouses in a suburb of the city. Romanian soldiers and police surrounded and torched the buildings, shooting any Jews attempting to escape. A horrified Romanian officer reported that:

> In an attempt to escape the agonies of the fire, some appeared at the windows and signaled to the soldiers to shoot them, pointing to their heads and hearts. But when they saw the guns pointed at them, they disappeared from the window for a brief moment, only to reappear a few seconds later and signal to the soldiers once again. Then they turned their backs to the window in order not to see the soldiers shooting at them ... Some women threw their children out the window.[28]

On October 24, Marshal Antonescu issued a personal order, No. 563, that a group of Jews be forced into a building full of explosives and then blown up, in symbolic retaliation for the bombing of the headquarters. This order was dutifully carried out the next day at the precise time the original Soviet bomb had exploded.[29] Romanians murdered approximately 20,000 Jews from Odessa during this massacre. The remainder was placed in ghettos.

Yet this killing paled in comparison to the larger plans that Antonescu had for Romanian Jews. Unlike the Nazis, who viewed the peoples they conquered in the East as primarily foreign and inferior, many Romanians saw the return of Bukovina and Bessarabia as the return of ancestral Romanian land. They also found much greater local support from ethnic Romanians.[30] Thus, Antonescu sought to cleanse this Romanian territory of the Jews, whom he considered disloyal and alien. This had been his plan for quite some time. In September 1940, he had proclaimed that

> I will solve the Jewish problem simultaneously with my reorganization of the state by gradually replacing Jews in the national economy with Romanian public servants ... Jewish property shall be largely nationalized in exchange for indemnities ... Jews will be allowed to live, yet they will not be allowed to capitalize on the resources of this country. Romanians must benefit first.[31]

By 1941, this plan had become even more radical. Antonescu decided that all Jews living in the reclaimed Romanian territories of Bessarabia and Bukovina should be killed or deported to Transnistria, which would serve as a dumping ground in much the same way as the Nazis envisioned the *Generalgovernment* earlier. On July 8, Antonescu told his ministers, "I am for the forced migration of the entire Jewish element from Bessarabia and Bukovina, which must be thrown over the border."[32] This planned ethnic cleansing is further apparent in the orders passed on by Romanian Army and police officials. The inspector General of the Gendarmerie, General Constantin Vasiliu told his men in Bessarabia that "The first measure you must undertake is cleansing the land. By cleansing the land we understand: exterminate on the spot all Jews in rural areas; imprison in ghettos all Jews in urban areas."[33] Such killings took place as early as July 9, after the Army was given an order "for the removal of the Judaic element from Bessarabian territory."[34] Throughout the newly occupied territories, Romanian forces murdered Jews. Yet carrying out an ethnic cleansing of Bessarabia and Bukovina was no small task; it would require the murder or deportation of 277,000 Jews as well as the Roma, who were also targeted by the regime for removal.[35] Transit camps and ghettos were established in Bessarabia and elsewhere in anticipation of deportations to Transnistria.

While local pogroms and mass killings continued, between 147,712 and 170,737 Romanian Jews were deported to Transnistria from newly reoccupied territories.[36] Both the journey and the conditions in Transnistria were appalling and lethal. Romanian soldiers and police forced the Jews on long, forced marches to crossing points over the Dniester and Bug rivers into Transnistria. Guards shot those who could not keep up and roving bands of local villagers robbed the marchers. The roads were littered with bodies, which the Germans noted disapprovingly. Organized rape occurred regularly during the deportations. In other instances, Jews were placed in sealed freight cars without food and water for days for the trip to Transnistria. As in other parts of Eastern Europe, the deportation of the Jews was accompanied by a massive program of individual and systematic looting. The National Bank of Romania facilitated this, receiving the currency and valuables stolen from Jews from the areas to be "cleansed." It also carried out a systematic defrauding of Jews forced to turn in valuable and exchange currency below market value.

Several concentration camps were established in Transnistria to receive incoming Jews, the most notorious being the Bogdanovka camp. When the Germans refused to accept Romanian Jews into their occupied territory, the Romanian government ordered the execution of 30,000. Interestingly, the commander of the gendarmerie at Bogdanovka, Sgt. Maj. Nicolae Melinescu, though a brutal antisemite, refused to obey orders to murder the thousands of prisoners in the camp and was fired.[37] At the end of August 1941, the provincial governor of Bessarabia could proclaim, "The Jewish problem has been solved in Bessarabia. Today, in the Bessarabian villages there are no longer any Jews, while in towns, ghettos have been set up for those remaining."[38]

Conditions in Transnistria for deportees—both in camps and without— were simply unfit for survival. A representative example of this is the Golta District in northern Transnistria. The prefect in charge of the district, Modest Isopescu, described a "Jewish nightmare" as he was overwhelmed with sick, malnourished, and exhausted Jews while still trying to cope with the corpses of earlier arrivals. His November 1941 report to the governor of Transnistria echoes those from the GG. He notes that 8,000 Jews died in one village from typhus and starvation and laments another "9,000 Yids were sent from Odessa. This means that, counting those who were already there and those who have meanwhile arrived, there are currently 11,000 Yids housed on the state farm in pigsties that could barely accommodate 7,000 pigs." After noting that the police could not keep pace with the burials required, Isopescu concludes by pleading with his superior, "Implore you to stop ordering Yids to be sent to this region."[39] An analysis of the available documentation indicates that by November 15, 1943, Romanian authorities murdered between 104,522 and 120,810 Romanian Jews in Transnistria via starvation, illness, and execution.[40] The region became known as the Kingdom of Death.

However, by 1943, Romanian anti-Jewish policy changed drastically. At a meeting in October 1942, the forced deportation of Jews to Transnistria was stopped. Mihai Antonescu passed on Marshal Antonescu's "decision to suspend the deportations of Jews to Transnistria."[41] Already in 1942, Antonescu had postponed the deportation of Romanian Jews to the Bełżec extermination center (from pre-war Romania), despite intense German pressure. By 1944, the Romanian government allowed Jews to return from Transnistria and emigrate to Palestine. Despite its unhappiness with this behavior, Germany could not force a change in Romanian behavior, not least because it still relied heavily on Romanian oil.

Why did Romania execute such a reversal in its support of the Holocaust in the East? It should be emphasized that these decisions did *not* stem from a sudden humanitarian change of heart in the Romanian government. Rather, from a much more pragmatic standpoint, Romanian and German goals had simply diverged. As noted earlier, anti-Jewish policy never held the prime importance for Romania that it did for Germany. Romania had also sacrificed many soldiers and resources for the Nazis in exchange for little of value and little hope of additional territory in the future. In addition, Romania faced pressure from a variety of sources, which probably combined to end its cooperation with Nazi Germany. First, prominent Jewish leaders in Romania marshaled not inconsiderable political opposition to Antonescu's policies. Dr. Wilhelm Filderman, a former classmate of Antonescu, led the Jewish community and was instrumental in the shift in policy. As the Romanian minister for internal affairs remarked, "The eyes of all the Jews were turned toward Filderman."[42]

Filderman rallied support from other political parties and from those close to Antonescu. Chief Rabbi Alexandru Safran assisted him by lobbying contacts in foreign governments. Some Romanian intellectuals also opposed the anti-Jewish policies, penning a 1942 memorandum that asked "How can we condemn the oppression of our brothers, who are living outside Romania's current borders, when we are about to exterminate a minority population whose right to live has been guaranteed by those same visionaries who sanctified our national borders?"[43] This memorandum allegedly also had a strong impact on King Michael and the queen mother. The United

States also began to pressure Romania to depart from its current course, demonstrating its interest in the deportations to Transnistria.

Deputy Minister Mihai Antonescu, largely responsible for carrying out Romanian anti-Jewish policy, began to enact a series of concessions, including an end to extermination policy in Transnistria, permission for more aid to deportees, repatriation of expelled Jews, and financial support for Jewish relief efforts in Romania and Transnistria (taken, of course, from money already extorted from Jewish communities).[44] Such political change was possible because Romania remained an independent state, free—to a large degree—from German control, and remaining important due to Nazi dependence on its oil. Thus, domestic political forces could still have considerable influence. Nothing illustrated this more clearly than the arrest of Marshal Antonescu in August 1944 by King Michael, when Antonescu had refused to accept a peace offer from the Allies.[45] Antonescu's arrest ended the alliance with Hitler and Romania became an allied country for the remainder of the war. While these measures did save a large number of Jews, Romania under Antonescu murdered around 220,000 Romanian Jews and 180,000 Ukrainian Jews in its occupied territories.[46] The Romanian state was, therefore, second only to Nazi Germany in numbers of Jews murdered.

Hungary: The Admiral and the Sinking Ship

I find the evolution of the Jewish question of such far-reaching importance that it may have a decisive impact on German-Hungarian relations, nay ... I must state in full knowledge of my responsibility that it will in fact become decisive.

Hungarian Ambassador to Germany, DÖME SZTÓJAY, 1940[47]

When the Nazis occupied Hungary in March 1944, Admiral Miklós Horthy stoically proclaimed, "I have sworn to the country not to forsake it. I am still an admiral. The captain cannot leave his sinking ship."[48] As captain, Horthy was naturally also responsible in large part for steering his nation's course. This included determining the degree of participation in German anti-Jewish measures as his ambassador noted above. Hungary's involvement, like that of Hitler's other allies, was also complex in its own ways, but it also had similar interests. Even into 1944, the vast majority of its Jews remained untouched and it became a haven for those fleeing the Nazis.

Since the interwar period, the new state of Hungary (created by the destruction of the Austro-Hungarian Empire) had been led by Miklós Horthy—an aristocratic admiral without a navy in a landlocked state serving as the regent to an absent king. Horthy, however, had ensured that before taking this position, he had secured all the powers of a monarch. He was described as an "absolutely honest and sincere man ... of sterling honesty but of no great cleverness."[49] Like many in Eastern Europe, Horthy feared and despised Bolshevism and the Soviet Union. The brief rule by the communist government of Bela Kun exacerbated this anti-Bolshevik sentiment in Hungary, as did the prominence of some Jews in his government. Horthy desired the removal of Jews as a self-proclaimed antisemite, and yet he likely did not support their physical extermination. He was also pragmatic and once noted that in a war between England and Germany, the former "will inevitably win."[50]

Like Romania, Hungary also harbored territorial ambitions and grudges it hoped could be remedied through an alliance with Nazi Germany. With the end of World War II, where Hungary had been part of the defeated Austro-Hungarian Empire, it lost two-thirds of its territory, a third of its ethnic Hungarian (Magyar) community, and three-fifths of its total population.[51] These painful losses kindled right-wing agitation throughout the country. Despite Hitler's anger over Hungary's refusal to participate in the Polish campaign and its sheltering of Polish soldiers, he developed a close relationship with Hungary, recognizing its utility in the forthcoming campaign against the Soviet Union. For his part, Horthy sought an opportunity to regain territory and to receive protection from a menacing Soviet Union. A close relationship with Hitler began to remedy Hungary's territorial losses in 1938, when it received the Carpatho-Ruthenia region of Czechoslovakia. In August 1940, Hungary received the contested region of Northern Transylvania from Romania. Hungary joined the Axis on November 23, 1940. In 1941, it would also receive territory from the defeated Yugoslavia. In return, Hungary supplied troops for the invasion of the Soviet Union in June 1941.

At home, Horthy faced a similar situation as the Romanians. While he represented a conservative, aristocratic, anti-Communist, and antisemitic ruling class, more extreme right-wing groups that identified more closely with Nazi ideology consistently challenged him. The most prominent of these was the Arrow Cross party. Headed by Ferenc Szálasi, a retired army officer and diagnosed schizophrenic psychopath, the Arrow Cross clamored for both more radical action against Jews, an ethnic Magyar state, and a social revolution threatening the position of the old guard like Horthy.[52] For both the Arrow Cross and many ordinary Hungarians, foreign "unassimilated" Jews, characterized as "Eastern" or "Galician" were not considered Hungarian and needed to be removed from the nation.[53] The Arrow Cross was not as dominant as the Iron Guard, but gained enough of a following that Horthy and his government felt that the passage of antisemitic legislation would appease them and decrease their popular support.

An early example of Hungarian antisemitic measures was the 1920 "Numerus Clausus" Act, which limited access to universities for Jews to only 6 percent of total enrollment. As relations with Germany became closer, antisemitic legislation and discrimination increased. A series of three so-called "Jewish Laws" represent this escalation in anti-Jewish discrimination. The First Jewish Law (May 1938) limited the number of Jews in the professions and in financial, commercial, and industrial businesses to 20 percent. The Second Jewish Law (May 1939) reduced the acceptable percentage to 6 percent and also attempted to provide a legal definition for who was a Jew. The Third Jewish Law (August 1941), a replication of the Nazi 1935 Nuremberg Laws, prohibited marriages and sexual relationships between Jews and non-Jews.[54] While these measures were certainly detrimental to Jewish economic concerns, they still left much of Hungarian Jewish life relatively unaffected. Indeed, Hungary would serve as a destination for Jews fleeing other areas of Eastern Europe for much of the war.

One area in which Hungarian Jews *did* suffer in a particularly extreme fashion was in the military labor system. Unlike most countries, beginning in 1919, the Hungarian military operated a quasi-military labor service for "unreliable elements" (Communists, other nationalities, and Jews) who could not be trusted to serve "honorably" in the Hungarian Army. Their tasks consisted largely of building roads and fortifications, carrying supplies, and clearing minefields. Initially, this system operated relatively fairly, limiting forced service to three months and offering the same pay, rations, and family benefits as it did to Christian recruits in the army.[55] However, over time, the system became radicalized. With a new series of regulations, all Jews of military age were eligible to be conscripted for at least two years. Their identification cards were marked with a "Zs" identifying them as a "Zsidó," (Jew) and they were forced to wear an armband for the same purpose.[56] Jews served in separate companies from Christians and their treatment and living conditions were far more brutal. Members of the Labor Service dug fortifications in freezing conditions, pulled wagons, received grossly inadequate clothing, and cleared minefields by marching through them or with their bare hands. One Labor Service base commander "allegedly instructed his company commanders to make sure the labor servicemen did not come back home alive, since they were the enemies of the state."[57] This particularly Hungarian form of annihilation through military labor was terribly effective. Of the 50,000 Jews conscripted between 1942 and 1944, approximately 42,000 died or were murdered.[58]

Jews in the Labor Service were not the only ones at great risk in Hungary. With the start of the war against the Soviet Union, antisemitic authorities in the Hungarian National Central Alien Control Office (KEOKH) prepared a plan to deport "foreign" Jews from the territories recently added to Hungary, in particular, from the Carpatho-Ruthenia region in what is now western Ukraine. The KEOKH sought to "expel from Carpatho-Ruthenia all persons of dubious citizenship and to hand them over to the German authorities in Eastern Galicia."[59] These "dubious" citizens consisted of Jews from Poland, Austria, Germany, Slovakia, and quite a few Hungarian Jews unable to prove their citizenship in the short time allowed. As in Romania, this deportation action was justified in terms of creating an ethnically homogenous Magyar state. These Jews were rounded up and deported via freight car to the border with the Nazi General Government, newly enlarged to

FIGURE 17 *Hungarian Jews stand by the open door of a cattle car while awaiting deportation to a forced labor battalion. Hungary, November 1940.*
Source: United States Holocaust Memorial Museum.

include Galicia. By the end of August 1941, approximately 18,000 had been forced across the border to Kamenets-Podolsk. German authorities were surprised and overwhelmed by the numbers and requested an end to the deportations. The Hungarians agreed to stop the deportations but refused to accept any Jews back into the country.

The Higher SS and Police Leader for the area, Friedrich Jeckeln, then agreed to carry out the murder of these Jews by September 1. True to his word, mass executions took place from August 27 to 28. Jeckeln's personal SS staff company and Police Battlion 320 murdered the around 18,000 deported Hungarian Jews at a former munitions depot near Kamenets-Podolsk. A local inhabitant recalled "a group of 8,000 defenseless Hungarians [Jews], who came to us in Kamenets-Podolsk from Hungary. They walked in rows of four and had their children with them or carried them in their arms."[60] A former German policeman recalled that at the end of the execution, Jeckeln himself "pointed specifically to one Jew, who was wearing a grey suit and who made an especially respectable impression. In very dramatic way he called this Jew by name and declared essentially: 'Look at this man. He is a typical Jew who must be exterminated so that we Germans can live.' "[61] A local Jew remembered that "Several days afterward, both day and night frightful noises were heard from the graves."[62] However, when the Hungarian Minister of the Interior, Ferenc Keresztes-Fischer, learned of the massacre, he immediately ordered an end to the deportations. The Hungarian Army carried out a mass killing in Délvidék (Yugoskavia) that targeted both Jews and Serbs and also was widely condemned in government circles. Such conflicting policies within the Hungarian government characterized internal differences in attitudes toward the Holocaust not present in Germany.

As in Romania, the fortunes of war and increasing Nazi pressure for more cooperation in anti-Jewish policy began to strain relations between Hungary and Germany. On the Eastern front in January 1943, the 2nd Hungarian Army lost 50 percent of its men in the Soviet Union and was practically destroyed.[63] After the loss of Stalingrad, it became increasingly clear that Germany would lose the war. In addition, Hitler's closest ally, Mussolini, was deposed later that year and Italy joined the allies. Admiral Horthy and his Prime Minister, Miklós Kállay, began looking for ways to distance themselves from the Nazis. First and foremost, they wanted to avoid Soviet occupation.

As Hitler became more and more concerned with the lack of Hungarian enthusiasm for both the war and the Final Solution, he summoned Horthy to the Klessheim Palace in Salzburg, Austria on April 16, 1943. The Führer reiterated the importance of the Jewish question but Horthy stated, "I had done everything I could against the Jews within the limits of decency, but I can hardly murder them or do away with them in some other way."[64] While Nazi Germany attempted to apply pressure on the Horthy government by increased support for the Arrow Cross, Kállay repeatedly declined German requests for the deportation of Hungarian Jews, citing their necessity in industry and therefore their importance to the German war effort as well.[65] He made this clear in a speech he gave in June 1943. While agreeing that Hungary had to solve its Jewish "problem," Kállay declined to "keep this problem on the agenda so long as the basic prerequisite of the solution, namely the answer to the question where the Jews are to be resettled is not given. Hungary will never deviate from those precepts of humanity which, in the course of history, it has always maintained in racial and religious questions." As the great Holocaust historian, Raul Hilberg, summarizd: "In the shrouded terminology of the Axis world, a man could not have said 'no' more clearly than Kállay had done in this speech."[66] In addition, Prime Minister Kállay began to seek a possible negotiated surrender to the Allies. In March 1944, Horthy was again summoned to the Klessheim Palace where Hitler informed him that the Germans would be occupying Hungary. Horthy agreed to the transfer of 300,000 Jewish "workers" to Germany.

German troops occupied Hungary on March 19, 1944. The relatively moderate Prime Minister Kállay resigned and was replaced by the pro-German Döme Sztójay, the former ambassador to Germany. Horthy's decision not to resign as Kállay did had several decisive repercussions for Hungarian Jews. First, he "contributed to the placement of the entire Hungarian state apparatus at the service of the Germans." Second, he calmed the population and "assured the maintenance of law and order that the Germans desired." Third, he became complicit in the crimes of the extremist Arrow Cross, which he had hoped to prevent by remaining part of the government. Lastly, while remaining part of the government, he effectively withdrew from the day-to-day decision-making, abandoning Hungarian Jews to German policies by his inaction.[67] As one historian described it, "Horthy abstained from any kind of political activity of practical importance for three months."[68] Nor did he appear to be opposed to German measures. Indeed, a Nazi official testified at his trial that:

> Horthy himself told me that he was interested only in protecting those who were prosperous, the economically valuable Jews in Budapest, those who were well off. However, as to the remaining Jewry—and he used a very ugly term there—he had no interest in them and was quite prepared to have them go to the Reich or elsewhere for labor.[69]

While Horthy did not explicitly consent to their murder, he certainly was aware by this point of the exterminationist form that the Final Solution had taken, and this statement has been corroborated by a variety of sources.[70]

In addition, more right wing extremists took up important positions in the cabinet. The new Sztójay government was, therefore, receptive to the arrival of two key Nazi functionaries, Edmund Veesenmayer and Ernst Kaltenbrunner, who were to assure Hungary's continued cooperation with Germany. Vessenmayer in particular was tasked with the overall deportation of Hungarian Jews. In addition, the Nazis sent in a special SS detail, led by their deportation specialist, SS-Obersturmbannführer Adolf Eichmann. He and his team immediately got to work in the spring and summer of 1944 on the task of deporting Hungarian Jews to Auschwitz. Eichmann and his staff divided Hungary into zones and began deporting Jews by zone by the end of April. From May 14, roughly four trains left the country each day, packed with 3,000 people each. The victims were mainly Jews from the provincial zones. By the beginning of July 1944, 437,000 Jews had been deported to Auschwitz, with most of them being murdered upon arrival.[71]

At this point, Horthy reemerged on the scene demanding an end to the deportations. It appears that a combination of outside pressures brought about this policy rather than a change of heart. At the end of June, Horthy had received requests from Pope Pius XII and the King of Sweden to end the deportations. The United States under President Roosevelt had been more insistent, demanding an end to the deportations and a "cessation of all

FIGURE 18 *Hungarian soldiers look at the corpses of eight Jews they have just executed on the bank of the Danube. Hungary, 1944.*
Source: United States Holocaust Memorial Museum.

anti-Jewish measures" and then underscoring these demands with "an unusually heavy air raid on Budapest" on July 2.[72] In what was perhaps some calculated theatrics, Horthy told his Council of Ministers that "I shall not tolerate this any further! I shall not permit the deportations to bring further shame on the Hungarians! . . . The deportations of the Jews of Budapest must cease! The Government must take the necessary steps!"[73] Even after Horthy's decree, Eichmann sought with mixed success to circumvent it by deporting more Jews. At this point, the Budapest zone was the only one untouched by Eichmann's handiwork.

Once again, Himmler and the SS found their plans for Hungarian Jews stymied. The situation came to a head with Horthy's official overtures to the Soviets and intent to surrender Hungary, knowing that the Allies could not support him. On October 15, 1944, before Horthy could broadcast Hungary's surrender, his son was arrested by the Nazis and used to force Horthy's abdication. He was replaced by Arrow Cross leader Ferenc Szálasi the next day. The Nazis were less than enthusiastic about their new ally. Hitler was unimpressed and famed general Heinz Guderian aptly described him having "little ability and less tact." In describing the meeting with Hitler, he recalled, "The conversation was awkward. The new man did not give the impression of one from whom much might be expected. He seemed to have risen in the world almost against his will. We had no allies anymore."[74]

The new truly puppet government under Szálasi authorized the restarting of deportations, which, while still deadly, were less catastrophic due to logistical difficulties and the dismantling of the gas chambers in Auschwitz.[75] The Jews in the Budapest ghetto still suffered mass killings at the hands of the Arrow Cross but, 163 days after Szálasi took power, the Red Army conquered Budapest, liberating over 100,000 Jews.

Bulgaria: The Reluctant Accomplice

> AGREEMENT
> for the deportation of the first 20,000 Jews from the new Bulgarian lands Thrace and Macedonia into the German eastern regions
> *attained between*
> Bulgarian Commissar for Jewish Questions, Mr. Aleksandur Belev, on one side, and German plenipotentiary, Captain of the Defense Detachment [SS-Hauptsturmführer] Theodor Dannecker, on the other side.
> 1. After confirmation by the Council of Ministers, in the new Bulgarian lands Thrace and Macedonia will be prepared
> 20,000 Jews without regard to age and sex-for deportation.
> The German Reich is ready to accept these Jews in their eastern regions.
>
> DANNECKER-BELEV AGREEMENT, February 22, 1943[76]

If Romania was quite willing to murder its Jews within its own borders and Hungary content to allow the Nazis to do the killing, Bulgaria was a most reluctant partner in the Holocaust. While allied with Nazi Germany, Bulgaria was the only Axis nation that did not send troops to aid in the invasion of the Soviet Union. Even volunteers were not permitted to participate. In fact, Bulgaria never even declared war on the Soviet Union.[77] It also managed to refuse implementation of the Final Solution more successfully than either Romania or Hungary. As a result, some have attempted to compare Bulgaria favorably to Denmark, which through extraordinary efforts rescued most of its Jewish population. One Bulgarian historian went so far as to claim that his country could recall its "history with pride, thanks to the collective protection they provided the Jews under the control." He refers to this as a "miraculous occurrence of goodness."[78] This "miracle" would be cold comfort to the over 11,000 Macedonian and Thracian Jews the Bulgarians deported in the Dannecker-Belev Agreement above, the majority of whom died in the gas chambers of Treblinka and Auschwitz. The situation in Bulgaria was more complex and this characterization may well represent wishful thinking more than reality. On the other hand, Bulgaria stands out both in its position in the Nazi solar system and its refusal to carry out most Nazi directives regarding the Final Solution.

The reluctance of Bulgaria to become a more active partner in Nazi genocidal policy stems in part from the less virulent and widespread antisemitism in the country. Leading historian on Bulgaria, Frederick Chary, has concluded that "On the whole, Bulgaria had less antisemitism than other countries of the Western World."[79] The Nazis themselves recognized this, as the German representative for Jewish Affairs in Bulgaria reported to Berlin that: "Having lived all their lives with Armenians, Greeks and gypsies, the Bulgarians see no harm in the Jew to justify special measures against him."[80] Bulgaria was home to 63,400 Jews, most of whom were Sephardic, having fled Spain in the 16th and 17th centuries.[81] The relatively small number of Jews (1 % of a more ethnically diverse population) likely contributed to the decreased strength and frequency of antisemitism in Bulgaria.[82] In addition, Jewish life in Bulgaria was "peculiar," as Jews were not nearly as visible in professional life or connected to a ruling nobility.[83] In addition, while there *was* an antisemitic, right wing, fascist organization, the *Ratsnitsi*, its numbers were relatively small and its focus lay on recovering territory. Unlike the Iron Guard or the Arrow Cross, it played little role in government at any point.

If Bulgaria was somewhat unlike Romania and Hungary in its attitude toward the Jews, it was similar to its neighbors in its politics. A dictatorial king, Boris III, governed Bulgaria as of 1935. His was a conservative regime, but not completely authoritarian; via a weak parliament, the people could provide *some* input to their government. Boris III's most pressing concerns were primarily territorial as well. Bulgaria sought the return of the Dobruja region in eastern Romania as well as Thrace and Macedonia. All of these territories had been reconquered during World War I and then lost due to Bulgaria's participation on the side of Germany. Many Bulgarians viewed these as traditional Bulgarian territories and demanded that they once again become part of the mother country. In these designs, Bulgaria resembled Romania and Hungary. Apart from Dobruja which brought it in conflict with Romania, however, most of Bulgarias's territorial claims were directed west against Greece and the newly formed nation of Yugoslavia.

King Boris III viewed an alliance with Nazi Germany as a relatively inexpensive way to retrieve these territories. The two nations were already economically close after all. Bulgaria began to enter Germany's sphere of influence in the 1930s via closer and closer economic ties. Nazi Germany became Bulgaria's chief trading partner, accounting for 65.5 percent of its imports and 67.8 percent of its exports by 1939. Perhaps more importantly, Bulgaria received much of its military equipment from Germany, strengthening its Nazi ties almost automatically in case of war.[84] After a series of negotiations and through pressure exerted by Germany, Bulgaria rejoiced over the return of Dobruja as a result of the Vienna Award of September 7, 1940.[85] In addition, most Bulgarians viewed the Soviet Union as a natural enemy. As the Bulgarian Prime Minister Bogdan Filov noted in his diary, "We cannot gain anything from an English victory, for a failure of German arms inevitably means we shall be 'Bolshevized.' "[86] Still, Boris III remained reticent to fully commit to Hitler, only signing the Tripartite Pact in March 1941, four months after Romania and Hungary. Bulgaria's delay in declaring war on England until December 1941 further illustrates the King's reluctance. However, after the Nazi invasion of Yugoslavia and Greece in April 1941, Bulgaria received the territories of Thrace and Macedonia. It now stood firmly in the Nazi camp, but limited its participation in the Nazi war effort to the passage of troops and supplying its allies. No Bulgarian troops entered the Soviet Union.

A shift to the right in the Bulgarian government in 1940 accompanied its closer connections to Germany. Indeed, both public and official antisemitism increased beginning in 1939. A new government was formed, headed by Prime Minister Bogdan Filov. Filov was an art historian and had previously served as the Minister of Education. He was also German-educated and retained close ties with the country.[87] Filov was not an extremist, but he certainly identified with some elements of the right and with Nazi goals. For example, he promoted Petar Gabrovski to the position of Minister of the Interior even though Gabrovski had been a member of the *Ratnitsi* and was a rabid antisemite. Filov also oversaw the passing of the first antisemitic law in Bulgaria: the Law for the Protection of the Nation (abbreviated ZZN in Bulgarian). This law, which took effect on January 23, 1941, was explicitly modeled on the Nuremberg Laws and other Nazi official discrimination against Jews. The ZZN prohibited marriage between Jews and non-Jews, but took a "fundamentally religious approach in defining Jews, excluding converts to Christianity and those [already] married to ethnic Bulgarians."[88] This legislation and others persecuted Jews and expelled them from Bulgarian society. A *numera clausus* or quota was established in many professions, limiting Jewish membership. Jewish businesses and employment were curtailed and property confiscated. Jewish men between 20 and 40 were condemned to forced labor, where they did construction work.[89] Gabrovski created a Commissariat for Jewish Questions and appointed his friend, Alexander Belev, as Commissioner. Belev was a die-hard *Ratnitsi* member and antisemite. In fact, he had traveled to Nazi Germany to research its anti-Jewish laws in preparation for similar measures in Bulgaria.

Official acts of discrimination were certainly devastating to the Bulgarian Jewish community, but they were "unenthusiastically" supported by King Boris III.[90] Communications from top Nazi officials themselves prove their irritation with this lack of enthusiasm. A high-level SS counterintelligence officer in the Reich Security Main Office (RSHA) complained in 1942 that Boris "himself has intervened through various people of his intimate circle directly in various cases in favor of the Jews." He also lamented the relatively sporadic wearing of the yellow star and believed that the Jews "are now actually proud of their badges."[91]

The same cannot be said of Bulgarian treatment of Jews in their newly occupied territories of Thrace, and Macedonia. In these places, Jews were not seen as Bulgarian citizens at all and enjoyed no protection from the government. Indeed, like Romania and Hungary, Bulgarian policy sought to "purify" these lands in order to better absorb them into the "Old Kingdom." Still, drastic actions against the Jews in these regions did not begin immediately. The Commissioner for Jewish Affairs, Alexander Belev, reported to Grabovski from Berlin in June 1942 that "The radical solution of the Jewish problem in our country would be the deportation of the Jews and simultaneous confiscation of their property." Though uncertain of the final disposition of the Jews, he emphasized that, "In the meantime until conditions for deportation of the Jews are created it is imperative that the measures concerning the Jews be strengthened . . . "[92] These measures extended to the newly occupied territories and seriously impacted Jewish life there. Jews here could not become Bulgarian citizens (as other ethnicities could if they wished). As one survivor from the small town of Monastir in Macedonia wrote, "Thus life was so greatly changed and there were no more get-togethers, no festivals, no weddings, no celebrations."[93]

The task of the disposition of Bulgaria's Jews fell to *SS-Hauptsturmführer* Theodor Dannecker who arrived in the capital, Sofia, in January 1943. Dannecker, one of Adolf Eichmann's deportation experts, had previously organized the rounding up and deportation of 13,000 French Jews to Auschwitz and hoped to do the same in Bulgaria. To that end, he met with Commissioner Belev on February 22, 1943, and arranged for the deportation of 20,000 Jews: 12,000 from the newly occupied territories of Thrace and Macedonia and a further 8,000 from the "Old Kingdom" of Bulgaria itself.

On March 4, Bulgarian police and other authorities began rounding up the approximately 4,000 Jews of Thrace, who were then confined to warehouses until the round up was completed two weeks later. They were then taken by train and ship to Vienna. From Vienna, the Nazis deported by them to the Treblinka extermination center on March 26 and 28, gassing them on arrival. The Bulgarian military and police were quite enthusiastic in their actions against Jews in the occupied territories. In the town of Pirot, taken from eastern Yugoslavia (now Serbia), Sarah Alkalaj recalled that the Bulgarians conducted house-to-house searches. She was 22 when she and her family "were taken to the Gymnasium. We were locked there for more than a week. No one could come or leave. There they took our valuable things, money, jewelry, etc. Then we were transferred to another building."[94] They narrowly escaped death by sneaking away from the train during a halt.

In Macedonia, approximately 8,000 Jews were not as fortunate. They were rounded up on March 11. Survivor Albert Sarfati recalled the deportation: "They loaded us into cattle wagons, fifty to sixty people per wagon, including luggage. There wasn't enough space and many had to stand. There was no water. The children were crying . . . A woman in one wagon was giving birth . . . but there was no doctor."[95] The Macedonian Jews were then confined in four warehouses belonging to the Monopol tobacco company in Skopje. Bulgarian authorities deprived their prisoners of sufficient food and water while robbing and abusing them. They also sexually assaulted the women and girls. A survivor described the mood in the Monopol warehouses, saying, "We were in a terrible mood. The youngsters tried to sing every so often, but the adults and the elderly people were in deep depression.

We did not know what awaited us, but the dreadful treatment we received from the Bulgarians showed the value of the promises given us that we would only be taken to a Bulgarian work camp."[96] The Jews of Macedonia were deported eleven days later in three trains. Albert Sarfati, who escaped deportation, watched the second train boarding and later described the scene: "Each wagon carried between 60 and 70 people with all their baggage. The people came out of the building carrying their belongings on their backs. Everyone was carrying things, from the oldest person to the youngest. With bowed heads, all approached the black train. In front of each wagon stood a German and a Bulgarian policeman checking off a list. It was impossible to sit down in the freight cars . . . Hands were waving goodbye from the small wagon windows and all of us in the building were shedding tears."[97] All three trains traveled to Treblinka where almost all the Jews of Macedonia were gassed upon arrival. The dead included more than 2,000 children under the age of 16.[98]

As the experience of the Thracian and Macedonian Jews demonstrates, Bulgarian authorities could be just as brutal and murderous as their Nazi allies. However, when Dannecker and Belev turned to preparations for the deportation of Jews from the "Old Kingdom" of pre-war Bulgaria, they encountered a surprising amount of resistance. News of the pending deportations leaked to prominent members of the Bulgarian community. Leaders in the Jewish community could and did still lobby the government against the planned actions. On their behalf, the Vice President of the Bulgarian Parliament, Dmitar Peshev, led a political campaign against the deportations. Even though he had supported the alliance with Hitler, Peshev could not tolerate the extermination of Bulgarian Jews. He mobilized 42 other members of parliament to sign his letter of protest addressed to Prime Minister Filov. In the letter, which he submitted to Parliament on March 17, 1943, Peshev wrote "It is impossible for us to accept that plans have been made to deport these people." He also made the utilitarian argument that participating in Nazi genocidal policy could have dire repercussions for Bulgaria when the war was over. Peshev closed his letter by saying "Good government requires basic legal principles, just as life requires air to breathe. The honor of Bulgaria is not just a matter of sentiment, it is also and above all a matter of policy."[99] Peshev's actions caused a great deal of debate both political and public, eventually leading to a parliamentary confrontation, which he lost along with his position. The Bulgarian Church and its leadership joined Peshev in opposition to the deportations. Its three highest leaders visited the King and Prime Minister Filov on April 15, 1943 to deliver their protests in person. Though more concerned with Jews who had converted to Christianity, they still lobbied on behalf of all Bulgarian Jews.[100] In addition, Americans and British issued a joint protest. The outrage generated by the deportations caused King Boris III to hesitate and eventually to oppose any deportations of Bulgarian Jews. In April, he told the Nazi Foreign Minister, Ribbentrop, of his "hope that deportations would remain limited to Jews in Macedonia and Thrace."[101] The Nazis were naturally displeased and increased pressure on Bulgaria to hand over its Jews. This resulted in the expulsion of Jews from the capital, Sofia, a move which both Dannecker and Belev hoped would lead to future deportation. While this measure was successful in forcing Jews into the countryside in May, it also generated protests and outrage as well. Two prominent politicians, for example, wrote a letter to the King in which they condemned the "cruel measures against our fellow citizens of Jewish origin."[102] In the end, no Bulgarian Jews were deported to the extermination centers. King Boris III has often been seen as a hero as a result, but his legacy is more complex. He supported both antisemitic legislation against Bulgarian Jews and knowingly agreed to the murder of Jews in the new territories under Bulgarian control. One historian has aptly summarized his role in rescuing Bulgarian Jews by noting that, previously, he had allowed events to take place, but in March 1943 "when he had to take a decision, he changed his policy." This, then, set a precedent from which he could not retreat.[103] Dmitâr Peshev was honored in 1973 by the Israeli Holocaust Museum, Yad Vashem, with its highest award for rescuers during the Holocaust: Righteous Among the Nations.[104]

The role played by Hitler's eastern allies exposes the complexity of the involvement of local governments and institutions in the Holocaust. The behavior and choices of Romania, Hungary, and Bulgaria demonstrate a wide range of complicity in genocide, but they have several characteristics in common. First, Hitler's allies were usually more concerned with resolving territorial claims than with participation in a racial war against the Jews. Second, they were far more willing to participate in the Holocaust when it supported their goal of "purifying" or "cleansing" newly acquired territories. Finally, each country retained the ability to negotiate its participation in the Nazi genocidal project and, often, to refuse. Only Hungary was truly occupied and forced to comply. Collectively, the histories of these countries illustrate the ways in which they used the Holocaust for their own purposes, and also the degree to which they could control their participation.

Selected Readings

Ancel, Jean. *The History of the Holocaust in Romania*. Lincoln: University of Nebraska Press, 2011.

Ancel, Jean. *Prelude to Mass Murder: the Pogrom in Iași, Romania, June 29, 1941 and Thereafter*. Translated by Fern Seckbach. Jerusalem: Yad Vashem, 2013.

Braham, Randolph L. *The Politics of Genocide the Holocaust in Hungary (Condensed Edition)*. Detroit, MI: Wayne State University Press, 2000.

Chary, Frederick B. *The Bulgarian Jews and the Final Solution, 1940–1944*. Pittsburgh: University of Pittsburgh Press, 1972.

Weinberg, Gerhard L. *A World at Arms: A Global History of World War II*. Cambridge: Cambridge University Press, 2005.

9

The Final Solution

Introduction

On the other hand, I have sufficiently strong nerves and a sufficiently strong sense of duty . . . that if I consider something to be necessary then I will carry it out uncompromisingly. I did not consider myself justified—I'm referring here to the Jewish women and children—in allowing avengers to grow up in the shape of the children who will then murder our fathers and grandchildren. I would have considered that a cowardly thing to do. As a result the question was solved uncompromisingly.

HEINRICH HIMMLER, speech to German generals, May 24, 1944[1]

They were crammed in so tightly against one another that the smallest and weakest were inevitably suffocated. At a certain moment, under that pressure, that anguish, you become selfish and there's only one thing you can think of: how to save yourself. That was the effect the gas had. The sight that lay before us when we opened the door was terrible; nobody can even imagine what it was like.

Auschwitz *Sonderkommando* member SCHLOMO VENEZIA[2]

Sometime in the late summer to early fall of 1941, Hitler decided to solve the so-called Jewish Question through the physical extermination of the Jews of Europe. This decision set in motion a period of intense preparation and activity that ended in the of murder extraordinary numbers of Jews in a short period of time . . . and which would place Schlomo

Venezia in a place of unimaginable horror: this "Final Solution" completed the evolution of the Nazi state into a genocidal one. In the spring of 1942, 75–80 percent of the victims of the Holocaust were still alive and 20–25 percent had already been murdered. Eleven months later, these percentages had been reversed.[3] This was Himmler's uncompromising solution that he referred to in 1944.

This was the Holocaust of the gas chambers, the crematoriums, and train journeys to annihilation. While mass shootings continued, this more "industrial" form of killing became, for a time, the primary method of murdering Jews and the most deadly. This chapter explains how this program of mass murder developed and was carried out. It will briefly examine earlier plans for solving the "Jewish Problem," before discussing the timing of the decision for murder and the planning involved in creating a system capable of murdering millions relatively quickly and efficiently. We will also examine the operation of some of these killing centers. As part of this discussion, we will focus on the extermination center of Treblinka. We will close with an exploration of the final liquidations of ghettos and the closing of most of the extermination centers.

The Evolution of the Final Solution

Today I will again be a prophet and say, if international finance Jewry in and outside Europe succeeds in plunging nations into another world war, then the end result will not be the Bolshevization of the planet and thus the victory of the Jews—it will be the annihilation of the Jewish race in Europe.

ADOLF HITLER to the Reichstag, January 30, 1939[4]

As we have begun to see already in this book, the movement from discriminatory policies against Jews to their physical extermination was more evolutionary than preordained. However, few topics have created more intense debate about the Holocaust than the nature and timing of the plan to murder all the Jews in Europe (and really the world). In 1939, when Hitler made his prophecy above, it was still unclear what the "annihilation of the Jewish race" meant to him and others in the regime. Therefore, it is important to examine in some depth how this decision came about . . . and how we can deduce that timing. The "twisted path" leading to the gas chambers resulted from a combination of innovation, experimentation, and previous experience; it was also modified both at the ground level and in the upper echelons of the Nazi system. In short, it demonstrates how an incredibly diverse group of people worked together to create a system to murder other human beings.

There are, of course, those who contend that Hitler intended to murder the Jews from the very beginning. Hitler did write in *Mein Kampf* in 1925,

"If, at the beginning of the War and during the War, twelve or fifteen thousand of these Hebraic corrupters of the nation had been subjected to poison gas . . . then the sacrifice of millions at the front would not have been in vain."[5] However, to read into this statement a concrete plan to murder Jews in the future is foolish. Hitler refers to the stab-in-the-back myth and the false assumption that Jews did not fight in proportional numbers during World War I. (They did.) He is not laying out a step-by-step plan that ends in the gas chambers. Hitler does expound upon antisemitic theories but only once (above) suggests the killing of Jews.

For these and other reasons, it is unlikely that Hitler entered office in 1933 with the intention of murdering all Jews. The policy developed through a process of "cumulative radicalization," in which ever more severe and extreme measures were favored by Hitler and Himmler. This explanation also fits well with the concept of "working toward the Führer," where Hitler gave vague guidance and then encouraged those who brought him plans that moved in the direction he wanted. He himself acknowledged this, saying he relied on "tough people of whom I know they take the steps I would take myself. The best man is for me the one who bothers me least by taking upon himself 95 out of 100 decisions."[6] Even the future chief architect of the Final Solution, Reinhard Heydrich, stated in the summer of 1940 regarding the Jews: "Biological extermination is undignified for the German people as a civilized nation."[7]

In addition to Hitler's leadership style and the habits of his subordinates, very real alternate plans demonstrate that the murder of the Jews culminated from a long process influenced by both situation and ideology. The first solution was the Lublin/Nisko plan in which Jews would be deported and concentrated on a reservation in Poland. As we have seen, this plan failed due to objections from local Nazi leaders as well as logistical difficulties. The second major plan was the Madagascar Plan, to deport the Jews of Europe to the island off the east coast of Africa. With the fall of France, this territory became available to the Germans. Far from being a fantasy, the Madagascar Plan attracted very real attention in the summer of 1940. Franz Rademacher, head of the Jewish Desk (Section D-III) in the German Foreign Office, personally took up the planning with great zeal. Hitler himself informed the chief of the German Navy that he intended to resettle European Jews there.[8] Even ghetto Chairman Adam Czerniakow in Warsaw was told that his Jews would be resettled to the African island. As one historian has written, there can be "no doubt that during this period both Rademacher and Eichmann tackled the [Madagascar] plan in full earnest."[9] While the Madagascar plan remained a territorial one, the displacement of millions of Jews to the rugged island would clearly lead to a decimation of the population that was not viewed unfavorably. In the end, however, the circumstances of war meant that the plan was scrapped. The failure to defeat Britain left it in control of the oceans, making any deportations from Europe impossible.

The final territorial solution proposed for dealing with the "Jewish Question" appeared in 1941 and involved the deportation of Jews to a "territory yet to be determined." This was the soon to-be-occupied Soviet Union, potentially beyond the Ural Mountains, into Siberia and Asian Russia. This plan, which also unapologetically acknowledged high mortality rates, remained undeveloped as events of the war soon overtook it.

Deciding for Murder

I hereby charge you with making all necessary preparations in regard to organizational and financial matters for bringing about a complete solution of the Jewish question in the German sphere of influence in Europe.
REICHSMARSCHALL GÖRING to Reinhard Heydrich, July 31, 1941[10]

It was in the context of the invasion of the Soviet Union and the massive demographic engineering already planned that, sometime in the late summer or early fall of 1941, Hitler decided that Europe's Jews should be murdered rather than resettled.[11] First, it should be made clear that the reason the timing is not conclusively known is that unlike the "euthanasia" program, no written order from Hitler exists for the Final Solution . . . and likely never did. Rather, he informed his high-ranking subordinates of his decision and they began to carry it out. The closest evidence to a direct order is the above memo giving Reinhard Heydrich the freedom to prepare for the Final Solution. Thus, historians must track the decision for the murder of the Jews through Nazi actions taken across Europe and the changes in policy.

With the war in the East going relatively well, it seems that Hitler abandoned his previous plans to delay implementing any permanent Jewish policy until the end of the war. This decision's repercussions gradually emerged throughout 1941 and into 1942. The events that heralded the coming of the Final Solution are scattered geographically and temporally, but they can be placed in a clear historical context. At the upper levels of the Nazi bureaucracy, Göring signed Heydrich's July 31, 1941 order:

> Complementing the task that was assigned to you on 24 January 1939, which dealt with arriving at-through furtherance of emigration and evacuation-a solution of the Jewish problem, as advantageously as possible, I hereby charge you with making all necessary preparations in regard to organizational and financial matters for bringing about a complete solution of the Jewish question in the German sphere of influence in Europe.[12]

This order (drafted by Heydrich himself) represented nothing less than an authorization for Heydrich (and the SS) to oversee all the necessary requirements for a physical solution to the "Jewish Question." With this mandate, Heydrich began planning an entirely different system of mass murder. At the same time, anti-Jewish actions in the Soviet Union began to change as well. In Chapter 6, we saw that the *Einsatzgruppen* were initially tasked with killing military-aged male Jews and communist functionaries (which Heydrich reiterated in a July 2 memorandum). However, we also saw that this directive expanded quickly via verbal orders from Himmler and other high-ranking SS officials so that, by September, the *Einsatzgruppen*—reinforced by additional Police Battalions, local auxiliaries, and the *Wehrmacht*—were systematically murdering Jews of all ages and sexes. This shift in targeting and scale also signaled that something had changed in Nazi policy toward Jews. Elsewhere in Nazi territory, it appears that others sensed change in the air. The head of the resettlement office in Poznań, Poland, wrote Eichmann on July 16, expressing concern about the food situation in Łódź and asking if "the most humanitarian solution would not be to finish off those Jews who are unfit for work by some *expedient means* [emphasis mine]."[13] In addition, it appears that Hitler decided in September 1941 to proceed with the deportation of German Jews to Eastern ghettos and killing sites.

A final high-level signal of a change from a policy of deportation and expulsion to murder came with an October 18 notation in Himmler's phone log: "No emigration by Jews to overseas."[14] Considering that Nazi policy to this point had sought to force Jews to leave Europe, preventing them from doing so indicates that emigration was no longer the Nazi course of action. Rather, Jews were to remain confined in Europe where they could be "resettled to the East," a euphemism that would shortly come to mean "killed in mass gassing operations." Indeed, by this time, rumors and insinuations were already flying. On October 23, a Nazi friend of Rademacher's wrote him regarding a conversation with "an old party comrade, who works in

TABLE 7 *Final Solution decision and execution timeline.*

Date	Event
July 1941	Himmler deploys additional Police Battalions to the East to assist in killing.
July 16, 1941	Eichmann receives request from SS officer Hoeppner in Poland for a "quick-acting agent" to serve as a "humane solution to dispose" of non-working Jews of Łódź.
July 31, 1941	Heydrich receives authorization to plan and carry out Final Solution.
August 1, 1941	Himmler orders SS Cavalry Brigade in USSR: "All Jews must be shot. Drive the female Jews into the swamps."

Date	Event
August 15–6, 1941	Himmler visits Minsk; observes mass shooting. EK 3 begins killing children.
September 3, 1941	Zyklon B first used at Auschwitz as gassing agent in Block 11 (Auschwitz I)
September 6, 1941	900 Soviet POWs gassed with Zyklon B in converted morgue at Auschwitz (Crematorium I).
October 1, 1941	SS begin planning Auschwitz II- Birkenau and design larger gas chambers.
October 15, 1941	First deportations of German Jews to Polish ghettos (Łódź); Himmler observes second mass shooting.
October, 18 1941	Emigration of Jews from Nazi territory halted.
October 21, 1941	Himmler visits Mogilev, discusses installation of gas chambers in camp there.
Late October/early November 1941	40 Russian prisoners killed in gas vans at Sachsenhausen concentration camp.
November 1, 1941	Construction begins of Bełzec Extermination Center.
November 1941	Gas van expert Herbert Lange establishes a permanent base in Chełmno.
December 1941	Chełmno Extermination Center begins gassing Jews.
December 16, 1941	Himmler orders extermination of all "Gypsies" in Europe.
January 20, 1942	Wannsee Conference.
March 17, 1942	Gassing begins at Bełzec.
March 20, 1942	Mass gassing of Jews begins in "little red house" at Auschwitz.
March 1942	Construction begins on Sobibor Extermination Center.
May 16/18, 1942	Gassing begins at Sobibor.
May 1942	Construction begins on Treblinka Extermination Center.
End of Jun 1942	Gassing begins at the "Bunker 2" gas chamber at Auschwitz.
July 13, 1942	Gassings begin at Treblinka.
March 13, 1943	First mass exterminations begin in Auschwitz II-Birkenau, Crematorium II

the east on the settlement of the Jewish question." This person apparently hinted that, "In the near future many of the Jewish vermin will be exterminated through special measures." Historian Christopher Browning noted the "extraordinary coincidence" that on that same day, Adolf Eichmann met with his deportation experts concerning the deportation of German Jews.[15] Table 7 notes some of the key moments that indicate the turn toward a full genocide against the Jews of Europe.

Building the Apparatus of Death

One day in the winter of 1941 Wirth arranged a transport [of euthanasia personnel] to Poland. I was picked together with about eight or ten other men and transferred to Bełżec . . . I don't remember the names of the others. Upon our arrival in Bełżec, we met Friedel Schwarz and the other SS men, whose names I cannot remember. They supervised the construction of barracks that would serve as a gas chamber. Wirth told us that in Bełżec "all the Jews will be struck down."

—SS-Scharführer ERICH FUCHS[16]

The actual design and construction of what would become the extermination centers, like Bełżec, began in the late fall/winter of 1941. As Fuchs notes, these were purpose-built for murder. The first, Chełmno, became operational by December 8, 1941. Note that the term "extermination center" is used rather than concentration camp. While the Nazis murdered Jews and others in both places, the extermination centers served only as mass killing sites while concentration camps could also serve as punishment and slave labor locations.

There were four "pure" extermination centers: Chełmno, Bełżec, Sobibor, and Treblinka. To these, we add the "hybrid" camps of Auschwitz and Majdanek, both of which operated as dedicated killing centers similar to the others; in Auschwitz, mass gassing occurred in several locations, eventually using four crematoria/gas chamber buildings in Auschwitz II (Birkenau). Majdanek repeatedly conducting mass killings, but they tended to be more sporadic. Bełżec, Sobibor, and Treblinka formed part of what became known as "Operation Reinhard" and were relatively similar, as we will discuss later. In July 1941, the mass killing apparatus had not yet been assembled.

The Nazis benefited, however, from distinct experiences that, when combined, would make the Final Solution possible. First, they had proficiency in the gassing of victims and disposal of bodies. This came from the Operation T-4 "euthanasia" program which had gassed 70,000 Germans. Moreover, many of those personnel involved were idle, as Hitler had been forced to "officially" end and decentralize the program. These experts were, therefore, available to assist in the design, building, and operation of extermination centers. Second, the Nazi state had perfected the concentration camp as a space of confinement and control. All that was lacking was the addition of a killing apparatus. Third, men like Adolf Eichmann and Franz Rademacher had gained invaluable experience in planning and coordinating the movement and deportations of large numbers of people by rail including Jews, Poles, and ethnic Germans. A further motivation for a change in killing methods was the very real mental damage being done to the Nazi killers, particularly those in the *Einsatzgruppen*. As the vast majority of these men were not sociopaths or insane, they suffered psychological damage approaching PTSD from the relentless murder of civilians, often regardless of how much they themselves approved or disapproved of the overall policy. Himmler himself had observed at least two mass shootings (August 15 and October 15, 1941).[17] He was visibly upset and some witnesses claimed he vomited. In any case, after the August killing, he began issuing orders to find a less traumatic method of killing. At this event, the Higher SS and Police Leader, Erich von dem Bach-Zelewski (who later suffered from PTSD himself) told Himmler: "*Reichsführer*, those were only a hundred . . . Look at the eyes of the men in this Kommando, how deeply shaken they are! These men are finished for the rest of their lives. What kind of followers are we training here? Either neurotics or savages!"[18] A method of killing which distanced killers from their victims was clearly preferable. Further, throughout Eastern Europe, Jews were already conveniently confined in ghettos as the Nazis deliberated on their fate and capitalized on their labor.

However, even with all these helpful experiences, a good deal of improvisation and experimentation was still required to perfect the execution of the Final Solution. Across the Greater Reich, Nazi experts had already begun experimenting with different methods of murder. In September 1941, commander of *Einsatzgruppe* B, Arthur Nebe, requested the services of Dr. Albert Widmann, SS chemist and gassing expert from the T-4 program. Widmann arrived to assist in the murder of mental patients. Explosives were tried with unsuccessful results. An observer testified that "The sight was atrocious . . . Body parts were scattered on the ground and hanging in the trees."[19] Nebe then suggested the use of automobile exhaust (carbon monoxide) inspired by his own close encounter of passing out in a running vehicle in his garage after a night of drinking.[20] This led to two tests involving exhaust pumped into sealed rooms from vehicles running outside.

At roughly the same time, in Berlin, Heydrich asked his technical chief of Department II-D, Walter Rauff, to investigate the feasibility of creating mobile gas vans. Rauff oversaw the conversion of a Saurer model cargo truck into a mobile gas chamber by sealing the cargo space and rerouting the exhaust gas. In late October/early November 1941, three chemists from the SS crime lab tested the gas vans in the Sachsenhausen concentration camp, killing forty Russian prisoners.[21] The SS commissioned the construction of thirty such "gas vans."

The Chełmno extermination center relied solely on these vans. In November 1941, the chief of a mobile gassing unit, Herbert Lange, established a killing center in a local mansion there. He told his men that "absolute secrecy is crucial . . . We have a tough, but important job to do."[22] Victims from the surrounding area, and especially Łódź, were trucked to the site where they entered the house, surrendered their valuables, and descended into the basement. Once in the basement, they undressed and climbed stairs leading into the back of a gas van. The van then drove a short distance into the forest where the driver attached the exhaust hose to the cargo compartment and waited until all Jews were dead. A Jewish *Sonderkommando* then unloaded and buried or burned the bodies. Among those murdered were also the Sinti/Roma (gypsies) who had been interned in the Łódź Ghetto. An SS man at Chełmno described the scene in the forest:

> We could see a clearing in the forest and a gray van that was parked there with the rear doors open. The van was full of bodies, which were taken out by a Jewish labor squad and thrown into a mass grave. The dead people looked like Gypsies. There were men, women and children there.[23]

In this way, at least 152,000 Jews and Sinti/Roma were murdered between December 1941 and June/July 1944. There were four survivors.

In September 1941, SS officials began experimenting with Zyklon-B as an alternate form of gassing. Zyklon-B was a chemical agent used as fumigant to kill insects, particularly lice, in living areas, ship holds, and large amounts of clothing. When exposed to heat and humidity, it changed from a solid, pellet form to hydrogen cyanide gas. Zyklon B kills by preventing oxygen uptake in red blood cells, leading to suffocation. The first tests of this substance on humans occurred in Block 11 at Auschwitz on September 3, 1941 and three days later in a converted morgue space known as Crematorium I, where 900 Soviet prisoners of war were murdered. The commandant of Auschwitz, Rudolf Höss personally observed the testing and testified regarding these experimental killings at Auschwitz:

> I must even admit that this gassing set my mind at rest, for the mass extermination of the Jews was to start soon, and at that time neither Eichmann nor I was certain as to how these mass killings were to be carried out. It would be by gas, but we did not know which gas and how it was to be used. Now we had the gas, and we had established a procedure.[24]

While Zyklon-B was famously used at Auschwitz and Majdanek, all other extermination centers used carbon monoxide gas generated from vehicle engines, often from submarines, tanks, or trucks.

Himmler commissioned the odious Higher SS and Police Leader in the Lublin District of the General Government, *SS-Brigadeführer* Odilo Globocnik, with the construction of the killing centers in Poland that would later be named Operation Reinhard after Heydrich's assassination in May 1942. Operation Reinhard encompassed the eventual construction of Bełzec, Sobibor, and Treblinka. Globocnik and his staff identified suitable locations for these camps and oversaw their construction. In order to avoid the public nature of the *Einsatzgruppen* killings, these extermination centers were located away from major population centers but on key railroad lines, allowing easy deportation of Jews to the camp by train. We will examine one camp, Treblinka, in more detail.

Globocnik also needed staff for the Operation Reinhard camps and found a ready pool of capable men in the former members of the T-4 program. Viktor Brack, who had organized the T-4 killing operations, testified at his trial that:

> In 1941, I received an order to discontinue the euthanasia program. In order to retain the personnel that had been relieved of these duties and in order to be able to start a new euthanasia program after the war, Bouhler [a co-conspirator in the T-4 program] asked me-I think after a conference with Himmler- to send [these] personnel to Lublin and place [them] at the disposal of *SS Brigadeführer* Globocnik.[25]

The unemployed T-4 men heeded the call. They "compose[d] almost the entire personnel of the extermination camps of Operation Reinhard." At least ninety worked in Bełzec, Sobibor, and Treblinka.[26] These men brought with them the experience of managing and working in gassing facilities and disposing of large numbers or bodies. The move to extermination was hardly a stretch.

On January 20, 1942, an important meeting took place in a villa on the idyllic Wannsee Lake outside Berlin. Reinhard Heydrich had originally scheduled the meeting for December 8, 1941, but more pressing events such as a Soviet counter-offensive and the American entry into the war forced a change of date. This daylong meeting became known as the Wannsee Conference and had important repercussions for the implementation of the Final Solution. Contrary to popular belief, the conference sought *not* to decide on the Final Solution, but rather to coordinate all the government offices in the task of *carrying out* the mass murder of Jews. As we have seen, the decision to kill, the methods, and the locations had already been agreed upon. Indeed, while the attendees met in an ornate dining room, some of the extermination centers to which they would send Jews to be murdered were already being built. The meeting was important enough, however, to require the presence of high-level Nazi officials and was led by Himmler's right-hand man, Reinhard Heydrich. The fifteen attendees represented the government departments who would be most involved in the deportation and murder of Jews. Some notable attendees were:

- Heinrich Müller, chief of the Gestapo
- Adolf Eichmann, head of RSHA office IV-B-4, deportation expert
- Dr. Rudolf Lange, former leader of *Einsatzkommando* 2 in the Baltic
- Dr. Eberhard Schöngarth, former *Einsatzkommando* leader in Galicia and then Commander of Security Police and SD in the Generalgovernment
- Dr. Josef Bühler, deputy of Hans Frank, Governor of the Generalgovernment[27]

These men gathered in the villa for approximately an hour and a half. Heydrich had appended to the initial November 29, 1941, invitation his authorization from Göring to plan the Final Solution, presumably to clearly establish his authority at the table.[28] Only one copy of the minutes of the Wansee Conference survived, and it lays out in detail the topics of discussion and outcomes of the meeting. After a brief summary of previous actions against the Jews, the minutes note that Hitler had given his approval for the "evacuation of the Jews to the East," a euphemism which stood for mass murder. The next page contained estimates of Jewish populations to be exterminated (including in yet-to-be-conquered countries such as England and Ireland). The population of Jews to be murdered was estimated at 11 million. The fate of "mixed race" Jews (*Mischlinge* 1st and 2nd Class) was also settled. The majority of *Mischlinge* 1st Class was to be killed while the majority of the *Mischlinge* 2nd Class was not. Indeed, it appears that a substantial amount of time was devoted to this issue and possible exceptions. The meeting minutes concluded with a recognition of SS authority in the Final Solution and the pledged support of the government agencies in attendance.[29] On January 31, 1942, SS deportation expert Adolf Eichmann sent a memo to SS authorities in Germany and Austria, instructing them to prepare for the "beginning of the Final Solution" and the "evacuation" of German and Austrian Jews.[30] By this time, gassing had already begun at Chełmno and would begin within months at Bełzec, Auschwitz, and Sobibor. Thus, at all levels—from methods to personnel to bureaucracy—the Nazi state had committed itself to a program of mass murder and genocide.

"The Terrible Smallness of the Place": Inside Treblinka[31]

"Here no one remains alive," he said. "Pray for them." Then we knew.

STANISLAW SZMAJZNER, Treblinka survivor[32]

The Treblinka extermination center fifty miles northeast of Warsaw serves as a good example of the history of the Reinhard camps and as a vehicle through which to examine in detail the most deadly of them. The Nazis

SELECTED FEATURES

LIVING AREA
1. Main Entrance
2. Camp Command & Commandant's Living Quarters
3. Ukrainian Guards' Living Quarters
4. Zoo
5. Service Building for the SS
6. Barracks for the Domestic Staff
7. Building for Sorting Gold and Valuables
8. SS Living Quarters
9. Service & Storage Buildings
10. Stables and Livestock Area
11. Barracks for Kapos & Women Prisoners
12. Barracks for Male Prisoners
13. Latrine
14. Assembly Area for Prisoners (Roll Call)
15. Entrances to Reception Area & Station Square
16. Entrance for Guards

RECEPTION AREA
17. Station Platform, Ramp & Square
18. Storehouse for Victims' Property (Disguised as a Train Station)
19. Burial Pits
20. Execution Site (Disguised as Hospital)
21. Reception Square (Sorting Area)
22. Latrine
23. Main Entrance to Deportation Area
24. Deportation Area
25. Barracks Where Women Undressed, Surrendered Valuables, and had Heads Shaved
26. Barracks Where Men Undressed
27. "The Tube" - Approach to Gas Chambers

EXTERMINATION AREA
28. 10 New Gas Chambers
29. 3 Old Gas Chambers
30. Cremation Pyres
31. Barracks for Prisoners

TREBLINKA CAMP SPRING 1943

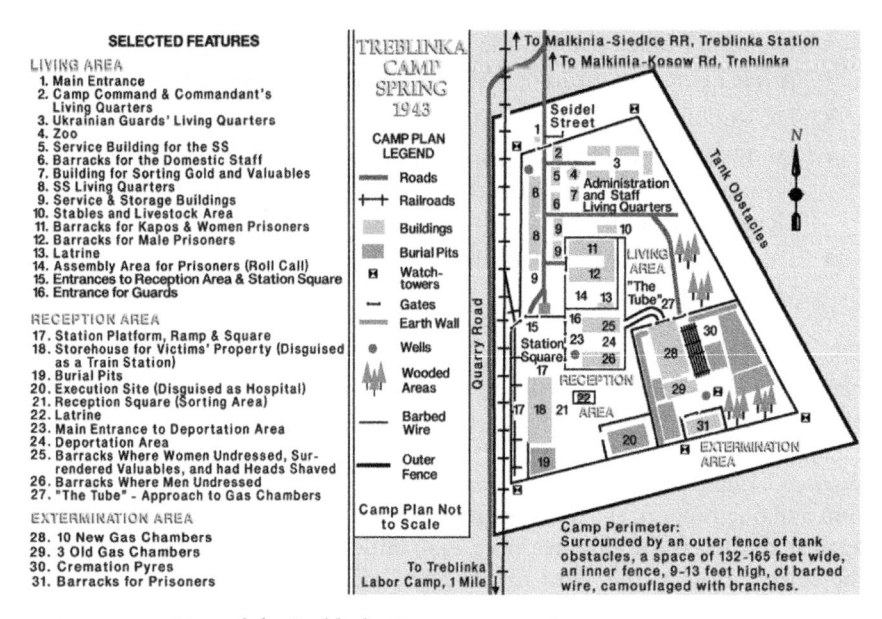

CAMP PLAN LEGEND
— Roads
+—+ Railroads
▓ Buildings
▓ Burial Pits
⌂ Watchtowers
— Gates
— Earth Wall
● Wells
🌲 Wooded Areas
— Barbed Wire
— Outer Fence

Camp Plan Not to Scale

To Treblinka Labor Camp, 1 Mile

↑ To Malkinia-Siedlce RR, Treblinka Station
↑ To Malkinia-Kosow Rd, Treblinka

Camp Perimeter:
Surrounded by an outer fence of tank obstacles, a space of 132-165 feet wide, an inner fence, 9-13 feet high, of barbed wire, camouflaged with branches.

FIGURE 19 *Map of the Treblinka Extermination Center*
Source: United States Holocaust Memorial Museum.

murdered between 870,000 and 925,000 Jews in the sixty acres that constituted the camp.[33] For inmates of the camp, like Stanislaw, the inconceivable magnitude of the crime taking place there became clear by way of initiation to their new surroundings. Treblinka ranks second only to Auschwitz in numbers of Jews murdered. In many ways, it represents the pinnacle of achievement for planners of the Final Solution, surpassed only by the later crematoria complexes of Auschwitz II-Birkenau.

The construction of the Treblinka extermination camp began in May 1942, likely upon the personal order of Himmler who had visited the Higher SS and Police Leader in Warsaw, Arpad Wigand, on April 17, 1942. Labor was provided by the nearby Treblinka I slave labor camp (the extermination camp would officially be named "Treblinka II," but we will use Treblinka as a shorthand here). The work was supervised by two German construction firms. The future commandant, Dr. Irmfried Eberl, a T-4 veteran, and 30–40 SS men, arrived as well. They were accompanied by 90–120 "Trawniki" men, Ukrainian guards recruited from German camps for Soviet POWs.[34]

The camp itself was divided into three sections: Camp I- the reception Area, Camp II- the "death camp" with gas chambers and burial sites, and Camp III- the living quarters for the SS and Ukrainians as well as barracks and workshops for the small contingent of Jews kept alive to help run the camp and craft items for the SS. The camp underwent renovations and upgrades, including the construction of a larger gas chamber complex, but its layout and function would remain mostly the same. A rail line was built off the main route so that trains could directly enter the camp. This area would later be improved into a "ramp," complete with a fake train station. This rail spur could accommodate twenty freight cars at a time, though frequently the trains arriving were 50–60 cars long, carrying around 5,000 people. These trains were simply broken up and twenty cars were then backed in by a Polish engineer who was forbidden to enter the camp.

Once on the ramp, the trains unloaded in front of the fake train station in order to deceive the victims as long as possible. This was at least partially effective. As one survivor, Richard Glazar, recalled, "I saw a green fence, barracks, and I heard what sounded like a farm tractor. I was delighted."[35] Arriving Jews would leave their baggage, be separated by sex, and be led into the reception area of Camp I. Children generally stayed with their mother. They undressed, and camp prisoners shaved all body hair for later use in the German economy. An SS memorandum from August 1942 explicitly stated that men's hair would be used to create "industrial felt" and women's hair would become "liners and socks for U-boat crews and railway workers." Camps were to report the total amount of men's and women's hair on the fifth of each month.[36] All currency and valuables were surrendered here as well. Next, a selection took place in which a few new arrivals (and often none) were selected to work in the camp. Those unable to move were taken away. The SS guard responsible, Willi Mentz, described this job: "There were always some ill and frail people on the transports . . . These ill, frail, and wounded people . . . would be taken to the hospital area. When no more ill or wounded were expected it was my job to shoot these people. I did this by shooting them in the neck with a 9mm pistol."[37] SS and Ukrainian guards then drove able-bodied victims down a barbed-wire corridor, camouflaged with branches, leading to the gas chamber complex. This corridor was known as "the Tube" or "Road to Heaven." At the end, climbing a few stairs, they would enter a long central corridor with ten gas chambers, five located on either side. Once the chambers were filled, the SS would start two tank engines that pumped carbon monoxide gas through pipes and out fake showerheads in the gas chambers. It took approximately 20 minutes for victims to suffocate.

After all had died, the Jewish squad (*Sonderkommando*) responsible for clearing the bodies began their work. Through larger exterior doors, they untangled and removed the bodies. Prisoners also were forced to remove gold teeth from the corpses, which were initially buried in large pits. Later, when numbers became too great, the bodies were exhumed and burned on long railroad ties, forming a sort of grill and referred to as "roasts." Other members of this group were responsible for cleaning the gas chambers in preparation for their next use. A former commandant of the camp, Franz Stangl, testified that "when the gas chambers were running for fourteen hours, approximately 12,000–15,000 people could be disposed of."

He added that "there were many days when we worked from morning to evening."[38]

Between 750 and 1,500 Jewish prisoners worked in the camp at any given time, divided into groups based on the labor they carried out. The most privileged group was the craftsmen, who ran small workshops for the SS. The "Water Kommando" lived and worked solely in the killing section, Camp II, and was segregated from the rest of the prisoners. There was a "Blue Kommando" who met the transports upon arrival and cleared the ramp area of their possessions. The "Red Kommando" included SS men and operated in the Reception Area (Camp I) overseeing the undressing of victims, sorting of the clothes, selections of those unable to walk to the gas chambers, and their execution in the so-called Hospital. The "Rag Kommando" sorted clothing by quality and searched for any hidden valuables. Lastly, the

FIGURE 20 *Pages from the album of Treblinka deputy, Kurt Franz, titled "Beautiful Times." Commandant Stangl can be seen in the bottom photo (left) next to Franz. Treblinka, Poland, 1942–43.*
Source: United States Holocaust Memorial Museum.

"Camouflage Kommando" was responsible for the constant refreshing of the branches that covered the camp's fencing, including the "Tube" to the gas chambers.[39]

The first commandant, psychiatrist Dr. Irmfried Eberl, epitomized the connection between the Final Solution and the T-4 program, as he had formerly been the director of the Brandenburg and Bernburg "euthanasia" centers in Germany before being assigned to Treblinka. However, the task of running the extermination center appears to have exceeded Eberl's abilities and the camp rapidly spun out of control. Odilo Globcnik, the man responsible for the Reinhard camps, discovered Eberl's incompetence and the lack of valuables being sent on from the camp. On August 28, 1942, he reassigned the commandant of the Sobibor killing center, Franz Stangl, to relieve Eberl and assume command of Treblinka. Ironically, Eberl had been Stangl's superior at the Bernburg T-4 killing hospital. Stangl described his first visit to Treblinka in a 1971 prison interview. "It was Dante's Inferno," he said, "I waded in notes, currency, precious stones, jewelry, clothes. They were everywhere, strewn all over the square. The smell was indescribable; the hundreds, no, the thousands of bodies everywhere, decomposing, putrefying."[40] Eberl was unceremoniously returned to the Bernburg hospital. Shortly thereafter, Stangl streamlined operations in the camp and created a more disciplined environment there. By all accounts, he was a conscientious and efficient commander. He himself stated, "That was my profession; I enjoyed it. It fulfilled me. And yes, I was ambitious about that; I won't deny that." Stangl coldly divorced himself from the horror of his "profession." Jews became "cargo" or a "huge mass" to him.[41] He also avoided visiting the gas chambers as much as possible. Stangl was transferred in August 1943 after a prisoner revolt in the camp and was sent to fight partisans in Italy.

Gassings continued for a short while in the camp under Stangl's deputy, Kurt Franz, before the killing stopped in October 1943. The Nazis razed the camp, planted trees, and installed a Ukrainian family in a farmhouse on the site. During the sixteen months the camp was in operation, between 750,000 and 900,000 Jews had been murdered, including over 250,000 from the Warsaw ghetto. During the period of that ghetto liquidation, the camp averaged 5,000 arrivals a day.[42]

Auschwitz: The Apex of the Final Solution

Prominent guests from Berlin were present at the inauguration of the first crematorium in March 1943. The "program" consisted of the gassing and burning of 8,000 Cracow Jews. The guests, both officers and civilians, were extremely satisfied with the results and the special peephole fitted into the door of the gas chamber was in constant use. They were lavish in their praise of this newly erected installation.

RUDOLF VRBA and ALFRED WETZLER, Auschwitz survivors[43]

For both the Nazis, like the prominent guests mentioned above, as well as the modern public, Auschwitz more than any other place, perhaps, serves as the public face of the Holocaust. But it is deserving of a brief discussion here not because of its notoriety, but because of the way in which it combined or represented most of the facets of the Nazi genocidal project and the Holocaust in the East that we have discussed in this book. Nazi planners envisioned transforming the town of Oswieçim (Auschwitz) into a model of German settlement and agricultural achievement. The camp itself was not to be a blemish on this exhibition of German superiority but a model of success; Himmler himself planned an apartment in the town. The commandant of the camp remembered Himmler's plans for the camp: "Every necessary agricultural experiment was to be attempted there. Massive laboratories and plant cultivation departments had to be built."[44]

The camp itself was simultaneously a prison to "convict" and punish political opponents, primarily Poles. It became a massive slave labor camp and the hub of many subcamps whose mainly Jewish labor was intended to support the Nazi state. It contained its own factory complex of the massive Nazi conglomerate I. G. Farben. And, finally, it served as the largest and most deadly of the centers for the extermination of Jews, a place where the process was perfected, streamlined, and constantly being improved. Compared to Treblinka, only 60 acres in size with a combined SS/Ukrainian staff of less than 200, Auschwitz was immense. It covered a territory of 9,600 acres with a staff of over 7,000. The Auschwitz camp was a product both of the Nazi imagination of the East and its conquest, *and* the accompanying genocidal project, directed first and foremost against the Jews.

The site itself began as a Polish Army camp, first noticed by the future Higher SS- and Police Leader, Bach-Zelewski on a search for concentration camp sites in January 1940. The former ammunition depot would become the future first gas chamber. The Army, who controlled all Polish military installations, handed the area over to the SS and on April 27, Himmler decided that a concentration camp would be built there.[45] Three days later, the thirty-nine year old new commandant, *SS-Hauptsturmführer* (Captain) Rudolf Höss arrived. He was described later as looking like "a normal person, like a grocery clerk."[46] After an apprenticeship at the Dachau concentration camp in Germany, Höss came to Poland believing that "true opponents of the state must be locked up."[47]

But the site at Auschwitz was in no way ready to be the iconic site of evil it would become. Höss lacked the most basic materials to create a prison camp. He candidly recalled that, "Whenever I found depots of material that was needed urgently I simply carted it away without worrying about the formalities. I didn't even know where I could get a hundred meters of barbed wire. So I just had to pilfer the badly needed barbed wire."[48] In short, Auschwitz was built, at least initially, out of stolen property. Höss worked dutifully, and was prepared to receive the first prisoners in June 1940 who were neither Polish nor Jewish, but German career criminals who would become the first *kapos* or overseers of the camp's prisoners. The old Polish army portion of the camp (known as Auschwitz I) soon received large numbers of Polish political prisoners. As mentioned, gassing experiments took place in Block 11 but soon the crematorium in Auschwitz I was converted into a gas chamber/crematorium.

The scope of the planning for Auschwitz broadened throughout 1941. In October, construction began on a much larger camp a few kilometers from Auschwitz I, which would come to be known as Auschwitz II-Birkenau. Himmler's notes state that it was intended to hold up to 100,000 Soviet POWs. However, this massive new camp soon came to hold predominantly Jews and the extermination apparatus. The barracks were made up predominantly of pre-fabricated German Army horse stables designed to hold 52 horses; SS planners determined that they would hold 774 prisoners.[49] Finally, in October 1942, a factory slave labor camp called Auschwitz III-Monowitz was built by camp labor for the I. G. Farben corporation to manufacture synthetic rubber. Primo Levi would be an inmate in this section of the camp.

In March 1942, Jews arrived in Birkenau as the first prisoners. By this time, a small farmhouse known as Bunker 1 or the "Little Red House" had been modified into a gas chamber with a capacity of 800 and was used to murder non-working Jews from the surrounding areas. By July 1942, the first selections of a transport of Slovakian Jews were gassed on arrival in Bunker 1 and in a second converted cottage known as Bunker 2 or the "Little White House." This marked a transition to systematic killing at Auschwitz. It was not, however, without its problems. There were as yet no crematoria, so bodies had to be burned in the open, which was slow, dirty, and difficult to conceal. Throughout the summer of 1942, men like Theodor Dannecker, then posted in France, arranged the deportation of thousands of western European Jews to Auschwitz.

On August 10, 1942, work began on the gas chambers and crematoria that would make Birkenau infamous. Existing plans for massive ovens to be built as morgue and crematoria complexes were modified, with the addition of undressing rooms and gas chambers, to become self-contained killing locations. Eleven German civilian companies participated in the building of Auschwitz's killing infrastructure, from furnaces to chimneys to waterproofing to roofing to ventilation systems to electrical wiring.[50] All knew precisely the purpose of the buildings they were constructing. Ultimately, four crematoria were constructed (II-V). The gas chambers could accommodate 2,000 victims at a time. Three to five bodies could be burned simultaneously in one oven over the course of thirty minutes. 2,500 corpses could be burned per day in Crematoria II and III and 1,500 per day in Crematoria IV and V. However, the Nazis still faced the dilemma of body disposal as the limiting factor on killing capacity and tempo. More victims could be killed than could be cremated. Thus, when the camp was running at full capacity, murdering 9,000 Jews a day, the ovens could not keep up, leading to open-air burning as a supplementary measure.[51]

In March 1943, the first of the crematoria (II) opened at Birkenau and began the mass extermination of Jews at Auschwitz. Prisoners arrived via train *outside* of Birkenau and walk a short distance into the camp where, after a brief selection, the majority would be directed to one of four crematoria where, in the case of Crematoria II and III, they would undress in an underground room and then proceed into the gas chamber, which had a capacity of 2,000. An SS man wearing a gas mask then walked along the roof of the gas chamber, pouring Zykon-B pellets into mesh columns down into the chamber. The pellets aerosolized and asphyxiated the victims. Next, as in the Reinhard camps, prisoners of the *Sonderkommando* removed the

FIGURE 21 *View from atop a train of Hungarian Jews lined up for selection on the ramp at Auschwitz-Birkenau. Photo taken by an SS photographer for a photo album. Auschwitz, Poland, 1944.*
Source: United States Holocaust Memorial Museum.

bodies to the furnaces to be burned, cleaned the chambers, and prepared for the next arrival. Other camp Jews collected and sorted clothing and belongings of the victims with currency and precious metals being turned over to the guards for deposit in SS coffers. Camp architects built the iconic "ramp" and railroad tracks running directly into the camp in preparation for the murder of Hungarian Jews. In the summer of 1944, deportation expert Adolf Eichmann arranged for the transporting of approximately 400,000 Hungarian Jews to Auschwitz, where most were gassed upon arrival. Gassing at Auschwitz ended in November 1944 and the gas chambers and crematoria were demolished by the Nazis a day before the camp's liberation by the Soviets in January 1945.

Ghetto Liquidations and the Attempted Destruction of Evidence

I order that all Jews still remaining in ghettos in the Ostland area be collected in concentration camps . . . Inmates of the Jewish ghettos who are not required are to be evacuated to the East.

Himmler order, June 21, 1943[52]

More than 12,000 bodies were taken out—men, women, children. These bodies were piled up together, 300 at a time, to be burned. What was left after the burning (charcoal and bones) was ground down to powder in pits. This powder was then mixed with earth so that no trace of it should remain.

Collective statement by escapees from *Sonderkommando* in Kaunas, Lithuania, December 26, 1943[53]

Ghettos throughout Eastern Europe constituted one of the major sources of victims for the extermination centers. They had already suffered a "Second Wave" of killings as the Nazis continued to reduce the populations to only those Jews capable of working or otherwise supporting the war effort. After several high-profile acts of resistance, the Nazis became increasingly uncomfortable with maintaining large populations of increasingly well-informed Jews. This was one of the reasons for Himmler's directive above and the so-called Third Wave of killings that eliminated almost all of the ghettos in the east, with the exception of small numbers of laborers and a few ghettos converted into short-lived concentration camps. Another reason for the final liquidation of ghettos in the east was the increasingly desperate nature of the war and the accelerating German retreat. SS officials wished to finish their task and also leave no witnesses. This program of mass killings, too, represents part of the Final Solution.

TABLE 8 *Major deportation Aktions to killing centers in the East.*

Date	Location	Approximate Number
January–September 1942	Łódź	70,000
March–April 1942	Lublin	34,000
July–September 1942	Warsaw	265,000
August 1942	Lwów	65,0000
October 1942	Krakow	6,000
February 1943	Bialystok	10,000
March 1943	Krakow	3,000
August 1943	Bialystok	7,600
May–July 1944	Budapest	440,000
August 1944	Łódź	75,000

Depending on date and location, some ghettos were liquidated through multiple Aktions and deportations to the killing centers. This was the case particularly for the largest Polish ghettos of Łódź, Warsaw, Lublin, and Lwów, as well as those in other large cities such as Budapest. Most of the mass deportations had taken place in the summer of 1942. Table 8 above shows some of the deportations from the larger cities.

Of course, some smaller ghetto populations were liquidated in the gas chambers, such as the last 3,500 Jews of the town of Lida in Belarus—who were sent to the Sobibor killing center on September 18, 1943.[54] However, the majority of the last killings in the East took the form of the first killings. Most ghettos were liquidated through mass shooting operations. The town of Peremyshliany in Ukraine is a good example. Some of its Jews were sent to Bełzec in 1942. However, that extermination center had closed by May 22–23, so German Police Regiment 23 and the Ukrainian Police murdered the remaining 2,000 Jews in the ghetto and in the surrounding forest.[55] Throughout the East, small ghetto populations were murdered, with only a few survivors who either escaped or were sent to various concentration camp systems. Importantly, however, many of these ghetto liquidation operations met with fierce resistance by the remnants of the surviving Jewish populations.

The closing of the extermination centers and the liquidation of the ghettos ushered in the last phase of the Final Solution: the eradication of the evidence. This operation, Operation 1005, was carried out across the occupied East by multiple squads known as *Sonderkommando* 1005. The Nazis had murdered almost six million Jews throughout Eastern Europe and had left many mass graves behind. As early as February 1942, a Foreign Office official wrote Heinrich Müller, head of the Gestapo, concerning an anonymous report of mass graves being discovered in occupied Poland. Müller nonchalantly dismissed these concerns, saying "In a place where wood is chopped splinters must fall, and there is no avoiding this."[56] However, in June, Müller tasked former *Einsatzkommando* leader, SS-*Standartenführer* (Colonel), Paul Blobel, with eradicating any traces of the Final Solution in Eastern Europe. Rather than beginning with the mass graves he was most familiar with, Blobel started unearthing, burning, and reburying the ashes of victims at the extermination centers, beginning with Chełmno. He then visited Auschwitz, advising the commandant on how best to dispose of corpses that had not been burned in the early period of the camp. Blobel's *Sonderkommando* 1005 units then spread out to work in the other extermination centers. The camps were leveled and trees planted to forever hide their existence.

TABLE 9 *Closing of extermination centers.*

Date	Camp
December 1942	Bełzec
March 1943	Chelmno (1st closing)
August 1943	Treblinka
November 1943	Sobibor
May 1944	Majdanek
June 1944	Chelmno (2nd closing)
January 1945	Auschwitz

After the mass graves in these camps had been disposed of, the *Sonderkommando* 1005 staff faced the much larger and more difficult task of the identifying and clearing of thousands of mass shooting sites across the occupied Soviet Union. Blobel first began work on the mass graves of the Janowska camp in Lwów, Ukraine. SS-*Unstersturmführer* (Second Lieutenant) Walter Schallock, a man described as "always drunk but never rowdy ... shrewd and an excellent administrator" commanded local operations.[57] Policemen from the 23rd Police Regiment were allocated as additional manpower. These men had to sign a document swearing them to secrecy.[58] Killings continued at the site as Schallock and 129 Jewish prisoners from the camp began the gruesome task of unearthing the bodies, burning them, grinding any remaining bones into dust, searching for any valuables remaining, and then reburying the ashes. The *Sonderkommando*

TABLE 10 *Extermination centers and their death tolls.*

Killing Center	Number of Victims
Auschwitz	1,100,000
Treblinka	870,000–925,000
Bełzec	434,500
Sobibor	170,000
Chełmno	152,000
Majdanek	78,000

Source: Numbers from USHMM with the exception of Majdanek whose numbers are from Tomasz Kranz, "Ewidencja zgonów i śmiertelność więźniów KL Lublin," *Zeszyty Majdanka* 23 (2005).

was divided into different squads for these various tasks. Survivors of the SK1005 group in Janowska recalled their awful work in postwar statements. Heinrich Chamaides described the process: "We laid a layer of wood between each layer of bodies and then soaked it in old oil and gas. When the bodies were burned, we ground the bones to ashes and spread the ashes on the fields. While the bodies burned, an orchestra played."[59] Another survivor, Moische Korn, recalled recognizing the body of his own wife. He asked Schallock to shoot him; Schallock replied that "I would remain alive as long as I was needed and as long as I could work. Then [Schallock] forced me to throw the body of my wife into the fire."[60] The SS men even dressed up a prisoner in a hat with horns, called him "the Devil," and placed him in charge of keeping the fires burning.[61] Frequently, groups of future SK1005 SS men would visit the camp. A member of the *Sonderkommando* at Janowska recalled that "10 day special courses" were held in the SK for officers and sergeants. There they learned how to exhume and burn bodies, disguise the gravesites, and bury any remaining evidence. He recalled at least ten such courses.[62] Some members of the SK1005 at Janowska escaped and survived, but in most places in the East, the *Sonderkommando* Jews were murdered immediately upon completion of their tasks.

The "Final Solution," the physical extermination of the Jews, evolved as a series of developments affected by time and situational factors; yet, at the same time, it *was* driven from the beginning by the ideological dedication of the Nazis to removing Jews from society. As we have seen, it was the method of removal that changed from expulsion to extermination over the course of the war. In many ways, the Final Solution—as it was carried out in the extermination centers—represents the unholy combination of a state political system with industrial methods and pseudoscientific theories. The Nazis created a streamlined process capable of murdering horrifyingly large numbers of human beings in a relatively efficient manner.

However, it is also important to remember that 1.5–2 million Jews were killed in open-air shootings as part of the Final Solution, and that thousands died of disease, starvation, and maltreatment before and after the decision to physically exterminate the Jews.

The Nazis were most successful at this task in Europe, but the genocide known as the Holocaust had no geographic limits. It is, therefore, important to recognize that there were *Einsatzgruppen* allocated to Rommel's "chivalrous" Afrika Korps in North Africa, and that the Wannsee Conference targeted Jews outside Europe. We must also remember that the majority of Western European Jews murdered during the Holocaust were killed in the extermination centers of the East. These facilities were located there not because Eastern Europeans were more antisemitic than those in the west, but because the majority of the victims (ca. 5.6 million) were there.

Selected Readings

Arad, Yitzhak. *Bełżec, Sobibor, Treblinka: The Operation Reinhard Death Camps*. Bloomington: Indiana University Press, 1987.

Browning, Christopher R., and Jürgen Matthäus. *The Origins of the Final Solution: The Evolution of Nazi Jewish Policy, September 1939–March 1942*. Lincoln: University of Nebraska Press, 2004.

Montague, Patrick. *Chełmno and the Holocaust: The History of Hitler's First Death Camp*. Chapel Hill: University of North Carolina Press, 2012.

Rees, Laurence. *Auschwitz: A New History*. New York: Public Affairs, 2005.

Sereny, Gitta. *Into That Darkness: An Examination of Conscience*. New York: Vintage Books, 1983.

10

The Kaleidoscope of Jewish Resistance

Introduction

We want to survive so much, to see the pogrom turned on the beast. We want to live to see light triumph over darkness, justice over tyranny, and freedom over oppression and terror. We yearn to live to build a better world. But will we make it? Is it not too late?

STANISLAW SZNAPMAN, diary, Warsaw, 1943[1]

Sznapman expressed in this diary entry the fervent desire to overcome the genocidal system in which he was trapped. Yet, how to resist that system was debated during the Holocaust and ever since. The nature of Jewish resistance to the Holocaust remains a sensitive and controversial topic. The definition of "resistance" itself varies according to the beholder, both scholarly and public. Indeed, the very goal of resistance also has been debated. It has created bitter confrontations between Jews, scholars, and even nations. However, perhaps the most important takeaway from this chapter is that resistance of some kind occurred in almost all places at all times during the Holocaust. One need only look.

This chapter addresses the spectrum of Jewish resistance during the Holocaust in Eastern Europe, beginning with the very definition itself. What is resistance? What was the goal? How did different people, both during and after the Holocaust conceive of resistance? We will then move on to examine the many forms this resistance took and the place of resisting in the minds of Jews.

Defining Resistance

> Of the twenty-four Judenrat members, four decided to meet the Germans and offer themselves as sacrificial victims to deflect the wrath of the enemy. With the ghetto empty and silent, the four men sat and waited for their executioners. While they were waiting one of them faltered. The others told him to go and hide. The three men of Kosów prepared to meet the Nazis on Passover of 1942. Was their act less than firing a gun?
>
> Historian YEHUDA BAUER[2]

The actions of the Judenrat members in Kosów exemplify almost at once the complexity of defining resistance in the Holocaust. Bauer rightly asks us to question whether the bravery and selfless behavior of those remaining Jews is any less significant than armed battle against the Nazis. In so doing, he engages in a highly contentious debate about Jewish resistance that began during the war and continued to generate heated reactions. For a long time, disputes ensued over whether only armed actions against the Nazis constituted resistance or whether other behaviors could be included. Wrapped up in any discussion of Jewish resistance must be the significant challenges to resistance in the first place.

First, while Jews had faced discrimination and even murder before in the form of pogroms, they had never faced an ideology intent on eliminating them from the face of the earth, supported by all the power of the modern nation state. Previous modes of coping with anti-Jewish violence simply were not effective. Second, Jews were under the complete physical control of that nation state intent on murdering them, with little means to physically resist. Third, decisions about physical resistance in particular were greatly complicated by potential reprisals against family and other members of the community. Fourth, even escape became a difficult choice because it often meant leaving behind young, old, and sick family members who could not survive the rigors of flight. Fifth, location was an important factor for the attitudes of the outside non-Jewish community, and/or the proximity to friendly partisans often dictated whether or not both escape and support for resistance was likely. All of these factors made choosing to resist much more difficult than some might assume.

The unspoken question behind discussions of resistance is often "why did it appear that so many Jews had not taken any action to save themselves?" Even Emanuel Ringelblum, the famed historian imprisoned in the Warsaw ghetto, lamented in October 1942, "Why didn't we resist when they began to resettle 300,000 Jews from Warsaw? Why did we allow ourselves to be led like sheep to the slaughter? Why did everything come so easy to the hangman?"[3] Hannah Arendt, writing at the Eichmann Trial in Jerusalem in 1961, went further, accusing the trial itself of avoiding asking of wartime Jewish authorities, "Why did you cooperate in the destruction of your own people and, eventually, in your own ruin?"[4] Even the noted scholar of Holocaust studies, Raul Hilberg, defined resistance only in terms of violence against Germans. In his pivotal work, he wrote that "the reaction pattern of the Jews is characterized by almost complete lack of resistance ... the documentary evidence of Jewish resistance, overt or submerged, is very slight." He notes there was no large-scale "blueprint for armed action" and goes as far as to quote a high-level SS man as saying that "Never before has a people gone as unsuspectingly to its disaster."[5]

Not surprisingly, others disagreed with this quite negative appraisal of Jewish reactions to the Holocaust. They argued for a variety of reasons that limiting resistance to its armed form overlooked many important ways in which Jews struggled against their oppression and eventual annihilation. This view of resistance borrows from the Jewish concept of *amidah* or "standing against." One scholar described this *amidah* as "'all expressions of Jewish 'non-conformism' and for all the forms of resistance and all acts by Jews aimed at thwarting the evil design of the Nazis,' a design that included not only physical destruction, but also to 'deprive them of their humanity, and to reduce them to dregs before snuffing out their lives.'"[6] This much broader definition reflects the complexity of the situation in which Jews found themselves, as well as the difficulty in even being able to participate in armed resistance. As such, it tends to be a more useful definition (and one which I will follow here.) In short, because the Nazis sought to destroy Jews physically, culturally, and spiritually, one can convincingly argue that anything they did to oppose this annihilation, even the act of staying alive, can be considered to be resistance.

Finally, it is important to note that beyond the value of a definition of resistance for our own understanding, it had important meanings in other contexts. For the perpetrators, portraying the behavior of the victims as passive, organized, and without violence was almost always an attempt to convince others of the "humaneness" of their actions and to, in some way, forget their own trauma and assuage their own guilt. For Jews, particularly those in Israel, a focus on armed resistance against the Nazis and a valorization of those who fought served more utilitarian purposes in the creation of the Jewish state. Many Israeli politicians did not want the world to see the Jews as victims going to their deaths without protest. They wanted Jews, and by extension the new state of Israel, to be seen as a collective of hardened fighters, prepared to defend it against the very real threats it faced from 1948 to 1973. Therefore, the Jewish partisans and those who had risen up in the ghettos, particularly Warsaw, received almost mythic idolization while others and other forms of resistance were marginalized. This often also resulted from the "survivor historians from Warsaw," who were able to shape the story of the Holocaust as told at Israel's Holocaust Museum and memorial, Yad Vashem. The law that established the institution in 1954 tasked it with commemorating and "gather[ing] material regarding all those members of the Jewish people who laid down their lives, who fought and rebelled against the Nazi enemy and his collaborators." While the law recognizes a mission to remember those murdered, three of the nine missions of the memorial were to commemorate:

(4) the fortitude of Jews who gave their lives for their people;
(5) the heroism of Jewish servicemen, and of underground fighters in towns, villages and forests, who staked their lives in the battle against the Nazi oppressors and their collaborators;
(6) the heroic stand of the besieged and fighters of the ghettoes, who rose and kindled the flame of revolt to save the honour of their people;[7]

For the purposes of this chapter, however, I will adopt a broader view of Jewish resistance along a spectrum from maintaining one's dignity to armed attacks against Nazi perpetrators.

Specifically, I divide resistance into three general categories: social and cultural, non-violent, and violent resistance. Social and cultural resistance covers a wide variety of behaviors, from maintaining dignity before death as the Judenrat members of Kosów did to maintaining religious and artistic life in the face of Nazi oppression. Non-violent resistance constitutes acts aimed directly against the Nazis, but not involving violent attacks upon them. This category includes such actions as documenting, escaping, smuggling, hiding, and sabotaging. Finally, the category of violent resistance requires physical attacks against the Nazis. Each of these kinds of opposition to the Holocaust took place in a variety of places, from concentration and extermination camps to ghettos large and small, to the forest. Certainly, some behaviors do not fit easily into these categories and those that are discussed are not to meant to be a comprehensive list. Rather, the goal is to provide a brief introduction to the complexity and diversity of Jewish resistance to the Holocaust in Eastern Europe.

Social and Cultural Resistance

For the Germans they were badges of shame and degradation. We proposed to wear them with pride and dignity. Jewish women did their utmost to make the armlets as fine as possible. The best possible material was used, and the blue Star of David was carefully embroidered on it in silk.

ADOLF FOLKMANN, survivor from Lwów[8]

For Jews like Adolf Folkmann, acts of resistance could be undertaken even in the face of German attempts to marginalize and oppress them. These acts could even take place in the mind. When we discuss social and cultural resistance, it is important to realize that the psychological impact on the individual and community could often be more important than any impact on chances of survival. The Nazis attempted to systematically degrade, humiliate, and disrupt Jewish communities in myriad ways in order to reduce Jews to a substandard existence and deprive them of a "normal" life. However, many Jews fought against this cultural genocide in a variety of ways, some of which will be discussed here. As Chaim Kaplan wrote in the Warsaw Ghetto, "everything is forbidden to us; and yet we do everything! We make our 'living' in ways that are forbidden, and not by permission."[9]

Socially, Jews under Nazi control fell back on more traditional forms of social support, which became resistance in the context of the Holocaust. The *kahal* system of communal welfare that had sustained Jewish communities in previous centuries reappeared in the ghettos, albeit in a weakened state. Jewish councils struggled to arrange for services that the modern state had taken over but that were denied under the Nazis. As we have seen, for example, the Warsaw and Łódź ghettos contained massive bureaucratic apparatuses to attempt to provide for their malnourished and sick populations. Jews in ghettos large and small faced a daily struggle for food that was at least partly alleviated by the soup kitchens created by the Jewish councils. The same was true for hospitals, where doctors and nurses fought a losing battle against illness and injury with insufficient instruments and perpetual shortages of medical supplies.

Jews in ghettos established orphanages to care for children whose parents had been deported or had died. The most famous of these was the Orphans' Home in the Warsaw ghetto. Dr. Janusz Korzcak, a renowned children's writer and educator who had managed orphanages before the war, continued his service in the ghetto. He and his staff cared for 200 children, with Korzcak personally supplying the teaching aids and arranging for different inhabitants of the ghetto to give talks to the children.[10] The Orphans' Home was one of thirty orphanages in the Warsaw ghetto. He even gave public puppet shows depicting "beautiful, gentle fairy tales."[11] Korzcak's dedication to his profession and to the health and welfare of the orphaned children must be recognized as a selfless act of resistance. In attempting to create as normal a life as possible for the children, Korzcak subverted Nazi oppression. The energy poured into social welfare certainly represents resistance against the Nazis, who were at best indifferent to suffering in the ghettos and at worst, approving of high death rates, particularly of the most vulnerable inhabitants unable to work. Simply staying alive thwarted Nazi plans.

In fact, simply the education itself that Korzcak provided was resistance, as it violated Nazi prohibitions against education. This was a common form of resistance throughout the ghettos of the East. In August 1942, the Nazis outlawed and closed schools in the Kaunas ghetto in Lithuania. The order read, "Existing schools are to be closed immediately; the staff employed in the schools is to be directly integrated into the labor brigades.

Any form of instruction as well as conducting religious exercises is immediately prohibited."[12] As inhabitant and historian of the ghetto, Avraham Tory wrote in 1943, "It is often truly heartbreaking to look at the young people. These 16- and 17-year old boys and girls—just children and just developing themselves –their place is on a school bench."[13] However, the authorities in the Kaunas ghetto subverted this order by creating "vocational schools," ostensibly only to teach trades but, in reality, these schools taught a wide variety of subjects. In the Łódź ghetto, Dawid Sierakowiak wrote in 1942, "I still want to read and to study. I borrow books, make plans and have projects, but there is nothing that I can turn into tangible reality. I used to blame it all on the winter, but it's quite warm now, and those winter obstacles are gone. Unfortunately, hunger is the real reason for my 'laziness.' "[14] The Warsaw ghetto in 1942 had 48,207 children of school age; at least half of them received some kind of education either in clandestine schools, children's organizations (daycare, orphanages, etc.), or in private lessons at home.[15] One survivor who was a student in the ghetto recalled that most of the classes "took place at the homes of pupils, in permanent readiness for visits."[16] In the labor and concentration camps of the East, such education was far more rare, and rarer still in the extermination centers, but did occur. However, in ghettos, the classroom became simultaneously a place of resistance: providing education, and a "normal" life for Jewish children, despite Nazi efforts to the contrary.

Another form of opposition can be placed under the umbrella of cultural defiance, that is, the maintenance of and creation of art of all kinds from visual art to literature, music, and theater. Accounts of ghetto life abound with references to performances of all kinds. Dawid Sierakowiak wrote in his diary on May 27, 1942: "Today I went to the concert on Krawiecka Street again. It was the first concert worth seeing in the ghetto: a Beethoven evening."[17] Many of the larger ghettos imprisoned nationally and internationally renowned artists and musicians who contributed to the cultural life of the community. The Eldorado Theater in the Warsaw ghetto performed classic and original works. A ghetto newspaper wrote that in the theater "again we are surrounded by an atmosphere of joyful oblivion for a few hours."[18] In Warsaw, there was also a Jewish Symphony Orchestra, many of whose members had previously played for the prestigious Warsaw Philharmonic.[19] Poets and writers continued to write, often smuggling their work outside of the ghetto. Underground newspapers provided information and entertainment to ghetto residents. Though the Nazis often closed libraries, underground versions sprang up, where Jews could borrow and read books.

Not all ghettos offered the same opportunities. In Minsk, most intellectuals and artists were gone either as a result of Soviet repression, flight, or Nazi actions. The Nazis themselves were more repressive there, making cultural gatherings much more difficult.[20] Even in the concentration camps, some cultural life remained and could sustain inmates. Many had their own orchestras and, while these men were forced to play at official events by the Nazis, they could also play on their own for the prisoners. Even in the *Sonderkomando* of the Janowska camp in Lwów, responsible for burning bodies, musicians were supplied with a fiddle and harmonica with which to make music.[21] The Janowska camp orchestra was led by renowned members of the Lwów musical community until they were all executed, one by one, while still playing.[22] Across the Holocaust landscape of the East, Jewish artists, writers, and musicians continued to devote themselves to their art as a form of both personal and communal resistance to Nazi dehumanization.

Not all Jews supported such cultural activities. When the director of the Ghetto Theater in Vilna, Israel Segal, was asked to reopen his theater by the head of the Jewish Council, Jacob Gens, he hesitated. After the war, Segal described the opening of the theater as "a daring beginning to the forced normalization of ghetto life." Indeed, he remembered the performance had taken place "despite the great protest of various influential persons and community activists."[23] The Socialist Bund reacted even more angrily, posting flyers throughout the ghetto stating that "In a cemetery no theater ought to be performed."[24] Yet, despite such strong initial reluctance, those who attended the performances found them to be enjoyable. One diarist wrote:

> people laughed and cried. They cast off the depression that had been weighing on their spirits. The alienation that had hitherto existed among the ghetto population seemed to have been thrown off . . . people awoke from a long, difficult dream.[25]

The diverse reception of this cultural performance demonstrates the varied ways in which culture was (or was not) seen as resistance by Jews themselves. For many artists and audiences, these events allowed a brief escape from the terrors and privations of daily life.

A final form of cultural resistance (most poignant for us historians) is the act of documenting the Holocaust experience, both by professional and amateur historians. The most famous of these is Emanuel Ringelblum of the Warsaw Ghetto, an historian and social activist before the Holocaust. He had been in Geneva when the war broke out in 1939, but decided to return home to Warsaw. Once in the ghetto, Ringelblum resisted in the best way possible for him: by acting as an historian and documenting every aspect of life and death in the ghetto. Many scholars and diarists in other ghettos also sought to fight the Nazis by documenting and leaving behind evidence of the crimes against them. In Vilna, Hermann Kruk wrote "if I am staying anyway and if I am going to be a victim of fascism, I shall take pen in hand and write a chronicle of a city."[26] Avraham Tory, Secretary of the Jewish Council in Kaunas, also determined to document the Holocaust in the hopes of later retribution. He wrote his *Last Will and Testament* in December 1942. He began

> Driven by a force within me, and out of fear that no remnant of the Jewish community of Kaunas will survive to tell of its final death agony under Nazi rule, I have continued, while in the Ghetto, to record my diary which I began on the first day of the outbreak of the war. Every day I put into writing what my eyes had seen and my ears had heard, and what I had experienced personally.[27]

Tory also collected German orders and a variety of other documents, which he hid in wooden crates that he buried within the ghetto before his successful escape in 1944. Avraham survived the war and retrieved the crates, which form a vital record of the Holocaust in Kaunas.

In Warsaw, Ringelblum eventually formed a group known as Oneg Shabbat (Hebrew for "Joy of the Sabbath"). This group brought together a collection of historians, intellectuals, academics, and others to compile an archive, which they hid in milk cartons and buried before the ghetto was liquidated. The work of groups like Oneg Shabbat was not designed only for posterity; indeed, they often served a vital purpose by bringing news of the outside world and the Holocaust into the ghettos. Though only some of the archive was recovered after the war, its documents and studies give us a much better understanding of the experience of the Warsaw Ghetto. The process of recording the life and death of the ghetto was not one of emotional detachment; when one of his friends was murdered by the SS, Ringelblum wrote in his diary about adding that name to the list of those killed:

> My hand shakes as I write these words; who knows if a future historian, reviewing this list, will not add my name, Emanuel Ringelblum? But so what, we have become so used to death that it can no longer scare us. If we somehow survive the war, we'll wander around the world like people from another planet, as if we stayed alive through a miracle or through a mistake.[28]

Ringelblum escaped the ghetto with his wife and son. They survived in hiding until betrayed and captured by the Nazis. Fellow prisoners in the infamous Pawiak prison offered to save him, but Ringelblum refused when they could not also save his family. His last words to a fellow prisoner were "Is death difficult?" The Nazis shot Ringelblum, his wife, and young son shortly thereafter, in the ruins of the ghetto.[29]

In most camps and ghettos, Nazi administrators forbade religious practice. This was another form of "cultural genocide"—of destroying another aspect of Jewish life. The prohibitions ranged from outlawing services to banning ritual slaughter of animals to the physical destruction of synagogues. However, many religious Jews fought against these prohibitions. Underground synagogues and religious observances took place in camps and ghettos across Eastern Europe, even in the worst of circumstances. In the Kishinev ghetto (in lands occupied by the Romanians), the chairman of the Jewish Council formally requested (and received) an exemption from forced labor for ghetto inhabitants so that they could observe religious holidays by fasting and not working.[30] In the Warsaw ghetto, Ringelblum wrote that "In a Jewish house, they study the holy books ... The place is disguised; the door is opened only to those who are trusted and know the password."[31] At least four clandestine ritual *mikvahs* or bathhouses operated within the ghetto.[32] The ghetto itself was divided into twenty-eight rabbinical districts with sixteen rabbis to preside over religious affairs.[33] Ghettos across Eastern Europe fought to maintain religious opportunities for the believers.

Even in the worst situations, observant Jews fought to practice their religion. Rivka Liebeskind, an Auschwitz survivor, recalled her first *Shabbat* in Birkenau. "We lit the candles and quietly began singing the songs for the Sabbath. We did not know what was happening around us, but after a few minutes we heard stifled crying from all the shelves around us ... They gathered around us and listened to our prayer and singing; soon there were those who came off their own shelves and asked to be allowed to bless the candles."[34] One survivor of Treblinka remembered that in the extermination area of the camp, "[weddings] were performed according to Jewish law."[35] Even in the gruesome Janowska "Death Brigade" tasked with burning bodies, Leon Wells recalled that the religious Jews among them "kept to their way of life despite all difficulties." He added that prayer books and religious materials were "much more dangerous to possess than money or gold." During Yom Kippur 1944, the non-religious Jews kept watch as the religious Jews observed the holiday.[36] Of course, religious experience was not the same everywhere. Renowned rabbi, David Kahane, noted of the Lwów ghetto that, "Religious life has not been resumed. In this respect, the situation in Lwów was worse than in outlying towns ... when [an underground service] was discovered, all the participants and the apartment owner were taken to the prison, and no one has yet returned from there."[37] The Holocaust deeply affected religious belief, either by destroying it or by deepening it.

A final form of individual, social resistance was the simple maintenance of dignity as recalled by Adolf Folkmann at the beginning of this section. Where the Nazis attempted to humiliate or terrify their victims, Jews could fight back, even at the last moments, by refusing to be degraded. This was naturally a symbolic form of resistance, likely mistaken by the perpetrators and some Jews as acquiescence. Yet, for many, maintaining their composure even in the face of their own violent deaths was clearly important, if only for themselves. We must recognize that some resistance was deeply personal and never meant to serve any larger cause. German factory manager, Hermann Graebe, observed such courage at a mass shooting in Dubno, Ukraine in 1943. He saw a father and son heading toward their imminent deaths. As Graebe recalled in a 1945 affidavit, "The father held the hand of a boy about 10 years old and spoke to him softly; the boy was fighting his tears. The father pointed toward the sky, fondled his hand, and seemed to explain something to him."[38] In this intensely personal moment, the father overcame his own fear to comfort his son, even in the face of the most awful of circumstances.

Perhaps the most poignant example of this kind of comfort and sense of duty can be seen by the actions of Dr. Janusz Korzcak and his staff of the orphanage in the Warsaw ghetto. On August 5, 1942, the children were all selected for deportation. Though Korzcak, being a prominent member of Warsaw's pre-war society, had many Poles willing and desperate to hide him, he chose to stay with his children as they were deported. He wanted to lessen the trauma of the experience as much as possible and so told the children to dress up as they were going on a field trip to the countryside. He then led them to the trains. An eyewitness recalled, "It was a march of a kind that had never taken place before. All the children were formed in fours, with Korzcak at their head, and with his eyes directed upward he held two children by their tiny hands, leading the procession."[39] Other witnesses recalled that the children were singing. Władisław Szlengel, a poet in the ghetto, remembered the event in verse, writing:

He was the only proud soldier
Janusz Korzcak, the orphan's guardian.[40]

FIGURE 22 *Janusz Korczak (center) with children and younger staff members in his orphanage, approximately 1930–39. Korczak ran a large orphanage in the Warsaw ghetto and voluntarily accompanied his children to Treblinka.*
Source: United States Holocaust Memorial Museum.

Korzcak's extraordinary courage in voluntarily going with his children to his death highlights the power of resistance that ultimately did not affect the killing process. However, for Korzcak (and many other teachers, doctors, and nurses like him), it was essential that he protect his children from being afraid up to the last moment. He saw it as his duty that they not experience their last moments alone and terrified. Korzcak and his two-hundred orphans arrived at Treblinka, likely on August 7, where they were gassed on arrival. While the commandant, Franz Stangl, was allegedly not present in the camp at the time, the story of Korzcak's arrival must have reached him; when in prison in Germany, a visitor gave him one of Korzcak's books and "his color changed and he bowed his head." The visitor left him "a badly shaken man."[41]

Non-Violent Resistance

During the trip, some other prisoners and I tore a plank out of the train car and then jumped out. I was naked. The people I met were afraid of me, no one could decide to give me some clothes. A woman finally gave me clothes. At first, I hid myself alone and then returned to the ghetto where I hid myself in the ghetto area.

> Survivor EDMUND SEIDEL describing his escape from a train to Bełzec and his return to the Lwów ghetto[42]

Edmund's harrowing escape from certain death at Bełzec is only one form of what we can call non-violent resistance; meaning it did not entail an assault on his oppressors. However, actions such as smuggling, escape, hiding, sabotage, and even suicide were ways in which some Jews chose to fight back against the Nazi program of persecution and, ultimately, extermination. These actions constituted concrete behavior opposing Nazi policy. We have already seen how smuggling was vital to the very survival of Jews in camps and ghettos and can thus be viewed as a form of resistance. However, as one historian has pointed out, "everything in the ghettos was permeated by ambiguity and duplicity. Were the smugglers heroes or merely rapacious exploiters?"[43] This is to say that resistance may be the result of activities sometimes designed to only benefit, in this case, the smugglers. By providing food to people who the Nazis were consciously attempting to starve, smugglers were resisting—whether that was their primary intention or not.

Where Jews were forced to perform forced labor, particularly for the German military, sabotage was one method of resistance. These "working Jews" could sometimes create faulty products that would fail when used in combat. This form of resistance was also incredibly dangerous if detected. Sabotage could also entail the theft of food and supplies from the workplace that could be used in the ghetto or for resistance. Therefore, the most important form of sabotage was the theft of weapons that could be smuggled into the camp or ghetto or given to the partisans. An exasperated German official in Belarus reported in 1942 that, "The Jews played a large role in all the destruction and sabotage . . . They were active in supplying stolen weapons and in stealing medicines from hospitals [on behalf of the partisans]."[44]

Escape was another form of high-risk (but usually non-violent) resistance. Escaping from a camp, a ghetto, or a train was naturally a clear rejection of Nazi attempts to murder Jews. Nazi authorities in Lwów made it policy that Jews like Edmund being sent to the extermination centers be stripped naked in order to impede escape attempts. This was done precisely because there were so many escapes. An official report from the Order Police guarding one train to Bełzec indicates the extent of these train escapes. The company commander wrote that "In the darkness of the night, many Jews escaped, after removing the barbed wire from the air holes" and that "The slow journey was exploited by those Jews who still had strength to slip through the openings and find rescue in escape, which was not dangerous on the slow-moving train."[45] Some Jews escaped from multiple deportation trains and became known as "parachutists." Often, these escapees found that returning to the ghetto was the only safe course of action.

Escapes took a variety of forms and could be only temporary—as in escaping a selection. In Warsaw, Emanuel Ringelblum would tirelessly wait at the deportation area of the ghetto, using his influence in an attempt to save "a chosen few—intellectuals, writers, teachers, and artists—from among the masses waiting their turn to enter the death trains."[46] He was also able to provide food to those waiting to be deported. In Treblinka, Jews working with the reception of incoming trains could sometimes save others from death, at least temporarily, by hiding them under clothing or secretly adding them to work details.[47]

Some Jews managed to escape from even the open-air shootings. In Rovno, Leah Bodkier ran from the Sosenki forest near Rovno as guards shot at her. She made it to a haystack and hid inside. She survived the war in hiding with a Pole.[48] Lisa and Pola Nussbaum ran from a massacre in the town of Slonim in Belarus, escaping both the Nazis and hostile local children who screamed, ""Jewesses, Jewesses, you took off your yellow stars! The Nazis will kill you! The Nazis will kill you!"[49] They collapsed in the barn of a local woman, who hid them until the massacre was over. Not infrequently, victims of these mass shootings would not be hit at all or would be only wounded. They climbed out of the pits and escaped.

Some escapes were more organized. The Jewish Council in Minsk worked closely with the non-Jewish Resistance and managed to send more than 10,000 Jews out of the ghetto and into the forests, where they were taken in by partisan units.[50] In 1943, 250 Jews escaped from Novogrudok, Belarus via a tunnel just before the Nazis liquidated the ghetto.[51] The chances of success for escapees often depended on local conditions, and whether the non-Jewish population was receptive, or at least not openly hostile to Jews.

Unfortunately, in many parts of Eastern Europe, this was not the case. The Minsk ghetto, for example, was so successful in getting Jews out, in part due to the proximity of deep forests and receptive partisan groups.

Others resisted by preparing hiding places in anticipation of Nazi roundups. These were known as *malinas* and throughout the ghettos of Eastern Europe, they appeared as the meaning of deportations became clear to the Jews. The *malinas* or hideouts could range from the simple to the incredibly complex. With sufficient warning, Jews could hide during raids and hope to avoid deportation. Yitzhak Rudashewski described the experience of hiding in the Vilna ghetto in September 1941:

> The hiding place was entered through a hole in the wall of the apartment . . . We are like animals surrounded by hunters . . . The knocking of smashed locks, doors creaking, axes . . . Suddenly the sound of a baby crying from somewhere above. A desperate groan issues forth from everyone's mouth. We're finished.[52]

Yitzhak was not, however, discovered and survived the raid. The chances of success in hiding increased greatly if Jews were assisted by non-Jews. In Vilnius, it is estimated that 7,000 Jews survived the first mass killings in hiding.[53] For those hiding on their own, refuge was usually only temporary, unless they were able to escape the ghetto permanently. For those in the camps, hiding was only an option when the camps were evacuated; some inmates were able to hide themselves and remain behind to be liberated. In the Starachowice camp (and others), prisoners hid sick inmates and children during selections to protect them from death.[54]

Perhaps the most personal (and often controversial) mode of resistance for some was suicide. One prominent historian has argued that suicide constitutes resistance because "death itself is a form of rebellion."[55] Many Jews concluded that choosing the time and manner of their own deaths—rather than allowing themselves to be murdered by the Nazis—was their only way to fight back. We have seen that Adam Czerniakow, Chairman of the Jewish Council in Warsaw, chose this course of action when confronted with the deportation of children. However, many ordinary citizens also committed suicide rather than face death at the hands of the Nazis. Not all observers agreed that suicide was resistance. Stefan Ernest, in the Warsaw ghetto, wrote in his diary that "in our circumstances nothing was easier than choosing to die; deciding to survive was harder by far."[56] The decision for suicide and its meaning remained an individual one.

Regardless, it was popular enough that the black market price of poison skyrocketed in ghettos such as Rovno and Lwów in Ukraine where, in the latter, "many people, especially intellectuals, used their last money in order to buy poison."[57] Christine Keren, in hiding with her parents in Lwów, recalled that cyanide was "very valuable in that time," and that her mother always kept three vials, one for each child, saying that the Germans "will not take us alive."[58] In the camps as well, prisoners often chose suicide as an escape when they could no longer bear the torture of camp life. A survivor of the Janowska camp remembered inmates tied to poles and left to die "yelling to us 'Cyanide!' so that they might be delivered from that agony."[59] Finally, some simply found their lives and the things they cared about too irreparably damaged to go on. In the Warsaw ghetto, Lejb Szur dedicated himself to saving as many Jewish books as possible from across the city and ghetto. When ordered to leave his apartment during the large deportation Aktion in August 1942, Lejb chose to remain with his books, hanging himself in front of his bookshelves.[60]

Armed Resistance

That is how they took our brothers, sisters, fathers, mothers, our children.
That is how they took tens of thousands away to their death.
But we will not go!
We will not let them take us like animals to slaughter.
Jews, prepare for armed resistance!
. . .
Jews, we have nothing to lose.
Death is certain. Who can still believe that he will survive when the murderers kill systematically? The hand of the hangman will reach out to each of us. Neither hiding nor cowardice will save lives.
Only armed resistance can save our lives and honor.

Proclamation of the United Partisan Organization, Vilna Ghetto,
September 1, 1943[61]

The above call to arms by the underground in the Vilna Ghetto simultaneously highlights the resolve of many Jews to fight and the challenges to armed, violent resistance against the Nazis. The decision to take violent physical action against the Nazi occupiers or camp personnel raised serious concerns that may not always be clear at first glance. However, Eastern European Jews fought their oppressors in ghettos, camps, and with the partisans to an extent rarely recognized. Each situation brought its own challenges and not all armed resistance dramatically affected the overall outcome of the Holocaust, but nonetheless, the ability and will of the Jews to fight deserves recognition.

Several very real factors hampered efforts to organize armed resistance in the ghetto. First, many Jews did not believe that the Nazis intended to murder them. Stansilaw Sznapman reported from the Warsaw ghetto that "Until October 1942, the Jews didn't know where people were being deported. They held on to the illusion that at least some might survive."[62] Yitzhak Cukierman in the Warsaw ghetto reported "But [the Jews of] Warsaw did not believe it! Common human sense could not understand that it was possible to exterminate tens and hundreds of thousands of Jews." "More than once," he went on, " the reaction to the information we had about the liquidation of the Jews was: 'that cannot happen to us here.' "[63] Though reports of mass murder came into Warsaw, many simply could not comprehend the scale of the danger or make life-changing decisions based on what they often considered rumors or isolated incidents. Even the Jews of Hungary, among the last to be targeted, seemed "almost oblivious to what was happening to the other Jewish communities in Nazi-dominated Europe."[64] Of course, those already in camps knew the truth, but were hampered by other factors.

The second factor that constrained armed resistance was closely linked to the first. For much of the period of the Holocaust, the Jews of Eastern Europe in ghettos lived with their families. The old, young, and infirm could neither escape nor fight and their presence often complicated the decision making of those most capable of resistance, particularly if they were unsure of the realities of Nazi policy. Certainly, few relished the idea of escaping or fighting alone, leaving their families in the hands of the Nazis. The most stark and poignant example of this attitude can be found in Mir, Belarus. A Jewish boy, Oswald Rufeisen, was ordered to work as an interpreter for the German police in the town, as they believed him to be Polish. Rufeisen was thus able to warn the ghetto of the date and time of the coming liquidation. The Jewish council did not believe him; one member stated emphatically that "A liquidation of the ghettos is out of the question!" Others in the ghetto were convinced, but did not want to escape without the permission of the council.[65] This is one reason that much armed resistance developed after the young and old had already been killed and Nazi plans became abundantly clear.

Third, many Jewish councils themselves were not only reluctant to support resistance movements, but actively worked against them. They feared German reprisals against the community that would target everyone or even lead to the liquidation of the ghetto. Jacob Gens in Vilna believed that the Nazis needed Jews to work and so opposed the smuggling of arms into the ghetto for fear of retaliation. He told his leadership in 1943 regarding attempted smuggling of pistols, "Don't cause trouble yourselves. If they do not provoke us, then we must not do it ourselves. Because it is we alone who pay!"[66] He was not alone in this stance. Many ghetto leaders, drawing on historical Jewish responses to persecution, pursued a policy of accommodation intended not to further antagonize the Nazis and cause potentially greater killing. While this policy may have been successful during pogroms in the past, it was doomed against the intended extermination of all Jews. It also hamstrung efforts by underground groups to prepare to fight the Nazis. Not all ghetto leaders took this approach. Dr. Elkes and his police force in Kaunas supported the underground, providing information and money for weapons.[67] A former Kaunas partisan recalled that "An atmosphere of solidarity with the underground was created in Kaunas . . . different than the atmosphere in Vilna."[68] The Minsk ghetto leadership also worked closely in providing fighters for the partisans outside the ghetto and weapons.

Lastly, those in the ghettos often found it extremely difficult and dangerous to acquire the weapons necessary to fight invariably better armed and organized Nazi forces. Local underground groups were often reluctant to provide arms from their own supplies to Jews either out of self-interest or due to antisemitism. This was the general rule, but there were exceptions, such as the Minsk ghetto's relationship with the non-Jewish underground.

Despite these challenges, a significant number of Jews did take the fight to the enemy. The United States Holocaust Memorial Museum estimates that ghetto uprisings broke out in one hundred Eastern European ghettos, or about 25 percent of the ghettos there.[69] Certainly, the most famous of these revolts was in Warsaw. The first attacks on German forces took place in January 1943, effectively stopping a deportation action. Although only around twelve Germans were killed, the resistance was shocking enough to cause them to avoid the ghetto until April. During this time, the ZOB, or Jewish Fighting Organization, prepared for the coming German assault. They trained fighters, and the noncombatants prepared bunkers and hiding places. The ZOB, led by Mordecai Anielewicz, a twenty-three year old youth group leader, also tried to acquire weapons from the Polish Home Army (AK) resistance group, but without much success. The ZOB wrote to the AK in March 1943 requesting more weapons and commenting acidly that "Sending us guns without ammunition gives the impression of a cynical playing with our fate and confirms the suspicion that the poison of antisemitism still affects Polish governing circles despite the cruel, tragic experiences of the past three years."[70]

Nonetheless, the larger ghetto uprising began on April 19, 1943, as German forces entered to round up the remaining Jews. A ghetto fighter described their entrance saying, "Tanks, armored cars, cannon, and columns of SS-men on motorcycles. 'They look as though they were going to war,' I said to the girl standing beside me. I felt then how very weak we were, how insignificant our forces were. We had only revolvers and hand grenades."[71] Regardless, 750 Jews of the fighting forces fought bravely for almost a month against overwhelming odds. Even Nazi propaganda chief, Josef Goebbels, exclaimed in his diary, "the Jews are putting up a desperate resistance."[72] In the end, the Germans crushed the uprising. They suffered at least sixteen killed and eighty-five wounded, though the actual casualty count is likely much higher. The commander of German forces, SS General Jürgen Stroop, reported 7,000 Jews killed during the fighting and 56,065 captured. The Nazis deported the remaining 42,000 Jews of Warsaw to the Majdanek and other camps, where most perished.

The Warsaw ghetto uprising was the largest armed ghetto revolt, but there were many others in ghettos of all sizes. In the ghetto of Baranovichi in Belarus, an underground headed by the Jewish police commander determined to break out if the Nazis attempted to liquidate the ghetto. They stole German weapons and prepared. Then, on September 22, 1942, when the Germans came, they fought back and, as a result, 450 people escaped to the deep forests nearby.[73] Similarly, inhabitants of the Lwów ghetto in Ukraine prepared to fight. A survivor recalled that "There were men who were determined to organize resistance at the last." They bought weapons from sympathetic Italian and Hungarian soldiers who were "always willing to sell whatever arms they could get hold of."[74] This small resistance group attacked German forces during the liquidation in June 1943. Jürgen Stroop, who had liquidated the Warsaw ghetto, was called in to help. Stroop noted that the Jews were "excellent military engineers" and almost admiringly praised them, saying they were "courageous, strong and imaginative" and "the Jews fought like tigers . . . none surrendered."[75] The Higher SS and Police Leader for Galicia, Friedrich Katzmann, reported eight dead and twenty-three wounded, but this may have been low given Stroop's comments.[76]

Opportunities for resistance in the extermination centers and at killing sites were scarce, yet serious revolts occurred in four out of the six extermination centers, and individual attacks occurred at both type of sites.[77] Jews arriving in these camps and at killing sites often fought back individually, with no hope of success. A survivor from Treblinka recalled that "people resisted, they refused to undress, they attacked the Germans with their fists."[78] Also in Treblinka, a prisoner named Meir Berliner hid a knife and attacked an SS guard, killing him. It was an "act of heroism and despair" that "aroused shock and fear amongst the SS personnel."[79] Even at mass killing sites, individual Jews both escaped and attacked their killers in their final moments. During the mass shooting of Jews from Slonim, Belarus, a German soldier witnessed a Jew attack a German policeman with a knife, wounding him in the face.[80] Members of SK1005 units in Lwów, Kaunas, Vilna and elsewhere attacked and killed guards during escapes.

In Sobibor, Treblinka, and even Auschwitz, inmates planned carefully orchestrated revolts. Prisoners in the small working sections of Sobibor and Treblinka were most successful. By October 1943, prisoners at Sobibor believed that they soon would be murdered and Alexander Pechersky, a Jewish Red Army prisoner of war, planned and led a revolt. Jewish prisoners lured individual SS guards to their workshops and then killed them, before storming the fences and running through a minefield into the forests. Survivor Thomas Blatt recalled, "I was behind the last of the fugitives. I went down a few times, each time thinking I had been hit. Each time I got up and ran farther . . . Behind us, blood and and ashes. In the grayness of the approaching evening, the tower's machine guns shot down their last victims."[81] Around half the camp, three hundred Jews, survived the escape and made it to the forest. The prisoners killed twelve SS men and two Ukrainian guards. Forty-seven of the escapees survived the war, including Blatt.[82] In Treblinka, prisoners took advantage of the absence of a large number of guards (who had gone swimming) to rise up in August 1943. While only one SS man was wounded and five or six Ukrainian guards killed, 200 out of 700 managed to escape and it is thought that seventy survived the war.[83]

In Auschwitz, 450 members of the *Sonderkommando,* believing themselves about to be killed, rose up in October 1944. They were able to kill a kapo and three SS men and to destroy one crematorium, but all were killed.[84] Despite the low survival rates of those who fought at these extermination centers, the very fact of resistance in these extremely oppressive environments powerfully illustrates the Jewish will to resist.

The final (and most extreme) version of armed resistance was fighting German military and police forces in guerilla groups operating in the forests and villages of Eastern Europe. Like their counterparts within the ghettos and camps, those Jews wishing to fight Germans in a more military fashion faced several obstacles. Thomas Blatt, who had escaped from the Sobibor extermination camp, realized that "daily life for a prisoner in Sobibor was actually in some ways more secure than that of Jews who were . . . in the forest . . . In Sobibor we knew what to expect."[85]

The transformation from civilian to partisan was fraught with many difficulties even before a Jewish fighter fired his or her first shot. First, Jews had to successfully escape captivity *and* survive long enough outside the ghetto or camp to find a partisan group. The geography of the surrounding areas could complicate this. Ghettos and camps closer to forests offered better chances for hiding and survival than those in areas that were more populated with non-Jews, many of whom were antisemitic and hostile. Second, most partisan groups were reluctant to take additional members who could not fight. Therefore, potential new members were expected to arrive with weapons, those same weapons being difficult to acquire in the ghetto or camp. Women were at a particular disadvantage in this regard. Lastly, Jews wishing to join the partisans had to find the *right* group of fighters. Throughout Eastern Europe, multiple groups of guerillas of various political ideologies fought the Nazis. Those that were nationalist often killed Jews as willingly as they killed Germans. Communist and official Soviet groups were less likely to do so, but still did on occasion. A Soviet intelligence officer reported on Jews in the forests in Belarus in November 1942: "The partisans do not help them, and they accept Jewish youngsters into their ranks unwillingly. There were cases of partisans from the Bogatirev unit . . . taking weapons from the Jews who came to them and sending them back. Anti-Semitism among the partisans is quite strongly developed."[86] Regardless, Belarus remained one of the areas that were more friendly to Jewish partisans.

With its deep forests and important German supply routes, it formed the heart of the partisan movement, though groups existed throughout the occupied Soviet Union. Jews typically joined either Soviet units or the less numerous Jewish partisan groups. After her family was murdered, twenty-year old Faye Schulman, joined a Soviet group where she was initially forced to do "women's work," serving as a nurse. However, she later was allowed to fight the Germans.[87] In Belarus, women made up 16 percent of non-Jewish partisan units and 26.5 percent of Jewish units.[88] Treatment of Jews in Soviet units varied depending on the commander, but was usually better than in nationalist units, where Jews often had to hide their identity. One member of such a group recalled that during an attack, he started taking fire from behind and that "I had a ... sneaky suspicion that they were shooting not at them, they were shooting at me."[89] Unsurprisingly, he left that unit as soon he could.

Perhaps the clearest form of armed resistance during the Holocaust was that of Jewish partisan units. Historian Yitzhak Arad estimates that there were between 18,000 and 20,000 Jewish partisans operating in the forests of the occupied Soviet Union. A further 10,000–13,000 non-fighters lived in family camps hidden deep within the forests with underground bunkers.[90] The most famous of these was the family camp operated by the Bielski brothers in Belarus. While the group did fight, its leader, Tuvia Bielski, maintained,

FIGURE 23 *Jewish partisan Faye Schulman in the forest. Near Pinsk, Belarus (Winter 1943)*
Source: Second Story Press.

FIGURE 23A *Portrait of female partisan, Sara Ginaite at the liberation of Vilna. The photograph was taken by a Jewish, Soviet major who was surprised to see a female, Jewish partisan standing guard, August 1944*
Source: United States Holocaust Memorial Museum.

"Don't rush to fight and die. So few of us are left, we need to save lives. It is more important to save Jews than to kill Germans."[91] The Bielski partisans entered ghettos and brought Jews out to the forest. When the Red Army arrived in the region, the Bielski camp contained 1,200 Jews, making it "the largest partisan group in the Soviet Union and all of German- occupied territory [and] one of the largest rescues of Jews by fellow Jews during WWII."[92]

Other Jewish partisan groups dedicated all their efforts to killing Nazis. One good example is the 51st Brigade, formed initially from the ghetto underground in Slonim, Belarus. Just establishing the unit was difficult. Jewish men and women from the ghetto began escaping to the forest before the major liquidation on June 29, 1942. On that day, the Germans burned the ghetto and rounded up survivors. In the forest, the survivors joined the 51st Brigade, which had been created after Soviet units refused to accept Jews. Relations were not exactly cordial between the Soviet and Jewish partisans. Non-Jews who had been in the 51st fled on July 1, 1942, stealing weapons that the Jews themselves had smuggled out of the Slonim ghetto when they escaped.[93] Typical of a partisan operation was the Battle of the Tenth Dam on September 13, 1942. The 51st desperately sought to escape a German anti-partisan operation near Pinsk in Belarus. They found a crossing point across the Oginski canal at the tenth dam. Believing it lightly guarded, the partisans advanced, only to discover that the dam had been reinforced with more German troops. A vicious firefight followed in which at least 100 Germans were killed. The 51st's commander, Feodorovitch, was mortally wounded, however. One survivor recalled his final words as he was dying: "Very few of you will survive, but you will be heroes."[94] The 51st eventually dissolved and dispersed among three Soviet units. However, the Jews of Slonim continued to serve. Indicative of the fierce fighting they carried out is the award certificate for Jacob Shepetinski, awarded June 22, 1944:

> He participated in 22 major battles against the German forces and police. He took part 5 times in blowing up railroad ties and in sabotage of telephone and telegraph lines, and has derailed three enemy military trains ... In all these actions he exhibited daring and bravery.[95]

Indeed, the Jews who fought the Nazis in battle paid a heavy price for their bravery. According to one study, "Jews served in disproportionately high numbers" in the partisans. Around 20,000–30,000 served in Soviet partisan units, where 80 percent died. Throughout the course of the war, there were at least thirty Jewish partisan groups.[96]

Jews in the occupied Soviet Union during the Holocaust continually faced "choiceless choices." Certainly, some of the most difficult involved the timing and manner of resistance in the face of overwhelming odds in opposing a structure of systematic oppression set against a background of often unsympathetic non-Jews. Resistance took many forms. What is, perhaps, most important is how Jews at the time viewed their actions through the lens of resistance. If we allow ourselves to examine resistance from their perspective, we find that many modes of behavior, public and private, violent and non-violent, represented the will of the Jewish community to fight against its persecutors.

Selected Readings

Blatt, Thomas Toivi. *From the Ashes of Sobibor: A Story of Survival*. Evanston, IL: Northwestern University Press, 1997.

Epstein, Barbara Leslie. *The Minsk Ghetto, 1941–1943: Jewish Resistance and Soviet Internationalism*. Berkeley: University of California Press, 2008.

Gutman, Israel. *Resistance: The Warsaw Ghetto Uprising*. Boston: Houghton Mifflin, 1994.

Marrus, Michael Robert, ed. *The Nazi Holocaust: Historical Articles on the Destruction of European Jews: Jewish Resistance to the Holocaust*. Vol. 7. Westport: Meckler, 1989.

Tec, Nechama. *Defiance: The Bielski Partisans*. New York: Oxford University Press, 1993.

11

Perpetrators, Collaborators, and Rescuers

Introduction

The active anti-Semitism which flared up quickly after the German occupation did not falter. Lithuanians are voluntarily and untiringly at our disposal for all measures against Jews, sometimes they even execute such measures on their own.

Report from OTTO STAHLECKER, commander of *Einsatzgruppe A*[1]

Stahlecker's report highlights the complexity of understanding the behavior of perpetrators and collaborators in the East: an SS officer praising the readiness of local Lithuanians to participate in the murder of their Jewish neighbors. This development particularly pleased Stahlecker as he had previously noted the relative difficulty of "organizing" pogroms. Naturally, he does not mention those who helped or rescued Jews. Yet one must understand each of these groups to truly view the Holocaust in Eastern Europe in its proper historical context. This requires empathy, the ability to view the world through their eyes and worldviews; empathy differs from sympathy in that we are not required to feel pity, sadness, or concern (at least not for perpetrators and collaborators).

The report above explicitly mentions perpetrators ("German occupation"), collaborators ("Lithuanians"), and victims ("Jews"). It does not mention bystanders. I argue that there is no such thing as a bystander and will abandon the "perpetrators, victims, bystanders" paradigm followed by many prominent historians.[2] "Bystander" implies a neutral observer not taking part yet everyone exposed to the Holocaust took part in some way, albeit on a broad spectrum from rescue to murder. Put another way, a man in a crowd watching the Lietūkis garage massacre in Kaunas *is* participating as an onlooker. He gives approval as a spectator by not leaving. If we view acts of genocide as communal behavior, this approval is an important factor. Our observer's actions certainly do not equal a killer's, but they move him toward to the perpetrator side. Conversely, if the same observer threw up his hands in disgust and walked away, we would not consider him a rescuer or resister, but his actions move him toward him to that side. Neither action killed or saved a victim, but nor are they neutral. One cannot, simply put, ever be completely neutral.

Those non-Germans choosing to side with the invaders also placed themselves along a spectrum of complicity for a variety of reasons. Only recently have researchers examined this group more closely. Unlike German perpetrators, Eastern Europeans who collaborated with the Nazis occupy a more complicated place in their own national histories as well.

Indeed, many Holocaust survivors have more bitter memories of neighbors and local populations who ignored, victimized, or marginalized them than of Nazis that sought to kill them. Paradoxically, there are *very* few Jews who survived the Holocaust without the help of at least one (and quite often many) non-Jews who frequently did so in the face of very real danger. Studies into these rescuers, those who helped or saved Jews, are also complex. All kinds of people became rescuers and saved Jews for a variety of reasons.

This chapter offers a brief overview of behaviors and motivations of perpetrators, collaborators, and rescuers in Eastern Europe. This discussion must be, by its very nature, somewhat sweeping, for scholars have dedicated mountains of research and countless studies to all three groups. Indeed, while sharing important similarities, specific places and times and longer histories inextricably link the phenomena of perpetration, collaboration, and rescue. Thus, I will not attempt to present an exhaustive treatment of any group but will rather sketch out the important roles individuals and groups played in the Holocaust in the East as well as some of the scholarly explanations for why they made the choices they did.

Killers and Desk Murderers

"I never saw Stangl hurt anyone," he said at the end. "What was special about him was his arrogance. And his obvious pleasure in his work and his situation. None of the others—although they were, in different ways, so much worse than he—showed this to such an extent. He had this perpetual smile on his face . . . No, I don't think it was a nervous smile; it was just that he was happy."

STAN SZMAJZNER, Treblinka survivor, on camp commandant, Franz Stangl[3]

Studies of perpetrators initially dominated Holocaust history. After all, without perpetrators, there would have been no Holocaust. Perpetrator studies sought to understand or explain the behavior of men such as Stangl and the seemingly inexplicable mentalities that Szmajzner observed. How could someone responsible for a camp that murdered thousands each day be "happy?" Addressing the behavior and motivations of the killers requires an understanding not only of history but also of psychology.

The label of "perpetrator" encompasses a broad array of positions, organizations, and behaviors. For our purposes, a perpetrator (or a perpetrator organization) directly furthered the Nazi genocidal project, including primarily the Holocaust, but also other policies directed against Sinti/Roma, Slavs, Soviet POWs, the handicapped, homosexuals, and others. Many of these individuals were not German, and will be discussed in the section on collaborators.

Who *were* the perpetrators? We have already encountered many: the *Einsatzgruppen*, the German Army, the SS, and camp personnel. Yet, others were not engaged directly in the physical murder of Jews but were still responsible for their deaths. Adolf Eichmann, the deportation expert, arranged the complicated logistics of moving large numbers of Jews from across Europe to extermination centers. Most famously, Hannah Arendt held him up as an example of a "desk murderer," those individual bureaucrats who facilitated the Holocaust without ever directly confronting it. She even coined the term "banality of evil" to describe what she saw as faceless officials performing mundane (but vital) tasks without the fervor of other killers. Christopher Browning has noted that Arendt correctly identified this group of people, but was wrong in believing Eichmann to be one of them. Further examination found that "Eichmann exemplified willful evil: a man who consciously strove to maximize the harm he did to others."[4] Various "population experts" involved in planning the mass starvation of Slavic peoples provide another example. Thousands of people from secretaries to railway officials to architects knowingly acted as accessories to the murder of millions.

Another excellent example of this kind of "desk murderer," both at the individual and organizational levels, was the company Topf and Sons. Topf and Sons was an established firm in Erfurt, Germany, which manufactured, among other things, crematoria for funeral homes and industrial incinerators beginning in 1914. The owners, Ludwig and Ernst Topf, and their crematorium engineer, Kurt Prüfer, were all party members. The company's complicity in the Holocaust began with Prüfer designing and supplying the Buchenwald concentration camp with a mobile oven to burn bodies.[5] Topf and Sons became the primary supplier of ovens to the Nazi camp system, with at least twenty-five installations completed.[6] Soon, however, it became far more involved in the process of murder as the oven contractor to Auschwitz. More ominously, Topf began building ventilation systems into its designs, proving that designers knew their ovens were being used in an integrated gas chamber complex from which poison gas needed to be extracted. Company employees installed the ovens and ventilation systems on-site in Auschwitz and one of them testified after that the war that:

After returning from Auschwitz, I reported to the head of the company, Ludwig Topf, that I had successfully completed testing the fan and exhaust systems in the second crematorium of Auschwitz Camp [Crematoria II in Birkenau]. In passing, I reported to him that the SS men had gassed a group of inmates in the gas chamber and their corpses had been burned in the crematory ovens. L. Topf showed no reaction. (Moscow, March 11, 1948)[7]

The firm's complicity peaked with an application for a patent imagining a four-story "continuous-operation corpse incineration oven for mass use."[8] Engineers at Topf and Sons recognized that corpse disposal slowed the extermination process and proposed solutions for their clients.

One area of perpetrator studies that historians have only recently begun to investigate is the role of women as participants in the Nazi genocidal project. Some fell into the category of the desk murderer or functionary. Nevertheless, we should not overlook the importance of the support these women lent their husbands, even simply knowing the nature of their work.

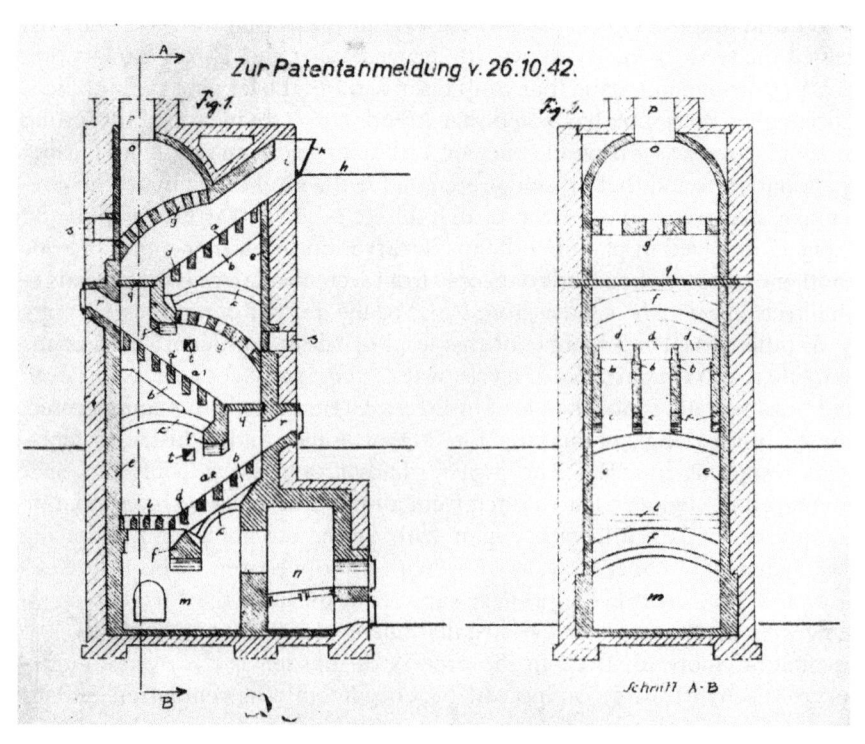

FIGURE 24 *Diagram of "continuous-operation corpse incineration oven for mass use" from Topf and Sons patent application, October 16, 1942.*
Source: Bundesarchiv Dahlwitz/Hoppegarten.

Historian Claudia Koonz aptly summarized the value of the moral support offered by perpetrators' wives, writing

> Nazi wives did not offer a beacon of strength for a moral cause, but rather created a buffer zone from their husbands' jobs. Far from wanting to share their husbands' concerns, they actively cultivated their own ignorance and facilitated his escape.[9]

They provided a respite and a sanctuary enabling their husbands to continue their "difficult" work. Indeed, Franz Stangl's wife admitted that "I believe that if I had ever confronted Paul with the alternatives: Treblinka—or me; he would . . . have chosen me."[10] She never put that question to the man who presided over the murder of between 870,000 and 925,000 human beings. Stangl's interviewer also concluded "that he was profoundly dependent on her approval of him as a husband, a father, a provider, a professional success—and also as a man."[11]

Other wives *did* want to participate in their husbands' careers. Some benefited financially, as with Hans Frank's wife in Poland. Other women, many single, were secretaries writing the *Einsatzgruppen* reports tallying Jews murdered in the East or serving in offices engaged daily in the persecution of Jews. Liselotte Meier, a secretary to the Nazi administrator in Lida, Belarus, accompanied her boss as he personally shot Jews. Despite strong evidence, Meier denied that she had also shot Jews, claiming not to remember.[12] Other women, too, became killers like Meier. Liesel Willhaus, the wife of the Janowska camp commandant in Lwów, enjoyed shooting prisoners from her balcony. One survivor recalled her leaning on the balcony and shooting while SS men sat behind her on stools laughing as she apparently hit a prisoner in the neck, killing him.[13] Another commandant's wife "ordered her dog to attack the Jewish children who worked in the camp garden"; a survivor recalled the task of retrieving the victims' limbs.[14]

In one final example, Erna Petri, wife of a German manager of an agricultural estate, murdered six Jewish children who had been seeking refuge there . . . after feeding them first.[15] Petri told the court that "I wanted to prove myself to the men."[16] In this sense, Erna sought to be seen as an equal perpetrator with the men around her. Historian Wendy Lower presents these female perpetrators and others to refute the idea that "violence is not a feminine characteristic and that women are not capable of mass murder." Moreover, she warns that "minimizing the violent behavior of women creates a false shield against a more direct confrontation with genocide and its disconcerting realities" while introducing an understudied class of perpetrators.[17]

What did the perpetrators *do*? The most obvious and well-covered actions were, of course, the murder of Jews and others. However, victimization took many forms, depending on individual, organization, and situation. Rampant theft of Jewish property occurred on both individual and group levels. For example, one German Army officer sent a train car of looted Jewish goods from Belarus to his home in Bavaria. One of his men observed that his comrades returning from a killing site had "acted as grave robbers. They had taken 10–15 rings, watches, valuable pieces of clothing." They then mailed these items home to their families in Germany.[18] As Jews moved into ghettos, Nazi officials systematically looted the bulk of their belongings left behind. In Lwów, one survivor in the Janowska camp recalled that Germans stole carpets, bedclothes, tablecloths and all manner of so-called "Jewish residue" and delivered them to be cleaned in the camp laundry where she worked.[19] Throughout the East, Nazi administrators continually extracted exorbitant "ransoms" from the population in attempts to steal as much wealth from the Jewish communities as possible before their liquidation. As early as July 1941, German authorities in Bialystok demanded a ransom of 5kg of gold, 100kg of silver, and 2 million rubles in exchange for the release of 4,000 men taken prisoner by Police Battalion 316. Inhabitants, mainly women, desperately raised the money. One survivor recalled that "women are roaming the streets, weeping and begging us: Give us gold, silver, money, in order to save our husbands and sons." The ransom was collected but, unfortunately, the 4,000 men had already been shot.[20] Sometimes, theft was blatant and petty. In Kaunas on August 20, 1942, two Nazi civil administrators visited the Jewish council, stole 31,000 marks from the cashbox, and left.[21]

Sexual violence against Jewish women accompanied many other crimes during the Holocaust in Eastern Europe. This topic is only now beginning to receive the attention it deserves. Perpetrators across Eastern Europe raped and sexually victimized their victims as a matter of course in ghettos, camps, mass shooting sites, and elsewhere. These attacks ranged from violent assaults to coerced sex to sexualized violence. For example, when Himmler visited Sobibor in February and March 1943, three hundred attractive young Jewish women were specifically selected to be gassed as a demonstration.[22] Not infrequently, Jewish women were raped at mass shooting sites prior to their deaths. Often, evidence of rape is not direct. A non-Jewish witness near the Ponary Forest wrote in his diary that a group of pretty young Jewish women was brought to the site. However, "the Germans, after bringing the Jewish women, removed the [Lithuanian collaborators] as far as the gate; nearly an hour elapsed from the arrival until the first shots were fired."[23] In Ukraine, the local Gestapo chief, Hummel, took two Jewish girls to his house on the day of the mass shooting, presumably killing them later.[24] In both instances, the implication is clear that these women were raped before their death. In Romania, officers arranged "orgies" during the deportation of Jews.[25] Sexual violence took place in the camps as well. Franz Stangl recalled that, on his first visit to Treblinka, camp personnel told him that then commandant Dr. Eberl "had naked Jewesses dance for them, on the tables."[26] In an act of sexualized violence, an SS man at the Janowska camp ordered two prisoners to have sex in public while the guards stood around and laughed. Both prisoners were shot when the SS grew bored of the spectacle.[27] What is critical about such crimes beyond their sheer horror is that they were never part of the Nazi genocidal plan. Indeed, Nazi laws prohibited sexual contact between Jews and Germans. Sexual violence of all kind was completely *voluntary*, as was theft. This insight demonstrates the degree to which some perpetrators were most definitely *not* following orders, but making their own choices to victimize Jews to further their own interests.

What caused perpetrators to willingly participate in the Nazi genocidal project? Identifying perpetrator motivation is an incredibly complicated endeavor. We must look at two scales: the macro, societal level and the micro individual/group scale. Many scholars of different disciplines (historians, sociologists, anthropologists, social psychologists, political scientists) have addressed the question of what makes societies capable of mass atrocities. Earlier research suggested authoritarian societies and personalities were to blame. Later research added more complexity. Sociologist Harald Welzer argues convincingly that a change in the nature of social belonging sets the stage for atrocities. He writes:

> Its alteration consists in the categorical redefinition of who belongs to one's own moral universe and who does not – who belongs to one's own group ("us") and who, as a member of a different group ("them"), is an "other," a stranger, and ultimately a deadly enemy.[28]

This process of "othering" is not unique to the Holocaust, but is present in all genocides. Drawing on this, historian Thomas Kühne adds that in Germany after World War I,

> the ethical code revolving around individual responsibility . . . was displaced by a moral system in which the only thing counting as "good" is that which appears good for one's own community, whilst everything figures as "bad" which is detrimental to it.[29]

Thus, we can see that group norms at a societal level helped create the conditions that dehumanized the victims and placed them outside the usual protections of "civil" society. This also applies at the micro level. Finally, social psychologist Albert Bandura provides us with a helpful framework for summarizing how some societies create and tolerate perpetrators in their midst. He states that three conditions create the moral disengagement necessary for perpetrators (and their societies) to distance themselves from the immorality of their behavior:

1. *Moral Justification*: The perpetrator society views the victimization and killing of the targeted group as a necessary, indeed, vital service for the survival of the community.

2. *Euphemistic Labeling of Evil Actions*: Vague and innocuous speech is used to both mask the immoral actions being committed and relieve perpetrators from confronting their own moral misgivings.

3. *Exonerating Comparisons:* Societies and perpetrators justify the necessity of criminal actions by the great threat (often imagined) posed by the "enemy." A utilitarian calculus then justifies immoral behavior in contrast with the much greater danger posed by the victim group.[30]

Taken together, these frameworks help us understand how German society (as well as some Eastern European societies and perpetrators) justified their actions against Jews and others on a state or national level. While it may seem odd, it is critical to recognize that no ideologically motivated perpetrator of genocide believes they are doing something wrong; on the contrary, genocidal ideologies always promise to improve society or save it from existential threats, even if the methods used cause moral discomfort.

At the individual or small group level, a diverse set of goals, beliefs, and environmental factors influence perpetrators to commit murder. These can be divided into dispositional (internal motivations and beliefs) and situational (external factors).[31] Earlier debates considered whether ideological or circumstantial factors drove participation in killing but now, historical consensus recognizes that *both* influence each other. Therefore, while an individual may be *more* or *less* moved by one factor or another, neither is sufficient alone to explain perpetrator behavior.

Thus, some perpetrators *were* definitely radical antisemites who saw the murder of Jews as completely acceptable. Eichmann, the so-called banal bureaucrat, was secretly recorded in hiding, reminiscing about telling his staff at the end of the war that "I will gladly jump into my grave in the knowledge that five million enemies of the Reich have already died like animals." In Theresienstadt, he told the Jewish Council that "Jewish death lists are my favorite reading matter before I go to sleep."[32] A *Wehrmacht* soldier described his commander as a "Jew hater;" this commander supervised the murder of 8,000–10,000 Jews in the town of Slonim in what is now Belarus.[33] An *Einsatzgruppen* commander in Ukraine led by example at one killing; he murdered an infant and mother saying "you have to die for us to live."[34] These kinds of behavior and language represent the powerful antisemitism embraced by some of the killers. For others, particularly collaborators, antisemitism also combined with anti-Bolshevism as powerful motivation.

For others, antisemitic prejudices may have been present, but did not form the primary motivation. In its own perverse way, the Holocaust provided previously unavailable career opportunities. The Topf example is a good one, but career prospects were also important for the killers. Many ambitious SS officers saw service in the *Einsatzgruppen* as a path to more rapid advancement. Conversely, those Nazi officials who had failed or disgraced themselves in the Reich often flocked to the East attempting to revive dead careers. One Nazi press officer noted that many of the civil administrators in the East (responsible for ghettos, Jewish policy, etc.) were:

> The idle and worthless type of . . . bureaucrat . . . the eternally hungry "Organizer" with a swarm of like- minded Eastern hyenas, his whole multitudinous clique, recognizable by the two big "Ws"—women and wine . . . [35]

We have already seen that those who began in the T-4 euthanasia program found further employment in the extermination centers of the East.

Perhaps the most mundane and yet most thoroughly disturbing motivation for killing was simple peer pressure. In July 1942, the commander of Reserve Police Battalion 101, informed his men that they would be murdering Jews. He then gave them the opportunity to refuse. Only around thirteen chose this moment to step out—without consequence.[36] The vast majority proceeded into the woods where they murdered almost 2,000 Jewish men, women, and children. Yet, these were not die-hard Nazis; they were middle-aged family men from one of the least Nazi-friendly areas in Germany.

Most simply could not resist the power of peer pressure and the expectations of the group. One scholar has called this "The Extraordinary Nature of the Collective."[37] It was common across the East for perpetrators to justify their participation on the grounds that they did not want to appear weak in front of their comrades or did not want their comrades to think they were avoiding "work" and passing it along to them. This reasoning also explains why most of those who refused used their own weakness as the excuse (at least publicly). They could then remain a part of the group; had they expressed their opposition in moral terms, they would be accusing their comrades of evil and would likely have been shut out of the only community available. One scholar has hypothesized that the very act of killing or transgressing standard morality created its own form of comradeship which "lived off collective breaches of the norm."[38] None of the preceding motivations for participation provides the only answer, but rather, they represent some ingredients present in varying amounts in a dangerous cocktail of spiraling violence.

We must close our brief overview of perpetrators by examining how they rationalized and coped with their own behavior. Why? Because the overwhelming majority of perpetrators in the Holocaust, including the killers themselves, were not insane and were not sociopaths. While initial studies had hoped to find that Holocaust perpetrators were psychologically abnormal, the truth is that most of them were quite healthy. This explains why so many experienced trauma as a result of their actions. Though perhaps hard to believe, some of the most dedicated, antisemitic murderers (such as Himmler) were disturbed by the experience. An SS officer in an *Einsatzgruppen* "suffered a nervous breakdown, because he couldn't stand the killing any more, particularly his own part in the shootings, and he requested a transfer back home."[39] His request was granted. Many other leaders and also low-level perpetrators experienced similar trauma, what one might call today post-traumatic stress, yet continued to kill or to participate. Already in 1939, a low-level *Einsatzgruppen* member from the Polish campaign reported being "depressed" about whether he would be able to leave behind his "criminal habits" that he had picked up.[40] By November 1941, Himmler had established mental hospitals, including one near Berlin, "where SS men are cared for who have broken down while executing women and children." A designer of the gas vans testified that one reason for their construction was that "the firing squads could not cope with the psychological and moral stress of the mass shootings indefinitely."[41] These perpetrators and others relied on a variety of techniques in order to rationalize and assuage their own discomfort.

The theory of cognitive dissonance neatly explains some of this trauma and one method of alleviating it, even among deeply committed Nazis. The theory says that when our actions and our belief systems are not in alignment, we experience mental and emotional stress and must change one or the other to bring our psyches back into balance. For many, it was far easier to change beliefs to justify behavior than to alter or end their participation in murder. Reserve Police Battalion 101 provides an extreme example of this rationalization, where a policeman testified that he intentionally shot *only* children after the mothers were killed. He explained this saying, "It was supposed to be, so to speak, soothing to my conscience to release children unable to live without their mothers."[42]

Other perpetrators sought to avoid the repercussions of their behavior by compartmentalizing or separating their murderous behavior from the rest of their lives. One scholar called this "doubling," where perpetrators attempted to live two separate lives. Franz Stangl tried this approach. In her interview, reporter Sereny attempted to understand why he dressed up in a formal uniform to meet arriving trains at the ramp. "I tried once more," she wrote. She asked him, "but to attend the unloading of these people who were about to die, in white riding clothes . . . ?" Stangl replied simply, "It was hot."[43] Stangl's reply indicates his complete detachment from the event and that he could not or did not wish to explain why he would treat arrivals as such important events. Stangl claimed that "the only way I could live was by compartmentalizing my thinking. By doing this I could apply it to my own situation."[44] Stangl was not alone in this approach.

Language, as mentioned above, also played an important role in the "sanitizing" of crimes. Words like "Final Solution," "Cleansing Actions," "special measures/special handling (*Sonderbehandlung*)," "resettlement to the East," among others provided perpetrators with a vocabulary allowing them to avoid facing their own actions. Stangl referred to victims as "cargo." *Einsatzgruppen* and army units involved in killing often reported their victims as either partisans, which gave the appearance of legitimate military targets or with a variety of euphemisms such as "partisan helper," "suspect civilian," "stranger to village," "wanderers," and "civilians without identification."[45] Such linguistic camouflage attempted to create mental/emotional distance from troubling activities.

To cope with their actions and the trauma they created, some perpetrators painted *themselves* as the victims, not the Jews. They stressed the difficult nature of their duties that they carried out in the service of others. In this characterization, Germans steeled their own emotions in order to sacrifice for the greater good of cleansing Europe of the threat posed by Jews and others. A killing unit member told his men forcefully, "'Good god! Damn it! A generation has to go through this for our children to have some peace."[46] Himmler himself proclaimed it was a "holy duty" for commanders to ensure that men who carried out the "burdensome duty" of killing never "suffer damage to the spirit."[47] The implication again is that the murder of the Jews was a deep sacrifice in which killers were victims.

Perhaps the final and most mundane solution for many was alcohol. Just as it had been in the euthanasia killing centers, alcohol and excessive drinking played a vital role in deadening the senses of killers and helping them fulfill their tasks. One scholar has concluded that "SS and police forces operating in the occupied territories abused alcohol on a tremendous scale."[48] As an *EK* leader, remarked to an Army officer, "We have to carry out this unhappy task, shooting all the way to the Urals. As you can imagine, it's not pretty and one can bear it only with alcohol."[49] If the abuse of alcohol at shooting sites helped soothe the shooters' consciences, it often resulted in poor performance leaving victims wounded but not dead. In the camps as well, alcohol figured prominently as a way to escape the tedium and also the trauma of living in a factory of death. Alcohol, despite Himmler's wishes that it not be used, not only perhaps temporarily assuaged mental trauma, but it also caused perpetrators to become even more violent. At the Janowska camp in Lwów, a drunken SS-man fired wildly into prisoners waiting for their meal, killing fifteen Jews.[50] Similar behavior and levels of drunkenness could be found at all the extermination centers in the East as well.

Perpetrator behavior, motivations, and coping mechanisms varied widely in time and space and this brief introduction certainly cannot be all-inclusive. However, the vast majority of perpetrators, whether direct or indirect, were not insane, sociopathic, or even particularly abnormal psychologically. They were, in most ways, ordinary individuals. Certainly, some were sadists drawn to violence, but most were not. This is and should be an uncomfortable truth highlighted by the quite different motivations and modes of participation sketched out above. As Christopher Browning closes his path-breaking book on the "ordinary men" of Reserve Police Battalion

101 "if [these] men . . . could become killers under such circumstances, what group of men cannot?"[51]

Local Collaborators in the Holocaust in Eastern Europe

For me, the situation was even more tragic because the orgy of murders was not only the deed of the Germans, and their Ukrainian and Latvian helpers. It was clear that our dear policemen would take part in the slaughter (one knows that they are like animals) but it turned out that normal Poles, accidental volunteers, took part as well.

Polish witness, STANISŁAW ŻEMIŃSKI, Łuków, Poland[52]

Local collaboration with Nazi occupiers in Eastern Europe is, perhaps, one of the most contentious histories for the modern populations of these countries. For a relatively small group of local non-Jews, then and now, this collusion with the enemy against the Jews was as tragic as it was to Żemiński (later murdered at Majdanek). His words are all the more damning as Poland is reluctant to recognize collaboration during the Holocaust. In this case, one author astutely notes that Poland is very proud not to have had a collaborationist government like Bulgaria, Romania, Hungary, and the German puppet states. However, he explains that this phenomenon was "not because a sufficiently prominent person could not be persuaded to cooperate, but because the Germans had no interest in granting the Poles authority."[53] Poland is not at all alone in this regard, however. Starting almost immediately after the war, even as the Soviets tried and executed collaborators, the official history largely buried the issue of local collaboration. The approved "dominant view" was that "the entire 'Soviet population' stood up to face the Nazi invader."[54] To recognize otherwise would be admitting that nationalities and ethnicities had rejected the Soviet system so strongly that they sided with the Nazis. While exact numbers are difficult to determine, they are significant. By 1942, 8,000 Lithuanians served in mobile police battalions, ten of which directly participated in the murder of Jews.[55] In the Baltic States, Belarus, and Ukraine, over 75,000 locals had volunteered to become "policemen" serving the Nazis by July 1942.[56] In Ukraine, "the ratio of Germans to local collaborators in many departments and police organizations ran from one to five in 1941, to 1 to 20 or more by 1943. The SS there consisted of 15,000 Germans and 238,000 native police at the end of 1942, reflecting a ratio of nearly 1 to 16, a rate that rose to 1:25 or even 1:50 in some eastern regions by 1944."[57] Another scholar estimated that at least one million Soviet citizens collaborated with the Nazis.[58] These numbers do not begin to include countless individual collaborators of all kinds.

Ironically, Jewish survivors usually hold their non-Jewish neighbors in higher contempt than the Nazis. Lithuanian survivor, Leib Garfunkel, wrote that "One of the factors that so exacerbated the suffering and pain of the Jewish population in Lithuania, and intensified their tragic fate, was the inhuman attitude toward the Jews on the part of many of their Lithuanian co-nationals, on all social levels."[59] For many Jews, the Nazis were like a natural disaster. They murdered Jews; that was their nature. But when non-Jewish neighbors joined in, the personal betrayal cut far deeper. This pain was felt not least because local collaboration was terribly important to the success of the Nazi genocidal project. One can argue that "without the active support of mayors, city councils, housing offices, and a plethora of local administrators, the identification, expropriation, and ghettoization of the Jewish population especially in rural areas would have exceeded the limited logistic capabilities of German occupation agencies."[60]

While a minority of non-Jews actively assisted the Nazis and an even smaller minority participated in killing, the majority of non-Jews in the East were passive observers at best or approving beneficiaries. For this reason, no discussion of the Holocaust in Eastern Europe would be complete without an examination of local complicity. These collaborators operated under different conditions and had their own objectives set deeply in the local context. While I will use the term "collaborator" in this section, many of these individuals' actions made them perpetrators as well, in that they actively participated in killing Jews.

First, not all regions of Eastern Europe collaborated with the same frequency or zeal as others. Generally, areas which had strong and enduring nationalist movements exhibited more intense collaboration. This is why the experience of Soviet occupation is so important in understanding the Holocaust. It neither solely explains collaboration nor solely caused it, but it did create fear, anger, and hatred in nationalist circles, many of which were already antisemitic. Garfunkel himself noted that Lithuanian antagonism toward Jews was "a side effect of the miserable downward slide in relations between the Lithuanians and the Jews, especially during the first year of Soviet rule and the annexation of Lithuania to the Soviet Union."[61] Such conditions made collaboration more likely with the Nazis who dangled vague prospects of national independence before these groups. By contrast, in areas like Belarus, which lacked a strong history of nationalist sentiment due to its multinational population and relatively short history, collaboration was not as widespread, though certainly not absent.

What did collaboration look like? Collaborators assisted the Nazis in a variety of ways, from providing information to committing murder themselves. But they also distinguished themselves from German perpetrators by acting out of sheer self-interest, often economic in nature. First and foremost, individuals willing to cooperate with Nazi occupiers could provide important information that was often deadly to Jews. One scholar has noted that in Ukraine "without local knowledge it would have been difficult for the Germans even to identify the Jews."[62] One informant in Kharkov told authorities "I am hereby informing you . . . that the Jewess Raissa Nikolayevna Yakubovich is registered in the house registry as a Jew. She now refuses to show her passport and claims to have lost it. I insist that Raissa Yakubovich is a Jew . . ."[63] It is not difficult to imagine Raissa's fate. In the tiny village of Krupki in Belarus, it was the Belarusian mayor who stood and read out the names of his Jewish citizens to ensure that all were present for the *Einsatzgruppen* to murder.[64]

Information gathering took a more sinister form when collaborators actively sought out Jews in hiding, like Raissa, and turned them over to the authorities. This often surpassed simple informing. Many collaborators escalated victimization into blackmail by uncovering Jews in hiding and extorting money under threat of betrayal. In Lwów, a survivor observed that "blackmailers learned of . . . hiding places and demanded large sums of money for keeping quiet, almost on a monthly basis." He described the dangers faced by Jews attempting to "pass" or hide in the local population, writing "individual blackmailers, crooks, and even children wandered the streets and had reached such a degree of expertise that they could identify at a glance a Jew in disguise."[65] This kind of collaboration could be quite lucrative.

Hunting Jews and turning them in to authorities represented a more extreme mode of informing. Both individuals and organizations engaged in this behavior. Jan Grabowski, a Polish historian, has quite bravely detailed the actions of the so-called Blue Police in Poland. This organization was formed from pre-war Polish policemen and augmented with new recruits, including those who had not been qualified to serve under the Polish state.[66] By 1943, there were around 16,000 Polish policemen working with German authorities.[67] While a good number of these police were members of the resistance, many others actively collaborated to the extent that the underground kept lists of them. German occupiers needed these police to fulfill "normal" police functions so that the Nazis could carry out their racial policy; however, the Blue Police often took part in anti-Jewish actions as well. This often included uncovering Jews in hiding. One former officer testified, for example, that "in the fall of 1942 . . . we went to the village of Żdżary where we caught four Jews (among them one Jewess), who were hiding in the house of one Szkotak. The Jews were later brought to Radgoszcz, and shot by the Germans."[68] Grabowski emphasizes that "the deadly efficiency of the 'blue' police in the process of exterminating the Jews was linked, on the one hand, to their excellent knowledge of the area and, on the other, to the dense network of available informers."[69] Jew hunting was a pastime not limited, of course, to Poland. Throughout the occupied East, individuals and organizations assisted the Nazis in uncovering Jews in hiding either in the hopes of financial gain or to curry favor.

Local populations invariably sought to benefit financially from the plight of their neighbors. This behavior uniformly transcended national boundaries. Often, participants belonged to no official local or German organization, but were simply opportunistic civilians. Non-Jews from the Baltic to the Crimea routinely stole from Jews under cover of the Holocaust. In its most passive form, this kind of theft occurred as Jews were removed from their homes and killed. Sara Gleich, a survivor from Mariupol', Ukraine wrote in her diary that, when she and her family were rounded up, "the neighbors waited like vultures for us to leave the apartment ... They all rushed into the apartment. Mama, Papa, and Fanya with her children immediately kept going, they could not bear to watch it. The neighbors quarreled over things before my eyes, snatching things out of each other's hands and dragging off pillows, pots and pans, and quilts."[70] Ukrainian authorities in the town imitated German authorities, demanding a ransom of two kilograms of pepper, 2,500 tins of black shoe polish, and seventy kilograms of sugar from the Jewish Council.[71] Two days later, between 8,000 and 16,000 Jews from Mariupol' had been murdered by *Einsatzgruppe* D.[72] In Poland, a local peasant was ordered to bury murdered Jews. Afterward, the Nazis gave him a dress, shoes, and a scarf as compensation but he complained, "only afterwards did I [find] out that there was a bullet hole in the back of the dress."[73] In Łódź, a Jewish school boy remembered that local Poles would frequently point out wealthy Jews to Germans in return for a portion of the loot.[74]

FIGURE 25 *A member of the Lithuanian auxiliary police who has just returned from taking part in the mass execution of the local Jewish population in the Rase Forest, auctions off their personal property in the central market. Utena, Lithuania, July–August 1941.*
Source: United States Holocaust Memorial Museum.

The most damning form of collaboration, however, resulted directly in the murder of Jews. This usually fell into two categories: at mass killing sites and at extermination centers. During the "Holocaust by Bullets," German killers often sought precisely this kind of assistance to alleviate the stress of killing. By the end of 1941, local auxiliaries did much of the shooting while German authorities supervised and directed them. These auxiliary units, called *Schutzmannschaften* (or *Schuma* battalions), were made up of young volunteers. The 13th Belarusian Battalion is one example. This group of young men represented some of the 130,000 Belarusians who collaborated with the Nazis.[75] Formed in 1943 (much later than similar units elsewhere) the 13th guarded POW and concentration camps and participated in ghetto clearing operations in at least three towns in Belarus. The 13th Battalion also participated in Operation Cottbus, a "large antipartisan action" in June 1943. While purportedly directed against partisans, this operation intentionally killed far more civilians (and Jews) than actual enemy combatants. The results tell the tale: around 10,000 killed—6,087 "fell in battle," 3,709 "executed," 599 captured (who likely were murdered shortly thereafter). German losses? 89 killed. Non-German (collaborator) losses? 40 killed. Enemy weapons captured? Around 900 for 10,000 enemies.[76] What is borne out of this and similar operations is that Jews and civilians were murdered when (most often) partisans could not be found or killed. If this operation is suggestive, others were not.

The commander of *Einsatzgruppe* A reported in October 1941 that "in all anti-Jewish steps, the Lithuanians take a stand alongside us, willingly and unreservedly."[77] Certainly, some embellishment adorns these reports. However, Lithuanian *Schutzmannschaften* were deployed across the East to directly participate in the murder of Jews. During the December 1941 massacre of 5,000 Jews in Nowogrodek, Belarus, a German sergeant observed that the actual shooting was done by a Lithuanian auxiliary unit.[78] In March 1942, an Estonian Police Battalion murdered the remnants of the ghetto and, in February 1943, a Lithuanian Battalion helped murder another 5,500 Jews from Nowogrodek.[79] Lithuanian *Schutzmannschaften* also killed Jews during large actions in Słonim and many other towns and villages throughout north and central Eastern Europe. Ukrainian auxiliaries were equally active. 1,200 of the roughly 1,500 shooters at the Babi Yar massacre were Ukrainian police.[80] By July 1942, 75,000 *Schutzmannschaften* were assisting the Nazis.[81]

Beyond supporting Nazi mass shooting operations, collaborators also served as guards at extermination centers, where they formed the overwhelming majority of armed personnel preventing Jewish escapes or uprisings. By the end of 1941, the SS began searching through the masses of Soviet POWs for volunteers to assist them in controlling the East, particularly in anti-Jewish policy. Only non-Russian ethnicities (ethnic Germans, Ukrainians, Lithuanians, Belarusians, etc.) could volunteer; the Germans did not trust "bolshevized" ethnic Russians. By July 1941, SS officer

Hermann Höfle had established a camp to receive these potential collaborators from the Red Army at a place called Trawniki, near Lublin.[82] There, the SS trained them to serve as camp guards and executioners. These "Trawniki men" were often referred to by both prisoners and Germans as "Askaris," after local East African contingents that had supported German colonial forces in the early 1900s. The goal of the education at Trawniki was quite clear, as remembered by one former member: "When we completed training ... the Germans ordered each of us to shoot a Jew. They apparently did this in order to be better able to rely on our loyalty to them."[83] Approximately 5,000 men served as Trawniki men, all of them directly engaged in the murder of Jews; they operated as guard forces in all the extermination centers, they participated in mass executions, and they assisted with ghetto liquidations (including the Warsaw ghetto.) Other auxiliaries, particularly Ukrainians and Lithuanians, also served.

Often, motivations differed for those in collaborationist organizations vs. individuals. Underlying much collaboration, however, was a foundation of antisemitism that saw Jews as inferior, a threat, or as complicit in Soviet oppression. Nazi occupation did not create these conditions, but certainly exacerbated them. Many were at best indifferent if not happy to see their own "Jewish question" resolved. As the famous Polish resistance fighter, Jan Karski, noted, "dislike of the Jews created a narrow bridge on which the

FIGURE 26 *Ukrainian SS auxiliaries in the Plaszow concentration camp outside of Krakow. They served as guards and in other camp roles, 1943.*
Source: United States Holocaust Memorial Museum.

[German] occupier and a significant part of the Polish society could meet."[84] Even a Polish underground newspaper wrote that " . . . every true Pole knows that in a reborn Poland there will be room neither for a German nor for a Jew."[85] Collaborators in other regions expressed similar sentiments.

To many Eastern Europeans in small towns, the price of one's soul was relatively cheap. Financial rewards could be great and immediate, as we have observed above; it should be pointed out that the value of a coat, household goods, and so on, was much higher for the relatively poorer Eastern Europeans than in the West. In the town of Iodi in Belarus, for example, while Germans were murdering the Jews, "the local population looted all the [Jewish] homes."[86] Extortion all too often accompanied murder as well. In Poland, a man named Kozik hid three Jews, who paid him for this service. When they ran out of money, he killed them with an axe.[87] These behaviors were not uncommon, as Jews in hiding were helpless against such attacks.

For those who joined collaborationist organizations (*Schuma* battalions, Trawniki, Iron Guard, Arrow Cross, etc.), financial gain was also a motivation. Members received higher pay, uniforms, food allowances, additional privileges, protection from their own potential victimization by the Nazis, and the opportunity to do their own robbing of Jews. Collaborators slightly higher in the chain of command individuals also received substantial compensation. A Ukrainian working for the German intelligence section in Krakow would receive a "beautiful, two-room, fully furnished apartment, including a telephone and radio."[88] This would have been the height of luxury. In uncertain times, financial stability and even advancement were powerful motivators.

For other collaborators, particularly those who joined organizations, political aspirations were an important motivation. Many were nationalists who had seen their countries occupied and victimized by the Soviets. They hoped, naively, that cooperation with the Nazi state would lead to independence. In almost all occupied areas however, the Nazis swiftly dispersed or marginalized nationalist groups. Virulent nationalist leaders often found themselves in forced exile in Germany or in prison. Yet, for many of the rank and file, simply the feeling of combating the Soviets alongside the Nazis left a glimmer of hope for national rebirth, even if it were an entirely unrealistic one. Organizations such as the Latvian Legion, a unit of the *Waffen-SS*, were extreme examples of this kind of thinking, often made up of men who had previously served in the *Schutzmannschaften* and who had murdered Jews.

The vast majority of Nazi collaborators in the Holocaust were Eastern European, either as individuals or as organizations. Without their help, the murder of the Jews there would have been much more difficult. From providing information to seeking individual rewards to refusing to shelter Jews, many locals intentionally or unintentionally made the task of the Nazis easier. Like perpetrators (a category which must extend to many collaborators as well), however, they did so for a variety of reasons stemming from the mundane to the ideological.

"Brave People": Helping and Rescue in Eastern Europe

I thought deeply, I wondered about the miracle of rescue
And I found the answer—you are good people.
Today I know that my survival comes only from the miracle
That such brave people are found on earth.
      "Memorable Sunday," survivor EDMUND KESSLER, 1942–44, Lwów[89]

Edmund Kessler survived hidden in a secret cellar by a Pole and nicely sums up one of the fundamental paradoxes of the Holocaust: most non-Jews did not help or rescue a single Jew, yet practically every Jew who survived was helped or rescued at some point by a non-Jew. The choice to rescue or even aid Jews carried great risk for non-Jews, particularly in Eastern Europe where they were far more likely to be executed along with their families, unlike in the West. The instinct of most human beings in a situation such as Nazi occupation is to avoid scrutiny and protect those closest to them. This natural tendency made each rescuer a rather unique individual and each rescue a unique event, conducted according to the circumstances on the ground. Rescuers formed a tiny minority of those encountering Jews during the Holocaust, but they critically show us that not everyone lost their humanity or stood idly by as their neighbors and the Nazis murdered Jews. To the contrary, the bravery of rescuers demonstrates that it *was* possible to save Jews and casts a harsh light on those who chose to benefit from the occupation instead.

Before exploring how and why some individuals risked their lives to save Jews, we must define what "rescue" and "helping" mean in the context of the Holocaust. Yad Vashem of the Israeli Holocaust Museum officially recognizes some rescuers as "Righteous Gentiles" or "Righteous Among the Nations" using a relatively strict definition. First, they recognize four main forms of rescue: "hiding Jews in the rescuers' home or on their property, providing false papers and false identities, smuggling and assisting Jews to escape, and the rescue of children."[90] Moreover, Yad Vashem withholds the designation if rescuers saved Jews for financial gain, religious conversion, for adoption, or as a result of other resistance activities. Lastly, in order to qualify, rescuers *must* have actively risked their lives.[91] These conditions, not always unreasonable, do, however, limit the number of individuals who become "Righteous." Not infrequently, monetary exchanges lead to a disqualification from consideration for the award of Righteous.[92] A well-known scholar has critiqued the Yad Vashem standards, arguing they "also [provide] a misleading model of what is required in order to assist those in need, even those in dire need."[93]

TABLE 11 *Righteous Gentiles by country (Eastern Europe).*

Country	Righteous
Poland	6620
Ukraine	2544
Lithuania	889
Hungary	837
Belarus	618
Russia	197
Latvia	135
Moldova	79
Romania	60
Bulgaria	20
Estonia	3
Total	12,002

Source: "Names and Numbers of Righteous among the Nations—Per Country & Ethnic Origin, as of January 1, 2016," Yad Vashem, http://www.yadvashem.org/righteous/statistics.

The numbers and national breakdowns for Eastern European awardees can be found in Table 11. The Righteous in Western Europe are overrepresented likely due to more documentation, the lack of Soviet interference, and general societal acceptance of rescue behavior, something often lacking in the East (France, for example, has nearly 4,000 names.)

Certainly, the numbers are even higher if we include without moral judgment those who saved Jews for less than ideal reasons. We must also recognize that many rescuers remain unknown due to their own wishes or having simply been lost in time. Thus, we may consider a more inclusive definition that counts those who actively prevented the murder of Jews. To this category, we should add that of "helper." Very few rescuers acted in isolation. In fact, research shows that successful rescue depended upon a network of people working together, either knowingly or unknowingly. For example, one person may have helped a Jew escape the ghetto, another provided food and housing for a night or two, another supplied false documentation and took the Jew to a hiding place while the rescuers there protected him/her. In addition, we should consider those who knew about such behavior and out of sympathy did not report it.

What did rescue look like? As with everything in the Holocaust, rescue was inevitably a local affair. The options, methods, and likelihood of success often depended on local conditions, time period, and environment—sometimes in surprising ways. It could be more difficult to hide one Jew in a small village than to hide twenty in a large city. Helping behavior carried perhaps the lowest level of risk, but was important nonetheless. Many survivors recall a moment's temporary hiding or a gift of food and clothing as critical to their survival. In Ukraine, Leah Bodkier fled a killing action and was fed and clothed by local Ukrainian peasants before she found a permanent hiding place.[94] Two girls fleeing a mass shooting in Belarus recalled being taken in by a Christian woman who told them, "You do not have to tell me where you are coming from. I know. God has brought you to the right house." She fed them, treated their wounds, and hid them until the next morning, when the girls left of their own volition, fearing for the safety of their rescuer.[95] Edmund Seidel escaped a death train bound for Bełżec but found himself naked in the snow. He survived only thanks to a local woman who gave him clothing.[96] A German soldier in Słonim hid a young Jewish boy in his headquarters during an Aktion.[97] He later brought the boy and his family food in the ghetto. His actions were not secret and were at least accepted by his comrades.

Even during frequently vicious and chaotic pogroms, individuals tried to intervene to save Jews. In Lwów, several individual German soldiers protested, one shouting that "we are not Bolsheviks, after all."[98] Of course, being German protected them from the reactions of the crowd. Others were not as lucky. During the Iasi Pogrom, a former professor was shot trying to save a Jew along with a priest attempting to do the same.[99]

The most dangerous but most vital forms of rescue were escape and permanent hiding. These actions were riskiest, but also most likely to ensure survival. Many rescuers saved Jews by enabling their escape from the Nazis, either from ghettos and camps or from Nazi territory itself. In the latter category fall, for example, two diplomats in Lithuania: the Japanese consul, Chiune Sugihara and the Dutch consul, Jan Zwartendijk. These diplomats saved Jews in 1940, before Lithuania came under Nazi control but at a crucial point when Jews were attempting to flee Soviet persecution and fleeing Nazi occupation. Together, they helped around 8,000 Jews escape Europe.[100] Most famously, Swedish diplomat Raoul Wallenberg, assisted by other diplomats, established an "international ghetto" in Budapest, Hungary, and helped issue documents protecting around 50,000 Jews from deportation. Individuals also smuggled Jews across borders and out of ghettos and camps. A most extraordinary example of this is German Sergeant Anton Schmid. He worked in a rear area unit in Vilnius, Lithuania that used Jewish slave labor from the ghetto. He filled a cargo truck weekly with Jews from the ghetto which he drove across the border into Belarus where he released them in safer areas.[101] Oskar Schindler is a more famous example, managing to transport several thousand Jews to his own factory in Czechoslovakia, away from Nazi killing. In the Ukranian town of Chernivtsi, the mayor and other citizens "stood up for the Jews and managed to retain 20,000

FIGURE 27 *Portrait of Japanese Consul Chiune Sugihara. Sugihara saved over 2,000 Polish Jewish refugees by issuing Japanese transit visas allowing them to escape to the Far East. Kaunas, Lithuania, 1940.*
Source: United States Holocaust Memorial Museum.

individuals [from deportation] by identifying them as being 'important for the war effort.'"[102]

The most difficult form of rescue was hiding Jews. Rescuers contended not only with the difficulty of creating hiding places, but they also had to devise clever ways to supply their Jews with food without raising the suspicions of neighbors who might well turn them in for a reward. Frequent Nazi (and local collaborator) searches for Jews also made hiding them an incredibly stressful and perilous endeavor. Hiding took many forms. In Vilnius, a Catholic priest and a nun hid eleven of their Jewish archive workers in the monastery.[103] The director of the zoo in Warsaw, Jan Zabinski, used his empty complex to hide Jews and personally hid twelve Jews in his own house, where his wife and son helped.[104] Pavel Gerasimchik, a poor Ukrainian peasant and father of three, volunteered to hide a Jewish family he had known before the war. It was a difficult decision, but he and his family worked to provide the additional food necessary and successfully hid the family until the end of the war. Gerasimchik even returned a gold watch the Jews had given him.[105]

Rescuers providing hiding places also placed their families in danger, for all would be shot if they were caught. In Kharkov, a journalist, Alexandra Byelova, was caught hiding a Jewish girl and executed. The Nazis executed Lithuanian Joudka Vytautas along with two Jewish women she had hidden.[106] A survivor recalled that, after the liquidation of the Lwów ghetto and subsequent search for hidden Jews, "the corpses of Poles who had been discovered giving shelter to Jews and the corpses of the Jews themselves could be seen all over the town, in the streets, in the squares and in all residential quarters."[107] One historical study identified at least 700 Poles executed for hiding Jews.[108] Rescuers had more to fear than the Nazis. Local non-Jews often murdered their neighbors for hiding Jews, as was the case for Lithuanian carpenter Jonas Paulavicius. His family hid twelve Jews. His neighbors only discovered his actions at the end of the war. They called him "Father of Jews" and murdered him in 1952.[109]

Why did rescuers do what they did? What motivated them to take such incredible risks, often for strangers? These questions are central to understanding why individuals chose to behave humanely in the face of overwhelming danger and the Eastern European context in which they acted. Some rescuers, particularly clergy and religious personnel, were driven more by their Christian faith. These individuals often baptized Jewish children and gave them to Christian families or attempted to convert them. One survivor from Kaunas described the priest who hid her, saying, "I understood from what he said that he was interested in rescuing children younger than me, so he could teach them Christianity . . . He would issue birth certificates and arrange for children to be placed with farmers in the villages . . . He said to me once, after liberation, that his profit consisted of sixty or seventy children who had been baptized into Christianity and whose parents were no longer alive."[110] Even a devoutly religious Catholic antisemite in Warsaw illegally secured the safety of 300 Jewish children by placing them in Christian orphanages and convents.[111]

Of course, moral or positive reasons did not motivate all rescuers. Many hid Jews simply for the financial opportunities they represented. One survivor described her feelings toward her rescuer: "Why should I be grateful? . . . He loved money . . . He did it only for money, besides every week he kept raising the price . . . and threatened that if the war would drag on, he would not keep me."[112] She was lucky. Other "rescuers" of this kind often killed Jews when their money ran out. Other would-be rescuers murdered or denounced their charges if they feared they would be discovered. Rescuers motivated by personal greed were also more likely to sexually or physically abuse their protectees.

Yet, in her study of rescuers, scholar Nechama Tec found that only 16 percent of the rescuers were "motivated by financial gain."[113] In fact, many rescuers chose to help Jews out of their own moral understanding of right and wrong. Tec has done the most extensive research on these altruistic rescuers. Her path-breaking work gives us the best insight, so far, into what made some people choose the difficult path in helping Jews. She identified six common elements of their personalities and motivations:

1) Individuality or separateness, which means that they did not quite fit into their respective social environments
2) Independence or self-reliance to act in accordance with personal convictions, regardless of how these were viewed by others.
3) Broad commitments to stand up for the needy and an enduring history of performing charitable acts.
4) A tendency to perceive aid to Jews in a matter-of-fact, unassuming way, with consistent denials of heroic or extraordinary qualities of rescue.
5) Unpremeditated, unplanned start of rescue, that is, a rescue that was extended gradually or suddenly, even impulsively.
6) Universalistic perceptions about the Jews. Rather than seeing Jews in those they were about to protect, they saw them as people totally dependent on aid from others. Such perceptions come with an ability to disregard all attributes except those expressing extreme suffering and need.[114]

Tec's rubric, derived from interviews with 309 survivors who described 565 rescuers, gives us perhaps our best understanding of what kinds of people became rescuers.[115] Like perpetrators, one factor alone, such as personal beliefs or circumstance, cannot explain rescuer motivation and behavior. Rather, as we have seen, rescuers came from all walks of life and were influenced by both personal beliefs and situational factors. Not all rescuers had pure motives, and yet, in the end, many of them *did* rescue Jews. Others *were* guided by a moral compass, but acted only when they suddenly found themselves confronted with the opportunity to help. Anton Schmid best expressed the simple humanity and courage of most rescuers. He wrote his sister before his execution for smuggling Jews to safety: "my dearest Steffi and Gerta, it is a terrible blow for us, but please, please forgive me. I acted only as a human being and did not want to hurt anyone."[116]

This examination of the complicated phenomenon of perpetrators, collaborators, and rescuers shows us several important characteristics about the human response to the Holocaust in Eastern Europe. In all three cases, we see that individuals involved were motivated not by one particular factor, be it ideology, personal gain, antisemitism, or situational and environmental factors. Rather, these men and women chose to behave as they did due to the complex interplay of all of these factors, with some being more influential at different times and places. Perhaps more importantly, we learn that most perpetrators were not insane and more ordinary than not. Likewise, rescuers show us that it was possible, even in the face of incredible danger and overwhelming difficulty to retain one's humanity and help others in need. In both cases, the actors may well have more much in common with us than not.

Selected Readings

Grabowski, Jan. *Hunt for the Jews: Betrayal and Murder in German-Occupied Poland*. Bloomington, IN: Indiana University Press, 2013.

Hilberg, Raul. *Perpetrators, Victims, Bystanders: The Jewish Catastrophe, 1933–1945*. New York: Aaron Asher Books, 1992.

Lower, Wendy. *Hitler's Furies: German Women in the Nazi Killing Fields*. New York: Houghton Mifflin Harcourt, 2013.

Sakowicz, Kazimierz, and Yitzhak Arad. *Ponary Diary, 1941–1943: A Bystander's Account of a Mass Murder*. New Haven: Yale University Press, 2005.

Tec, Nechama. *When Light Pierced the Darkness: Christian Rescue of Jews in Nazi-Occupied Poland*. New York: Oxford University Press, 1986.

Conclusion

The ghosts of the past still roam freely in the hills and valleys, clutter the unpaved streets, and congregate in synagogues transformed into garbage dumps and in cemeteries grazed by goats. And the inhabitants walk among the ruins and the ghosts, awakened to their presence only when asked by a stranger and forgetting them just as soon as he leaves. It is a region suspended in time . . .

Historian OMER BARTOV[1]

American author William Faulkner famously wrote, "The past is never dead. It's not even past."[2] During his travels in present-day Galicia and to his family's hometown, Omer Bartov echoes this sentiment. Unlike Germany—which was in many ways forced to confront its role in the Holocaust from having its citizens paraded through concentration camps to the series of famous trials held there—Eastern Europe has for the most part *not* confronted the totality of its Holocaust experience in any meaningful way. The ghosts of the Holocaust haunt the region both metaphorically, and for some inhabitants who report actual hauntings, literally.[3] Synagogues often symbolize this haunting. Those in Eastern European towns are often in ruins or have been repurposed as barns, movie theaters, and libraries. Many of them stand in towns without a single Jewish inhabitant, reflecting physically the absence of a group of people who once existed in large communities.

Yet immediately after the Holocaust, significant numbers of Jews lived in Eastern Europe. Many emerged from the forests, hiding places, or various Eastern camps. Others began returning from camps in Germany. They often tried to discover the whereabouts and fate of their relatives. Survivor Leon Wells, for example, recalled returning to Lwów and finding his way to a school that was being used as a shelter for Jews. Outside the school, thousands of slips of paper were posted requesting information on loved ones.[4] In 1944, the local Jewish committee in Lwów determined that 823 of the 2,500 Jews in the city were actual citizens.[5] The pre-war population had been over 150,000. Similar events played out across Eastern Europe as survivors returned home usually to find that their entire families had been murdered or at least were scattered and missing. Still, some Jews tried to

FIGURE 28 *Ruins of the synagogue built in 1852 in Dzialoszyce, Poland. In 1940–41, 1,000 of the 10,000 Jews in the town were confined in the synagogue. The majority of the population was murdered in the gas chambers at Bełżec in 1942. Dzialoszyce, Poland (2009)**
Source: The author.

reestablish their lives in the East. In Brzezany, Ukraine, a small group of survivors prayed in a single apartment as the synagogue had been turned into a grain depot. There was at least one wedding there as well. And, while some of the child survivors had pleasant memories of the time, the remaining Jews of Brzezany mostly left by 1945.[6]

The reception of neighbors and non-Jewish inhabitants of these towns added to the trauma of these returns. Given their knowledge of the Holocaust, most locals did not expect any Jews to still be alive. Wells wrote that he was exhausted and sat in the middle of the sidewalk. All around him "Passers-by stopped to look at me. Some stopped only for a second, others for a little longer. They talked among themselves. The only thing I heard them saying was, 'It is a Jew.'"[7] Many Eastern European locals were not particularly happy to see Jews return, looking for their relatives but also for

---

*Megargee, Geoffrey P., ed. *The United States Holocaust Memorial Museum Encyclopedia of Camps and Ghettos, 1933–1945*. Vol. II, vol. A. Bloomington: Indiana University Press in association with the United States Holocaust Memorial Museum, 2009, pp. 503–5.

their property and homes that they had been forced to leave. One survivor in Poland recalled approaching the neighbors and friends he had divided his property among for safe-keeping. He said, "now after our return they didn't want to give them back. They said that Germans or Russians took them away, but the neighbors said that it was not true, because they did not see and did not hear about it. Three-fourths of our goods were taken by the locals."[8] Wells returned to find a Ukrainian family living in his family's apartment. The father refused to return it, telling the Holocaust survivor that "I shouldn't think that only the Jews had had a hard time; true, his family had not been killed, but 'we didn't have it too easy either.'"[9] Across Eastern Europe, many locals feared that returning Jews would attempt to reclaim property that they had stolen from them. Indeed, at war's end, many believed that Jewish possessions rightfully belonged to them.

Often, they were concerned about much more, for, as we have seen, local collaborators had murdered Jews on their own initiative. One survivor in Ukraine remembered that a friend in hiding with him had run into the street to celebrate with the Red Army soldiers. According to the survivor, local Ukrainians recognized him at once and started shouting in dismay, "Pejsach's son, Pejsach's son!" They were terrified, because every Jew who survived was a witness to all the murders committed by the Ukrainians."[10] They also knew that Soviet officials would not look kindly on those who had collaborated with the Germans. For many Eastern Europeans, returning Jews became a very visible and painful reminder of their own guilt in collaborating with the Nazis, victimizing Jews, or profiting from their deaths. This, along with existing antisemitism, created a dangerous environment for the small numbers of Jews trickling back into the East.

Not infrequently, this environment turned violent. Thomas Blatt, who had survived the escape from the Sobibor extermination center and the war, planned to return home to Izbica. A Polish man warned him that there were no Jews there and that "they are looking for you, they are looking. Run, run today to Lublin, before it's too late." He managed to escape on a Red Army vehicle.[11] Other returning Jews were not so lucky. The most infamous example of postwar violence against Jewish survivors is likely the pogrom which took place on July 4, 1946 in Kielce, Poland. On July 1, a Polish boy disappeared; he returned two days later but his drunken father reported that his son had been kidnapped by Jews, echoing the centuries old Blood Libel. The boy falsely claimed that he had been held in the basement of the Jewish community center housing Holocaust survivors; the building had no basement. Regardless, an angry crowd gathered outside of the building. Some of the Polish Security Service personnel recognized the pogrom for what it was and attempted to protect the Jews, but were soon overwhelmed by a combination of local police, Polish soldiers, and civilians who stormed the building. A Polish policeman recalled that "Jews were brought from the building into the square, where the population cruelly murdered them, and the armed soldiers did not react, they only covered their ears and fled somewhere, and some went back into the building and kept bringing out other Jews."[12] A Jewish witness recalled "how policemen threw two Jewish girls off the second-floor [third-floor] balcony and the crowd in the courtyard finished them off."[13] At least 42 Jews were murdered in Kielce by a broad cross-section of Polish society. The postwar murder of Jews was not limited to Poland. In Romania, the Security Service reported in August 1946 that "Hatred of the Jewish element is on the rise." In Moldova, dozens of Jews were similarly murdered trying to return to their homes.[14]

But it was the Kielce Pogrom that made headlines around the world. The *New York Times* placed the massacre on the front page. Its reporter wrote that Polish government spokesmen "frankly and ashamedly declare that it is not safe for Jews to live in small Polish towns."[15] This was a message not lost on the Jews in Poland themselves. For example, survivor Jack Ahrens recalled that many Jews came to Lwów "because there is a safety in numbers and safety in a big town."[16] These were temporary measures for self-protection, however. The Kielce Pogrom made it clear to Eastern European Jews, particularly in Poland, that it was simply not safe to return home. As a result, the numbers of Jews fleeing the East greatly increased after Kielce. Many of these refugees made their way to displaced persons camps in Germany before emigrating elsewhere. Soviet rule also contributed to the desire to leave, as it cracked down on religious practice and became increasingly antisemitic in Stalin's last days. Ironically, not a few local collaborators also took the opportunity to pose as refugees and to join the flow of immigrants out of the East, escaping what they knew would be swift and severe Soviet justice.

Indeed, the Soviets began investigations into Nazi crimes in the East in 1944, before the war was even over. A special body known as the Extraordinary State Commission to Investigate German-Fascist Crimes Committed on Soviet Territory from the USSR or more simply Extraordinary State Commission (ESC) had already been created in 1942 for this express purpose. These investigators compiled thousands of statements and other documentation of Nazi crimes, including exhumations of killing sites. It also was responsible for uncovering those Soviet citizens who had been "disloyal" to the regime.[17] The Commission was a huge undertaking, involving over 30,000 individuals.[18] The Commission reached even small villages, accounting in exhaustive detail the physical and property destruction wrought by the Third Reich. The relationship of the ESC to Jewish suffering was ambivalent, however. The Soviet Jewish Anti-Fascist Committee (JAFC) wished to be involved in the investigations when they involved the murder of Jews, but seems to have been rejected.[19] This fell in line with the Soviet desire not to single out any particular group, but to include all victims of the Nazis as "Soviet Citizens." Initially, however, crimes against Jews *were* specifically documented by many investigators, often as a result of direct questioning.[20] Only later would Jews as a victim group slowly be subsumed into the larger death toll of Soviet citizens.

These initial Soviet investigations are, however, vitally important as the first legal examinations of the Holocaust. They also led to the first Nazi war crimes trials. The first took place at Krasnodar in July 1943 and tried eleven Russian and Ukrainian collaborators. These men had been auxiliaries for *Sonderkommando 10a*.[21] One reporter venomously described the defendants as monstrous: "Not human beings but filth, scum . . . They stood before a Soviet court, before the whole Soviet people naked as worms."[22] The proceedings clearly smacked of earlier Soviet show trials with little legal rigor, as all defendants confessed their guilt. The court convicted all of them of treason and eight were executed. In Kharkhov in December 1943, three Germans and one Russian collaborator were tried. Yet, Soviet coverage of the perpetrators' defenses and motivations was prescient, with one reporter writing, "But let them not seek excuses in the fact that they are rank and file murderers."[23] Moreover, the ESC investigations provided a large amount of evidence to the postwar International Military Tribunals at Nuremberg Prosecution of local Eastern European collaborators in the postwar years, unless driven by the Soviets, dropped off precipitously. For the Soviets, it became increasingly important to portray the Great Patriotic War as a unified effort by all of the nations behind the Iron Curtain; embarrassing public trials of Soviet collaborators with the Nazis would have worked against this message.

Trials of German perpetrators (*Einsatzgruppen* members, camp guards, *Wehrmacht* killers, civil administrators and others) also had mixed success. The Nuremberg trials successfully prosecuted the main offenders at the highest levels, and the subsequent Nuremberg trials prosecuted medical, military, business, and SS perpetrators, again at a high level. The Dachau trials conducted by the Americans targeted some lower level officials from concentration camps in Germany, but were hampered by accusations of legal irregularities including the use of torture, which turned out to be true. In spite of these immediate Allied trials, many of the worst Nazi criminals escaped prosecution by fleeing Europe, often with the help of the Red Cross and the Catholic Church.[24] Franz Stangl, commandant of Treblinka, was one of these.

Other war criminals from the East escaped justice due to the inconsistent and flawed nature of the German system itself. Despite some of the largest postwar German trials such as the Ulm Einsatzgruppen Trial (1958), Frankfurt Auschwitz Trial (1963–67), and Stuttgart Lwów Trial (1968), most perpetrators remained at large. The Allied process of denazification, intended to remove former Nazis from positions of authority in society, largely fell short of that goal. Both the judiciary and the police often contained former Nazis and, worse, actual war criminals. In Bavaria in 1949, 81 percent of judges on the bench were former Nazis.[25] It got worse. When senior police officials were also war criminals, they were often in a position to be very informed about cases against them. When German police burst into the home of Ludwig Hahn, former SD chief in Warsaw (and current police official), they were astonished to discover "not just ten binders of photocopied witness statements [in the case against him] but also photocopies of the most recent notes of the States Attorney's office [in the case against him] from which he could learn the names and addresses of witnesses who had not yet been interviewed."[26]

When the system itself was not corrupted, legal constraints often prevented many middle- and low-level perpetrators from standing trial. By 1960, a statute of limitations limited prosecution to the crime of first-degree murder, which placed a very high bar in front of prosecutors, requiring them to prove the perpetrator had acted out of base motives such as antisemitism, to prove his mindset. This is always a difficult legal challenge, doubly so regarding the Holocaust. In addition, even conscientious authorities faced a lack of witnesses and documentation, an obstacle exponentially greater for crimes committed in Eastern Europe, where both distance and politics inhibited cooperation. As a result, the bulk of Nazi participants in the Holocaust in Eastern Europe remained unpunished. Only recently have trials against the lowest level perpetrators such as Oskar Groening, the "bookkeeper of Auschwitz," moved forward, now that the German legal code has determined that presence at a camp constituted participation in its crimes. Of the many Eastern European perpetrators who fled to the United States, only a small number have been uncovered and deported for lying on their immigration documents about their Nazi past. The most famous of these was John Demjanjuk, a Ukrainian Trawniki man who served at the Sobibor extermination center. He was eventually deported from the United States, tried (and found innocent) in Israel before being extradited to Germany where he was convicted as an accessory to murder.

Trials and prosecutions are only one form of confronting the past. In the case of most of Eastern Europe, that past was not confronted either in trials or in public and private spaces. A Polish ethnomusicologist working in small villages there wrote sadly:

> The most painful thing for me is the attitude in the countryside towards Jews, and a universal sense of triumph because they are no longer there. Universal. And one more thing, which I rarely wrote about, and which weighs terribly on my conscience: the killings of Jews who were hiding in forests by the peasants. The number of these crimes and incidents that I know about it *[sic]* is a terrible burden.[27]

In small communities across Eastern Europe, not just in Poland, the crimes of the Holocaust remain very present. Scholar Jan Gross describes this as "a collective deed, implicating all those present, a group experience of ultimate transgression marking forever the local community where it took place, especially that people later had to live alongside the murderers."[28] These transgressions continued even after the war, as locals dug up the grounds of extermination centers and tore apart formerly Jewish houses in search of gold and valuables. Thus, the collective knowledge and guilt often remains a hidden undercurrent of local history and likely contributes, along with continuing antisemitism, to the silence regarding the Holocaust in the East.

In most of Eastern Europe, this silence began with the return of Soviet rule, which refused to distinguish between Jews and other victims of the Nazi genocidal project, adhering to a policy of "Don't divide the dead." As a result, memorials to murdered Jews, where they were allowed to be built at all, only mentioned "peaceful Soviet citizens," as on the monument to the murdered Jews of Krupki in Belarus.[29] The official monument to the 33,000 Jews murdered at Babi Yar in Ukraine also defined them as "Soviet citizens." Worse still, hundreds of mass gravesites across Eastern Europe remain unmarked, though they are fixed in the memory of the local communities, who can easily take a visitor there if asked. During the Soviet years, small groups of Jews remaining in the East often visited killing sites, cemeteries, and memorials for small, impromptu remembrances, but no official ceremonies were sanctioned.

With the fall of the Soviet Union in 1991, it appeared that some space had opened for returning the Jews as specific victims of the Holocaust. Memorials were updated or new ones built, often with money from Jewish communities of emigrés. However, in many formerly Soviet states that were now independent, nationalist commemorations overshadowed remembrance of Jewish victims. In Latvia, the government instituted a national day of remembrance (since abolished) for the Latvian Legion, a *Waffen-SS* unit whose members included Latvian auxiliary war criminals. To this day, marches to commemorate this deeply problematic unit continue. In Kaunas, Lithuania, the museum at the Ninth Fort Massacre site focuses more on the Soviet deportation of Lithuanians than on the murder of Jews that took place a hundred yards from its doors. Worse are the nationalist commemorations at the Ponary Forest killing site where 100,000 people were murdered, including 70,000 Jews. Here, right-wing groups commemorate the murder of around 100 members of the Lithuanian Territorial Self-Defense Force (an organization that actively collaborated with the Nazis) . . . and who were only killed when they refused to continue. In Ukraine, the OUN and its leader, Stepan Bandera, are commemorated with statues and marches, ignoring the antisemitism of the OUN and its role in murdering Jews—both with the Nazis and on its own initiative—during the Holocaust. In present-day (2016) Lwów, adjacent to the ruins of the famous Golden Rose Synagogue is a "Jewish-themed" restaurant where Ukrainians dress up as Jews and customers must barter for their meals. A lawsuit forced the new memorial at the site of the ruins to remove language that condemned Poles and Ukrainians.[30] Finally, as of the printing of this book, Poland has passed a law making it illegal to refer to death camps in Poland as "Polish" or to claim that Poles collaborated with the Nazis in exterminating Jews. Violations of this could lead to a prison sentence of up to three years. Famed

Holocaust historian Yehuda Bauer replied that, "A law that imposes punishment on someone who says Poles participated in the murder of Jews contains a total lie."[31] This Polish law aptly summarizes the failure of many other Eastern European countries to come to terms with their own participation in the Holocaust. Poland, of course, suffered greatly under the Nazis who murdered 3,000,000 non-Jewish Poles, but it has chosen to focus on that suffering and literally outlaw discussion about its own collaboration, which, as we have seen, was widespread, not as a state or ally of Germany, but through the actions of individuals.

This book has sought to examine the history of the Holocaust in Eastern Europe both chronologically and from a variety of perspectives. It situates the events of the Holocaust as experienced by perpetrators, victims, and collaborators in the complex times and places in which it took place as well as in the longer-term history of the region. We have seen how and why Eastern Europe became the epicenter of the Holocaust, the home of the extermination centers, and is the land in which the developmental steps toward the Final Solution can most easily be seen. In addition, this text has endeavored to explain and give examples of the diverse responses and behaviors that individuals and groups displayed when faced with the horrors of the Nazi

FIGURE 29 *Memorial to the victims of the Lietūkis Garage Massacre in what is now a parking lot behind a school. The monument is very recent. A commemoration ceremony was held in 2015, but no officials from the Lithuanian government attended. Kaunas, Lithuania, 2017.*
Source: The author.

genocidal project. It is only by applying this kind of local analysis that we can begin to look more broadly at a region as large as Eastern Europe. The East is, naturally, critical to our understanding of the Holocaust, as the overwhelming majority of victims, perpetrators, and collaborators were located there. However, it is also vitally important to understand the events of 1939–45 due to the frightening increase in xenophobic and antisemitic behavior there today. This is but one symptom of a past yet to be fully confronted. If Eastern Europe seems haunted by the Holocaust, it is because, as one scholar has written, "Endings that are not over is what haunting is about."[32]

In May 2006, a Polish man appeared at the Bełzec extermination center museum and memorial. He had been born in the town of Bełzec and, when he was 18, his grandmother had given him a woman's gold ring which had obviously been taken by someone digging in the remains of the camp. A Jewish girl appeared to him in a dream after he had a near death experience on the highway asking him to return the ring to the extermination site. He traveled there shortly thereafter to do so. "One usually forgets dreams," he wrote in a letter accompanying the ring, "but this one is fixed in my memory forever."[33] Perhaps the passing of time will allow Eastern Europe to confront its own dreams and memories of the Holocaust with more clarity.

Selected Readings

Bartov, Omer. *Erased: Vanishing Traces of Jewish Galicia in Present-Day Ukraine.* Princeton; Oxford: Princeton University Press, 2007.
Desbois, Patrick. *The Holocaust by Bullets: A Priest's Journey to Uncover the Truth Behind the Murder of 1.5 Million Jews.* New York: Palgrave Macmillan, 2008.
Gross, Jan Tomasz. *Fear: Anti-Semitism in Poland after Auschwitz- an Essay in Historical Interpretation.* Princeton, NJ: Princeton University Press, 2006.
Himka, John-Paul, and Joanna Beata Michlic, eds. *Bringing the Dark Past to Light the Reception of the Holocaust in Postcommunist Europe.* Lincoln: UNP – Nebraska, 2013.
Steinacher, Gerald. *Nazis on the Run: How Hitler's Henchmen Fled Justice.* Oxford: Oxford University Press, 2011. Book.

NOTES

Prelims

1 Reprinted from *Points of Departure* by Dan Pagis, translated by Stephen Mitchell, by permission of the University of Nebraska Press. English translation copyright 1982 by the Jewish Publication Society, Philadelphia.

Introduction

1 Zwi Bachrach and Batsheva Pomerantz, *Last Letters from the Shoah* (Jerusalem: Yad Vashem, 2013), p. 196.
2 Ernst Klee, Willi Dressen, and Volker Riess, *"The Good Old Days:" The Holocaust as Seen by Its Perpetrators and Bystanders*, 1st American ed. (New York: Free Press, 1991), pp. 39, 42.
3 Timothy Snyder, *Bloodlands: Europe between Hitler and Stalin* (New York: Basic Books, 2012), ix.
4 "holocaust, n.," *Oxford English Dictionary*, http://www.oed.com/view/Entry/87793?isAdvanced=false&result=1&rskey=a18MC9&.
5 Ibid.
6 USHMM, "Holocaust Encyclopedia: Introduction to the Holocaust," United States Holocaust Memorial Museum, http://www.ushmm.org/wlc/en/article.php?ModuleId=10005143.
7 Yad Vashem, "The Holocaust: Definition and Preliminary Discussion," http://www.yadvashem.org/yv/en/holocaust/resource_center/the_holocaust.asp.
8 A. Dirk Moses, "The Holocaust and Genocide," in *The Historiography of the Holocaust*, ed. Dan Stone (New York: Palgrave Macmillan, 2005), p. 533.
9 Donald L. Niewyk and Francis R. Nicosia, *The Columbia Guide to the Holocaust* (New York: Columbia University Press, 2000), p. 45.
10 Larry Wolff, *Inventing Eastern Europe: The Map of Civilization on the Mind of the Enlightenment* (Stanford, CA: Stanford University Press, 1994), p. 4.
11 For such a political study, see R. J. Crampton, *Eastern Europe in the Twentieth Century– and After* (New York: Routledge, 1997).
12 Both Larry Wolff and Maria Todorova argue that Eastern Europe and the Balkans are both in many ways imagined regional divisions. Many books on Eastern Europe do not include the Balkans, and certainly not Greece, but some do. See, for example: Mariia͡ Nikolaeva Todorova, *Imagining the*

Balkans (New York: Oxford University Press, 2009); Wolff, *Inventing Eastern Europe: The Map of Civilization on the Mind of the Enlightenment*.

1 Beyond the Pale: Pre-War Jewish Life in Eastern Europe

1. Aaron Liebermann, "The Jewish Question in Eastern Europe (1877)," in *The Jew in the Modern World: A Documentary History*, ed. Paul R. Mendes-Flohr and Jehuda Reinharz (New York: Oxford University Press, 1995), p. 386.
2. Note: I use the unhyphenated term "antisemitism" rather than "anti-Semitism" because "Semitism" has never been a meaningful concept and certainly not a meaningful movement, political or otherwise.
3. Phyllis Goldstein, *A Convenient Hatred: The History of Antisemitism* (Brookline, MA: Facing History and Ourselves, 2012), p. 108.
4. Ibid., p. 107.
5. John Efron et al., *The Jews: A History* (Upper Saddle River, NJ: Pearson, 2009), p. 157.
6. Klaus-Peter Friedrich, "Antisemitism in Poland," in *Antisemitism in Eastern Europe*, ed. Hans Christian Petersen and Samuel Salzborn (Frankfurt am Main: Peter Lang GmbH, 2010), pp. 9–10.
7. Goldstein, *A Convenient Hatred: The History of Antisemitism*, p. 147.
8. Mordechai Zalkin, "Antisemitism in Lithuania," in *Antisemitism in Eastern Europe*, ed. Hans Christian Petersen and Samuel Salzborn, Politische Kulturforschung (Frankfurt am Main: Peter Lang GmbH, 2010), pp. 138–9.
9. Hans Christian Petersen and Samuel Salzborn, eds., *Antisemitism in Eastern Europe*, vol. 5, Politische Kulturforschung (Frankfurt am Main: Peter Lang GmbH, 2010), p. 177.
10. Elissa Bemporad, *Becoming Soviet Jews: The Bolshevik Experiment in Minsk* (Bloomington: Indiana University Press, 2013), p. 3.
11. Numbers from the United States Holocaust Memorial Museum (Poland, Soviet Union, Romania, Latvia, Lithuania, Estonia, Bulgaria, Hungary, Yugoslavia, Albania) USHMM, "Jewish Population of Europe in 1933: Population Data by Country," United States Holocaust Memorial Museum, http://www.ushmm.org/wlc/en/article.php?ModuleId=10005161.
12. David Assaf, ed. *Journey to a 19th Century Shtetl: The Memoirs of Yekhezkel Kotik* (Detroit: Wayne State University Press, 2008), p. 286.
13. Howard Morley Sachar, *A History of the Jews in the Modern World* (New York: Knopf, 2005), p. 315.
14. Mirosława M. Bułat, "Warsaw Yiddish Art Theater," *YIVO Encyclopedia of Jews in Eastern Europe* (2010), http://www.yivoencyclopedia.org/article.aspx/Warsaw_Yiddish_Art_Theater.
15. *Oxford English Dictionary*. Alternately, the word can be spelled "anti-Semitism" but this gives the false impression that there is or was an actual movement of "Semitism." Therefore, I choose to use "antisemitism."
16. See Gavin I. Langmuir, *Toward a Definition of Antisemitism* (Berkeley: University of California Press, 1990), chapter 14.
17. King James Bible, Gospel According to John 8:44–7.

18 Goldstein, *A Convenient Hatred: The History of Antisemitism*, p. 37.
19 Steve Hochstadt, ed. *Sources of the Holocaust* (New York: Palgrave Macmillan, 2004), p. 13.
20 "Gregory X: Letter on Jews, (1271–6)—against the Blood Libel," Fordham University, http://legacy.fordham.edu/halsall/source/g10-jews.asp.
21 "The Czar on Trial," *New York Times*, October 12, 1913, p. 12.
22 King James Bible, Ezekiel 22:12–13.
23 Michael Hagemeister, "'The Antichrist as an Imminent Political Possibility' Sergei Nilus and the Apocalyptical Reading of the Protocols of the Elders of Zion," in *The Paranoid Apocalypse: A Hundred-Year Retrospective on the Protocols of the Elders of Zion*, ed. Richard Allen Landes and Steven T. Katz (New York: New York University Press, 2012), p. 79.
24 Serei Nilus, *The Jewish Peril: Protocols of the Learned Elders of Zion* (London: "The Britons", 1920), ii.
25 Ibid., p. 9.
26 Philip Graves, ""Jewish World Plot"—an Exposure—the Source of the Protocols—Truth at Last," *The Times*, August 16, 1921, p. 9.
27 Texe Marrs, ed. *Protocols of the Learned Elders of Zion* (Austin, TX: Rivercrest Publishing, 2010), p. 28. Note: this is an unannotated, antisemitic text that purports to be real. It does contain articles from Henry Ford's newspaper.
28 USHMM, "Holocaust Encyclopedia: Protocols of the Elders of Zion," United States Holocaust Memorial Museum, http://www.ushmm.org/wlc/en/article.php?ModuleId=10007058.
29 Goldstein, *A Convenient Hatred: The History of Antisemitism*, p. 243.
30 "Page from the Anti-Semitic German Children's Book, 'Der Giftpilz'" (United States Holocaust Memorial Museum: Photo #40014).
31 Alfred Rosenberg, "The Jewish Question as World Problem (28 March 1941)," in *The Third Reich Sourcebook*, ed. Anson Rabinbach and Sander L Gilman (Berkeley: University of California Press, 2013), p. 729.
32 Adolf Hitler, "Letter to Adolf Geimlich, 16 September 1919," ibid., ed. Anson Rabinbach and Sander L. Gilman (Berkeley: University of California Press, 2013), p. 6.
33 John Connelly, "Nazis and Slavs: From Racial Theory to Racist Practice," *Central European History* 32, no. 1 (1999): 17.
34 Hochstadt, *Sources of the Holocaust*, p. 29.
35 Andre Mineau, *SS Thinking and the Holocaust* (Amsterdam: Rodopi B.V., 2012), p. 47.
36 Ibid.

2 The Origins of the Nazi State

1 Adolf Hitler, *Mein Kampf*, trans. Alvin Johnson (Boston, MA: Houghton Mifflin, 1939), p. 601.
2 Ibid., p. 845.
3 Ibid., p. 73.
4 Ibid., p. 84.

5 Ibid., p. 99.
6 Thomas Weber, *Hitler's First War: Adolf Hitler, the Men of the List Regiment, and the First World War* (Oxford: Oxford University Press, 2010), p. 97.
7 Ibid., p. 141.
8 Hitler, *Mein Kampf*, p. 266.
9 Ibid., p. 210.
10 Andre Mineau, *SS Thinking and the Holocaust* (Amsterdam: Rodopi B.V., 2012), p. 76.
11 Hitler, *Mein Kampf*, p. 261.
12 Ian Kershaw, *Hitler: A Biography* (New York: W.W. Norton, 2008), p. 72.
13 Ibid., p. 74.
14 Ibid., p. 132.
15 Wilfrid Bade, "The Hitler Trial," in *The Third Reich Sourcebook*, ed. Anson Rabinbach and Sander L Gilman (Berkeley: University of California Press, 2013), p. 27.
16 Kershaw, *Hitler: A Biography*, p. 135.
17 "Results of Elections to the German Reichstag, 1919–1933," in *Documents on the Holocaust: Selected Sources on the Destruction of the Jews of Germany and Austria, Poland, and the Soviet Union*, ed. Yitzhak Arad, Israel Gutman, and Abraham Margaliot (Jerusalem: Yad Vashem, 1999), p. 31.
18 Kershaw, *Hitler: A Biography*, p. 275.
19 Ibid., p. 276.
20 Otto Wels, "Speech against the Enabling Act, 28 March 1933," in *The Third Reich Sourcebook*, ed. Anson Rabinbach and Sander L Gilman (Berkeley: University of California Press, 2013), p. 51.
21 "Decrees Excluding Jews from Cultural and Public Life (1933–1942)," in *The Jew in the Modern World: A Documentary History*, ed. Paul R. Mendes-Flohr and Jehuda Reinharz (New York: Oxford University Press, 1995), pp. 723–6.
22 Joseph Goebbels, "Radio as the Eighth Great Power," in *The Third Reich Sourcebook*, ed. Anson Rabinbach and Sander L. Gilman (Berkeley: University of California Press, 2013), p. 612.
23 Kershaw, *Hitler: A Biography*, p. 171.
24 Goebbels, "Radio as the Eighth Great Power," p. 613.
25 Peter Longerich, *Goebbels: A Biography*, trans. Alan Bance, Jeremy Noakes, and Lesley Sharpe (New York: Random House LLC, 2015), p. 578.
26 Ian Kershaw, *Hitler, the Germans, and the Final Solution* (Jerusalem: International Institute for Holocaust Research, Yad Vashem, 2008), p. 31.
27 Ibid., p. 35.
28 This concept was introduced by historian Ian Kershaw.
29 Kershaw, *Hitler, the Germans, and the Final Solution*, p. 42.
30 This concept originated with the work of historian Hans Mommsen.
31 Peter Longerich, *Heinrich Himmler: A Life* (New York: Oxford University Press, 2012), p. 152.
32 Robert Gerwarth, *Hitler's Hangman: The Life of Heydrich* (New Haven, CT: Yale University Press, 2011), p. 50.
33 Longerich, *Heinrich Himmler: A Life*, p. 195.
34 Kershaw, *Hitler: A Biography*, p. 312.

35 Steve Hochstadt, ed. *Sources of the Holocaust* (New York: Palgrave Macmillan, 2004), pp. 29–40.
36 "Law for the Restoration of the Professional Civil Service," in *The Third Reich Sourcebook*, ed. Anson Rabinbach and Sander L Gilman (Berkeley: University of California Press, 2013), p. 53.
37 "Law for the Protection of German Blood and German Honor, 15 September 1935," in *The Third Reich Sourcebook*, ed. Anson Rabinbach and Sander L Gilman (Berkeley: University of California Press, 2013), p. 209.
38 Lucy S. Dawidowicz, *The War against the Jews, 1933–1945*, 1st ed. ed. (New York: Holt, Rinehart and Winston, 1975), p. 316.
39 "Decrees Excluding Jews from Cultural and Public Life (1933–1942)," 723–6.
40 Gerwarth, *Hitler's Hangman: The Life of Heydrich*, p. 165.
41 Reinhard Heydrich, "Instructions for Kristallnacht (10 November 1938)," in *The Third Reich Sourcebook*, ed. Anson Rabinbach and Sander L. Gilman (Berkeley: University of California Press, 2013), pp. 231–2.
42 USHMM, "Holocaust Encyclopedia: Kristallnacht," United States Holocaust Memorial Museum, http://www.ushmm.org/wlc/en/article.php?ModuleId=10005201.
43 Randall L Bytwerk, *Landmark Speeches of National Socialism*, 1st ed. (College Station: Texas A&M University Press, 2008), p. 89.
44 Henry Friedlander, *The Origins of Nazi Genocide: From Euthanasia to the Final Solution* (Chapel Hill: University of North Carolina Press, 1997), p. 39.
45 Clemens August von Galen, "Sermon on Euthanasia (2 August 1941)," in *The Third Reich Sourcebook*, ed. Anson Rabinbach and Sander L. Gilman (Berkeley: University of California Press, 2013), p. 345.
46 *Nazi Conspiracy and Aggression*, vol. V (Washington, DC: U.S. G.P.O., 1946), p. 689.
47 Adolf Hitler and Gerhard L Weinberg, *Hitler's Second Book: The Unpublished Sequel to Mein Kampf*, trans. Krista Smith (New York, NY: Enigma Books, 2006), x.
48 Kershaw, *Hitler: A Biography*, p. 354.
49 Jeremy Noakes and Geoffrey Pridham, eds., *Nazism, 1919–1945: A Documentary Reader*, vol. 3 (Exeter, UK: University of Exeter Press, 1995), p. 670.
50 Adolf Hitler, "Secret Memorandum on the Four Year Plan (1936)," in *The Third Reich Sourcebook*, ed. Anson Rabinbach and Sander L. Gilman (Berkeley: University of California Press, 2013).
51 Hitler and Weinberg, *Hitler's Second Book: The Unpublished Sequel to Mein Kampf*, 101.
52 Kershaw, *Hitler: A Biography*, p. 336.
53 Noakes and Pridham, *Nazism, 1919–1945: A Documentary Reader*, p. 724.
54 Gerhard L Weinberg, *Germany, Hitler, and World War II: Essays in Modern German and World History* (Cambridge: Cambridge University Press, 1995), p. 120.
55 Kershaw, *Hitler: A Biography*, p. 482.
56 Weinberg, *Germany, Hitler, and World War II: Essays in Modern German and World History*, p. 127.
57 Noakes and Pridham, *Nazism, 1919–1945: A Documentary Reader*, p. 745.

58 Kershaw, *Hitler: A Biography*, p. 483.
59 Adolf Hitler, "Speech to the Great German Reichstag, 30 January 1939," in *The Third Reich Sourcebook*, ed. Anson Rabinbach and Sander L. Gilman (Berkeley: University of California Press, 2013), pp. 723–4.
60 *Proceedings, 17 December 1945–8 January 1946*, vol. 4, Trial of the Major War Criminals before the International Military Tribunal (Nuremberg: U.S. Government Printing Office, 1947), pp. 242–3.
61 Noakes and Pridham, *Nazism, 1919–1945: A Documentary Reader*, p. 755.
62 Ibid., p. 757.

3 Nazis and the Imaginary East

1 Helmut Hieber, "Der Generalplan Ost," *Vierteljahrshefte für Zeitgeschichte* 6, no. 3 (1958): 281.
2 See, for example, Winson Chu, Jesse Kauffman, and Michael Meng, "A Sonderweg through Eastern Europe? The Varieties of German Rule in Poland during the Two World Wars," *German History* 31, no. 3 (2013).
3 Vejas G Liulevicius, *The German Myth of the East: 1800 to the Present* (Oxford: Oxford University Press, 2009), p. 25.
4 Tacitus, *Agricola. Germania. Dialogue on Oratory*, trans. M. Hutton and W. Peterson, vol. 35, Loeb Classical Library (Cambridge, MA: Harvard University Press, 1914).
5 Christopher B. Krebs, "An Innocuous yet Noxious Text: Tacitus's Germania," *Historically Speaking* 12, no. 4 (2011): 2.
6 Ibid., p. 4.
7 Liulevicius, *The German Myth of the East: 1800 to the Present*, p. 26.
8 Ibid., p. 22.
9 Ibid., pp. 90–1.
10 Ibid., p. 39.
11 Ibid., pp. 39–40.
12 Renate Bridenthal, "Germans from Russia: The Political Network of a Double Diaspora," in *The Heimat Abroad: The Boundaries of Germanness*, ed. Krista O'Donnell, Nancy Ruth Reagin, and Renate Bridenthal (Ann Arbor: University of Michigan Press, 2005), 70.
13 Chu, Kauffman, and Meng, "A Sonderweg through Eastern Europe? The Varieties of German Rule in Poland During the Two World Wars," p. 325.
14 Ibid., p. 327.
15 Vejas G. Liulevicius, *War Land on the Eastern Front: Culture, National Identity and German Occupation in World War I* (Cambridge: Cambridge University Press, 2000), p. 248.
16 Chu, Kauffman, and Meng, "A Sonderweg through Eastern Europe? The Varieties of German Rule in Poland During the Two World Wars," p. 330.
17 Jan M. Piskorski, "The Medieval Colonization of Central Europe as a Problem of World History and Historiography," 22, no. 3 (2004): 338.
18 Moritz Wilhelm Heffter, *Der Weltkampf der Deutschen und Slaven seit dem Ende des fünten Jahrhunderts nach christlicher Zeitrechnung, nach seinem Ursprunge* (Hamburg: F. und A. Perthes, 1847), p. 462.

19 Liulevicius, *War Land on the Eastern Front: Culture, National Identity and German Occupation in World War I*, p. 255.
20 Piskorski, "The Medieval Colonization of Central Europe as a Problem of World History and Historiography," p. 333.
21 Larry Wolff, *Inventing Eastern Europe: The Map of Civilization on the Mind of the Enlightenment* (Stanford, CA: Stanford University Press, 1994), p. 4.
22 Liulevicius, *The German Myth of the East: 1800 to the Present*, p. 51.
23 Liulevicius, *War Land on the Eastern Front: Culture, National Identity and German Occupation in World War I*, p. 154.
24 Liulevicius, *The German Myth of the East: 1800 to the Present*, p. 123.
25 Liulevicius, *War Land on the Eastern Front: Culture, National Identity and German Occupation in World War I*, p. 155.
26 Ibid., p. 131.
27 Liulevicius, *The German Myth of the East: 1800 to the Present*, p. 120.
28 Ibid., p. 115.
29 Ibid., p. 140.
30 Ibid., p. 151.
31 Liulevicius, *War Land on the Eastern Front: Culture, National Identity and German Occupation in World War I*, p. 161.
32 John Connelly, "Nazis and Slavs: From Racial Theory to Racist Practice," *Central European History* 32, no. 1 (1999): 14.
33 Andre Mineau, *SS Thinking and the Holocaust* (Amsterdam: Rodopi B.V., 2012), p. 65.
34 Ibid.
35 Peter Longerich, *Heinrich Himmler: A Life* (New York: Oxford University Press, 2012), p. 273.
36 Krebs, "An Innocuous yet Noxious Text: Tacitus's Germania," p. 2.
37 See OKW, *Der Osten: Sonderlehrgang 1 Teil*, Soldatenbriefe Zur Berufsförderung (Breslau: F. Hirt, 1941).
38 Martin Winstone, *The Dark Heart of Hitler's Europe: Nazi Rule in Poland under the General Government* (London: I. B. Tauris, 2015), p. 30.
39 Norbert Götz, "German-Speaking People and German Heritage: Nazi Germany and the Problem of Volksgemeinschaft," in *The Heimat Abroad: The Boundaries of Germanness*, ed. Krista O'Donnell, Nancy Ruth Reagin, and Renate Bridenthal (Ann Arbor: University of Michigan Press, 2005), p. 61.
40 Ibid., p. 63.
41 Adolf Hitler and Gerhard L Weinberg, *Hitler's Second Book: The Unpublished Sequel to Mein Kampf*, trans. Krista Smith (New York, NY: Enigma Books, 2006), p. 47.
42 Ibid., p. 101.
43 Liulevicius, *The German Myth of the East: 1800 to the Present*, pp. 183–4.
44 Jürgen Matthäus and Frank Bajohr, eds., *The Political Diary of Alfred Rosenberg and the Onset of the Holocaust*, Documenting Life and Destruction: Holocaust Sources in Context (Lanham, MD: Rowman & Littlefield, 2015), p. 378.
45 Wolfgang Diewerge, *Deutsche soldaten sehen die Sowjet-union* (Berlin: W. Limpert 1941), Accessed online at: http://research.calvin.edu/german-propaganda-archive/feldpost.htm.

46 Connelly, "Nazis and Slavs: From Racial Theory to Racist Practice," p. 29.
47 Nicholas Markow, *Der Jude ist der Parasit des Bauerntums* (Frankfurt-Main: Welt-Dienst-Verlag, 1944), p. 10.
48 Mineau, *SS Thinking and the Holocaust*, p. 64.
49 Hitler and Weinberg, *Hitler's Second Book: The Unpublished Sequel to Mein Kampf*, p. 115.
50 Diewerge, *Deutsche soldaten sehen die Sowjet-union*, Accessed online at: http://research.calvin.edu/german-propaganda-archive/feldpost.htm.
51 Connelly, "Nazis and Slavs: From Racial Theory to Racist Practice," p. 13.
52 Friedrich Kopp, *Deutschland, Europas Bollwerk Im Osten: Germanische Leistungen für Europas Sicherheit*, vol. Heft 8, Bolschewismus (München: F. Eher, 1939).
53 Diewerge, *Deutsche soldaten sehen die Sowjet-union*, Accessed online at: http://research.calvin.edu/german-propaganda-archive/feldpost.htm.
54 *Proceedings, 27 August -1946–1 October 1946*, vol. 22, Trial of the Major War Criminals before the International Military Tribunal (Nuremberg: US Government Printing Office, 1948), p. 229.
55 Matthäus and Bajohr, *The Political Diary of Alfred Rosenberg and the Onset of the Holocaust*, p. 259.
56 Ibid., p. 264.
57 Longerich, *Heinrich Himmler: A Life*, p. 204.
58 "Excerpts from Four Policy Texts by Rosenberg's Office Regarding Propaganda and Public Relations Work with Reference to the Soviet Union (Typed, No Signature, Stamped "Dienststelle Rosenberg"), No Date (Spring 1941)," in *The Political Diary of Alfred Rosenberg and the Onset of the Holocaust*, ed. Jürgen Matthäus and Frank Bajohr, Documenting Life and Destruction: Holocaust Sources in Context (Lanham, MD: Rowman & Littlefield, 2015), p. 373.
59 *Judentum und Bolschewismus*, vol. Heft 27, Schriftenreihe Zur Weltanschaulichen Schulungsarbeit Der Nsdap (München: Franz Eher Nachf., 1943).
60 Carroll P. Kakel, *The Holocaust as Colonial Genocide: Hitler's 'Indian Wars' in the 'Wild East'* (New York: Palgrave Pivot, 2013), p. 46.
61 Liulevicius, *The German Myth of the East: 1800 to the Present*, p. 12.
62 Ibid., p. 106.
63 Longerich, *Heinrich Himmler: A Life*, p. 386.
64 Alfred Rosenberg, "Speech before Members of the Civil Administration in Riga, 16 May 1942," in *The Political Diary of Alfred Rosenberg and the Onset of the Holocaust*, ed. Jürgen Matthäus and Frank Bajohr, Documenting Life and Destruction: Holocaust Sources in Context (Lanham, MD: Rowman & Littlefield, 2015), p. 403.
65 Connelly, "Nazis and Slavs: From Racial Theory to Racist Practice," p. 29.
66 Ben Kiernan, *Blood and Soil: A World History of Genocide and Extermination from Sparta to Darfur* (New Haven: Yale University Press, 2007), p. 432.
67 Liulevicius, *The German Myth of the East: 1800 to the Present*, pp. 78–9.
68 Ibid., p. 80.
69 Ibid., pp. 104–5.
70 Ian Kershaw, *Hitler, 1936–45: Nemesis* (London: Allen Lane, 2000), p. 434.
71 Timothy Snyder, *Bloodlands: Europe between Hitler and Stalin* (New York: Basic Books, 2012), p. 160.

72 Carroll P. Kakel, *The American West and the Nazi East: A Comparative and Interpretive Perspective* (New York: Palgrave Macmillan, 2011), p. 1.
73 Richard Rhodes, *Masters of Death: The SS-Einsatzgruppen and the Invention of the Holocaust* (New York: Vintage Books, 2003), p. 93.
74 Ibid.
75 Hitler and Weinberg, *Hitler's Second Book: The Unpublished Sequel to Mein Kampf*, p. 109.
76 The first concentration camps in the modern era were created by the British during the Boer War.
77 Liulevicius, *The German Myth of the East: 1800 to the Present*, p. 188.
78 Shelley Baranowski, "Against "Human Diversity as Such": Lebensraum and Genocide in the Third Reich," in *German Colonialism: Race, the Holocaust, and Postwar Germany*, ed. Volker Langbehn and Mohammad Salama (New York: Columbia University Press, 2011), p. 59.
79 Liulevicius, *The German Myth of the East: 1800 to the Present*, p. 7.
80 Liulevicius, *War Land on the Eastern Front: Culture, National Identity and German Occupation in World War I*.
81 Heinrich Himmler, "Document 1919-Ps: Himmler's Speech at Posen, 4 October 1943," in *Trials of the Major War Criminals before the International Military Tribunal: Documents and Other Material in Evidence, 1850-Ps to 2233-Ps* (Nuremberg: US Government Printing Office, 1948), pp. 171–2.
82 Kakel, *The Holocaust as Colonial Genocide: Hitler's 'Indian Wars' in the 'Wild East'*, p. 45.
83 Kiernan, *Blood and Soil: A World History of Genocide and Extermination from Sparta to Darfur*, p. 452.
84 Bridenthal, "Germans from Russia: The Political Network of a Double Diaspora," p. 197.
85 Liulevicius, *War Land on the Eastern Front: Culture, National Identity and German Occupation in World War I*, p. 271.
86 Ibid., p. 270.
87 "'Reflections on the Treatment of Peoples of Alien Races in the East' a Secret Memorandum Handed to Hitler by Himmler on 25 May 1940," in *Trials of War Criminals before the Nuernberg Military Tribunals under Control Council Law No. 10* (Washington, DC: Government Printing Office, 1952), p. 147.
88 Alex J. Kay, "The Purpose of the Russian Campaign Is the Decimation of the Slavic Population by Thirty Million": The Radicalisation of German Food Policy in Early 1941," in *Nazi Policy on the Eastern Front, 1941: Total War, Genocide, and Radicalization*, ed. Alex J. Kay, Jeff Rutherford, and David Stahel (Rochester, NY: University of Rochester Press, 2012), pp. 187–8.
89 Christopher R. Browning, "Keynote: Science, Planning, Expulsion—the National Socialist General Plan for the East," (University of Toronto, 2008), p. 2.
90 Longerich, *Heinrich Himmler: A Life*, p. 578.
91 From "Response and Thoughts on the Reichsführer SS General Plan Ost" compiled by Dr. Erhard Wetzel from the RSHA, April 27, 1942, Hieber, "Der Generalplan Ost," p. 297.
92 Waitman Wade Beorn, *Marching into Darkness: The Wehrmacht and the Holocaust in Belarus* (Cambridge: Harvard University Press, 2014), p. 57.

93 Hieber, "Der Generalplan Ost," p. 289.
94 From "Report of Meeting, 4 February 1942" compiled by Dr. Erhard Wetzel from the RSHA, ibid., p. 295.
95 From "Response and Thoughts on the Reichsführer SS General Plan Ost" compiled by Dr. Erhard Wetzel from the RSHA, April 27, 1942, ibid., p. 307.
96 Heinrich Himmler, "Some Thoughts on the Treatment of Racial Aliens in the East, 15 May 1940," in *The Third Reich Sourcebook*, ed. Anson Rabinbach and Sander L. Gilman (Berkeley: University of California Press, 2013), p. 734.
97 Kay, "The Purpose of the Russian Campaign Is the Decimation of the Slavic Population by Thirty Million": The Radicalisation of German Food Policy in Early 1941," p. 190.
98 From "Response and Thoughts on the Reichsführer SS General Plan Ost" compiled by Dr. Erhard Wetzel from the RSHA, April 27, 1942, Hieber, "Der Generalplan Ost," p. 324.
99 From "Reichsführer SS Memo, 12 June 1942," ibid., p. 325.
100 Dietrich Eichholtz, ""Generalplan Ost" Zur Versklavung Osteuropäischer Völker," *Utopie Kreativ* 167, no. September (2004): 805.
101 Rosenberg, "Speech before Members of the Civil Administration in Riga, 16 May 1942," p. 401.
102 Eichholtz, ""Generalplan Ost" Zur Versklavung Osteuropäischer Völker," p. 804.
103 Himmler, "Some Thoughts on the Treatment of Racial Aliens in the East, 15 May 1940," p. 734.
104 Longerich, *Heinrich Himmler: A Life*, p. 599.
105 Götz, "German-Speaking People and German Heritage: Nazi Germany and the Problem of Volksgemeinschaft," p. 63.
106 Gesine Gerhard, "Food and Genocide: Nazi Agrarian Politics in the Occupied Territories of the Soviet Union," *Contemporary European History* 18, no. 01 (2009): 56.
107 Ibid., p. 48.
108 Ibid., p. 50.
109 Kay, "The Purpose of the Russian Campaign Is the Decimation of the Slavic Population by Thirty Million": The Radicalisation of German Food Policy in Early 1941," p. 175.
110 Ibid., p. 182.
111 Klaus Jochen Arnold and Gert C. Lübbers, "The Meeting of the Staatssekretäre on 2 May 1941 and the Wehrmacht: A Document up for Discussion," *Journal of Contemporary History* 42, no. 4 (2007): 616.
112 Snyder, *Bloodlands: Europe between Hitler and Stalin*, p. 162.
113 Kay, "The Purpose of the Russian Campaign Is the Decimation of the Slavic Population by Thirty Million": The Radicalisation of German Food Policy in Early 1941," p. 187.
114 Ibid., pp. 187–8.
115 Ibid., p. 191.
116 Longerich, *Heinrich Himmler: A Life*, p. 53.
117 Liulevicius, *The German Myth of the East: 1800 to the Present*, p. 171.
118 Browning, "Keynote: Science, Planning, Expulsion—the National Socialist General Plan for the East," p. 19.

4 The Soviet Interlude

1. Jan Tomasz Gross, *Revolution from Abroad: The Soviet Conquest of Poland's Western Ukraine and Western Belorussia* (Princeton, NJ: Princeton University Press, 1988), p. 22.
2. Geoffrey Roberts, *Stalin's Wars: From World War to Cold War, 1939–1953* (New Haven, CT: Yale University Press, 2006), p. 30.
3. Yitzhak Arad, *The Holocaust in the Soviet Union* (Lincoln: University of Nebraska Press, 2009), p. 37.
4. Roberts, *Stalin's Wars: From World War to Cold War, 1939–1953*, p. 32.
5. Ibid., p. 30.
6. Ibid.
7. "Secret Supplementary Protocol to the Non-Aggression Pact between Germany and the Soviet Union, 23 August 1939, Moscow," in *Katyn: A Crime without Punishment*, ed. Anna M. Cienciala, Natalia S. Lebedeva, and Wojciech Materski (New Haven: Yale University Press, 2007), p. 41.
8. Piotr J. Wróbel, "Class War or Ethnic Cleansing?" *Polish Review* 59, no. 2 (2014): 20.
9. "Order No. 005 of the Military Council of the Belorussian Front to the Troops on the Goals of the Red Army's Entry into Western Belorussia," in *Katyn: A Crime without Punishment*, ed. Anna M. Cienciala, Natalia S. Lebedeva, and Wojciech Materski (New Haven: Yale University Press, 2007), p. 43.
10. Gross, *Revolution from Abroad: The Soviet Conquest of Poland's Western Ukraine and Western Belorussia*, p. 12.
11. "Soviet Government Note Handed to the Polish Ambassador in the USSR, Waclaw Grzybowski, 17 September 1939, Moscow," in *Katyn: A Crime without Punishment*, ed. Anna M. Cienciala, Natalia S. Lebedeva, and Wojciech Materski (New Haven: Yale University Press, 2007), p. 44.
12. "Order No. 005 of the Military Council of the Belorussian Front to the Troops on the Goals of the Red Army's Entry into Western Belorussia," p. 42.
13. Timothy Snyder, *Bloodlands: Europe between Hitler and Stalin* (New York: Basic Books, 2012), p. 89.
14. Shimon Redlich, *Together and Apart in Brzezany: Poles, Jews, and Ukrainians, 1919–1945* (Bloomington: Indiana University Press, 2002), p. 87.
15. Gross, *Revolution from Abroad: The Soviet Conquest of Poland's Western Ukraine and Western Belorussia*, p. 25.
16. Ibid., p. 34.
17. Redlich, *Together and Apart in Brzezany: Poles, Jews, and Ukrainians, 1919–1945*, p. 80.
18. Ibid.
19. Gross, *Revolution from Abroad: The Soviet Conquest of Poland's Western Ukraine and Western Belorussia*, p. 33.
20. Chaim Kaplan, "Escape of Jews from Poland to the Soviet Union at the Beginning of the War," in *Documents on the Holocaust: Selected Sources on the Destruction of the Jews of Germany and Austria, Poland, and the Soviet Union*, ed. Yitzhak Arad, Israel Gutman, and Abraham Margaliot (Jerusalem: Yad Vashem, 1999), p. 189.

21 Gross, *Revolution from Abroad: The Soviet Conquest of Poland's Western Ukraine and Western Belorussia*, p. 50.
22 Halik Kochanski, *Eagle Unbowed: Poland and the Poles in the Second World War* (Cambridge: Harvard University Press, 2014), p. 121.
23 Dov Levin, *The Lesser of Two Evils: Eastern European Jewry under Soviet Rule, 1939–1941*, trans. Naftali Greenwood (Philadelphia: Jewish Publication Society, 1995), p. 38.
24 Joanna B. Michlic, "The Soviet Occupation of Poland, 1939–41, and the Stereotype of the Anti-Polish and Pro-Soviet Jew," *Jewish Social Studies* 13, no. 13 (2007): 140.
25 Kochanski, *Eagle Unbowed: Poland and the Poles in the Second World War*, p. 120.
26 Redlich, *Together and Apart in Brzezany: Poles, Jews, and Ukrainians, 1919–1945*, p. 86.
27 Gross, *Revolution from Abroad: The Soviet Conquest of Poland's Western Ukraine and Western Belorussia*, pp. 35, 37.
28 Christoph Mick, "'Only the Jews Do Not Waver'—L'viv under Soviet Occupation," in *Shared History, Divided Memory: Jews and Others in Soviet-Occupied Poland,1939–1941*, ed. Elazar Barkan, Elizabeth A. Cole, and Kai Struve (Leipzig: Leipziger Universitätsverlag, 2007), p. 47.
29 Alfred Erich Senn, *Lithuania 1940: Revolution from Above* (Amsterdam: Rodopi, 2007), p. 226.
30 Redlich, *Together and Apart in Brzezany: Poles, Jews, and Ukrainians, 1919–1945*, p. 86.
31 Senn, *Lithuania 1940: Revolution from Above*, p. 243.
32 "NKVD UPV Instruction to the Head of Putivl Camp on Detaining POWs with Various Specializations and Backgrounds, 23 October 1939, Moscow," in *Katyn: A Crime without Punishment*, ed. Anna M. Cienciala, Natalia S. Lebedeva, and Wojciech Materski (New Haven: Yale University Press, 2007), pp. 75–6.
33 Gross, *Revolution from Abroad: The Soviet Conquest of Poland's Western Ukraine and Western Belorussia*, p. 94.
34 Anna M. Cienciala, Natalia S. Lebedeva, and Wojciech Materski, *Katyn: A Crime without Punishment*, trans. Marian Schwartz, Anna M. Cienciala, and Maia A. Kipp (New Haven: Yale University Press, 2007), p. 25.
35 Karen Sutton, *The Massacre of the Jews of Lithuania: Lithuanian Collaboration in the Final Solution, 1941–1944* (Jerusalem: Gefen Publishing House, 2008), p. 82.
36 Arad, *The Holocaust in the Soviet Union*, p. 44.
37 Snyder, *Bloodlands: Europe between Hitler and Stalin*, p. 128.
38 Kochanski, *Eagle Unbowed: Poland and the Poles in the Second World War*, p. 127.
39 Sutton, *The Massacre of the Jews of Lithuania: Lithuanian Collaboration in the Final Solution, 1941–1944*, p. 89.
40 Senn, *Lithuania 1940: Revolution from Above*, p. 227.
41 Gross, *Revolution from Abroad: The Soviet Conquest of Poland's Western Ukraine and Western Belorussia*, p. 131.
42 Kochanski, *Eagle Unbowed: Poland and the Poles in the Second World War*, p. 125.

NOTES

43 Arad, *The Holocaust in the Soviet Union*, p. 43.
44 Ibid., p. 22.
45 Redlich, *Together and Apart in Brzezany: Poles, Jews, and Ukrainians, 1919–1945*, p. 91.
46 Arad, *The Holocaust in the Soviet Union*, p. 47.
47 Ibid., p. 48.
48 Ibid., p. 49.
49 Leon Weliczker Wells, *The Janowska Road* (New York: MacMillan, 1963), p. 26.
50 Sutton, *The Massacre of the Jews of Lithuania: Lithuanian Collaboration in the Final Solution, 1941–1944*, p. 89.
51 Snyder, *Bloodlands: Europe between Hitler and Stalin*, p. 137.
52 Krzysztof Bielawski, "Polish Jews—Victims of Katyn Massacre," POLIN Museum of the History of Polish Jews, http://www.sztetl.org.pl/en/cms/news/5141,polish-jews-victims-of-katyn-massacre/. Source is Goldhar J., My story, Tel-Aviv, 2012, translated by K. Bielawski
53 Kochanski, *Eagle Unbowed: Poland and the Poles in the Second World War*, p. 119.
54 Snyder, *Bloodlands: Europe between Hitler and Stalin*, p. 126.
55 Adolf Folkmann and Stefan Szende, *The Promise Hitler Kept* (New York: Roy Publishers, 1945), p. 28.
56 Gross, *Revolution from Abroad: The Soviet Conquest of Poland's Western Ukraine and Western Belorussia*, pp. 61–2.
57 "Conclusion of the Indictment in the Case of POW Szczepan Olejnik, 6 January 1940, Ostashkov," in *Katyn: A Crime without Punishment*, ed. Anna M. Cienciala, Natalia S. Lebedeva, and Wojciech Materski (New Haven: Yale University Press, 2007), p. 89.
58 Redlich, *Together and Apart in Brzezany: Poles, Jews, and Ukrainians, 1919–1945*, p. 80.
59 Gross, *Revolution from Abroad: The Soviet Conquest of Poland's Western Ukraine and Western Belorussia*, p. 157.
60 Redlich, *Together and Apart in Brzezany: Poles, Jews, and Ukrainians, 1919–1945*, p. 89.
61 Wróbel, "Class War or Ethnic Cleansing?" p. 28.
62 Lyn Smith, *Remembering: Voices of the Holocaust- a New History in the Words of the Men and Women Who Survived* (New York: Carroll & Graf, 2006), p. 90.
63 Ibid., p. 91.
64 Gross, *Revolution from Abroad: The Soviet Conquest of Poland's Western Ukraine and Western Belorussia*, p. 204.
65 Ibid., p. 206.
66 Levin, *The Lesser of Two Evils: Eastern European Jewry under Soviet Rule, 1939–1941*, p. 15.
67 Sutton, *The Massacre of the Jews of Lithuania: Lithuanian Collaboration in the Final Solution, 1941–1944*, p. 93.
68 Levin, *The Lesser of Two Evils: Eastern European Jewry under Soviet Rule, 1939–1941*, p. 265.
69 Ibid., p. 18.
70 Kochanski, *Eagle Unbowed: Poland and the Poles in the Second World War*, p. 129.

71 "NKVD UPV Instruction to the Head of Putivl Camp on Detaining POWs with Various Specializations and Backgrounds, 23 October 1939, Moscow," pp. 75–6.
72 Ibid.
73 "Beria Memorandum to Joseph Stalin Proposing the Execution of the Polish Officers, Gendarmes, Police, Military Settlers, and Others in the Three Special Pow Camps, Along with Those Held in the Prisons of the Western Regions of Ukraine and Belorussia, Accepted by the Politburo, 5 March 1940, Moscow," in *Katyn: A Crime without Punishment*, ed. Anna M. Cienciala, Natalia S. Lebedeva, and Wojciech Materski (New Haven: Yale University Press, 2007), p. 120.
74 This is a number of some debate but this range seems most reliable and is sourced from Simon Schochet, "Reflections on Soviet Documents Relating to Polish Prisoners of War Taken in September 1939," in *Focusing on the Holocaust and Its Aftermath*, ed. Antony Polonsky, Polin: Studies in Polish Jewry (Oxford: Littman Library of Jewish Civilization, 2000), p. 75.
75 Ibid.
76 Robert van Voren, *Undigested Past: The Holocaust in Lithuania* (New York: Rodopi, 2011), p. 57.
77 Gross, *Revolution from Abroad: The Soviet Conquest of Poland's Western Ukraine and Western Belorussia*, pp. 180–1.
78 Sutton, *The Massacre of the Jews of Lithuania: Lithuanian Collaboration in the Final Solution, 1941–1944*, p. 94.
79 Ibid.
80 van Voren, *Undigested Past: The Holocaust in Lithuania*, pp 58–9.
81 Michlic, "The Soviet Occupation of Poland, 1939–41, and the Stereotype of the Anti-Polish and Pro-Soviet Jew," p. 145.
82 Elissa Bemporad, *Becoming Soviet Jews: The Bolshevik Experiment in Minsk* (Bloomington: Indiana University Press, 2013), p. 3.
83 Michlic, "The Soviet Occupation of Poland, 1939–41, and the Stereotype of the Anti-Polish and Pro-Soviet Jew," p. 140.
84 van Voren, *Undigested Past: The Holocaust in Lithuania*, p. 52.
85 Sutton, *The Massacre of the Jews of Lithuania: Lithuanian Collaboration in the Final Solution, 1941–1944*, p. 69.
86 Saul Friedländer, *The Years of Extermination: Nazi Germany and the Jews, 1939–1945* (New York: Harper Collins, 2007), p. 47.
87 van Voren, *Undigested Past: The Holocaust in Lithuania*, p. 53.
88 Sutton, *The Massacre of the Jews of Lithuania: Lithuanian Collaboration in the Final Solution, 1941–1944*, p. 63.
89 Snyder, *Bloodlands: Europe between Hitler and Stalin*, p. 115.
90 Levin, *The Lesser of Two Evils: Eastern European Jewry under Soviet Rule, 1939–1941*, p. 43.
91 Redlich, *Together and Apart in Brzezany: Poles, Jews, and Ukrainians, 1919–1945*, p. 80.
92 Sutton, *The Massacre of the Jews of Lithuania: Lithuanian Collaboration in the Final Solution, 1941–1944*, p. 59.
93 van Voren, *Undigested Past: The Holocaust in Lithuania*, p. 56.
94 Ibid., p. 58.

95 Redlich, *Together and Apart in Brzezany: Poles, Jews, and Ukrainians, 1919–1945*, p. 89.
96 Ibid., p. 90.
97 Friedländer, *The Years of Extermination: Nazi Germany and the Jews, 1939–1945*, p. 48.

5 Poland: The Nazi Laboratory of Genocide

1 Saul Friedländer, *The Years of Extermination: Nazi Germany and the Jews, 1939–1945* (New York: Harper Collins, 2007), p. 4.
2 This figure from Peter Longerich, *Holocaust: The Nazi Persecution and Murder of the Jews* (Oxford: Oxford University Press, 2010), p. 148.
3 "Translation of Document 1014-PS: Second Speech by the Führer on 22 Aug 1939," in *Nazi Conspiracy and Aggression, vol. III* (Washington, DC: US Government Printing Office, 1946), p. 665.
4 "Document 2751-PS: Sworn Statement by Alfred Helmut Naujoks, 20 November 1945," in *Trials of the War Criminals before the International Military Tribunal: Documents and Other Material In Evidence, 2605-PS to 3054-PS, Vol. Xxxi* (Nuremberg: US Government Printing Office, 1948), pp. 91–2.
5 "Document 100-R: Memorandum on Statements by Hitler concerning his Political and Military Plans, made to Brauchitsch, 25 March 1939," in *Trials of the War Criminals before the International Military Tribunal: Documents and Other Material In Evidence, 185-L to 1216-RF, Vol. Xxxviii* (Washington, DC: US Government Printing Office, 1949), p. 274.
6 Max Hastings, *Inferno: The World at War, 1939–45* (New York: Alfred A. Knopf, 2011), p. 5.
7 Ibid., p. 15.
8 Ibid.
9 Ibid., p. 11.
10 Jürgen Matthäus and Jochen Böhler, eds., *War, Pacification, and Mass Murder, 1939: The Einsatzgruppen in Poland* (Lanham: Rowman & Littlefield, 2014), p. 8.
11 Timothy Snyder, *Bloodlands: Europe between Hitler and Stalin* (New York: Basic Books, 2012), p. 121.
12 Hastings, *Inferno: The World at War, 1939–45*, p. 9.
13 Lyn Smith, *Remembering: Voices of the Holocaust- a New History in the Words of the Men and Women Who Survived* (New York: Carroll & Graf, 2006), p. 76.
14 Friedländer, *The Years of Extermination: Nazi Germany and the Jews, 1939–1945*, pp. 28–9.
15 Hastings, *Inferno: The World at War, 1939–45*, p. 21.
16 Christopher R. Browning and Jürgen Matthäus, *The Origins of the Final Solution: The Evolution of Nazi Jewish Policy, September 1939–March 1942* (Lincoln: University of Nebraska Press, 2004), p. 170.
17 Matthäus and Böhler, *War, Pacification, and Mass Murder, 1939: The Einsatzgruppen in Poland*, pp. 12–13.

18 Ibid., p. 15.
19 Browning and Matthäus, *The Origins of the Final Solution: The Evolution of Nazi Jewish Policy, September 1939–March 1942*, pp. 55–6.
20 Adolf Hitler and Gerhard L Weinberg, *Hitler's Second Book: The Unpublished Sequel to Mein Kampf*, trans. Krista Smith (New York: Enigma Books, 2006), p. 50.
21 Matthäus and Böhler, *War, Pacification, and Mass Murder, 1939: The Einsatzgruppen in Poland*, p. 6.
22 Martin Winstone, *The Dark Heart of Hitler's Europe: Nazi Rule in Poland under the General Government* (London: I. B. Tauris, 2015), p. 69.
23 Ibid., p. 119.
24 "Agreement between the Wehrmacht and Sipo/SD Regarding "Guidelines for the Foreign Deployment of the Security Police and the SD," Undated (August 1939)," in *War, Pacification, and Mass Murder, 1939: The Einsatzgruppen in Poland*, ed. Jürgen Matthäus and Jochen Böhler (Lanham: Rowman & Littlefield, 2014), p. 32.
25 "Directive by the Army High Commander Regarding Activities and Tasks of the Einsatzgruppen, September 21, 1939," in *War, Pacification, and Mass Murder, 1939: The Einsatzgruppen in Poland*, ed. Jürgen Matthäus and Jochen Böhler (Lanham: Rowman & Littlefield, 2014), pp. 130–1.
26 Matthäus and Böhler, *War, Pacification, and Mass Murder, 1939: The Einsatzgruppen in Poland*, p. 16.
27 Friedländer, *The Years of Extermination: Nazi Germany and the Jews, 1939–1945*, pp. 12–3.
28 "Activity report by Einsatzgruppe IV in Warsaw, October 10, 1939," in *War, Pacification, and Mass Murder, 1939: The Einsatzgruppen in Poland*, ed. Jürgen Matthäus and Jochen Böhler (Lanham: Rowman & Littlefield, 2014), p. 75.
29 "Daily Reports by the Chief of the Sipo/SD, September 24 and 26, 1939," in *War, Pacification, and Mass Murder, 1939: The Einsatzgruppen in Poland*, ed. Jürgen Matthäus and Jochen Böhler (Lanham: Rowman & Littlefield, 2014), p. 136.
30 "Testimony by Zofia Semik on German Violence in Limanowa, May 13, 1977," in *War, Pacification, and Mass Murder, 1939: The Einsatzgruppen in Poland*, ed. Jürgen Matthäus and Jochen Böhler (Lanham: Rowman & Littlefield, 2014), pp. 47–8.
31 Halik Kochanski, *Eagle Unbowed: Poland and the Poles in the Second World War* (Cambridge: Harvard University Press, 2014), p. 98.
32 Matthäus and Böhler, *War, Pacification, and Mass Murder, 1939: The Einsatzgruppen in Poland*, p. 3.
33 "Interrogation of Kurt G., Former Member of Einsatzkommando 1/Iv, Regarding Anti-Jewish Violence in Białystok, November 13, 1965," in *War, Pacification, and Mass Murder, 1939: The Einsatzgruppen in Poland*, ed. Jürgen Matthäus and Jochen Böhler (Lanham: Rowman & Littlefield, 2014), p. 92.
34 Matthäus and Böhler, *War, Pacification, and Mass Murder, 1939: The Einsatzgruppen in Poland*, p. 93.
35 "Account by Berta Lichtig on the Burning of the Synagogue in Mielec Undated (Ca. 1943)," in *War, Pacification, and Mass Murder, 1939: The Einsatzgruppen*

in Poland, ed. Jürgen Matthäus and Jochen Böhler (Lanham: Rowman & Littlefield, 2014), p. 89.
36 Matthäus and Böhler, *War, Pacification, and Mass Murder, 1939: The Einsatzgruppen in Poland*, p. 90.
37 Ibid., p. 140.
38 Browning and Matthäus, *The Origins of the Final Solution: The Evolution of Nazi Jewish Policy, September 1939–March 1942*, p. 169.
39 "Report by General Petzel, Chief Defense Region (Wehrkreiskommando) XXI, to the Commander of the Reserve Army (Befehlshaber des Ersatzheeres), November 23, 1939," in *War, Pacification, and Mass Murder, 1939: The Einsatzgruppen in Poland*, ed. Jürgen Matthäus and Jochen Böhler (Lanham: Rowman & Littlefield, 2014), p. 143.
40 Browning and Matthäus, *The Origins of the Final Solution: The Evolution of Nazi Jewish Policy, September 1939–March 1942*, pp. 173–4.
41 Ibid., p. 175.
42 Ibid., p. 169.
43 Ibid., p. 59.
44 Ibid., p. 169.
45 Matthäus and Böhler, *War, Pacification, and Mass Murder, 1939: The Einsatzgruppen in Poland*, pp. 28–9.
46 Ibid., pp. 172–3.
47 Ibid., p. 28.
48 Ibid., p. 30.
49 "Directive by the Commander of the 14th Army, Generaloberst Wilhelm List, to Subordinate Commanders, October 1, 1939," in *War, Pacification, and Mass Murder, 1939: The Einsatzgruppen in Poland*, ed. Jürgen Matthäus and Jochen Böhler (Lanham: Rowman & Littlefield, 2014), p. 142.
50 Winstone, *The Dark Heart of Hitler's Europe: Nazi Rule in Poland under the General Government*, p. 158.
51 Martyn Housden, "Hans Frank- Empire Builder in the East, 1939–41," *European History Quarterly* 24, no. 3 (1994): 371.
52 Winstone, *The Dark Heart of Hitler's Europe: Nazi Rule in Poland under the General Government*, p. 105.
53 Ibid., p. 79.
54 Bradley Nichols, "Forging the Aryan Utopia: Nazi Racial Policy in Occupied Poland, 1939–1945," in *The Routledge History of the Holocaust*, ed. Jonathan C. Friedman (New York: Routledge, 2011), p. 127.
55 "Decree by the Higher SS and Police Leader, Posen, Regarding the Expulsion of Jews and Poles from the Warthegau, November 12, 1939," in *War, Pacification, and Mass Murder, 1939: The Einsatzgruppen in Poland*, ed. Jürgen Matthäus and Jochen Böhler (Lanham: Rowman & Littlefield, 2014), p. 113.
56 Kochanski, *Eagle Unbowed: Poland and the Poles in the Second World War*, p. 109.
57 Laurence Rees, *Auschwitz: A New History* (New York: Public Affairs, 2005), p. 16.
58 Browning and Matthäus, *The Origins of the Final Solution: The Evolution of Nazi Jewish Policy, September 1939–March 1942*, p. 106.
59 Ibid., p. 103.

60 Kochanski, *Eagle Unbowed: Poland and the Poles in the Second World War*, p. 105.
61 Winstone, *The Dark Heart of Hitler's Europe: Nazi Rule in Poland under the General Government*, p. 100.
62 Ibid., p. 121.
63 Ibid.
64 Tadeusz Nasierowski, "In the Abyss of Death," *International Journal of Mental Health* 35, no. 3 (2006): 51.
65 Ibid., p. 54.
66 "Interrogation of Max-Franz Janke, Former Member of Einsatzkommando 16 Stationed in Gdynia, July 10, 1969," in *War, Pacification, and Mass Murder, 1939: The Einsatzgruppen in Poland*, ed. Jürgen Matthäus and Jochen Böhler (Lanham: Rowman & Littlefield, 2014), p. 69.
67 Nasierowski, "In the Abyss of Death," p. 54.
68 Henry Friedlander, *The Origins of Nazi Genocide: From Euthanasia to the Final Solution* (Chapel Hill: University of North Carolina Press, 1997), p. 140.
69 Nichols, "Forging the Aryan Utopia: Nazi Racial Policy in Occupied Poland, 1939–1945," p. 128.
70 Kochanski, *Eagle Unbowed: Poland and the Poles in the Second World War*, p. 134.
71 Browning and Matthäus, *The Origins of the Final Solution: The Evolution of Nazi Jewish Policy, September 1939–March 1942*, p. 158.
72 Waitman Wade Beorn, *Marching into Darkness: The Wehrmacht and the Holocaust in Belarus* (Cambridge: Harvard University Press, 2014), p. 71.
73 Kochanski, *Eagle Unbowed: Poland and the Poles in the Second World War*, p. 106.
74 Winstone, *The Dark Heart of Hitler's Europe: Nazi Rule in Poland under the General Government*, p. 131.
75 Kochanski, *Eagle Unbowed: Poland and the Poles in the Second World War*, p. 106.
76 Nicholas Lane, "Tourism in Nazi-Occupied Poland: Baedeker's Generalgouvernement," *East European Jewish Affairs* 27, no. 1 (1997): 49.
77 Winstone, *The Dark Heart of Hitler's Europe: Nazi Rule in Poland under the General Government*, pp. 28–9.
78 Kochanski, *Eagle Unbowed: Poland and the Poles in the Second World War*, p. 116.
79 Housden, "Hans Frank- Empire Builder in the East, 1939–41," p. 372.
80 Rees, *Auschwitz: A New History*, p. 1.
81 Snyder, *Bloodlands: Europe between Hitler and Stalin*, p. 150.
82 Rees, *Auschwitz: A New History*, p. 20.
83 Kochanski, *Eagle Unbowed: Poland and the Poles in the Second World War*, p. 100.
84 Housden, "Hans Frank- Empire Builder in the East, 1939–41," p. 373.
85 Ibid., p. 382.
86 Chaim Kaplan, "Extracts from the Warsaw Ghetto Diary of Chaim A. Kaplan, 1940," in *Documents on the Holocaust: Selected Sources on the Destruction of the Jews of Germany and Austria, Poland, and the Soviet Union*, ed. Yitzhak Arad, Israel Gutman, and Abraham Margaliot (Jerusalem: Yad Vashem, 1999), p. 201.

87 Smith, *Remembering: Voices of the Holocaust- a New History in the Words of the Men and Women Who Survived*, p. 76.
88 "Interrogation of Lothar Beutel, former commander of Einsatzgruppe IV, in West Berlin, July 20, 1965," in *War, Pacification, and Mass Murder, 1939: The Einsatzgruppen in Poland*, ed. Jürgen Matthäus and Jochen Böhler (Lanham: Rowman & Littlefield, 2014), p. 103.
89 "Attack on the Jews of Wlocawek Following the German Occupation," in *Documents on the Holocaust: Selected Sources on the Destruction of the Jews of Germany and Austria, Poland, and the Soviet Union*, ed. Yitzhak Arad, Israel Gutman, and Abraham Margaliot (Jerusalem: Yad Vashem, 1999), p. 185.
90 Winstone, *The Dark Heart of Hitler's Europe: Nazi Rule in Poland under the General Government*, p. 148.
91 Kochanski, *Eagle Unbowed: Poland and the Poles in the Second World War*, p. 103.
92 "Four Decrees Issued in Occupied Poland, 1939–1941," in *The Third Reich Sourcebook*, ed. Anson Rabinbach and Sander L Gilman (Berkeley: University of California Press, 2013), p. 725.
93 Smith, *Remembering: Voices of the Holocaust- a New History in the Words of the Men and Women Who Survived*, p. 74.
94 Longerich, *Holocaust: The Nazi Persecution and Murder of the Jews*, p. 159.
95 Friedländer, *The Years of Extermination: Nazi Germany and the Jews, 1939–1945*, p. 41.
96 Browning and Matthäus, *The Origins of the Final Solution: The Evolution of Nazi Jewish Policy, September 1939–March 1942*, p. 137.
97 "Policy and Operations Concerning Jews in the Occupied Territories, 21 September 1939 (Heydrich)," in *The Third Reich Sourcebook*, ed. Anson Rabinbach and Sander L Gilman (Berkeley: University of California Press, 2013), p. 749.
98 Winstone, *The Dark Heart of Hitler's Europe: Nazi Rule in Poland under the General Government*, p. 161.
99 Friedländer, *The Years of Extermination: Nazi Germany and the Jews, 1939–1945*, pp. 92–3.
100 Housden, "Hans Frank- Empire Builder in the East, 1939–41," p. 381.

6 War of Annihilation: The Invasion of the Soviet Union

1 "Metzner, Alfred Statement, 18 September 1947," (BA-ZS: B162/5088), pp. 141–2.
2 Saul Friedländer, *The Years of Extermination: Nazi Germany and the Jews, 1939–1945* (New York: Harper Collins Publishers, 2007), p. 197.
3 Yitzhak Arad, *The Holocaust in the Soviet Union* (Lincoln: University of Nebraska Press, 2009), p. 65.
4 Timothy Snyder, *Bloodlands: Europe between Hitler and Stalin* (New York: Basic Books, 2012), p. 168.
5 See Gerhard L Weinberg, *A World at Arms: A Global History of World War II* (Cambridge: Cambridge University Press, 2005), p. 188.

6 Snyder, *Bloodlands: Europe between Hitler and Stalin*, pp. 165–6.
7 Geoffrey Roberts, *Stalin's Wars: From World War to Cold War, 1939–1953* (New Haven, CT: Yale University Press, 2006), p. 90.
8 Weinberg, *A World at Arms: A Global History of World War II*, p. 264.
9 Snyder, *Bloodlands: Europe between Hitler and Stalin*, p. 175.
10 Waitman Wade Beorn, *Marching into Darkness: The Wehrmacht and the Holocaust in Belarus* (Cambridge: Harvard University Press, 2014), p. 56.
11 Ibid., p. 59.
12 Friedländer, *The Years of Extermination: Nazi Germany and the Jews, 1939–1945*, p. 129.
13 Weinberg, *A World at Arms: A Global History of World War II*, p. 264.
14 Snyder, *Bloodlands: Europe between Hitler and Stalin*, p. 169.
15 Jeff Rutherford, "The Radicalization of German Occupation Policies: The Wirtschaftsstab Ost and the 121st Infantry Division in Pavlovsk, 1941," in *Nazi Policy on the Eastern Front, 1941: Total War, Genocide, and Radicalization*, ed. Alex J. Kay, Jeff Rutherford, and David Stahel (Rochester, NY: University of Rochester Press, 2012), p. 243.
16 Friedländer, *The Years of Extermination: Nazi Germany and the Jews, 1939–1945*, p. 129.
17 Roberts, *Stalin's Wars: From World War to Cold War, 1939–1953*, p. 57.
18 Omer Bartov, *Germany's War and the Holocaust: Disputed Histories* (Ithaca: Cornell University Press, 2003), pp. 3–4.
19 Thomas Earl Porter, "Hitler's Forgotten Genocides: The Fate of Soviet Pows," *Elon Law Review* 5, no. 2 (2013): p. 366.
20 Alex J. Kay, "'The Purpose of the Russian Campaign Is the Decimation of the Slavic Population by Thirty Million': The Radicalisation of German Food Policy in Early 1941," in *Nazi Policy on the Eastern Front, 1941: Total War, Genocide, and Radicalization*, ed. Alex J. Kay, Jeff Rutherford, and David Stahel (Rochester, NY: University of Rochester Press, 2012), p. 184.
21 Norman J. W. Goda, "Black Marks: Hitler's Bribery of His Senior Officers during World War Ii," *The Journal of Modern History* 72, no. 2 (2000).
22 Jürgen Matthäus and Jochen Böhler, eds., *War, Pacification, and Mass Murder, 1939: The Einsatzgruppen in Poland* (Lanham: Rowman & Littlefield, 2014), p. 155.
23 "Translation of Document 884-PS: Treatment of Political and Military Russian Officials, p. 12 May 1941," in *Nazi Conspiracy and Aggression, Supplement A* (Washington, DC: US Government Printing Office, 1947), pp. 637–8.
24 "Richtlinien für das Verhalten der Truppe in Russland, 29 May 1941" (BA-MA: RH 26-252-91), p. 33.
25 "Guidelines for the Treatment of Political Commissars, 6 June 1941," in *The Third Reich Sourcebook*, ed. Anson Rabinbach and Sander L. Gilman (Berkeley: University of California Press, 2013), p. 822.
26 "Translation of Document 884-PS: Treatment of Political and Military Russian Officials, 12 May 1941," p. 352.
27 Christopher R. Browning and Jürgen Matthäus, *The Origins of the Final Solution: The Evolution of Nazi Jewish Policy, September 1939–March 1942* (Lincoln: University of Nebraska Press, 2004), p. 455.

28 Felix Römer, "The Wehrmacht in the War of Ideologies: The Army and Hitler's Criminal Orders on the Eastern Front," in *Nazi Policy on the Eastern Front, 1941: Total War, Genocide, and Radicalization*, ed. Alex J. Kay, Jeff Rutherford, and David Stahel (Rochester, NY: University of Rochester Press, 2012), pp. 152–3.
29 Browning and Matthäus, *The Origins of the Final Solution: The Evolution of Nazi Jewish Policy, September 1939–March 1942*, p. 444.
30 Ibid., p. 447.
31 Bartov, *Germany's War and the Holocaust: Disputed Histories*, p. 5.
32 Michael Burleigh, *The Third Reich: A New History* (New York: Hill and Wang, 2000), pp. 432–3.
33 Konrad Jarausch, *Reluctant Accomplice: A Wehrmacht Soldier's Letters from the Eastern Front* (Princeton: Princeton University Press, 2011), p. 291.
34 Kay, "The Purpose of the Russian Campaign Is the Decimation of the Slavic Population by Thirty Million": The Radicalisation of German Food Policy in Early 1941," p. 196.
35 Porter, "Hitler's Forgotten Genocides: The Fate of Soviet Pows," p. 371.
36 Snyder, *Bloodlands: Europe between Hitler and Stalin*, p. 182.
37 Christian Streit, *Keine Kameraden: die Wehrmacht und die sowjetischen Kriegsgefangenen, 1941–1945* (Stuttgart: Deutsche Verlags-Anstalt, 1978), p. 79.
38 "Document 1519-Ps: Okw Order No. 3058/41, 8 September 1941," in *Trials of the Major War Criminals before the International Military Tribunal: Documents and Other Material In Evidence, 1104-PS to 1739-PS*, vol. XXVII (Washington, D.C.: US Government Printing Office, 1946), p. 275.
39 "Erläuterungen zur Übergabe des Gefangenen-Durchgangslager 127 von Kdt. r.A.559 an A.O.K. 2/O.Q.2, 14 July 1941," (BA-MA: RH 23–124), Anl. 24.
40 Aleksei Gavrilovich Maslov and Harold S. Orenstein, "I Returned From Prison Part III," *Journal of Slavic Military Studies* 19, no. 2 (2006): 379.
41 Porter, "Hitler's Forgotten Genocides: The Fate of Soviet Pows," p. 362.
42 Snyder, *Bloodlands: Europe between Hitler and Stalin*, p. 176.
43 Beorn, *Marching into Darkness: The Wehrmacht and the Holocaust in Belarus*, p. 68.
44 Streit, *Keine Kameraden: die Wehrmacht und die sowjetischen Kriegsgefangenen, 1941–1945*, pp. 138–9.
45 Jarausch, *Reluctant Accomplice: A Wehrmacht Soldier's Letters from the Eastern Front*, p. 261.
46 Beorn, *Marching into Darkness: The Wehrmacht and the Holocaust in Belarus*, p. 68.
47 Maslov and Orenstein, "I Returned From Prison Part III," p. 382.
48 Porter, "Hitler's Forgotten Genocides: The Fate of Soviet Pows," p. 363.
49 Jarausch, *Reluctant Accomplice: A Wehrmacht Soldier's Letters from the Eastern Front*, p. 325.
50 Porter, "Hitler's Forgotten Genocides: The Fate of Soviet Pows," p. 383.
51 Snyder, *Bloodlands: Europe between Hitler and Stalin*, p. 184.
52 Jan Phillipp Reemtsma, Ulrike Jureit, and Hans Mommsen, eds., *Verbrechen der Wehrmacht: Dimensionen des Vernichtungskrieges 1941–1944: Ausstellungskatalog* (Hamburg: Hamburger, 2002), p. 207.

53 "rHGM Korpsbefehl 59, 10 Oct 1941," (BA-MA: RH 22–225), Anl. 116.
54 Snyder, *Bloodlands: Europe between Hitler and Stalin*, p. 184.
55 Jeffrey Burds, *Holocaust in Rovno: A Massacre in Ukraine, November 1941* (New York: Palgrave Macmillan, 2013), p. 54.
56 See Friedländer, *The Years of Extermination: Nazi Germany and the Jews, 1939–1945*, p. 209.
57 "Document 447-PS: Top-Secret Directive by the High Command of the Wehrmacht (Keitel), 13 March 1941, on Special Matters in Connection with Directive No. 21, Case Barbarossa," in *Trials of the Major War Criminals before the International Military Tribunal: Documents and Other Material In Evidence, 405-PS to 1063(d)-PS, vol. XXVI* (Nuremberg: US Government Printing Office, 1947), pp. 54–5.
58 "Extract from Guidelines by Heydrich for Higher SS and Police Leaders in the Occupied Territories of the Soviet Union, July 2, 1941," in *Documents on the Holocaust: Selected Sources on the Destruction of the Jews of Germany and Austria, Poland, and the Soviet Union*, ed. Yitzhak Arad, Israel Gutman, and Abraham Margaliot (Jerusalem: Yad Vashem, 1999), p. 378.
59 Guillaume de Syon, "The Einsatzgruppen and the Issue of "Ordinary Men"," in *The Routledge History of the Holocaust*, ed. Jonathan C. Friedman (New York: Routledge, 2011), 150.
60 Friedländer, *The Years of Extermination: Nazi Germany and the Jews, 1939–1945*, p. 135.
61 Browning and Matthäus, *The Origins of the Final Solution: The Evolution of Nazi Jewish Policy, September 1939–March 1942*, pp. 461–2.
62 Browning and Matthäus, *The Origins of the Final Solution: The Evolution of Nazi Jewish Policy, September 1939–March 1942*, p. 459.
63 Yitzhak Arad, Schmuel Krakowski, and Shmuel Spector, eds., *The Einsatzgruppen Reports: Selections from the Dispatches of the Nazi Death Squads' Campaign against the Jews, July 1941–January 1943* (New York: Holocaust Library, 1989), p. 34.
64 Ibid., p. 41.
65 Ibid., p. 45.
66 Ibid., p. 82.
67 Browning and Matthäus, *The Origins of the Final Solution: The Evolution of Nazi Jewish Policy, September 1939–March 1942*, p. 475.
68 Arad, *The Holocaust in the Soviet Union*, p. 131.
69 Franz Magill, "Report by Waffen-SS on Killing of Jews in the Pripet Marshes August 12, 1941," in *Documents on the Holocaust: Selected Sources on the Destruction of the Jews of Germany and Austria, Poland, and the Soviet Union*, ed. Yitzhak Arad, Israel Gutman, and Abraham Margaliot (Jerusalem: Yad Vashem, 1999), p. 415.
70 Browning and Matthäus, *The Origins of the Final Solution: The Evolution of Nazi Jewish Policy, September 1939–March 1942*, p. 469.
71 Ibid., p. 471.
72 Vladimir Solonari, "Patterns of Violence: The Local Population and the Mass Murder of Jews in Bessarabia and Northern Bukovina, July–August 1941," in *The Holocaust in the East: Local Perpetrators and Soviet Responses*, ed. Michael David-Fox, Peter Holquist, and Alexander M. Martin (Pittsburg, PA: University of Pittsburgh Press, 2014), p. 75.

73 "Excerpts from Four Policy Texts by Rosenberg's Office Regarding Propaganda and Public Relations Work with Reference to the Soviet Union (Typed, No Signature, Stamped "Dienststelle Rosenberg"), No Date (Spring 1941)," in *The Political Diary of Alfred Rosenberg and the Onset of the Holocaust*, ed. Jürgen Matthäus and Frank Bajohr, Documenting Life and Destruction: Holocaust Sources in Context (Lanham, MD: Rowman & Littlefield, 2015), pp. 373–4.

74 "Teletype, Heydrich to Einsatzruppen Leaders, 29 July 1941," in *Die Einsatzgruppen in der besetzten Sowjetunion, 1941/42: die Tätigkeits- und Lageberichte des Chefs der Sicherheitspolizei und des SD*, ed. Peter Klein (Berlin: Edition Hentrich, 1997), p. 319.

75 Lyn Smith, *Remembering: Voices of the Holocaust- a New History in the Words of the Men and Women Who Survived* (New York: Carroll & Graf, 2006), p. 94.

76 Solonari, "Patterns of Violence: The Local Population and the Mass Murder of Jews in Bessarabia and Northern Bukovina, July–August 1941," p. 64.

77 Browning and Matthäus, *The Origins of the Final Solution: The Evolution of Nazi Jewish Policy, September 1939–March 1942*, pp. 546–7.

78 Karen Sutton, *The Massacre of the Jews of Lithuania: Lithuanian Collaboration in the Final Solution, 1941–1944* (Jerusalem: Gefen Publishing House, 2008), p. 121.

79 Ernst Klee, Willi Dressen, and Volker Riess, *"The Good Old Days:" The Holocaust as Seen by Its Perpetrators and Bystanders*, 1st American ed. (New York: Free Press, 1991), p. 31.

80 Ibid., pp. 34–5.

81 Ibid., p. 35.

82 Ibid., p. 31.

83 Arad, Krakowski, and Spector, *The Einsatzgruppen Reports: Selections from the Dispatches of the Nazi Death Squads' Campaign against the Jews, July 1941-January 1943*, p. 17.

84 Friedländer, *The Years of Extermination: Nazi Germany and the Jews, 1939–1945*, p. 223.

85 Browning and Matthäus, *The Origins of the Final Solution: The Evolution of Nazi Jewish Policy, September 1939–March 1942*, p. 549.

86 Robert van Voren, *Undigested Past: The Holocaust in Lithuania* (New York: Rodopi, 2011), p. 77.

87 Jan Tomasz Gross, *Revolution from Abroad: The Soviet Conquest of Poland's Western Ukraine and Western Belorussia* (Princeton, NJ: Princeton University Press, 1988), pp. 179–80.

88 Christoph Mick, ""Only the Jews Do Not Waver "- L'viv under Soviet Occupation," in *Shared History, Divided Memory: Jews and Others in Soviet-Occupied Poland,1939–1941*, ed. Elazar Barkan, Elizabeth A Cole, and Kai Struve (Leipzig: Leipziger Universitätsverlag, 2007), p. 347.

89 Y. A. Honigsman, *The Catastrophy of Jewry in Lvov* (Lvov: Solom-Aleichem Jewish Society of Culture, 1997), p. 6.

90 "Lewi, Meier Statement, 22 September 1944," (USHMM: 1.2.7.7/82183313_0_1-82183317_0_1/ITS Digital Archive).

91 "Victims of Russian Massacre in the Baltics and Southern Russia (Film)," (United States Holocaust Memorial Museum: RG-60.0328).

92 Arad, *The Holocaust in the Soviet Union*, p. 90.
93 Tuviah Friedman, ed. *Love Letters of a Nazi Murderer in Lemberg and Drohobycz* (Haifa: Institute of Documentation in Israel for the Investigation of Nazi War Crimes, 1987), 4.
94 Arad, *The Holocaust in the Soviet Union*, p. 90.
95 "Translation of *Szkola Okuricienstwa* by Stanislawa Gogolowska, Wydanictwo Lubelskie, 1964," (StAL: EL 317 III, Bü 1720), p. 4.
96 "Goldberg, Abraham Trial Testimony, Band 77, 10 January 1967" (StAL: EL 317 III, Bü 1578), p. 2444.
97 Wendy Lower, "Pogroms, Mob Violence and Genocide in Western Ukraine, Summer 1941: Varied Histories, Explanations and Comparisons," *Journal of Genocide Research* 13 (2011): 223.
98 Adolf Folkmann and Stefan Szende, *The Promise Hitler Kept* (New York: Roy Publishers, 1945), p. 90.
99 Radu Ioanid, "The Holocaust in Romania: The Iasi Pogrom of June 1941," *Contemporary European History* 2, no. 2 (1993): 144.
100 Jean Ancel, *The History of the Holocaust in Romania* (Lincoln: University of Nebraska Press, 2011), p. 445.
101 Ioanid, "The Holocaust in Romania: The Iasi Pogrom of June 1941," p. 144.
102 Ibid., p. 122.
103 Ancel, *The History of the Holocaust in Romania*, p. 447.
104 Ioanid, "The Holocaust in Romania: The Iasi Pogrom of June 1941," p. 124.
105 Ibid.
106 Ibid., p. 125.
107 Ibid., p. 126.
108 Ibid., p. 128.
109 Ibid., p. 133.
110 Ancel, *The History of the Holocaust in Romania*, p. 452.
111 Ioanid, "The Holocaust in Romania: The Iasi Pogrom of June 1941," pp. 137, 42.
112 Ibid., p. 143.
113 Ibid., p. 128.
114 Ibid., p. 130.
115 Ibid., p. 129.
116 Ancel, *The History of the Holocaust in Romania*, p. 448.
117 Ioanid, "The Holocaust in Romania: The Iasi Pogrom of June 1941," p. 134.
118 Ibid., p. 123.
119 Browning and Matthäus, *The Origins of the Final Solution: The Evolution of Nazi Jewish Policy, September 1939–March 1942*, p. 552.
120 Arad, Krakowski, and Spector, *The Einsatzgruppen Reports: Selections from the Dispatches of the Nazi Death Squads' Campaign against the Jews, July 1941–January 1943*, p. 68.
121 Patrick Desbois, *The Holocaust by Bullets: A Priest's Journey to Uncover the Truth Behind the Murder of 1.5 Million Jews* (New York: Palgrave Macmillan, 2008), p. 81.
122 Paul Kubicek, *The History of Ukraine* (Westport, CT: Greenwood Press, 2008), p. 109.
123 Arad, *The Holocaust in the Soviet Union*, p. 174.

124 Karel C. Berkhoff, *Harvest of Despair: Life and Death in Ukraine under Nazi Rule* (Cambridge, MA: Belknap Press of Harvard University Press, 2004), pp. 30–1.
125 Ibid., p. 33.
126 Geoffrey P. Megargee, *War of Annihilation: Combat and Genocide on the Eastern Front, 1941* (Lanham, MD: Rowman & Littlefield, 2006), p. 95.
127 Wolfram Wette, *The Wehrmacht: History, Myth, Reality* (Cambridge, Mass.: Harvard University Press, 2006), p. 115.
128 Arad, Krakowski, and Spector, *The Einsatzgruppen Reports: Selections from the Dispatches of the Nazi Death Squads' Campaign against the Jews, July 1941–January 1943*, p. 165.
129 Berkhoff, *Harvest of Despair: Life and Death in Ukraine under Nazi Rule*, p. 33.
130 Ibid.
131 Wette, *The Wehrmacht: History, Myth, Reality*, p. 117.
132 James Waller, *Becoming Evil: How Ordinary People Commit Genocide and Mass Killing* (Oxford: Oxford University Press, 2002), p. 90.
133 Ibid., p. 91.
134 Burds, *Holocaust in Rovno: A Massacre in Ukraine, November 1941*, p. 58.
135 Berkhoff, *Harvest of Despair: Life and Death in Ukraine under Nazi Rule*, p. 77.
136 Wette, *The Wehrmacht: History, Myth, Reality*, p. 118.
137 "Document 411-D: Army Order from General Field Marshal Von Reichenau, 10 October 1941," in *Trials of the Major War Criminals before the International Military Tribunal: Documents and Other Material in Evidence, 039-D to 906-D* (Nuremberg: US Government Printing Office, 1949), p. 85.
138 Beorn, *Marching into Darkness: The Wehrmacht and the Holocaust in Belarus*, p. 65.
139 Ibid., p. 71.
140 Ibid., p. 73.
141 Ibid., p. 79.
142 Ibid.
143 Kazimierz Sakowicz and Yitzhak Arad, *Ponary Diary, 1941–1943: A Bystander's Account of a Mass Murder* (New Haven: Yale University Press, 2005), xiii.
144 Beorn, *Marching into Darkness: The Wehrmacht and the Holocaust in Belarus*, 100.
145 Friedländer, *The Years of Extermination: Nazi Germany and the Jews, 1939–1945*, p. 362.
146 Yitzhak Arad, *Belzec, Sobibor, Treblinka: The Operation Reinhard Death Camps* (Bloomington: Indiana University Press, 1987), p. 8.
147 Mark Mazower, *Hitler's Empire: How the Nazis Ruled Europe* (New York: Penguin Press, 2008), p. 208.
148 Arad, *The Holocaust in the Soviet Union*, p. 96.
149 van Voren, *Undigested Past: The Holocaust in Lithuania*, p. 89.
150 Arad, *The Holocaust in the Soviet Union*, p. 115.
151 Snyder, *Bloodlands: Europe between Hitler and Stalin*, p. 170.

152 Rutherford, "The Radicalization of German Occupation Policies: The Wirtschaftsstab Ost and the 121st Infantry Division in Pavlovsk, 1941," p. 224.
153 Snyder, *Bloodlands: Europe between Hitler and Stalin*, p. 172.
154 Ibid., p. 173.
155 Rutherford, "The Radicalization of German Occupation Policies: The Wirtschaftsstab Ost and the 121st Infantry Division in Pavlovsk, 1941," p. 231.
156 Ibid., p. 242.
157 Ibid., p. 241.

7 Ghetto Life and Death in the East

1 Saul Friedländer, *The Years of Extermination: Nazi Germany and the Jews, 1939–1945* (New York: Harper Collins, 2007), p. 196.
2 See Lawrence L. Langer, ed. *Art from the Ashes: A Holocaust Anthology* (New York: Oxford University Press, 1995), pp. 160–1.
3 Samuel D. Kassow, *Who Will Write Our History? Emanuel Ringelblum, the Warsaw Ghetto, and the Oyneg Shabes Archive* (Bloomington: Indiana University Press, 2007), p. 171.
4 For more, see Dan Michman, *The Emergence of Jewish Ghettos during the Holocaust* (Cambridge: Cambridge University Press, 2011).
5 Peter Longerich, *Holocaust: The Nazi Persecution and Murder of the Jews* (Oxford: Oxford University Press, 2010), p. 167.
6 Adam Czerniaków et al., *The Warsaw Diary of Adam Czerniakow: Prelude to Doom*, trans. Stanislaw Staron (New York: Stein and Day, 1979), p. 402.
7 "Express Letter by Reinhard Heydrich to the Einsatzgruppen on the "Jewish Question in the Occupied Territory," September 21, 1939," in *War, Pacification, and Mass Murder, 1939: The Einsatzgruppen in Poland*, ed. Jürgen Matthäus and Jochen Böhler (Lanham: Rowman & Littlefield, 2014), pp. 104–5.
8 Christopher R. Browning, *The Path to Genocide: Essays on Launching the Final Solution* (Cambridge: Cambridge University Press, 1992), p. 55.
9 Geoffrey P. Megargee, ed. *The United States Holocaust Memorial Museum Encyclopedia of Camps and Ghettos, 1933–1945*, vol. II (Bloomington: Indiana University Press in association with the United States Holocaust Memorial Museum, 2009), pp. 279–80.
10 Michman, *The Emergence of Jewish Ghettos During the Holocaust*, p. 61.
11 Christopher R. Browning and Jürgen Matthäus, *The Origins of the Final Solution: The Evolution of Nazi Jewish Policy, September 1939–March 1942* (Lincoln: University of Nebraska Press, 2004), p. 244.
12 Gordon J Horwitz, *Ghettostadt: Łódź and the Making of a Nazi City* (Cambridge, MA: The Belknap Press of Harvard University Press, 2008), p. 62.
13 Browning and Matthäus, *The Origins of the Final Solution: The Evolution of Nazi Jewish Policy, September 1939–March 1942*, p. 249.
14 Ibid., p. 257.

15 Horwitz, *Ghettostadt: Łódź and the Making of a Nazi City*, p. 66.
16 Waldemar Schön, "From a Lecture on the Steps Leading to the Establishment of the Warsaw Ghetto, January 20, 1941," in *Documents on the Holocaust: Selected Sources on the Destruction of the Jews of Germany and Austria, Poland, and the Soviet Union*, ed. Yitzhak Arad, Israel Gutman, and Abraham Margaliot (Jerusalem: Yad Vashem, 1999), p. 225.
17 Browning and Matthäus, *The Origins of the Final Solution: The Evolution of Nazi Jewish Policy, September 1939–March 1942*, pp. 280–1.
18 Martyn Housden, "Hans Frank- Empire Builder in the East, 1939–41," *European History Quarterly* 24, no. 3 (1994): 381.
19 Dieter Pohl, *Nationalsozialistische Judenverfolgung in Ostgalizien, 1941–1944: Organisation und Durchfuhrung eines staatlichen Massenverbrechens* (München: R. Oldenbourg, 1996), pp. 76–7.
20 Browning and Matthäus, *The Origins of the Final Solution: The Evolution of Nazi Jewish Policy, September 1939–March 1942*, p. 232.
21 "LG Saarbrücken Urteil gg. Fritz Gebauer, 29 June 1971," (BA-ZS: B162/ 14465), p. 24.
22 Y. A. Honigsman, *The Catastrophy of Jewry in Lvov* (Lvov: Solom-Aleichem Jewish Society of Culture, 1997), p. 11.
23 "Ahrens, Jack Interview, 5/11/1995," (USHMM: RG-50.030*0311).
24 Browning and Matthäus, *The Origins of the Final Solution: The Evolution of Nazi Jewish Policy, September 1939–March 1942*, p. 251.
25 Martin Winstone, *The Dark Heart of Hitler's Europe: Nazi Rule in Poland under the General Government* (London: I. B. Tauris, 2015), p. 149.
26 Heinrich Gottong, "Directives Issued by the Head of Department for Jewish Affairs on Policies Concerning Treatment of Jews in the Government-General, 6 April 1940," in *Documents on the Holocaust: Selected Sources on the Destruction of the Jews of Germany and Austria, Poland, and the Soviet Union*, ed. Yitzhak Arad, Israel Gutman, and Abraham Margaliot (Jerusalem: Yad Vashem, 1999), p. 196.
27 Helene Sinnreich, "Victim and Perpetrator Perspectives of World War II-era Ghettos," in *The Routledge History of the Holocaust*, ed. Jonathan C. Friedman (New York: Routledge, 2011), pp. 116–17.
28 Chaim Kaplan, *The Warsaw Diary of Chaim Kaplan*, trans. Abraham I. Katsh (New York: Collier Books, 1973), p. 261.
29 Christopher R. Browning, "Introduction," in *The United States Holocaust Memorial Museum Encyclopedia of Camps and Ghettos, 1933–1945*, ed. Geoffrey P. Megargee (Bloomington: Indiana University Press in association with the United States Holocaust Memorial Museum, 2009), xvii.
30 Martin Dean, "Editor's Introduction," ibid., ed. Geoffrey P. Megargee (Bloomington: Indiana University Press in association with the United States Holocaust Memorial Museum, 2009), xliii.
31 Megargee, *The United States Holocaust Memorial Museum Encyclopedia of Camps and Ghettos, 1933–1945*, pp. 412–13.
32 Yitzhak Arad, *The Holocaust in the Soviet Union* (Lincoln: University of Nebraska Press, 2009), p. 166.
33 Walter Laqueur and Judith Tydor Baumel-Schwartz, eds., *The Holocaust Encyclopedia* (New Haven: Yale University Press, 2001), p. 62.

34 Nachum Alpert, *The Destruction of Slonim Jewry: The Story of the Jews of Slonim During the Holocaust* (New York: Holocaust Library, 1989), p. 99.
35 Raul Hilberg, *The Destruction of the European Jews* (New York: Holmes & Meier, 1985), p. 83.
36 Shimon Redlich, *Together and Apart in Brzezany: Poles, Jews, and Ukrainians, 1919–1945* (Bloomington: Indiana University Press, 2002), p. 112.
37 Randolph L. Braham, *The Politics of Genocide the Holocaust in Hungary (Condensed Edition)* (Detroit, MI: Wayne State University Press, 2000), pp. 155–6.
38 Tim Cole, *Holocaust City: The Making of a Jewish Ghetto* (New York: Routledge, 2003), 83.
39 Paul A. Shapiro, ed. *The Kishinev Ghetto, 1941–1942: A Documentary History of the Holocaust in Romania's Contested Borderlands* (Tuscaloosa, AL: The University of Alabama Press, 2015), p. 17.
40 Ibid., pp. 145–6.
41 Czerniaków et al., *The Warsaw Diary of Adam Czerniakow: Prelude to Doom*, p. 261.
42 Arad, *The Holocaust in the Soviet Union*, p. 186.
43 Ibid., p. 168.
44 Czerniaków et al., *The Warsaw Diary of Adam Czerniakow: Prelude to Doom*, p. 191.
45 Kaplan, *The Warsaw Diary of Chaim Kaplan*, p. 384.
46 "Translation of Document 3666-PS: Heydrich Schnellbrief, 21 September 1939," in *Nazi Conspiracy and Aggression, vol. VI* (Washington, DC: US Government Printing Office, 1946), p. 97.
47 Michman, *The Emergence of Jewish Ghettos During the Holocaust*, p. 152.
48 Arad, *The Holocaust in the Soviet Union*, p. 166.
49 See Chapter 1 on the kahal. Friedländer, *The Years of Extermination: Nazi Germany and the Jews, 1939–1945*, pp. 40–1.
50 "Choiceless choices" was coined by Lawrence Langer in Lawrence L. Langer, *Versions of Survival: The Holocaust and the Human Spirit* (Albany: State University of New York Press, 1982).
51 Longerich, *Holocaust: The Nazi Persecution and Murder of the Jews*, p. 170.
52 See Isaiah Trunk, *Judenrat: The Jewish Councils in Eastern Europe under Nazi Occupation* (Lincoln, NE: University of Nebraska Press, 1996), p. 30.
53 See ibid., p. 34.
54 Josef Kermisz, "Introduction," in *The Warsaw Diary of Adam Czerniakow: Prelude to Doom*, ed. Adam Czerniaków, et al. (New York: Stein and Day, 1979), p. 1.
55 Barbara Engelking and Jacek Leociak, *The Warsaw Ghetto: A Guide to the Perished City*, trans. Emma Harris (New Haven, CT: Yale University Press, 2009), pp. 159–60.
56 Czerniaków et al., *The Warsaw Diary of Adam Czerniakow: Prelude to Doom*, p. 76.
57 Friedländer, *The Years of Extermination: Nazi Germany and the Jews, 1939–1945*, pp. 153–4.
58 Chaim Kaplan, "Extracts from the Diary of Chaim A. Kaplan on the Warsaw Judenrat, 1941," in *Documents on the Holocaust: Selected Sources on the Destruction of the Jews of Germany and Austria, Poland, and the*

Soviet Union, ed. Yitzhak Arad, Israel Gutman, and Abraham Margaliot (Jerusalem: Yad Vashem, 1999), p. 230.
59 Engelking and Leociak, *The Warsaw Ghetto: A Guide to the Perished City*, p. 162.
60 Friedländer, *The Years of Extermination: Nazi Germany and the Jews, 1939–1945*, pp. 153–4.
61 Engelking and Leociak, *The Warsaw Ghetto: A Guide to the Perished City*, p. 163.
62 Ibid., p. 164.
63 Ibid.
64 Ibid.
65 Czerniaków et al., *The Warsaw Diary of Adam Czerniakow: Prelude to Doom*.
66 Engelking and Leociak, *The Warsaw Ghetto: A Guide to the Perished City*, p. 164.
67 Ibid.
68 Stefan Ernest, "Warsaw Ghetto Diary, July 1942," in *The Third Reich Sourcebook*, ed. Anson Rabinbach and Sander L. Gilman (Berkeley: University of California Press, 2013), p. 765.
69 Friedländer, *The Years of Extermination: Nazi Germany and the Jews, 1939–1945*, p. 61.
70 Laqueur and Baumel-Schwartz, *The Holocaust Encyclopedia*, p. 399.
71 Raul Hilberg, *The Destruction of the European Jews*, 3rd ed., vol. 1 (New Haven, CT: Yale University Press, 2003), p. 230.
72 Horwitz, *Ghettostadt: Łódź and the Making of a Nazi City*, p. 14.
73 Ibid., p. 260.
74 Friedländer, *The Years of Extermination: Nazi Germany and the Jews, 1939–1945*, p. 62.
75 Laqueur and Baumel-Schwartz, *The Holocaust Encyclopedia*, p. 253.
76 Horwitz, *Ghettostadt: Łódź and the Making of a Nazi City*, p. 23.
77 Laurence Rees, *Auschwitz: A New History* (New York: Public Affairs, 2005), p. 90.
78 Laqueur and Baumel-Schwartz, *The Holocaust Encyclopedia*, p. 402.
79 Horwitz, *Ghettostadt: Łódź and the Making of a Nazi City*, p. 72.
80 Ibid., p. 58.
81 Ibid., p. 84.
82 Ibid., p. 58.
83 Ibid., p. 199.
84 Ibid., p. 145.
85 Ruth Linn, "Genocide and the Politics of Remembering: The Nameless, the Celebrated, and the Would-Be Holocaust Heroes," *Journal of Genocide Research* 5, no. 4 (2003): 580.
86 "Rumkowski's Address at the Time of the Deportation of the Children from the Łódź Ghetto, September 4, 1942," in *Documents on the Holocaust: Selected Sources on the Destruction of the Jews of Germany and Austria, Poland, and the Soviet Union*, ed. Yitzhak Arad, Israel Gutman, and Abraham Margaliot (Jerusalem: Yad Vashem, 1999), pp. 283–4.
87 USHMM, "Sara Rachela Plagier," United States Holocaust Memorial Museum, https://www.ushmm.org/wlc/en/article.php?ModuleId=10007293.

88 Lyn Smith, *Remembering: Voices of the Holocaust—a New History in the Words of the Men and Women Who Survived* (New York: Carroll & Graf, 2006), p. 111.
89 Horwitz, *Ghettostadt: Łódź and the Making of a Nazi City*, p. 295.
90 See, for example, Michael Checinski, "Observations: How Rumkowski Died," COMMENTARY, May 1979, p. 65.
91 Linn, "Genocide and the Politics of Remembering: The Nameless, the Celebrated, and the Would-Be Holocaust Heroes," p. 581.
92 Ibid.
93 Dennis B Klein, ed. *Hidden History of the Kovno Ghetto* (Boston, MA: Little, Brown and Co. with the United States Holocaust Memorial Museum, 1997), p. 83.
94 L. Garfunkel, "The Election of Elkes as Head of the Judenrat in Kovno (Kovna ha-Yehudit be-Hurbana, 1959)," in *Documents on the Holocaust: Selected Sources on the Destruction of the Jews of Germany and Austria, Poland, and the Soviet Union*, ed. Yitzhak Arad, Israel Gutman, and Abraham Margaliot (Jerusalem: Yad Vashem, 1999), p. 386.
95 Ibid.
96 Yitzhak Arad, Schmuel Krakowski, and Shmuel Spector, eds., *The Einsatzgruppen Reports: Selections from the Dispatches of the Nazi Death Squads' Campaign against the Jews, July 1941–January 1943* (New York: Holocaust Library, 1989), p. 17.
97 Avraham Tory, Martin Gilbert, and Dina Porat, *Surviving the Holocaust: The Kovno Ghetto Diary* (Cambridge, MA: Harvard University Press, 1990), p. 47.
98 Klein, *Hidden History of the Kovno Ghetto*, p. 32.
99 Ibid., p. 33.
100 Tory, Gilbert, and Porat, *Surviving the Holocaust: The Kovno Ghetto Diary*, p. 49.
101 Lucy S. Dawidowicz, *The War against the Jews, 1933–1945*, 1st ed. ed. (New York: Holt, Rinehart and Winston, 1975), p. 420.
102 Klein, *Hidden History of the Kovno Ghetto*, p. 83.
103 Tory, Gilbert, and Porat, *Surviving the Holocaust: The Kovno Ghetto Diary*, p. 250.
104 Dawidowicz, *The War against the Jews, 1933–1945*, p. 555.
105 Klein, *Hidden History of the Kovno Ghetto*, p. 214.
106 Hilberg, *The Destruction of the European Jews*, 1, pp. 236–7.
107 For information on Młynów, see Megargee, *The United States Holocaust Memorial Museum Encyclopedia of Camps and Ghettos, 1933–1945*, p. 1429.
108 Sinnreich, "Victim and Perpetrator Perspectives of World War II-era Ghettos," p. 118.
109 Laqueur and Baumel-Schwartz, *The Holocaust Encyclopedia*, p. 687.
110 Friedländer, *The Years of Extermination: Nazi Germany and the Jews, 1939–1945*, p. 147.
111 Alex Kozlowski, "Olec-as Told to Anne Marie Davies," (USHMM: 2015.165.1), p. 7.
112 Hilberg, *The Destruction of the European Jews*, 1, p. 264.
113 Ibid., p. 265.

114 Laqueur and Baumel-Schwartz, *The Holocaust Encyclopedia*, p. 686.
115 Trunk, *Judenrat: The Jewish Councils in Eastern Europe under Nazi Occupation*, p. 103.
116 "Hirschhorn, Bernhard Statement, 9 February 1948," (StAL EL 317, III Bü 1524), p. 4.
117 Barbara Leslie Epstein, *The Minsk Ghetto, 1941–1943: Jewish Resistance and Soviet Internationalism* (Berkeley: University of California Press, 2008), p. 89.
118 Samuel. Drix, *Witness to Annihilation: Surviving the Holocaust, a Memoir* (Washington: Brassey's, 1994), p. 35.
119 Friedländer, *The Years of Extermination: Nazi Germany and the Jews, 1939–1945*, p. 148.
120 Tory, Gilbert, and Porat, *Surviving the Holocaust: The Kovno Ghetto Diary*, p. 216.
121 Engelking and Leociak, *The Warsaw Ghetto: A Guide to the Perished City*, p. 232–3.
122 Trunk, *Judenrat: The Jewish Councils in Eastern Europe under Nazi Occupation*, p. 157.
123 Ibid., p. 169.
124 Klein, *Hidden History of the Kovno Ghetto*, p. 97.
125 Megargee, *The United States Holocaust Memorial Museum Encyclopedia of Camps and Ghettos, 1933–1945*, p. 45.
126 Hilberg, *The Destruction of the European Jews*, 1, pp. 272–4.
127 Smith, *Remembering: Voices of the Holocaust—a New History in the Words of the Men and Women Who Survived*, p. 111.
128 Friedländer, *The Years of Extermination: Nazi Germany and the Jews, 1939–1945*, p. 150.
129 Engelking and Leociak, *The Warsaw Ghetto: A Guide to the Perished City*, p. 547.
130 Lucjan Dobroszycki, ed. *The Chronicle of the Łódź Ghetto, 1941–1944*, Abridged ed. (New Haven, CT: Yale University Press, 1984), p. 102.
131 "Teodor Ryder," ORT, http://holocaustmusic.ort.org/places/ghettos/lodź/ryderteodor/.
132 Klein, *Hidden History of the Kovno Ghetto*, p. 189.
133 Engelking and Leociak, *The Warsaw Ghetto: A Guide to the Perished City*, p. 207.
134 Józef Zelkowicz, "Diary of the Łódź' Ghetto, September 1942," in *The Third Reich Sourcebook*, ed. Anson Rabinbach and Sander L Gilman (Berkeley: University of California Press, 2013), p. 772.
135 Dina Porat, "The Jewish Councils of the Main Ghettos of Lithuania: A Comparison," *Modern Judaism* 13, no. 2 (1993): 155.
136 Smith, *Remembering: Voices of the Holocaust—a New History in the Words of the Men and Women Who Survived*, p. 121.
137 Wendy Lower, ed. *The Diary of Samuel Golfard and the Holocaust in Galicia* (Lanham: Altamira Press in association with United States Holocaust Memorial Museum, 2011), p. 55.
138 Adolf Folkmann and Stefan Szende, *The Promise Hitler Kept* (New York: Roy Publishers, 1945), p. 97.
139 Drix, *Witness to Annihilation: Surviving the Holocaust, a Memoir*, p. 172.

140 Engelking and Leociak, *The Warsaw Ghetto: A Guide to the Perished City*, pp. 206–7.
141 "Ahrens, Jack Interview, 5/11/1995."
142 Abba Kovner, "A Summons to Resistance, Vilna Ghetto. January 1942," in *The Third Reich Sourcebook*, ed. Anson Rabinbach and Sander L Gilman (Berkeley: University of California Press, 2013), 7 p. 68.
143 Porat, "The Jewish Councils of the Main Ghettos of Lithuania: A Comparison," pp. 155–6.
144 "Moskva, Paulina Statement, 20 September 1944," (BA-ZS: B162/29309), p. 304.
145 Zelkowicz, "Diary of the Łódz' Ghetto, September 1942," p. 774.
146 Megargee, *The United States Holocaust Memorial Museum Encyclopedia of Camps and Ghettos, 1933–1945*, p. 1602.

8 Hitler's Eastern Allies

1 Saul Friedländer, *The Years of Extermination: Nazi Germany and the Jews, 1939–1945* (New York: Harper Collins, 2007), p. 227.
2 Frederick B Chary, *The Bulgarian Jews and the Final Solution, 1940–1944* (Pittsburgh: University of Pittsburgh Press, 1972), p. 194.
3 See Asher Cohen, "Petain, Horthy, Antonescu and the Jews,1942–4: Toward a Comparative View," in *The Nazi Holocaust: Historical Articles on the Destruction of European Jews: The "Final Solution" Outside Germany*, ed. Michael Robert Marrus (Westport: Meckler, 1989), p. 64. In addition, these places like part of Greece and the occupied Soviet Union had either Nazi military or civilian administration in place to facilitate the Holocaust.
4 Christian Leitz, *Nazi Foreign Policy, 1933–1941: The Road to Global War* (London: Routledge, 2004), p. 100.
5 Ibid., p. 99.
6 Jean Ancel, "The Romanian Way Solving the Jewish Problem in Bessarabia and Bukovina, June-July 1941," *Yad Vashem Studies* 19 (1988): 224.
7 Radu Ioanid, "The Holocaust in Romania: The Iasi Pogrom of June 1941," *Contemporary European History* 2, no. 2 (1993): 119.
8 Mark Mazower, *Hitler's Empire: How the Nazis Ruled Europe* (New York: Penguin Press, 2008), p. 334.
9 Friedländer, *The Years of Extermination: Nazi Germany and the Jews, 1939–1945*, p. 168.
10 Elie Wiesel et al., eds., *Final Report of the International Commission on the Holocaust in Romania* (Bucharest: International Commission on the Holocaust in Romania, 2004), p. 10.
11 Ronit Fischer, "Transnistria: The Holocaust in Romania," in *The Routledge History of the Holocaust*, ed. Jonathan C. Friedman (New York: Routledge, 2011), p. 277.
12 Rebecca Haynes, "Corneliu Zelea Codreanu: The Romanian 'New Man'," in *In the Shadow of Hitler: Personalities of the Right in Central and Eastern Europe*, ed. Rebecca Haynes and Martyn Rady (London: I. B. Tauris, 2011), pp. 173–4.

13 Ibid., p. 171.
14 Ibid., p. 179.
15 Ibid., p. 180.
16 Dennis Deletant, "Ion Antonescu: The Paradoxes of His Regime, 1940–44," ibid., ed. Rebecca Haynes and Martyn Rady (London: I. B. Tauris, 2011), p. 285.
17 Ibid., pp. 278–9.
18 Ibid., p. 280.
19 Dennis Deletant, "German-Romanian Relations, 1941–1944," in *Hitler and His Allies in World War II*, ed. Jonathan R. Adelman (New York: Routledge, 2007), p. 168.
20 Ibid., p. 171.
21 Gerhard L Weinberg, *A World at Arms: A Global History of World War II* (Cambridge: Cambridge University Press, 2005), p. 196.
22 Deletant, "Ion Antonescu: The Paradoxes of His Regime, 1940–44," p. 281.
23 Ibid., p. 278.
24 Fischer, "Transnistria: The Holocaust in Romania," pp. 279–80.
25 Jean Ancel, *The History of the Holocaust in Romania* (Lincoln: University of Nebraska Press, 2011), p. 218.
26 Fischer, "Transnistria: The Holocaust in Romania," p. 277.
27 Ancel, *The History of the Holocaust in Romania*, p. 355.
28 Wiesel et al., *Final Report of the International Commission on the Holocaust in Romania*, p. 55.
29 Ibid.
30 Vladimir Solonari, "Patterns of Violence: The Local Population and the Mass Murder of Jews in Bessarabia and Northern Bukovina, July–August 1941," in *The Holocaust in the East: Local Perpetrators and Soviet Responses*, ed. Michael David-Fox, Peter Holquist, and Alexander M. Martin (Pittsburg, PA: University of Pittsburgh Press, 2014), p. 53.
31 Wiesel et al., *Final Report of the International Commission on the Holocaust in Romania*, p. 11.
32 Friedländer, *The Years of Extermination: Nazi Germany and the Jews, 1939–1945*, p. 225.
33 Wiesel et al., *Final Report of the International Commission on the Holocaust in Romania*, p. 28.
34 Ibid., p. 24.
35 Solonari, "Patterns of Violence: The Local Population and the Mass Murder of Jews in Bessarabia and Northern Bukovina, July–August 1941," p. 56.
36 Wiesel et al., *Final Report of the International Commission on the Holocaust in Romania*, p. 87.
37 Ancel, *The History of the Holocaust in Romania*, p. 344.
38 Wiesel et al., *Final Report of the International Commission on the Holocaust in Romania*, p. 35.
39 Ancel, *The History of the Holocaust in Romania*, pp. 339–40.
40 Wiesel et al., *Final Report of the International Commission on the Holocaust in Romania*, p. 87.
41 Deletant, "Ion Antonescu: The Paradoxes of His Regime, 1940–44," p. 287.
42 Ancel, *The History of the Holocaust in Romania*, p. 495.
43 Ibid., p. 500.

44 Ibid., p. 508.
45 Cohen, "Petain, Horthy, Antonescu and the Jews,1942–1944: Toward a Comparative View," p. 89.
46 Ancel, *The History of the Holocaust in Romania*, p. 562.
47 Christopher R. Browning and Jürgen Matthäus, *The Origins of the Final Solution: The Evolution of Nazi Jewish Policy, September 1939–March 1942* (Lincoln: University of Nebraska Press, 2004), p. 429.
48 Attila Pok, "German-Hungarian Relations, 1941–1945," in *Hitler and His Allies in World War II*, ed. Jonathan R. Adelman (New York: Routledge, 2007), p. 162.
49 Ibid., p. 155.
50 Ibid., p. 156.
51 Randolph L Braham, *The Politics of Genocide the Holocaust in Hungary (Condensed Edition)* (Detroit, MI: Wayne State University Press, 2000), p. 22.
52 Martyn Rady, "Ferenc Szálasi, 'Hungarism' and the Arrow Cross," in *In the Shadow of Hitler: Personalities of the Right in Central and Eastern Europe*, ed. Rebecca Haynes and Martyn Rady (London: I. B. Tauris, 2011), p. 261.
53 Braham, *The Politics of Genocide the Holocaust in Hungary (Condensed Edition)*, 21.
54 Ibid., pp. 24–5.
55 Ibid., p. 40.
56 Ibid., p. 42.
57 Ibid., p. 44.
58 See Randolph L Braham, "A Post-Mortem of the Holocaust in Hungary: A Probing Interpretation of the Causes," in *Monna and Otto Weinmann Annual Lecture Series* (Washington, DC: United States Holocaust Memorial Museum, 2012), 3; Kinga Frojimovics, "The Special Characteristics of the Holocaust in Hungary, 1938–1945," in *The Routledge History of the Holocaust*, ed. Jonathan C. Friedman (New York: Routledge, 2011), p. 252.
59 Braham, *The Politics of Genocide the Holocaust in Hungary (Condensed Edition)*, p. 32.
60 "Soviet Extraordinary State Commission Report. 13 May 1944," (YVA: JM/19711).
61 Klaus-Michael Mallmann, Wolfram Pyta, and Volker Riess, eds., *Deutscher Osten 1939–1945: der Weltanschauungskrieg in Photos und Texten* (Darmstadt: Wissenschaftliche Buchgesellschaft, 2003), p. 87.
62 "Testimony of N.H.," (YVA: M.49.E/6848).
63 Pok, "German-Hungarian Relations, 1941–1945," p. 159.
64 Ibid.
65 Cohen, "Petain, Horthy, Antonescu and the Jews,1942–1944: Toward a Comparative View," p. 73.
66 Raul Hilberg, *The Destruction of the European Jews*, 3rd ed., vol. 2 (New Haven, CT: Yale University Press, 2003), p. 878.
67 Braham, *The Politics of Genocide the Holocaust in Hungary (Condensed Edition)*, p. 56.
68 Cohen, "Petain, Horthy, Antonescu and the Jews,1942–1944: Toward a Comparative View," p. 87.
69 Braham, *The Politics of Genocide the Holocaust in Hungary (Condensed Edition)*, p. 60.

70 Ibid.
71 Peter Longerich, *Heinrich Himmler: A Life* (New York: Oxford University Press, 2012), p. 693–4.
72 Braham, *The Politics of Genocide the Holocaust in Hungary (Condensed Edition)*, p. 161.
73 Ibid.
74 Rady, "Ferenc Szálasi, 'Hungarism' and the Arrow Cross," pp. 273–74.
75 Longerich, *Heinrich Himmler: A Life*, p. 706–7.
76 Chary, *The Bulgarian Jews and the Final Solution, 1940–1944*, p. 208.
77 R. J. Crampton, *Eastern Europe in the Twentieth Century– and After* (New York: Routledge, 1997), p. 207.
78 Tzvetan Todorov, *The Fragility of Goodness: Why Bulgaria's Jews Survived the Holocaust- a Collection of Texts* (Princeton, NJ: Princeton University Press, 2001).
79 Chary, *The Bulgarian Jews and the Final Solution, 1940–1944*, p. 34.
80 Ethan J. Hollander, "The Final Solution in Bulgaria and Romania: A Comparative Perspective," *East European Politics & Societies* 22, no. 2 (2008): 217.
81 Ibid., p. 215.
82 Browning and Matthäus, *The Origins of the Final Solution: The Evolution of Nazi Jewish Policy, September 1939–March 1942*, p. 433.
83 Hollander, "The Final Solution in Bulgaria and Romania: A Comparative Perspective," p. 215.
84 Chary, *The Bulgarian Jews and the Final Solution, 1940–1944*, pp. 12–13.
85 Ibid., p. 19.
86 Ibid., p. 21.
87 Ibid.
88 James Frusetta, "The Final Solution in Southeastern Europe," in *The Routledge History of the Holocaust*, ed. Jonathan C. Friedman (New York: Routledge, 2011), p. 271.
89 Walter Laqueur and Judith Tydor Baumel-Schwartz, eds., *The Holocaust Encyclopedia* (New Haven: Yale University Press, 2001), p. 99.
90 Michael Berenbaum, "The Rescuers: When the Ordinary Is Extraordinary," in *The Routledge History of the Holocaust*, ed. Jonathan C. Friedman (New York: Routledge, 2011), p. 323.
91 Hollander, "The Final Solution in Bulgaria and Romania: A Comparative Perspective," p. 219.
92 Chary, *The Bulgarian Jews and the Final Solution, 1940–1944*, p. 52.
93 "The Holocaust in Macedonia: Deportation of Monastir Jewry," *USHMM Holocaust Encyclopedia (online)* (2016), https://www.ushmm.org/wlc/en/article.php?ModuleId=10006804.
94 "Alkalaj, Sara Interview, 16 April 1997 (Transcript)," (USHMM: RG-50.459*0010), p. 13.
95 "The Holocaust in Macedonia: Deportation of Monastir Jewry".
96 Ibid.
97 Ibid.
98 Chaim Frank, "Anti-Semitism in Yugoslavia," in *Antisemitism in Eastern Europe*, ed. Hans Christian Petersen and Samuel Salzborn, Politische Kulturforschung (Peter Lang GmbH: Frankfurt am Main, 2010), p. 81.

99 Dmitar Peshev, "Protest Letter by the Vice-Chairman of the 25th Session of the National Assembly, Dmitâr Peshev, and Forty-Two Other Deputies," in *The Fragility of Goodness: Why Bulgaria's Jews Survived the Holocaust- a Collection of Texts*, ed. Tzvetan Todorov (Princeton, N.J.: Princeton University Press, 2001), 79–80.
100 Hollander, "The Final Solution in Bulgaria and Romania: A Comparative Perspective," p. 224.
101 Ibid.
102 Nikola Mushaniv and Petka Stainov, "Letter from Nikola Mushanov and Petko Stainov to King Boris," in *The Fragility of Goodness: Why Bulgaria's Jews Survived the Holocaust- a Collection of Texts*, ed. Tzvetan Todorov (Princeton, NJ: Princeton University Press, 2001), p. 104.
103 Joseph Benatov, "Debating the Fate of Bulgarian Jews During World War Ii," in *Bringing the Dark Past to Light the Reception of the Holocaust in Postcommunist Europe*, ed. John-Paul Himka and Joanna Beata Michlic (Lincoln: UNP – Nebraska, 2013), p. 116.
104 "Contesting the Deportations in Parliament, Dimitar Peshev (Bulgaria)," *The Righteous Among the Nations* (2016), http://www.yadvashem.org/yv/en/righteous/stories/peshev.asp.

9 The Final Solution

1 Peter Longerich, *Heinrich Himmler: A Life* (New York: Oxford University Press, 2012), 695.
2 Shlomo Venezia and Béatrice Prasquier, *Inside the Gas Chambers: Eight Months in the Sonderkommando of Auschwitz*, trans. Andrew Brown (Cambridge, UK: Polity, 2009), p. 65.
3 Christopher R. Browning, *Ordinary Men: Reserve Police Battalion 101 and the Final Solution in Poland* (New York: Harper Perennial, 1998), xv.
4 Adolf Hitler, "Speech to the Great German Reichstag, 30 January 1939," in *The Third Reich Sourcebook*, ed. Anson Rabinbach and Sander L Gilman (Berkeley: University of California Press, 2013), pp. 723–4.
5 Adolf Hitler, *Mein Kampf*, trans. Alvin Johnson (Boston, MA: Houghton Mifflin, 1939), p. 984.
6 Christopher R. Browning and Jürgen Matthäus, *The Origins of the Final Solution: The Evolution of Nazi Jewish Policy, September 1939–March 1942* (Lincoln: University of Nebraska Press, 2004), p. 495.
7 Laurence Rees, *Auschwitz: A New History* (New York: Public Affairs, 2005), p. 18.
8 Browning and Matthäus, *The Origins of the Final Solution: The Evolution of Nazi Jewish Policy, September 1939–March 1942*, p. 185.
9 Ibid., p. 195.
10 "Translation of Document 710-PS: Letter from Goering to Heydrich Concerning Solution of Jewish Question, 31 July 1941," in *Trials of War Criminals before the Nuernberg Military Tribunals (Einsatzgruppen and RuSHA Cases), Vol. Iv* (Washington, DC: US Government Printing Office, 1949).

11 There are other scholarly arguments for a different timeline: winter 1941 and even into 1942, for example. However, I find the summer-fall 1941 argument most compelling and so will focus on it here.
12 "Translation of Document 710-PS: Letter from Goering to Heydrich Concerning Solution of Jewish Question, 31 July 1941."
13 Lucjan Dobroszycki, ed. *The Chronicle of the Łódź ghetto, 1941–1944*, Abridged ed. (New Haven, CT: Yale University Press, 1984), lii.
14 Christopher R. Browning, "The Origins of the Final Solution," in *The Routledge History of the Holocaust*, ed. Jonathan C. Friedman (New York: Routledge, 2011), p. 165.
15 Browning and Matthäus, *The Origins of the Final Solution: The Evolution of Nazi Jewish Policy, September 1939–March 1942*, p. 742.
16 Yitzhak Arad, *Bełżec, Sobibor, Treblinka: The Operation Reinhard Death Camps* (Bloomington: Indiana University Press, 1987), p. 24.
17 Longerich, *Heinrich Himmler: A Life*, p. 534–47.
18 Rees, *Auschwitz: A New History*, pp. 51–2.
19 Ibid., p. 52.
20 Browning and Matthäus, *The Origins of the Final Solution: The Evolution of Nazi Jewish Policy, September 1939–March 1942*, p. 714.
21 Ibid., p. 716.
22 Rees, *Auschwitz: A New History*, p. 71.
23 Patrick Montague, *Chełmno and the Holocaust: The History of Hitler's First Death Camp* (Chapel Hill: University of North Carolina Press, 2012), p. 66.
24 Arad, *Bełżec, Sobibor, Treblinka: The Operation Reinhard Death Camps*, p. 10.
25 Ibid., p. 17.
26 Henry Friedlander, *The Origins of Nazi Genocide: From Euthanasia to the Final Solution* (Chapel Hill: University of North Carolina Press, 1997), p. 297.
27 Norbert Kampe, "Die Wannsee-Konferenz," in *Die Wannsee-Konferenz und der Völkermord an den europäischen Juden*, ed. Christa Schikorra (Berlin: Jütte-Messedruck Leipzig GmbH, 2006), pp. 103–9.
28 Ibid., p. 114.
29 Ibid., pp. 116–19.
30 Ibid., p. 112.
31 Gitta Sereny, *Into That Darkness: An Examination of Conscience* (New York: Vintage Books, 1983), p. 145.
32 Ibid., p. 126.
33 USHMM, "Holocaust Encyclopedia: Treblinka," United States Holocaust Memorial Museum, https://www.ushmm.org/wlc/en/article.php?ModuleId=10005193.
34 Jacek Andrzej Młynarczyk, "Treblinka- Ein Todeslager Der 'Aktion Reinhardt,'" in *"Aktion Reinhardt:" Der Völkermord an Den Juden Im Generalgouvernement 1941–1944*, ed. Bogdan Musial (Osnabrück: Fibre, 2004), p. 258.
35 Sereny, *Into That Darkness: An Examination of Conscience*, p. 148.
36 "Document 511-USSR: Letter from the SS-Economic and Administrative Main Office to the Commandants of the Concentration Camps, 6 August 1942," in *Trials of the Major War Criminals before the International Military*

Tribunal: Documents and Other Material In Evidence, 1218-RF to JN, vol. XXXIX (Nuremberg: US Government Printing Office, 1949), pp. 552–3.

37 Ernst Klee, Willi Dressen, and Volker Riess, *"The Good Old Days:" The Holocaust as Seen by Its Perpetrators and Bystanders*, 1st American ed. (New York: Free Press, 1991), p. 247.
38 Młynarczyk, "Treblinka- Ein Todeslager Der "Aktion Reinhard"," ff. 270.
39 Ibid., p. 274.
40 Sereny, *Into That Darkness: An Examination of Conscience*, p. 157.
41 Ibid., pp. 200–1.
42 Longerich, *Heinrich Himmler: A Life*, p. 573.
43 Rudolf Vrba and Alfred Wetzler, "Auschwitz Protocols, 25 November 1944," in *The Third Reich Sourcebook*, ed. Anson Rabinbach and Sander L Gilman (Berkeley: University of California Press, 2013).
44 Rees, *Auschwitz: A New History*, p. 24.
45 Deborah Dwork and R. J. van Pelt, *Auschwitz, 1270 to the Present*, 1st ed. (New York: Norton, 1996), pp. 167–8.
46 Rees, *Auschwitz: A New History*, p. 2.
47 Ibid., p. 6.
48 Ibid., p. 23.
49 Ibid., p. 64.
50 Dwork and Pelt, *Auschwitz, 1270 to the Present*, p. 318.
51 Annegret Schüle and Rikola-Gunnar Lüttgenau, *The Engineers of the Final Solution: Topf and Sons- Builders of the Auschwitz Ovens* (Weimar: Stiftung Gedamstätten Buchenwald und Mittelbau-Dora, 2005), pp. 49–50.
52 "Order by Himmler for the Liquidation of the Ghettos of Ostland, June 21, 1943," in *Documents on the Holocaust: Selected Sources on the Destruction of the Jews of Germany and Austria, Poland, and the Soviet Union*, ed. Yitzhak Arad, Israel Gutman, and Abraham Margaliot (Jerusalem: Yad Vashem, 1999), pp. 456–7.
53 "Evidence of Jewish Escapees from the Ninth Fort in Kovno on the Burning of the Bodies, 26 December 1943," in *Documents on the Holocaust: Selected Sources on the Destruction of the Jews of Germany and Austria, Poland, and the Soviet Union*, ed. Yitzhak Arad, Israel Gutman, and Abraham Margaliot (Jerusalem: Yad Vashem, 1999), p. 474.
54 Yitzhak Arad, *The Holocaust in the Soviet Union* (Lincoln: University of Nebraska Press, 2009), p. 325.
55 Wendy Lower, ed. *The Diary of Samuel Golfard and the Holocaust in Galicia* (Lanham: Altamira Press in association with United States Holocaust Memorial Museum, 2011), 156. See also Geoffrey P. Megargee, ed. *The United States Holocaust Memorial Museum Encyclopedia of Camps and Ghettos, 1933–1945*, vol. II (Bloomington: Indiana University Press in association with the United States Holocaust Memorial Museum, 2009), p. 816.
56 Schmuel Spector, "Aktion 1005-Effacing the Murder of Millions," *Holocaust Genocide Studies* 5, no. 2 (1990): 158.
57 Leon Weliczker Wells, *The Janowska Road* (New York: MacMillan Company, 1963), 165.
58 "Neubert, Wilhelm Statement, 13 January 1948," (BA-ZS: B162/29309), p. 124.

59 "Chamaides, Heinrich Statement, 13 September 1944," (USHMM: 1.2.7.7/ 82183301_0_1-82183305_0_1/ITS Digital Archive).
60 "Korn, Moische Statement, 13 September 1944," (BA-ZS: B162/29309), pp. 268–9.
61 "Wells (Welizcker), Leon Statement, 22 September 1944," (BA-ZS: B162/29309), p. 355.
62 "Manusevich, David Statement, 13 September 1944," (BA-ZS: B162/29309), p. 299. See also, A.F. Vysotsky et al., eds., *Nazi Crimes in Ukraine, 1941–1944: Documents and Materials* (Kiev: Naukova Dumka Publishers, 1987), p. 223.

10 The Kaleidoscope of Jewish Resistance

1 Stanislaw Sznapman, "Warsaw Ghetto Diary, 1943," in *The Third Reich Sourcebook*, ed. Anson Rabinbach and Sander L. Gilman (Berkeley: University of California Press, 2013), p. 777.
2 Yehuda Bauer, "Forms of Jewish Resistance," in *The Holocaust: Problems and Perspectives of Interpretation*, ed. Donald L. Niewyk (Boston: Houghton Mifflin, 2003), p. 165.
3 Emanuel Ringelblum and Jacob Sloan, eds., *Notes from the Warsaw Ghetto-the Journal of Emmanuel Ringelblum* (New York: McGraw-Hill, 1958), p. 310.
4 Hannah Arendt, *Eichmann in Jerusalem: A Report on the Banality of Evil* (New York: Viking Press, 1964), p. 124.
5 Raul Hilberg, *The Destruction of the European Jews*, 3rd ed., vol. 3 (New York: Holmes & Meier, 2003), pp. 1104–5.
6 John M. Cox, "Jewish Resistance against Nazism," in *The Routledge History of the Holocaust*, ed. Jonathan C. Friedman (New York: Routledge, 2011), p. 328.
7 "Martyrs' and Heroes Remembrance (Yad Vashem) Law 5713-1953," (YVA1953), Accessed at http://www.yadvashem.org/yv/en/about/pdf/YV_law.pdf.
8 Adolf Folkmann and Stefan Szende, *The Promise Hitler Kept* (New York: Roy Publishers, 1945), p. 68.
9 Chaim Kaplan, "Extracts from the Warsaw Ghetto Diary of Chaim A. Kaplan, 1940," in *Documents on the Holocaust: Selected Sources on the Destruction of the Jews of Germany and Austria, Poland, and the Soviet Union*, ed. Yitzhak Arad, Israel Gutman, and Abraham Margaliot (Jerusalem: Yad Vashem, 1999), p. 203.
10 Barbara Engelking and Jacek Leociak, *The Warsaw Ghetto: A Guide to the Perished City*, trans. Emma Harris (New Haven, CT: Yale University Press, 2009), p. 320.
11 Ibid., p. 601.
12 Dennis B. Klein, ed. *Hidden History of the Kovno Ghetto* (Boston, MA: Little, Brown and Co. with the United States Holocaust Memorial Museum, 1997), p. 191.
13 Ibid.

14 Dawid Sierakowiak, Alan Adelson, and Kamil Turowski, eds., *Diary of Dawid Sierakowiak* (Cary. Oxford University Press, 2006), p. 155.
15 Engelking and Leociak, *The Warsaw Ghetto: A Guide to the Perished City*, p. 344.
16 Ibid., p. 347.
17 Sierakowiak, Adelson, and Turowski, *Diary of Dawid Sierakowiak*, p. 174.
18 Engelking and Leociak, *The Warsaw Ghetto: A Guide to the Perished City*, pp. 556–7.
19 Ibid., p. 578.
20 Barbara Leslie Epstein, *The Minsk Ghetto, 1941–1943: Jewish Resistance and Soviet Internationalism* (Berkeley: University of California Press, 2008), p. 91.
21 Leon Weliczker Wells, *The Janowska Road* (New York: MacMillan, 1963), p. 187.
22 "Blai, Barbara Statement, 19 September 1944," (BA-ZS: B162/29309).
23 Solon Beinfeld, "The Cultural Life of the Vilna Ghetto," in *The Nazi Holocaust: Historical Articles on the Destruction of European Jews: The "Final Solution" Outside Germany*, ed. Michael Robert Marrus (Westport: Meckler, 1989), p. 95.
24 Ibid.
25 Ibid., p. 96.
26 Saul Friedländer, *The Years of Extermination: Nazi Germany and the Jews, 1939–1945* (New York: Harper Collins Publishers, 2007), pp. 198–9.
27 Avraham Tory, Martin Gilbert, and Dina Porat, *Surviving the Holocaust: The Kovno Ghetto Diary* (Cambridge, MA: Harvard University Press, 1990), pp. 167–8.
28 Samuel D. Kassow, *Who Will Write Our History? Emanuel Ringelblum, the Warsaw Ghetto, and the Oyneg Shabes Archive* (Bloomington: Indiana University Press, 2007), p. 357.
29 Ibid., p. 385.
30 "Memo to Military Command, Municipality of Chisinau, 14 September 1941," in *The Kishinev Ghetto, 1941–1942: A Documentary History of the Holocaust in Romania's Contested Borderlands*, ed. Paul A. Shapiro (Tuscaloosa, AL: University of Alabama Press, 2015), p. 158.
31 Engelking and Leociak, *The Warsaw Ghetto: A Guide to the Perished City*, p. 649.
32 Ibid., p. 648.
33 Ibid., pp. 656–7.
34 Stephen Howard Garrin, ""But I Forsook Not Thy Precepts (Ps. 119:87): Spiritual Resistance to the Holocaust," in *The Routledge History of the Holocaust*, ed. Jonathan C. Friedman (New York: Routledge, 2011), p. 342.
35 Yitzhak Arad, *Belzec, Sobibor, Treblinka: The Operation Reinhard Death Camps* (Bloomington: Indiana University Press, 1987), p. 217.
36 Wells, *The Janowska Road*, p. 200.
37 Yitzhak Arad, *The Holocaust in the Soviet Union* (Lincoln: University of Nebraska Press, 2009), p. 473.
38 *Nazi Conspiracy and Aggression*, vol. II (Washington, DC: US Government Printing Office, 1946), p. 269.

39 Engelking and Leociak, *The Warsaw Ghetto: A Guide to the Perished City*, p. 717.
40 Ibid., p. 547.
41 Gitta Sereny, *Into That Darkness: An Examination of Conscience* (New York: Vintage Books, 1983), p. 258.
42 "Record of Soviet Military Court of the Carpathian Military Region against Prichodjko et. al, 14 December 1966," (BA-ZS: B162/29309).
43 Tom Lawson, *Debates on the Holocaust* (Manchester, UK: Manchester University Press, 2010), p. 262.
44 Arad, *The Holocaust in the Soviet Union*, 493.
45 Ibid., pp. 250–1.
46 Kassow, *Who Will Write Our History? Emanuel Ringelblum, the Warsaw Ghetto, and the Oyneg Shabes Archive*, p. 338.
47 See the work of Chad Gibbs on this topic.
48 Jeffrey Burds, *Holocaust in Rovno: A Massacre in Ukraine, November 1941* (New York: Palgrave Macmillan, 2013), p. 66.
49 Waitman Wade Beorn, *Marching into Darkness: The Wehrmacht and the Holocaust in Belarus* (Cambridge: Harvard University Press, 2014), p. 2.
50 Epstein, *The Minsk Ghetto, 1941–1943: Jewish Resistance and Soviet Internationalism*, p. 191.
51 Arad, *The Holocaust in the Soviet Union*, p. 325.
52 Ibid., p. 454.
53 Ibid., pp. 455–6.
54 See, for example, Christopher R. Browning, *Remembering Survival: Inside a Nazi Slave-Labor Camp* (New York: W. W. Norton, 2010).
55 Lawson, *Debates on the Holocaust*, p. 253.
56 Stefan Ernest, "Warsaw Ghetto Diary, July 1942," in *The Third Reich Sourcebook*, ed. Anson Rabinbach and Sander L Gilman (Berkeley: University of California Press, 2013), p. 765.
57 Burds, *Holocaust in Rovno: A Massacre in Ukraine, November 1941*, 64; Y.A. Honigsman, *The Catastrophy of Jewry in Lvov* (Lvov: Solom-Aleichem Jewish Society of Culture, 1997), p. 46.
58 "Keren, Christine Interview, 10/25/2007," (USHMM: RG-50.030*0520, 2007.349).
59 "Kohn, Rosa Statement, 27 November 1958," (BA-ZS: B162/5726), p. 6.
60 Engelking and Leociak, *The Warsaw Ghetto: A Guide to the Perished City*, p. 550.
61 "Proclamation by the F.P.O. Calling for Revolt in Vilna, September 1, 1943," in *Documents on the Holocaust: Selected Sources on the Destruction of the Jews of Germany and Austria, Poland, and the Soviet Union*, ed. Yitzhak Arad, Israel Gutman, and Abraham Margaliot (Jerusalem: Yad Vashem, 1999), p. 459.
62 Sznapman, "Warsaw Ghetto Diary, 1943," p. 777.
63 Yitzhak Cukierman, "The Jewish Population Disbelieves Reports of the Extermination," in *Documents on the Holocaust: Selected Sources on the Destruction of the Jews of Germany and Austria, Poland, and the Soviet Union*, ed. Yitzhak Arad, Israel Gutman, and Abraham Margaliot (Jerusalem: Yad Vashem, 1999), pp. 277–8.

64 Randolph L. Braham, "A Post-Mortem of the Holocaust in Hungary. A Probing Interpretation of the Causes," in *Monna and Otto Weinmann Annual Lecture Series* (Washington, DC: United States Holocaust Memorial Museum, 2012), p. 1.
65 Nechama Tec, *In the Lion's Den: The Life of Oswald Rufeisen* (New York: Oxford University Press, 1990), 143, p. 45.
66 Jacob Gens, "Address by Gens, Head of the Ghetto at the Meeting of Brigadiers, Supervisors and Policemen, May 15, 1943," in *Documents on the Holocaust: Selected Sources on the Destruction of the Jews of Germany and Austria, Poland, and the Soviet Union*, ed. Yitzhak Arad, Israel Gutman, and Abraham Margaliot (Jerusalem: Yad Vashem, 1999), p. 455.
67 Arad, *The Holocaust in the Soviet Union*, p. 62.
68 Dina Porat, "The Jewish Councils of the Main Ghettos of Lithuania: A Comparison," *Modern Judaism* 13, no. 2 (1993): 156.
69 USHMM, "Holocaust Encyclopedia: Jewish Uprisings in Ghettos and Camps, 1941–1944," United States Holocaust Memorial Museum, https://www.ushmm.org/wlc/en/article.php?ModuleId=10005407.
70 Engelking and Leociak, *The Warsaw Ghetto: A Guide to the Perished City*, p. 770.
71 Ibid., p. 776.
72 Ibid., p. 779.
73 Arad, *The Holocaust in the Soviet Union*, p. 492.
74 Folkmann and Szende, *The Promise Hitler Kept*, p. 151.
75 Claudia Koonz, "Raul Hilberg Lecture: On Reading a Document: SS-Man Katzmann's 'Solution of the Jewish Question in the District of Galicia'" (University of Vermont, 2005), p. 11.
76 "Bericht des SS- und Polizeiführers über die Vernichtung der Juden Galiziens (Katzmann Bericht) reproduced by T. Friedman, October 1963" (USHMM: 1.2.7.8/82187874_0_1-82188051_0_1/ITS Digital Archive).
77 There is evidence of a revolt among the *Sonderkommando* at Bełzec that killed 4–6 guards, mentioned in a Polish Underground report at the end of July 1942. This is the only mention of such resistance there. See Arad, *Belzec, Sobibor, Treblinka: The Operation Reinhard Death Camps*, p. 275.
78 Ibid., p. 134.
79 Ibid., p. 99.
80 Beorn, *Marching into Darkness: The Wehrmacht and the Holocaust in Belarus*, p. 149.
81 Thomas Toivi Blatt, *From the Ashes of Sobibor: A Story of Survival* (Evanston, IL: Northwestern University Press, 1997), p. 153.
82 Jules Schelvis, *Sobibor: A History of a Nazi Death Camp*, trans. Karin Dixon (London: Bloomsbury in association with the United States Holocaust Memorial Museum, 2007), p. 168.
83 Arad, *Belzec, Sobibor, Treblinka: The Operation Reinhard Death Camps*, p. 294.
84 Donald L. Niewyk and Francis R. Nicosia, *The Columbia Guide to the Holocaust* (New York: Columbia University Press, 2000), p. 35.
85 Blatt, *From the Ashes of Sobibor: A Story of Survival*, p. 173.
86 Arad, *The Holocaust in the Soviet Union*, pp. 507–8.
87 Cox, "Jewish Resistance against Nazism," p. 327.

88 Tamara Vershitskaya, "Jewish Women Partisans in Belarus," *Journal of Ecumenical Studies* 46, no. 4 (2011): 567.
89 "Ahrens, Jack Interview, 5/11/1995" (USHMM: RG-50.030*0311).
90 Arad, *The Holocaust in the Soviet Union*, p. 515.
91 Nechama Tec, *Defiance: The Bielski Partisans* (New York: Oxford University Press, 1993), p. 112.
92 Franziska Reiniger, "Solidarity in the Forest—the Bielski Brothers" Yad Vashem, http://www.yadvashem.org/yv/en/education/newsletter/28/bielski_brothers.asp#01.
93 Sarah Shner-Nishmit, *The 51st Brigade: The History of the Jewish Partisan Group from the Slonim Ghetto*, trans. Judith Levi (New York: JewishGen in cooperation with the Museum of Jewish Heritage, NYC, 2015), p. 120.
94 Ibid., p. 177.
95 Ibid., p. 342.
96 Cox, "Jewish Resistance against Nazism," p. 34.

11 Perpetrators, Collaborators, and Rescuers

1 "Partial Translation of Document L-180, Prosecution Exhibit 34: Extracts from Report of Einsatzgruppe a Covering the Period from 23 June 1941 to 15 October 1941," in *Trials of the War Criminals before the Nuernberg Military Tribunals under Control Council Law No. 10, vol. IV: The Einsatzgruppen Case*," "*The RuSHA Case*" (Washington, DC: US Government Printing Office, 1949), p. 164.
2 Perhaps the most important of these was Raul Hilberg in Raul Hilberg, *Perpetrators, Victims, Bystanders: The Jewish Catastrophe, 1933–1945* (New York: Aaron Asher Books, 1992).
3 Gitta Sereny, *Into That Darkness: An Examination of Conscience* (New York: Vintage Books, 1983), p. 131.
4 Christopher R. Browning, *Collected Memories: Holocaust History and Postwar Testimony* (Madison, WI: The University of Wisconsin Press, 2003), p. 3.
5 Annegret Schüle and Rikola-Gunnar Lüttgenau, *The Engineers of the Final Solution: Topf and Sons- Builders of the Auschwitz Ovens* (Weimar: Stiftung Gedamstätten Buchenwald und Mittelbau-Dora, 2005), p. 25.
6 Ibid., p. 66.
7 Ibid., p. 45.
8 Ibid., p. 57.
9 Claudia Koonz, *Mothers in the Fatherland: Women, the Family, and Nazi Politics* (New York: St. Martin's Press, 1987), p. 420.
10 Sereny, *Into That Darkness: An Examination of Conscience*, p. 361.
11 Ibid., p. 78.
12 Wendy Lower, *Hitler's Furies: German Women in the Nazi Killing Fields* (New York: Houghton Mifflin Harcourt, 2013), p. 175.
13 "Barth, Pinkas Statement, 21 April 1964" (StAL: EL 317 III, Bü 1502), p. 67.
14 Lower, *Hitler's Furies: German Women in the Nazi Killing Fields*, p. 201.
15 Ibid., pp. 191–2.
16 Ibid., p. 155.

17 Ibid., p. 158.
18 Waitman Wade Beorn, *Marching into Darkness. The Wehrmacht and the Holocaust in Belarus* (Cambridge: Harvard University Press, 2014), pp. 162–3.
19 "Wieselberg, Teresa Statement, 10 March 1963" (StAL: EL 317 III, Bü 1516), p. 27.
20 Sara Bender, *The Jews of Białystok during World War II and the Holocaust* (Waltham, MA: Brandeis University Press, 2008), p. 97.
21 Avraham Tory, Martin Gilbert, and Dina Porat, *Surviving the Holocaust: The Kovno Ghetto Diary* (Cambridge, MA: Harvard University Press, 1990), p. 126.
22 Richard Rhodes, *Masters of Death: The SS-Einsatzgruppen and the Invention of the Holocaust* (New York: Vintage Books, 2003), p. 264.
23 Kazimierz Sakowicz and Yitzhak Arad, *Ponary Diary, 1941–1943: A Bystander's Account of a Mass Murder* (New Haven: Yale University Press, 2005), p. 21.
24 Patrick Desbois, *The Holocaust by Bullets: A Priest's Journey to Uncover the Truth Behind the Murder of 1.5 Million Jews* (New York: Palgrave Macmillan, 2008), p. 85.
25 Elie Wiesel et al., eds., *Final Report of the International Commission on the Holocaust in Romania* (Bucharest: International Commission on the Holocaust in Romania, 2004), p. 45.
26 Sereny, *Into That Darkness: An Examination of Conscience*, p. 160.
27 "Drix, Samuel, Tagebuch, 1942–1943" (StAL: EL 317 III, Bü 1721), pp. 62–3.
28 Harald Welzer, "On Killing and Morality: How Normal People Become Mass Murderers," in *Ordinary People as Mass Murderers: Perpetrators in Comparative Perspectives*, ed. Olaf Jensen and Claus-Christian W. Szejnmann (New York: Palgrave-MacMillan, 2008), 168.
29 Thomas Kühne, "Male Bonding and Shame Culture: Hitler's Soldiers and the Moral Basis of Genocidal Warfare," ibid., ed. Olaf Jensen and Claus-Christian W. Szejnmann (New York: Palgrave MacMillan, 2008), p. 58.
30 James Waller, *Becoming Evil: How Ordinary People Commit Genocide and Mass Killing* (Oxford: Oxford University Press, 2002), p. 186-190. Summary is mine.
31 Ibid., p. 175.
32 Alex Kershaw, *The envoy: the epic rescue of the last Jews of Europe in the desperate closing months of World War II* (Cambridge, MA: Da Capo Press, 2010), Book, p. 173.
33 Beorn, *Marching into Darkness: The Wehrmacht and the Holocaust in Belarus*, p. 140.
34 Andrej Angrick, "The Men of Einsatzgruppe D: An inside View of a State-Sanctioned Killing Unit in the 'Third Reich,'" in *Ordinary People as Mass Murderers: Perpetrators in Comparative Perspectives*, ed. Olaf Jensen and Claus-Christian W. Szejnmann (New York: Palgrave MacMillan, 2008), pp. 86–7.
35 Beorn, *Marching into Darkness: The Wehrmacht and the Holocaust in Belarus*, p. 157.
36 Christopher R. Browning, *Ordinary Men: Reserve Police Battalion 101 and the Final Solution in Poland* (New York: Harper Perennial, 1998), p. 57.

37 Waller, *Becoming Evil: How Ordinary People Commit Genocide and Mass Killing*, p. 29.
38 Kühne, "Male Bonding and Shame Culture: Hitler's Soldiers and the Moral Basis of Genocidal Warfare," p. 65.
39 Andrej Angrick, "The Men of Einsatzgruppe D: An inside View of a State-Sanctioned Killing Unit in the 'Third Reich'," ibid., ed. Olaf Jensen and Claus-Christian W. Szejnmann (New York: Palgrave MacMillan, 2008), p. 91.
40 "Interrogation of Fritz Liebl, Member of Einsatzkommando 3/I, by SS and Police Investigators, December 1939," in *War, Pacification, and Mass Murder, 1939: The Einsatzgruppen in Poland*, ed. Jürgen Matthäus and Jochen Böhler (Lanham: Rowman & Littlefield, 2014), p. 140.
41 Rhodes, *Masters of Death: The SS-Einsatzgruppen and the Invention of the Holocaust*, pp. 166–7.
42 Browning, *Ordinary Men: Reserve Police Battalion 101 and the Final Solution in Poland*, 73.
43 Sereny, *Into That Darkness: An Examination of Conscience*, p. 118.
44 Ibid., p. 164.
45 Beorn, *Marching into Darkness: The Wehrmacht and the Holocaust in Belarus*, p. 106.
46 Angrick, "The Men of Einsatzgruppe D: An inside View of a State-Sanctioned Killing Unit in the 'Third Reich,'" p. 89.
47 Rhodes, *Masters of Death: The SS-Einsatzgruppen and the Invention of the Holocaust*, 168.
48 Edward B. Westermann, "Stone-Cold Killers or Drunk with Murder? Alcohol and Atrocity During the Holocaust," *Holocaust and Genocide Studies* 30, no. 1 (2016): 13.
49 Beorn, *Marching into Darkness: The Wehrmacht and the Holocaust in Belarus*, p. 72.
50 "Vogel, Josef Statement, 1 September 1964" (StAL: EL 317 III, Bü 1502), p. 126.
51 Browning, *Ordinary Men: Reserve Police Battalion 101 and the Final Solution in Poland*, p. 189.
52 Jan Grabowski, *Hunt for the Jews: Betrayal and Murder in German-Occupied Poland* (Bloomington, IN: Indiana University Press, 2013), p. 52–3.
53 Halik Kochanski, *Eagle Unbowed: Poland and the Poles in the Second World War* (Cambridge: Harvard University Press, 2014), p. 98.
54 Jerzy Grzybowski, "An Outline History of the 13th (Belarusian) Battalion of the SD Auxiliary Police (Schutzmannschafts Bataillon der SD 13)," *Journal of Slavic Military Studies* 23, no. 3 (2010): 461.
55 Martin Dean, "Local Collaboration in the Holocaust in Eastern Europe," in *The Historiography of the Holocaust*, ed. Dan Stone (New York: Palgrave Macmillan, 2004), p. 122.
56 Ibid., pp. 126–7.
57 Jeffrey Burds, *Holocaust in Rovno: A Massacre in Ukraine, November 1941* (New York: Palgrave Macmillan, 2013), p. 13.
58 Grzybowski, "An Outline History of the 13th (Belarusian) Battalion of the SD Auxiliary Police (Schutzmannschafts Bataillon der SD 13)," p. 462.
59 Yitzhak Arad, *The Holocaust in the Soviet Union* (Lincoln: University of Nebraska Press, 2009), p. 424.

60 Christopher R. Browning and Jürgen Matthäus, *The Origins of the Final Solution: The Evolution of Nazi Jewish Policy, September 1939–March 1942* (Lincoln: University of Nebraska Press, 2004), p. 557.
61 Arad, *The Holocaust in the Soviet Union*, p. 424.
62 Dean, "Local Collaboration in the Holocaust in Eastern Europe," p. 127.
63 Arad, *The Holocaust in the Soviet Union*, p. 427.
64 Beorn, *Marching into Darkness: The Wehrmacht and the Holocaust in Belarus*, p. 74.
65 Arad, *The Holocaust in the Soviet Union*, p. 426.
66 Grabowski, *Hunt for the Jews: Betrayal and Murder in German-Occupied Poland*, p. 102.
67 Kochanski, *Eagle Unbowed: Poland and the Poles in the Second World War*, p. 275.
68 Grabowski, *Hunt for the Jews: Betrayal and Murder in German-Occupied Poland*, p. 103.
69 Ibid.
70 Sara Gleykh, "The Diary of the Student Sara Gleykh, 1941," in *The Unknown Black Book: The Holocaust in the German-Occupied Soviet Territories*, ed. Joshua Rubenstein and Ilya Altman (Bloomington, IN: Indiana University Press, 2008), p. 216.
71 Ibid., p. 215.
72 Geoffrey P. Megargee, ed. *The United States Holocaust Memorial Museum Encyclopedia of Camps and Ghettos, 1933–1945*, vol. II (Bloomington: Indiana University Press in association with the United States Holocaust Memorial Museum, 2009), p. 1757.
73 Grabowski, *Hunt for the Jews: Betrayal and Murder in German-Occupied Poland*, p. 57.
74 Lyn Smith, *Remembering: Voices of the Holocaust- a New History in the Words of the Men and Women Who Survived* (New York: Carroll & Graf, 2006), p. 76.
75 Grzybowski, "An Outline History of the 13th (Belarusian) Battalion of the SD Auxiliary Police (Schutzmannschafts Bataillon der SD 13)," p. 462.
76 Jan Phillipp Reemtsma, Ulrike Jureit, and Hans Mommsen, eds., *Verbrechen der Wehrmacht: Dimensionen des Vernichtungskrieges 1941–1944: Ausstellungskatalog* (Hamburg: Hamburger, 2002), p. 495.
77 Arad, *The Holocaust in the Soviet Union*, p. 422.
78 "Jörg, Johann Statement, 29 October 1964" (BA-ZS: B162/3454), p. 507.
79 Megargee, *The United States Holocaust Memorial Museum Encyclopedia of Camps and Ghettos, 1933–1945*, pp. 1248–9.
80 Burds, *Holocaust in Rovno: A Massacre in Ukraine, November 1941*, p. 58.
81 Dean, "Local Collaboration in the Holocaust in Eastern Europe," pp. 126–7.
82 Peter Black, "Foot Soldiers of the Final Solution: The Trawniki Training Camp and Operation Reinhard," *Holocaust and Genocide Studies* 25, no. 1 (2011): 6.
83 Ibid., p. 17.
84 Grabowski, *Hunt for the Jews: Betrayal and Murder in German-Occupied Poland*, p. 56.
85 Ibid., p. 58.
86 Arad, *The Holocaust in the Soviet Union*, pp. 424–5.

87 Grabowski, *Hunt for the Jews: Betrayal and Murder in German-Occupied Poland*, p. 50.
88 Burds, *Holocaust in Rovno: A Massacre in Ukraine, November 1941*, p. 59.
89 Edmund Kessler, *The Wartime Diary of Edmund Kessler: Lwow, Poland, 1942–1944* (Boston, MA: Academic Studies Press, 2010), p. 98.
90 "About the Righteous," Yad Vashem, http://www.yadvashem.org/righteous/about-the-righteous.
91 "Righteous among the Nations: Frequently Asked Questions," Yad Vashem, http://www.yadvashem.org/righteous/faq.
92 See, for example, Istvan Pal Adam, "Tipping the Rescuer? The Financial Aspects of the Budapest Building Managers' Helping Activity During the Last Phase of the Second World War," *Shoah: Intervention.Methods. Documentation* 2, no. 1 (2015).
93 Michael Berenbaum, "The Rescuers: When the Ordinary Is Extraordinary," in *The Routledge History of the Holocaust*, ed. Jonathan C. Friedman (New York: Routledge, 2011), 316.
94 Burds, *Holocaust in Rovno: A Massacre in Ukraine, November 1941*, p. 66.
95 Beorn, *Marching into Darkness: The Wehrmacht and the Holocaust in Belarus*, p. 2.
96 "Record of Soviet Military Court of the Carpathian Military Region against Prichodjko et. al, 14 December 1966" (BA-ZS: B162/29309), pp. 72–3.
97 Beorn, *Marching into Darkness: The Wehrmacht and the Holocaust in Belarus*, p. 174.
98 Tarik Cyril Amar, *The Paradox of Ukrainian Lviv: A Borderland City between Stalinists, Nazis, and Nationalists* (Ithaca, NY: Cornell University Press, 2015), p. 99.
99 Radu Ioanid, "The Holocaust in Romania: The Iasi Pogrom of June 1941," *Contemporary European History* 2, no. 2 (1993): 132.
100 Alfred Erich Senn, *Lithuania 1940: Revolution from Above* (Amsterdam: Rodopi, 2007), p. 23.
101 Arno Lustiger, "Feldwebel Anton Schmid- Judenretter in Wilna 1941–1942," in *Retter in Uniform: Handlungsspielräume im Vernichtungskrieg der Wehrmacht*, ed. Norbert Haase and Wolfram Wette (Frankfurt am Main: Fischer Taschenbuch Verlag, 2002).
102 Mariana Hausleitner, "Antisemitism in Romania: Modes of Expression between 1866 and 2009," in *Antisemitism in Eastern Europe*, ed. Hans Christian Petersen and Samuel Salzborn, Politische Kulturforschung (Peter Lang GmbH: Frankfurt am Main, 2010), p. 209.
103 Arad, *The Holocaust in the Soviet Union*, p. 433.
104 "Righteous among the Nations: Jan and Antonina Zabinski," Yad Vashem, http://www.yadvashem.org/righteous/stories/zabinski.
105 "Righteous among the Nations: Pavel and Lyubov Gerasimchik and Their Children Klavdiya Kucheruk, Galina Gavrishchuk and Nikolay," Yad Vashem, http://www.yadvashem.org/righteous/stories/gerasimchik-kucheruk-gavrishchuk.
106 Arad, *The Holocaust in the Soviet Union*, p. 438.
107 Adolf Folkmann and Stefan Szende, *The Promise Hitler Kept* (New York: Roy Publishers, 1945), p. 168–9.

108 Grabowski, *Hunt for the Jews: Betrayal and Murder in German-Occupied Poland*, p. 56.
109 Arad, *The Holocaust in the Soviet Union*, 432; "Righteous among the Nations: Paulavičius Family," Yad Vashem, http://db.yadvashem.org/righteous/family.html?language=en&itemId=4044789.
110 Arad, *The Holocaust in the Soviet Union*, p. 448.
111 Nechama Tec, "Who Dared to Rescue Jews, and Why?" in *Resisting Genocide: The Multiple Forms of Rescue*, ed. Jacques Andrieu Claire Semelin and Sarah Gensburger (New York: Columbia University Press, 2014), p. 108.
112 Ibid., p. 105.
113 Ibid., p. 106.
114 Ibid., p. 105.
115 Marnix Croes, "Researching the Survival and Rescue of Jews in Nazi Occupied Europe: A Plea for the Use of Quantitative Methods," ibid., ed. Jacques Andrieu Claire Semelin and Sarah Gensburger (New York: Columbia University Press, 2014), p. 74.
116 Beorn, *Marching into Darkness: The Wehrmacht and the Holocaust in Belarus*, p. 232.

Conclusion

1 Omer Bartov, *Erased: Vanishing Traces of Jewish Galicia in Present-Day Ukraine* (Princeton; Oxford: Princeton University Press, 2007), p. 9.
2 William Faulkner, *Requiem for a Nun*, 1st ed. (New York: Vintage Books, 2011), p. 73.
3 See Jeffrey Burds, *Holocaust in Rovno: A Massacre in Ukraine, November 1941* (New York: Palgrave Macmillan, 2013).
4 Leon Weliczker Wells, *The Janowska Road* (New York: MacMillan Company, 1963), p. 252.
5 Edmund Kessler, *The Wartime Diary of Edmund Kessler: Lwow, Poland, 1942–1944* (Boston, MA: Academic Studies Press, 2010), p. 14.
6 Shimon Redlich, *Together and Apart in Brzezany: Poles, Jews, and Ukrainians, 1919–1945* (Bloomington: Indiana University Press, 2002), pp. 149–50.
7 Wells, *The Janowska Road*, p. 239.
8 Jan Tomasz Gross, *Golden Harvest: Events at the Periphery of the Holocaust* (New York: Oxford University Press, 2012), p. 102.
9 Wells, *The Janowska Road*, p. 245.
10 Samuel. Drix, *Witness to Annihilation: Surviving the Holocaust, a Memoir* (Washington: Brassey's, 1994), p. 213.
11 Thomas Toivi Blatt, *From the Ashes of Sobibor: A Story of Survival* (Evanston, Ill.: Northwestern University Press, 1997), p. 223.
12 Jan Tomasz Gross, *Fear: Anti-Semitism in Poland after Auschwitz- an Essay in Historical Interpretation* (Princeton, NJ: Princeton University Press, 2006), p. 88.
13 Ibid., p. 89.
14 Jean Ancel, "'The New Jewish Invasion'—the Return of the Survivors from Transnistria," in *The Jews Are Coming Back: The Return of the Jews to Their*

Countries of Origin after WW II, ed. David Bankier (New York: Berghahn Books, 2005), p. 241.
15 W. H. Lawrence, "Poles Kill 26 Jews in Kielce Pogrom," *New York Times*, July 5, 1946.
16 "Ahrens, Jack Interview, 5/11/1995" (USHMM: RG-50.030*0311).
17 Marian R. Sanders, "Extraordinary Crimes in Ukraine: An Examination of Evidence Collection by the Extraordinary State Commission of the Union of Soviet Socialist Republics, 1942–1946," Ohio University, 1995, p. 73.
18 Ibid., p. 84.
19 Kiril Feferman, "Soviet Investigation of Nazi Crimes in the USSR: Documenting the Holocaust," *Journal of Genocide Research* 5, no. 4 (2003): 590.
20 See, for example, ibid., p. 596.
21 Ilya Bourtman, "'Blood for Blood, Death for Death': The Soviet Military Tribunal in Krasnodar, 1943," *Holocaust and Genocide Studies* 22, no. 2 (2008): 251.
22 Jeremy Hicks, "'Soul Destroyers': Soviet Reporting of Nazi Genocide and Its Perpetrators at the Krasnodar and Khar′Kov Trials," *History* 98, no. 332 (2013): 536.
23 Ibid., p. 540.
24 See, for example, Gerald Steinacher, *Nazis on the Run: How Hitler's Henchmen Fled Justice* (Oxford: Oxford University Press, 2011), Book.
25 Waitman Wade Beorn, *Marching into Darkness: The Wehrmacht and the Holocaust in Belarus* (Cambridge: Harvard University Press, 2014), p. 214.
26 Ibid.
27 Gross, *Golden Harvest: Events at the Periphery of the Holocaust*, pp. 62–3.
28 Ibid., p. 57.
29 Beorn, *Marching into Darkness: The Wehrmacht and the Holocaust in Belarus*, p. 90.
30 Alex Ulam, "What Went Wrong at the Golden Rose Synagogue?," *Foreign Policy* (2016), http://foreignpolicy.com/2016/12/01/what-went-wrong-at-the-golden-rose-synagogue/.
31 Daniel Blatman, "What Poland's New Holocaust Bill Gets Right—and What It Gets Very Wrong," *Haaretz* (2016), http://www.haaretz.com/opinion/.premium-1.739451.
32 Burds, *Holocaust in Rovno: A Massacre in Ukraine, November 1941*, p. 99.
33 Gross, *Golden Harvest: Events at the Periphery of the Holocaust*, pp. 123–4.

INDEX

Abrahamic religions 11
Abravanel, Isaac 10
Afrika Korps 223
amidah 227
anti-Bolshevik crusade 36, 59, 134, 189
anti-Bolshevik propaganda 36
anti-Jewish policies 4, 7, 19–20, 26, 38–40, 71, 90, 92–3, 95–6, 103, 108, 110, 115, 127–8, 133–4, 139, 147, 152–3, 159, 167, 176, 181, 184, 187–9, 192, 194, 197, 205, 232, 260, 262
antisemitism 9, 80, 141, 181, 242
 chimeric 18
 Christian 18–21
 in Eastern Europe 17–27
 economic 21–2
 forms of 17
 immigration policies 40, 116
 political 22–5
 racial 25–7
 realistic 17–18
 religious 18–19
 Romanian 138–41
 xenophobic 18
Antonescu, Ion 139, 183, 185, 188
Antonescu, Mihai 184, 187–8
Arad, Yitzhak 243
Arendt, Hannah 226
Arlt, Fritz 108
armed/violent resistance 238–45
 in extermination centers and at killing sites 241
 factors hampered efforts to organize 238–9
 partisan movement 242–5
 uprisings 240–1
Arrow Cross 189, 192–6, 264
Aryanization of businesses 116

Ashkenazi 10
Askaris 61
Auerswald, Heinz 162
Auschwitz concentration camp 215–19, 249–50
 construction 217–19
 killing infrastructure 217–18
Austria 5, 30, 41, 43, 80, 99, 105, 119, 181, 190, 192, 211
Austrian Jews 30, 108, 211
Austro-Hungarian Empire 15, 188–9

Babi Yar killings 142–4
Bach-Zelewski, Erich von dem 208, 216
Backe, Herbert 66
Balkans 283n. 12
Balkan wars of 1912–13 182
Baltic Barons 51
Baltic States 6, 46, 51, 63, 65, 67, 72–3, 75, 79, 83, 87, 93, 141, 258
Bandera, Stepan 279
Bandura, Albert 253
Barbarossa, Frederick 119
Barbarossa, Decree 123
Baruch, Bernard 24
Battle of the Tenth Dam, 1942 245
Bauer, Yehuda 166, 280
Beilis, Mendel 20
Belarus 5, 63–5, 67, 73–5, 78, 80, 85, 120, 127, 132, 144–7, 157, 220, 236, 239–42, 245, 251–2, 254, 258–60, 262, 264, 267, 279
Belorussian Soviet Socialist Republic 12
Bełżec 207, 210–11, 220–2, 235–6, 281
Beria, Lavrenty 88
Berliner, Meir 241
Beutel, Lothar 101
Bialystoker Stern 81
Biebow, Hans 154, 164–6

Blady-Szwajger, Dr 172
Blaskowitz, General Johannes 104
Blatt, Thomas 241–2, 275
Bodkier, Leah 236, 267
Bolshevik Revolution 59–60
Bolsheviks 24, 74, 91, 134, 137, 143, 148, 267
Bolshevism 15, 24, 43, 55, 58–9, 120, 123, 141, 149, 189, 254
Boris III, King 196, 200
Bouhler, Phillipp 41
Brack, Viktor 210
Brandt, Karl 41
Brauchitsch, Field Marshal 104
Browning, Christopher 153, 207, 249, 257
Bulgaria 7, 182, 195–200
  antisemitism 197–200
  Bulgarian military and police 198
  experience of the Thracian and Macedonian Jews 195–9
  Jewish life in 196
  reason for being an ally to Nazi 195–6
Byelova, Alexandra 269

Carol II, King 182–3
Catherine the Great, empress 12, 51
Catholicism 19
Chagall, Marc 17
Chamberlain, Neville 45–6
Chary, Frederick 196
Chelmno extermination center 166, 209, 220
chimeric antisemitism 18
"choiceless choices," category of 159–69
Christian antisemitism 18–21
  Christian prohibition on usury 21
  Jews as Christkillers, view of 18–19
  Jews as murder of Jesus, view of 18
Christian doctrine 18
Christianity 12, 18–19, 22, 181, 197, 199, 269
Christians 11
Citino, Robert 49
Codreanu, Corneliu 182
Columbus' voyage 10

Communism 24, 33
communism 16
Communist Jews 76
Communist Party 34, 74–5, 81, 91
Constantine, Emperor 18
Councils of Jewish Elders 160
Court Jews 11, 21
Criminal Police (*Kriminalpolizei* or *Kripo*) 37, 99
Cukierman, Yitzhak 238
Czechoslovakia 43–4, 99, 180
Czerniakow, Adam 161–3, 165, 169, 203, 237

Dachau trials 277
Dannecker, Theodor 198
Dannecker–Belev Agreement 195
Decree for the Protection of People and State 34
Demjanjuk, John 278
Der Stürmer 35
Drechsel, Hans 153
Durchgangslager or DULAG 126–7

East
  demographic engineering project in 63–9
  German conceptions of 53–5
  Nazis conceptions of 55–60
Eastern allies of Hitler 179–200
  Bulgaria 195–200
  Hungary 188–95
  Romania 181–8
Eastern Europe 1, 49
  definitions of 6
  history 5
Eastern European Jews 12, 15, 17, 26, 30, 55, 57, 175, 238, 276
Eberhard, Kurt 143
Eberl, Irmfried 212, 215
economic antisemitism 21–2
  Jews as economic parasites, view of 21
  reasons for 21–2
Ehlich, Hans 63
Eichengreen, Lucille 164
Eichmann, Adolf 116, 193–4, 198, 203, 208, 211, 249

Einsatzgruppen (EG units) 141, 205,
    254–7
  mass shooting of Jews 142–7
  in occupied Soviet Union 128–33
  in Poland (1939–41) 98–105, 110,
    124, 128
Einsatzkommandos (EKs) 99, 101,
    105, 130
Eldorado Theater 230
Elkes, Elkhanan 161, 166–7, 169
Ernest, Stefan 237
Erren, Gerhard 157
Estonians 75
ethnic German settlement of East 52
eugenics 25–6, 41
European Enlightenment 15
Extraordinary Pacification
    campaign 110
Extraordinary State Commission
    (ESC) 276–7

Farben, I. G. 216
Faulkner, William 273
Filderman, Wilhelm 187
Final Solution 7, 57, 95, 117, 121, 146,
    149, 152, 163, 167, 178, 192–3,
    195, 201–2, 280
  closing of extermination centers and
    liquidation of ghettos 219–23
  decision and execution
    timeline 205–6
  evolution of 202–4
  extermination centers for
    207–19, 222
  murder decision 204–7
  Operation Reinhard 207, 210
  Operation T-4 41, 207
  plans for culmination of Jews 203
  Wannsee Conference 210, 223
Folkmann, Adolf 137, 228, 233
France, invasion of 47
Frank, Anne 3
Frank, Hans 62, 106–7, 109–14,
    153–4
Frankfurt Auschwitz Trial (1963–67)
    277
Franz, Kurt 215
Friedländer, Saul 163

Galicia 107
Garfunkel, Leib 259
Generalgouvernement (GG) 106–9,
    153, 185
  attempted destruction of Polish
    culture in 112–13
  economic measures 114
  Nazi functionaries in 113–14
  occupation policies 109–14
General Jewish Labor Bund 16
Generalplan Ost (General Plan East)
    63–6, 68
Gens, Jacob 239
Gerasimchik, Pavel 269
German Communist Party (KPD) 34
Germanic territories 50–3
German immigration 61, 107–9
  in Mexico 66
  in Nebraska 66
German Invasion of Poland 96–8
  military brutality 97
  Polish reactions 97
  undisciplined looting following 98
Germanization 33, 50, 65, 96,
    107–8, 111
  attempt in
    Generalgovernment 109–14
  of incorporated territories 105–8
German killing squads 1
Germans 36, 38–42, 45, 49–51
  conceptions of East 53–5, 58
  in East 51–3
  ethnic 50–1, 65, 87, 97, 107–9, 111–
    12, 144, 208, 262
  Germanic warrior 51
  as liberators 59
  pre-Christian era 56
  as racial antisemites 25
  view of Eastern Europe 57
German Volk 39, 57
German Worker's Party (*Deutsche
    Arbeiter Partei*-DAP) 31
ghettos/ghettoization 116, 147, 151–2
  in Budapest 158
  Budapest ghetto 195
  Councils of Jewish Elders and 159–69
  cultural life in 173–5
  daily life for inhabitants 169–78

in East 156–9
in Eastern Europe 158
final liquidation of 219–23
Kishinev ghetto 158, 233
Kaunas ghetto 166, 172–3, 175, 177, 229–30
Krakow ghetto 156
Łodz ghetto 116–17, 153–5, 157, 163, 166, 170–1, 173, 177, 205, 220, 229–30
longer-lived ghettos 159
Lublin ghetto 220
Lwów ghetto 155, 157, 170–2, 176, 220, 233, 236–8, 241, 252, 257, 260, 267, 269, 273
Minsk ghetto 177–8, 237, 239–40
Nazi policy on purpose of ghettos 7, 152–6
official and unofficial smuggling of food 170–2
populations 158
sanitation and hygiene in 172–3
shorter-lived ghettos 159
sufferings 170–1
uprising in 240–1
Vilna ghetto 237–8
Vilnius ghetto 176–7
Vitebsk ghetto 158
Warsaw ghetto 153–4, 157, 166, 172, 176–7, 220, 229, 232, 240
Ghetto Theater 231
Glazar, Richard 213
Gleich, Sara 261
Globocnik, Odilo 210, 215
Goebbels, Josef 35–6, 40, 56, 105, 107, 119, 240
Golden Rose Synagogue 279
Göring, Hermann 32, 47, 64, 108, 183, 204
Grabowski, Jan 260
Graebe, Hermann 233
Greater Reich 106
Green Plan 148
Gregory X, Pope 19
Groening, Oskar 278
Gross, Jan 278
Grynzspan, Herschel 40
Guderian, Heinz 194
GULAGs (Soviet prison camps) 85

Halder, Franz 46, 120
Hashomer Hatzair 84
Hasidic Judaism 15
Hess, Rudolf 33
Heydrich, Reinhard 37, 101, 129, 152, 204–5, 208, 210–11
Hilberg, Raul 192, 227
Himmler, Heinrich 32, 37, 64, 101, 107, 109, 112, 146–7, 182, 194, 205, 208, 216, 256–7
Hirszenberg, Szmul 17
Hitler, Adolf 7, 24, 29–30, 32, 37–8, 42, 71–2, 122
  antisemitic measures 38–40
  as Chancellor of Germany 34
  as a corporal 30–1
  diplomatic alliances in Eastern Europe 179–200
  foreign policy, 1933–40 41–7
  Germanization of the population 33
  killing of Jews, see Final Solution
  as Leader 32
  Mein Kampf 30–1, 49, 202
  mistreatment of Soviet POWs 58–9
  monitoring of right-wing extremist organizations 31
  motivations for German–Soviet pact 72
  national revolution 32
  passage of Enabling Act 34
  rearmament and military buildup 43
  Reichstag Decree 34
  trial for high treason 32–3
  violation of Versailles Treaty 42–3
  wars won 41–7
  way of operating 36
  worldview 30, 42
  World War I, impact of 30–1
Hofer, Fritz 143
Höfle, Hermann 263
Holocaust perpetrators, collaborators, and rescuers in Eastern Europe 7, 247–8
  killers and desk murderers 248–58
  local collaboration with Nazi occupiers 258–65
  rescuers 265–71
Horthy, Miklós 188–9, 192–4
Höss, Rudolf 113, 209, 216–17

Hungarian National Central Alien
    Control Office (KEOKH) 190
Hungary 7, 182, 188–95
    antisemitic measures 189–90
    Hungarian military 190
    "Jewish Laws" 189–90
    Jews, sufferings of 190–2
    "Numerus Clausus" Act 189
    relationship with Hitler 189
Hunger Plan 63, 67–8, 148

Iasi pogrom 138–41
incorporated territories of
    Poland 106–9
    anti-Jewish policies in 114–18
    Generalgouvernement (GG)
        region 106–14
Iron Guard 181–3

Janowska concentration camp 171,
    176, 221–2, 231, 233, 238,
    251–2, 257
Jarausch, Konrad 127
Jewish Councils (*Judenräte*) 159–69,
    172, 176, 236, 254, 261
Jewish Courts of Honor 161
Jewish emancipation 16, 23
Jewish Enlightenment (*Haskalah*) 15
Jewish imprisonment, deportation, and
    murder 198, 204, 220, *see also*
    Final Solution
    during German ocuupation 87, 92,
        102, 107–9
    Nisko/Lublin plan 108
    of Romanian Jews 186
    during Soviet occupation from
        1939–40 82–9
Jewish life in Eastern Europe 7
    agricultural skills 17
    cultural and creative life, form of 17
    economic difficulties 14
    Jewish population of Europe,
        1933 13
    literacy rate 15
    living conditions 11
    political influence and
        participation 15–16
    religious beliefs 15
    in shtetls 14

traditional Jewish form of
    self-government 16
year 1492 10–12
Zionism and 16–17
Jewish manager 10
Jewish political mobilization and
    participation 24–5
"Jewish Question" in Europe 9, 22,
    96, 103, 106, 116, 121, 141, 201,
    204–5, 207, 263
Jewish resistance 7
    armed resistance 238–45
    challenges to 226
    defining 226–8
    non-violent resistance 235–8
    social and cultural resistance 228–35
Jewish self-help (*kehilla*) group 16,
    160–1, 171
Jewish Symphony Orchestra 230
Jews and non-Jews, relationships
    between 26
Judaism in Eastern Europe 15
Judenlagers or JULAGS 178
Judeo–Bolshevik myth 59, 89–93,
    141, 181
jüdische Ordnungsdienst (JOD) 176
Jurisdiction Order 122

Kadish, George 173
kahal system of communal welfare
    16, 229
Kahane, David 233
Kállay, Miklós 192
Kaltenbrunner, Ernst 193
Kaplan, Chaim 76, 157, 163, 229
Karski, Jan 83, 91
Kaunas pogrom 134–6
kehilla 16
Keren, Christine 237
Keresztes-Fischer, Ferenc 192
Kessler, Edmund 265
Kielce pogrom 276
Koonz, Claudia 251
Korzcak, Janusz 229, 234–5
Kaunas Jews 166–7
Kraków 107, 110, 112–13
Kristallnacht 40
Kruk, Hermann 231
Krupki killings 144–7

338   INDEX

Kruschev, Nikita 78
Kühne, Thomas 253

Langmuir, Gavin 17
Lasch, Karl 155
Latvia 51, 145, 147, 184, 279
Latvians 75
Law for the Protection of German
    Blood and German Honor 39
Law for the Restoration of the Civil
    Service 39
Lewin, Abraham 151
Liebermann, Aaron 9
Liebeskind, Rivka 233
Lietūkis garage massacre 134–5, 280
Lithuania 5, 12, 15–16, 51, 54, 73, 75,
    77–9, 82, 89, 91–2, 134–6, 139,
    145, 147, 229, 266–7
  annexation to Soviet Union 259
  Jewish businesses in 82
  Jewish imprisonment, deportation,
    and murder 87, 89
  Jewish population in 259
Lithuanian auxiliaries 1
Lithuanian Communist Party 91
Lithuanian Jews 1, 87, 92
Lithuanians 11, 53, 75, 87, 89–92, 112,
    136, 247, 258–9, 262–3, 279
Lithuanian *Schutzmannschaften* 262, 264
Lithuanian Territorial Self-Defense
    Force 279
Lublin 107
Ludendorff, Erich 31
Luther, Martin 19
Lvov 73, 75, 78–9, 81–2, 84, 87,
    89, 137
Lwów pogrom 136–7

Macedonia 195–8
Madagascar Plan 117, 203
malinas or hideouts 237
Marr, Wilhelm 25
Marxism, connection between
    Jews and 30
Maslov, Aleksei 126
May, Karl 61
Mazower, Mark 6
Meier, Liselotte 251

Melinescu, Nicolae 186
Mendelssohn, Moses 22
Mentz, Willi 213
Mexico 57, 66
Meyer, Konrad 63
Michael, King 187–8
Minority Treaties 15
missions of the memorial 228
Mitnagadim 15
Molotov, Vyacheslav 74
Molotov–Ribbentrop Pact 72–3, 95
  supplementary protocols and
    economic arrangements 73
Müller, Heinrich 108, 221
Munich Agreement 45
Mussolini, Benito 32
mythical position of Eastern Europe
    7, 49–50
  German conceptions of East 53–5
  Nazi expansion plans 63–9
  Nazis conceptions of East 55–60

National Socialist German Worker's
    Party (*Nationalsozialistische
    Deutsche Arbeiterpartei*-NSDAP)
    31, 33–4
Nazi 4, 7, 19–20, 26, 38–40, 71, 90,
    92–3, 95–6, 103, 108, 110, 115,
    127–8, 133–4, 139, 147, 152–3,
    159, 167, 176, 181, 184, 187–9,
    192, 194, 197, 205, 232, 260, 262
  conceptions of East 55–60
  decision to murder Jews 7, *see
    also* Final Solution; pogroms
    against Jews
  East, expansion plans for 60–3
  Eastern Europe, expansion plans
    for 63–9
  exploitation of land and resources 68
  genocidal project 1, 3, 6, 29, 47, 49,
    68, 96, 102, 110, 121, 179, 199–
    200, 249, 279
  independent allies of 7
  "Manifest Destiny" 60–3
  occupation and dissection of
    Poland 105–9
  policy toward Western Europe 67–8
  propaganda 33, 35, 97, 240

viewpoints on the purpose of ghettos 7, 152–6
vision of *Lebensraum* 105
Welfare Organization 65
worldview 125
Nazi-allied countries
  Bulgaria 195–200
  Hungary 188–95
  Romania 181–8
Nazi state 68
  antisemitic measures 38–40
  areas of authority 36
  chaotic nature of 37
  concept of "working towards the Führer" 36
  evolution of 35–41
  foreign policy, 1933–40 41–7
  Hitler's role 29–34
  important characteristics of 36–7
  killing of political enemies 37
  Nazi consolidation of power 38
  party apparatuses 37
  rise of 7, 29
  violence against Jews 40–1
Nebe, Artur 146, 208
Nilus, Sergei 23
Nisko/Lublin plan 108–9, 203
NKVD (Soviet Secret Police) 78, 83–90, 92, 136–7, 143
Non-Aggression Pact with the Soviet Union 46
non-violent resistance 235–8
Nuremberg Laws of 1935 26, 39
Nuremberg trials 277
Nussbaum, Lisa 236
Nussbaum, Pola 236

Ober Ost 52, 54
occupation of the Soviet Union
  German POW policy 125–7
  impact of 148
  mass killings 142–7
  mission of the EGs in 128–33
  occupation policies in occupied East 147–9
  Operation Barbarossa 121–4
  pogroms from Lithunia to Romania 133–41

Oneg Shabbat 232
On the Jews and their Lies 19
On the Origin of Species (Charles Darwin) 25
Operation Barbarossa 119, 129, 149
  Einsatzgruppen commanders, role of 128–33
  planning and preparations for 121–4
  pogroms against Jews 133–41
Operation Reinhard 207, 210
Operation T-4 41, 111, 207–8, 210, 215, 255
Operation Tannenberg 99
Organization of Ukrainian Nationalists (OUN) 84
Orphans' Home 229
Orthodox Judaism 14
Oshry, Rabbi Ephraim 175

Palčiauskas, Kazys 167
Pale of Settlement 12
Pechersky, Alexander 241
Peretz, I.L. 17
Peshev, Dmitar 199
Petri, Erna 251
Pilate, Pontius 18
Pius XII, Pope 193
pogroms against Jews 133–4, 167, *see also* Final Solution
  Babi Yar killings 142–4
  Iasi pogrom 138–41
  Kaunas pogrom 134–6
  Kielce pogrom 276
  Krupki killings 144–7
  Lwów pogrom 136–7
Poland 53, 93
  Einsatzgruppen (EG) in 98–105
  ethnicity and Catholicism 74
  ethnic violence 76–7
  German Invasion of 96–8
  invasion of 7, 45–7, 72–3
  issues with Soviet Union 74–5
  occupation and dissection of 105–9
  Soviet view of Poles 74
Polish prisoners of war 88
Polish resistance movements 113
political antisemitism 22–5
  connection of Jews and Bolsheviks 24

Jewish conspiracy to control the world, view of 24
Jews as driving force behind capitalism, view of 24
Protocols of the Elders of Zion and 23
Pre-World War II Europe, 1919–29 (map) 2
Prisoners of War (POWs) 88, 123, 143
  German policies towards Soviet 125–7
  Soviet 125–7, 212, 217, 249, 262
Protocols of the Elders of Zion 23
Prüfer, Kurt 249

racial antisemitism 25–7
  eugenics movement and 25–6
  Jews as biological contaminants 25
racial hygiene theories 25, 41
Rademacher, Franz 203, 208
Radom 107
Rauff, Walter 208
realistic antisemitism 17–18
Red Army troops 73–7
Reichskommissariat Weissruthenien occupation region 120
Reichssicherheitshauptamt (RSHA) 37, 64, 117, 129, 132, 197
religious antisemitism 18–19
Rhineland 42
Righteous Among the Nations 265
Righteous Gentiles 265–6
Ringelblum, Emanuel 151, 162, 175, 226, 231–3, 236
Röhm, Ernst 38
Roman Empire 18
Romania 7, 181–8
  in Axis powers 181
  Jewish population in 181
  loyalty to Hitler 184
  religious tradition in 181
  violence against Jews 184–7
Rosenberg, Alfred 24, 66
Rudashewsky, Yitzhak 237
Rufeisen, Oswald 239
Rumkowski, Chaim 161, 163–5, 169
Ryder, Theodor 175

Safran, Rabbi Alexandru 187
Sarfati, Albert 199
Schallock, Walter 221

Schindler, Oskar 267
Schmid, Anton 267, 270
Schönemann, Werner 145
Schulman, Faye 242
secret police (NKVD), *see* NKVD (Soviet Secret Police)
Secret State Police (*Geheime Staatspolizei* or *Gestapo*) 37, 99
Seidel, Edmund 267
sexual violence against Jewish women 252–3
Shabbat, Oneg 175
Shapiro, Rabbi 167
Shepetinski, Jacob 245
Shirer, William 72, 97
Sierakowiak, Dawid 230
Sima, Horia 183
Sobibor killing center 178, 207, 210–11, 215, 222, 241–2, 252, 275, 278
social and cultural resistance 228–35
  act of documenting the Holocaust experience 231
  maintenance of and creation of art 230
  orphanages to care for children 229–30
Social Democratic Party (SPD) 34
socialism 16
"Sovietization" of the state 78
Soviet Jewish Anti-Fascist Committee (JAFC) 276
Soviet occupation from 1939–40 7, 71–2
  anti-Zionist measures 81
  changes in education and school system 79–80
  claims of liberation and protection of Belorussians and Ukrainians 73–7
  economic turmoil and shortages following 79
  effects on local populations, Jewish and non-Jewish 72
  Jewish reaction to 75–6
  Jews under 80–2
  Judeo-Bolshevik antisemitism perspective 89–93
  loss of Jewish identity 80
  occupation policy 76–80

political control of newly acquired territories 76–80
religious life of Jews 81
role of Jews in 92
Soviet repression during (imprisonment, deportation, and murder) 82–9
Soviet prison massacres 137
Soviet Union 67
SS Race and Settlement Office (RuSHA) 111
St. Augustine 18
Stahlecker, Walter 134
Stalin, Josef 71–3, 83
  motivations for German–Soviet pact 73
Stangl, Franz 213, 215, 235, 251, 256–7, 277
Steinberg, Baruch 89
Stieff, Helmut 104
Strasser, Gregor 38
Stuttgart Lwów Trial (1968) 277
Sugihara, Chiune 268
Szálasi, Ferenc 189, 194
Szlengel, Władysław 173, 234
Sznapman, Stansilaw 238
Sztójay, Döme 193
Szur, Lejb 238

Tec, Nechama 270
Teutonic Order of Knights 51
Third Reich 32, 182, 276
Third Wave of killings 219
Thomas of Monmouth 19
Thrace 195–7
Tiergartenstrasse 4, 41
Topf and Sons 249
Tory, Avraham 175, 230–2
Transnistria 186–8
Transylvania 182
Treblinka extermination center 211–15, 241, 251, 277
  commandant of camps 213–14
  construction of 212
  sections of camps 212
Treuhandstelle Ost 114
Triumph of the Will 35
Trotsky, Leon 16
Trunk, Isaiah 161

Trzaskome, Father 102
Turner, Frederick Jackson 62
Turner thesis 62
tzedekah 16

Ukraine 5, 12, 15, 24, 57, 63, 66–7, 72–5, 78, 84–5, 93, 120, 132–3, 139, 142–4, 147, 157–8, 182, 190, 220, 233, 237, 241, 252, 254, 258–9, 261, 267, 274
Ukrainians 75–7, 136–7
Ulm Einsatzgruppen Trial (1958) 277
United States 61

Veesenmayer, Edmund 193
Versailles Treaty 15, 32, 42, 74, 99
Vilnius Jews 1
Volga Germans 51
Völkischerbeobachter 35
Volksdeutsche 112
Volksgemeinschaft 36, 65
vom Rath, Ernst 40
von Bismarck, Otto 50
von Brauchitsch, Walther 96
von Hinderburg, Paul 33–4
von Kahr, Gustav 38
von Leeb, Field Marshal 136
von Papen, Franz 34
von Ribbentrop, Joachim 45
von Seisser, Hans 32
Vytautas, Joudka 269

Wagner, General Eduard 124–5
Waldow, MAJ Johannes 145
Wallenberg, Raoul 267
"War of Annihilation" 7
Warsaw Philharmonic 230
Wartheland or *Warthegau* 106, 108
Way to Victory of Germanism over Judaism, The 25
Wehrmacht 43, 46, 67, 96–7, 99, 102, 104, 115, 120–2, 124, 127, 142, 145, 205
Weimar Constitution 34
Weimar Republic 34
Wells, Leon 233
Welzer, Harald 253
Werner, Kurt 144
Western European countries 67–8

Widmann, Albert 208
Wigand, Arpad 212

xenophobia 9, 183
xenophobic antisemitism 18

Yad Vashem 227, 265
Yakubovich, Raissa Nikolayevna 260

Yiddish Theater 17
Yom Kippur 1944 233

Zabinski, Jan 268
Żemiński, Stanisław 258
Zhukov, Marshal 120
Zionism 16–17, 81
Zwartendijk, Jan 267